Get the eBooks FREE!

(PDF, ePub, Kindle, and liveBook all included)

We believe that once you buy a book from us, you should be able to read it in any format we have available. To get electronic versions of this book at no additional cost to you, purchase and then register this book at the Manning website.

Go to https://www.manning.com/freebook and follow the instructions to complete your pBook registration.

That's it!
Thanks from Manning!

The Design of Web APIs

ARNAUD LAURET

Foreword by Kin Lane

MANNING

SHELTER ISLAND

Manning Publications Co.
20 Baldwin Road
PO Box 761
Shelter Island, NY 11964

Development editor:	Jenny Stout
Technical development editor:	Michael Lund
Review editor:	Ivan Martinović
Production editor:	Deirdre Hiam
Copy editor:	Frances Buran
Proofreader:	Melody Dolab
Technical proofreader:	Paul Grebenc
Typesetter:	Happenstance Type-O-Rama
Cover designer:	Marija Tudor

ISBN 9781617295102
Printed in the United States of America

brief contents

contents

foreword

For over a decade, API design has always meant REST to most developers. This reality has been constructed through regular waves of books and API-centered blogs that push RESTful design belief systems, leaving the discipline very focused and often times dogmatic. *The Design of Web APIs* by Arnaud Lauret is the beginning wave of the next generation of API design guidance, which will help us transcend this reality that has held us back for over a decade. His pragmatic approach to API design is still rooted in REST, but he has worked hard to bring real world API design knowledge to the table—minus the usual dogma.

Lauret takes us through the fundamentals of API design that you can easily find in other industry books, but he assembles the fundamental building blocks of this discipline in a very easy-to-access way and walks you through the vast landscape in a friendly and comfortable manner. I have known Arnaud personally for several years and consider him among a handful of top tier API talent that don't just understand how you do APIs technically, but also understand the human-centered challenges of delivering APIs and how APIs can positively or negatively impact your API experience among developers. Arnaud focuses his knowledge on not just the act of designing an API, but also the act of providing a well-designed API for your intended audience in a thoughtful way.

I have personally watched Arnaud sit in the front row of hundreds of API talks around the globe, absorbing the best-of-breed API wisdom. One just needs to visit his Twitter timeline or to follow the hashtag for a popular API event to understand what I am talking about. He has a unique approach to listening to API industry speakers, processing the API information they are sharing, while also live-tweeting the most important points of the talk as a steady stream of API insights. It makes me happy to see Arnaud take this accumulated knowledge and put it down in book form, continuing his approach to not just sharpening his own skills, but also making sure he is sharing what he knows and his unique approach to API design with the world. Arnaud is a rare breed of API analyst that listens, cares, understands, and distills API knowledge down into usable building blocks you can actually put to work in your business world.

After the API design world began to pick up momentum after 2012 and the OpenAPI (FKA Swagger) began to grow in dominance, Arnaud was one of just a handful of API experts who worked hard to understand the potential of this specification, while also developing innovative tooling and visualizations around the open source API specification standard. Doing the hard work to understand not just the specification, but how it can embody, represent, and even govern many of the API design principles you need to be successful in the space. It takes a lot of work to reach the point where you realize OpenAPI isn't just about documentation, a journey that most API developers end up not taking. Arnaud understands that OpenAPI isn't just about API documentation, but is the fundamental underpinning of API design for any platform—something that will help define every other stop along your API lifecycle. *The Design of Web APIs* is the first API design book I have seen that merges API design and OpenAPI together in such a thoughtful and pragmatic way, which is sure to help many developers along in their API journey.

Spend the time to understand what Arnaud is sharing with you here. This isn't a skimming book. This isn't a one-read book. This is a handbook. This is your guide to taking the design of your APIs to the next level. It brings that loose bucket of API concepts you are familiar with and provides you with the blueprints to build the Millennium Falcon or even the Death Star (if you so choose) from your bucket of API Lego building blocks. I recommend reading this book, then putting it down for a month. Then get to work building an API and moving it from design to actually being deployed and publicly available—sharing it with a handful of developers. Then while you wait for feedback, sit down and read the book again. You will begin to understand the depth of what you hold in your hands and the value of the knowledge Arnaud is sharing with you. Then repeat this process until you are satisfied with your ability to design not a perfect API, but exactly the API you need to reach the consumers you are looking to make an impact upon.

—*Kin Lane, The API Evangelist*

preface

For most of my career, I have worked on connecting software bricks together using various software interface technologies, from simple files and databases to remote software interfaces based on RPC, Corba, Java RMI, SOAP web services, and web APIs. Throughout these years, I have been fortunate to work on motley distributed systems, mixing very old mainframe technology with state-of-the art cloud systems and everything in between. I also have been fortunate to work on both sides of software interfaces in various contexts. I worked on IVR (Interactive Voice Response), websites, and mobile applications built on top of huge service-oriented architecture systems. I've built both private and public web services and web APIs for frontend and backend applications. During all these years, I complained a lot about the terrible software interfaces, and I fell into many traps and created terrible software interfaces too.

As years passed, and technology evolved from RPC to SOAP web services and web APIs, connecting software together became more and more simple from a technical point of view. But whatever the technology used, I have learned that a software interface is far more than technical plumbing or a by-product of a software project.

After attending my first API conferences in 2014, "API Days" in Paris, I realized that many other people were struggling with APIs just like me. That is why in 2015 I started my *API Handyman* blog and also started to participate in API conferences. I wanted to share my experiences with others and help them to avoid falling in the same traps I had fallen into. Writing and speaking about web APIs not only allowed me to help others, it also allowed me to learn even more about them.

After two years of blogging and speaking at conferences, the idea of writing a book came. I wanted to write a book for my old self who fell into so many traps. As luck would have it, Manning Publications was looking for someone willing to write a book about the OpenAPI Specification, an API description format (we'll talk about it in chapter 4, by the way). I took a chance and proposed my *Design of Everyday APIs* book, and it was accepted. This title was inspired by Don Norman's *Design of Everyday Things* (MIT Press, 1998), which is a book about design (you definitely should read it). My idea was later replaced by the more straightforward *The Design of Web APIs*. I have to admit that I am more comfortable with this title; I don't feel I'm borrowing from the fame of Don Norman anymore.

In the beginning, the book's content included the design of everyday things + API + REST vs. gRPC vs. GraphQL. It would have been quite indigestible, but I wanted to make a book whose principles could be used for any type of API. Month after month, the content was refined and enhanced to what is now *The Design of Web APIs*. I chose to focus on REST APIs and use those as a support example for you to learn web/remote API design principles, which would go beyond merely designing APIs. I think my old self would have been quite happy to read this book; I hope you like it too!

acknowledgments

Two years. It took me two years to finish this book. That's a very long time, but that is what helped me to make it a great book that I hope you will like. I was not alone while working on it. There are a few people I'd like to thank for helping me during this journey, and I also want to thank the people who made this journey possible.

First and foremost, I want to thank my wife, Cinzia, and my daughter, Elisabetta. Thank you so much for your support and your patience while I was spending my evenings and weekends on "the book." I love you so much.

Next, I would like to thank everyone at Manning Publications. You can't imagine how many people work on a book when you haven't written one yet, and every one of one them has done a wonderful job. I would like to especially thank my editor, Mike Stephens, who believed in the book. Very special thanks also to my two development editors, Kevin Harreld and Jennifer Stout, and my technical development editor, Michael Lund. You really helped me a lot! This book wouldn't have been the same without the three of you. And very special *merci beaucoup* to my ESL copyeditor, Rachel Head, who really, really, really has done an awesome job fixing my frenglish. Thank you to my production editor Deirdre Hiam, my copyeditor Frances Buran, proofreader Melody Dolab, and technical proofreader Paul Grebenc. I would also like to thank all the reviewers: Andrew Gwozdziewycz, Andy Kirsch, Bridger Howell, Edwin Kwok, Enrico Mazzarella, Mohammad Ali Bazzi, Narayanan Jayaratchagan, Peter Paul Sellars, Raveesh Sharma, Sanjeev Kumar Jaiswal, Sergio Pacheco, Shaun Hickson, Shawn Smith, Shayn Cornwell, Vincent Theron, and William Rudenmalm.

A special thanks to Ivan Goncharov, who on March 15, 2017, forwarded me an email from Manning Publications, looking for someone to write a book that later became *The Design of Web APIs*. As luck would have it, I'm glad we met at REST Fest 2015.

Thank you to all the people who took time to read the manuscript at various stages and provided invaluable encouragement and feedback. Special thanks to Isabelle Reusa and Mehdi Medjaoui for field-testing the book's content and providing their feedback. And thanks to all the API practitioners I have met and worked with over the years; I have put everything I have learned from you in this book.

And finally, a very big thanks to Mike Amundsen, Kin Lane, and Mehdi Medjaoui (again) for their encouragement and help when I started the *API Handyman* blog in 2015. This book wouldn't have existed without you.

about this book

The Design of Web APIs was written to help you design web APIs that do more than just cover expressed needs. This book will help you design outstanding web APIs that are usable by anyone in many different contexts, and those that are also secure, durable, evolvable, efficient, and implementable. It uncovers all aspects of web API design and gives a full overview of the web APIs ecosystem and how API designers can contribute to it.

Who should read this book

The Design of Web APIs is, obviously, for anyone who needs to design web APIs. They can be developers working on a backend for mobile applications or websites or needing to connect microservices together, or they can be product owners working on an API as a product, and everything in between. Actually, this book can be read by all people working on a project involving the creation of an API.

How this book is organized: a roadmap

This book has three parts that cover 13 chapters.

Part 1 teaches the most fundamental concepts and skills needed to design APIs.

Chapter 1 discusses what an API is, why its design matters, and what the elements of API design are.

Chapter 2 explains how to accurately determine an API's purpose—its real goals—by focusing on the point of view of API users and the software consuming the API, and by avoiding the point of view of the organization and software exposing the API.

Chapter 3 introduces the HTTP protocol, REST APIs, and the REST architectural style. It teaches how to design a web programming interface (comprising resources, actions on resources, data, parameters, and responses) based on the identified goals.

Chapter 4 introduces the OpenAPI Specification and demonstrates how to describe an API in a structured and standard way using such an API description format.

Part 2 focuses on how to design *don't make me think* APIs that will be easy to understand and easy to use.

Chapter 5 explains how to design straightforward data representations, error and success feedback, and flows of API calls that people will understand instantly and use easily.

Chapter 6 teaches how to design even more easy-to-understand and easy-to-use APIs, whose users (humans or machines) will be able to guess how APIs work, by making them consistent, adaptable, and discoverable.

Chapter 7 shows how to organize and size all aspects of APIs in order to keep them easy to understand and easy to use.

Part 3 shows that API designers must take into account the whole context surrounding an API and the whole context surrounding the API design process itself.

Chapter 8 describes API security and how to design secure APIs.

Chapter 9 teaches how to modify an API without unduly impacting its users, and when and how to version it. It also demonstrates how to design APIs that will be easy to evolve from the ground up.

Chapter 10 focuses on how to design network-efficient web APIs.

Chapter 11 exposes the whole context that API designers must take into account when designing APIs. It comprises adapting communication mechanisms (request/ responses, asynchronous, events, and batch or bulk processing), evaluating and adapting to consumers' or providers' limitations, and choosing an adequate API style (resource-, function- or data-based).

Chapter 12 explains how API designers participate in the creation of different types of API documentation, taking advantage of an API description format like the OpenAPI Specification.

Chapter 13 shows how API designers can participate in the growing of many APIs by participating along the whole API lifecycle and across many APIs. It especially focuses on API design guidelines and API reviews.

This book should be read from cover to cover, each chapter in order. Each new chapter expands what has been learned in previous ones. That being said, once you have finished chapters 1, 2, and 3, you can jump to any chapter covering a topic that you need to investigate urgently.

About the code

This book contains many examples of source code both in numbered listings and in line with normal text. In both cases, source code is formatted in a `fixed-width font like this` to separate it from ordinary text. Sometimes code is also **in bold** to highlight code that has changed from previous steps in the chapter, such as when a new feature adds to an existing line of code.

In many cases, the original source code has been reformatted; we've added line breaks and reworked indentation to accommodate the available page space in the book. In rare cases, even this was not enough, and listings include line-continuation markers (➥). Additionally, comments in the source code have often been removed from the listings when the code is described in the text. Code annotations accompany many of the listings, highlighting important concepts.

Source code for the examples in this book is available for download from the publisher's website at https://www.manning.com/books/the-design-of-web-apis.

liveBook discussion forum

Purchase of *The Design of Web APIs* includes free access to a private web forum run by Manning Publications where you can make comments about the book, ask technical questions, and receive help from the author and from other users. To access the forum, go to https://livebook.manning.com/book/the-design-of-everyday-apis/welcome/v-11/discussion. You can also learn more about Manning's forums and the rules of conduct at https://livebook.manning.com/#!/discussion.

Manning's commitment to our readers is to provide a venue where a meaningful dialogue between individual readers and between readers and the author can take place. It is not a commitment to any specific amount of participation on the part of the author, whose contribution to the forum remains voluntary (and unpaid). We suggest you try asking the author some challenging questions lest his interest stray! The forum and the archives of previous discussions will be accessible from the publisher's website as long as the book is in print.

Other online resources

There are so many online resources about APIs, but here are my two favorite ones:

- The *API Developer Weekly Newsletter* (https://apideveloperweekly.com/) is the best way to know what happens in the API world and to discover new sources of information about APIs.
- The Web API Events website (https://webapi.events/) will keep you updated about upcoming API conferences.

about the author

ARNAUD LAURET is a French software architect with 17 years of experience. He spent most of these years in the finance sector working on interconnecting systems in various ways, especially using web services and APIs. He runs the *API Handyman* blog and the API Stylebook web site and is a guest lecturer at multiple API conferences around the world. He is passionate about human-centered software design and loves to build and help to build systems that will provide a wonderful experience for all users, from developers and operations teams to end users.

about the cover illustration

The figure on the cover of *The Design of Web APIs* is captioned "Girl from Drniš, Dalmatia, Croatia." The illustration is taken from a reproduction of an album of Croatian traditional costumes from the mid-nineteenth century by Nikola Arsenovic, published by the Ethnographic Museum in Split, Croatia, in 2003. The illustrations were obtained from a helpful librarian at the Ethnographic Museum in Split, itself situated in the Roman core of the medieval center of the town: the ruins of Emperor Diocletian's retirement palace from around AD 304. The book includes finely colored illustrations of figures from different regions of Croatia, accompanied by descriptions of the costumes and of everyday life.

Dress codes and lifestyles have changed over the last 200 years, and the diversity by region, so rich at the time, has faded away. It's now hard to tell apart the inhabitants of different continents, let alone of different hamlets or towns separated by only a few miles. Perhaps we have traded cultural diversity for a more varied personal life—certainly for a more varied and fast-paced technological life. Manning celebrates the inventiveness and initiative of the computer business with book covers based on the rich diversity of regional life of two centuries ago, brought back to life by illustrations from old books and collections like this one.

Part 1

Fundamentals of API design

Every journey starts with a first step, and the API design journey is no exception. API designers need many skills and need to take many topics into account when creating APIs, but without a solid foundation, all advanced skills and topics are worth nothing. That is what you'll learn in this first part.

We will first set the scene by explaining what an API is, why it actually must be designed, and what *learning to design an API* actually means. You will discover that although these actually are programming interfaces, APIs are more than "technical plumbing" and that you must learn fundamental principles to design any type of API.

Even before thinking about the programming side, you will see that an API has to be thought of from its users' perspectives. An API is supposed to let your users easily achieve their goals, not the ones of the system exposing the API. Only once these goals are known and accurately described can the actual programming interface, such as a REST API, be designed. And like any programming, describing a programming interface should be done with an adapted tool like the OpenAPI Specification for REST APIs.

What is API design?

Web application programming interfaces (APIs) are an essential pillar of our connected world. Software uses these interfaces to communicate—from applications on smartphones to deeply hidden backend servers, APIs are absolutely everywhere. Whether these are seen as simple technical interfaces or products in their own right, whole systems, whatever their size and purpose, rely on them. So do entire companies and organizations from tech startups and internet giants to non-tech small and medium-sized enterprises, big corporations, and government entities.

If APIs are an essential pillar of our connected world, API design is its foundation. When building and evolving an API-based system, whether it is visible to anyone or deeply hidden, whether it creates a single or many APIs, design must always be a major concern. The success or failure of such a system depends directly on the quality of the design of all its APIs.

But what does designing APIs really mean? And what do you have to learn to design APIs? To answer these questions, we need to consider what an API is and for whom it's designed, and we also need to realize that designing an API is more than just designing a programming interface for applications.

1.1   What is an API?

Billions of people own smartphones and use them to share photos on social networks. This wouldn't be possible without APIs. Sharing photos using a mobile social networking application involves the use of different types of APIs, as shown in figure 1.1.

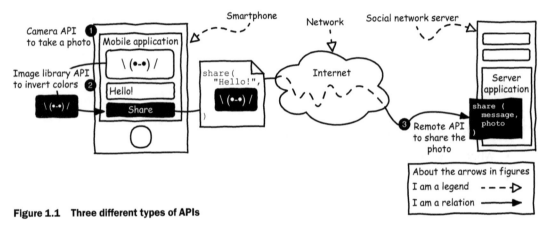

Figure 1.1   Three different types of APIs

First, to take a photo, the social networking mobile application uses the smartphone's camera via its API. Then, through its API, it can use some image library embedded in the application to invert the photo's colors. And, eventually, it shares the modified photo by sending it to a server application hosted on the social network server using a remote API accessible via a network, usually the internet. So, in this scenario, three different types of API are involved: respectively, a hardware API, a library, and a remote API. This book is about the latter.

APIs, whatever their types, simplify the creation of software, but remote APIs, and especially web ones, have revolutionized the way we create software. Nowadays, anyone can easily create anything by assembling remote pieces of software. But before we talk about the infinite possibilities offered by such APIs, let's clarify what the term *API* actually means in this book.

1.1.1   An API is a web interface for software

In this book, an API is a remote API and, more precisely, a *web API*—a web interface for software. An API, whatever its type, is first and foremost an interface: *a point where two systems, subjects, organizations, and so forth meet and interact.* The concept of an API might not be easy to grasp at first, but figure 1.2 makes it more tangible by comparing it to an application's user interface (UI).

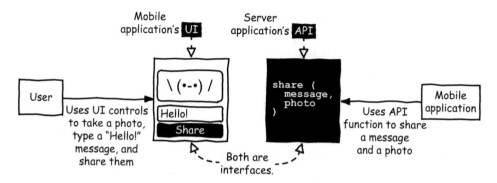

Figure 1.2 Comparing an application's user interface (UI) to an application programming interface (API)

As a user of a mobile application, you interact with it by touching your smartphone's screen, which displays the application's UI. A mobile application's UI can provide elements like buttons, text fields, or labels on the screen. These elements let users interact with the application to see or provide information, or to trigger actions such as sharing a message and a photo.

Just as we (human beings) use an application's UI to interact with it, that application can use another application through its programming interface. Whereas a UI provides input fields, labels, and buttons to provide some feedback that can evolve as you use them, an API provides functions that may need input data or that may return output data as feedback. These functions allow other applications to interact with the application providing the API to retrieve or send information or to trigger actions.

Strictly speaking, an API is *only* an interface exposed by some software. It's an abstraction of the underlying *implementation* (the underlying code—what actually happens inside the software product when the API is used). But note that the term *API* is often used to name the whole software product, including the API and its implementation. So APIs are interfaces for software, but the APIs we talk about in this book are more than just APIs: they are web APIs, as shown in figure 1.3.

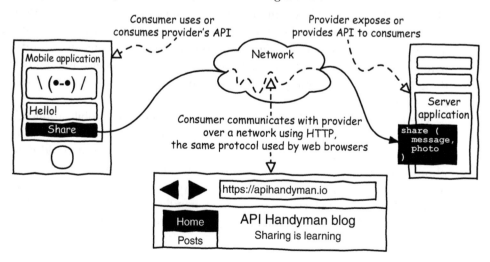

Figure 1.3 Web APIs are remote APIs that can be used with the HTTP protocol.

The mobile application running on a smartphone uses or consumes the API exposed or provided by the server application (often called a *backend application* or simply *backend*) that's hosted on a remote server. The mobile application is therefore called a *consumer*, and the backend is called a *provider*. These terms also apply respectively to the companies and the people creating the applications, or consuming or providing APIs. Here that means the developers of the mobile application are consumers and the ones developing the backend are providers.

To communicate with its backend, the mobile application usually uses a famous network: the internet. The interesting thing here is not the internet itself—such communication can also be done over a local network—but *how* these two applications communicate over the network. When a mobile application sends a photo and message to the backend application, it does so using the Hypertext Transfer Protocol (HTTP). If you've ever opened a web browser on a computer or a smartphone, you have used HTTP (indirectly). This is the protocol that is used by any website. When you type a website's address, like http://apihandyman.io or its secured version, https://apihandyman.io, into the address bar and press Enter or click a link in a browser, the browser uses HTTP to communicate with the remote server hosting the website in order to show you the site's content. Remote APIs, or at least the ones we're talking about in this book, rely on this protocol just like websites; that's why these are called *web APIs*.

So, in this book, APIs are web APIs. They are web interfaces for software. But why are such APIs so interesting?

1.1.2   *APIs turn software into LEGO® bricks*

Thousands, even millions, of mobile applications and their backends have been created thanks to web APIs, but there's more to the story. Indeed, web APIs unleash creativity and innovation by turning software into reusable bricks that can be easily assembled. Let's go back to our example and see what might happen when sharing a photo on a social network.

When a social network backend receives a photo and message, it might store the photo on the server's filesystem and store the message and the photo identifier (to retrieve the actual file later) in a database. It could also process the photo using some homemade facial recognition algorithm to detect if it contains any friends of yours before storing the photo. That's one possibility—a single application handling everything for another solitary application. Let's consider something different, as shown in figure 1.4.

The backend API could be used by both a social network mobile application and a website, and its implementation could be totally different. When the backend receives a photo and message to share (whichever application sent it), it could delegate the photo's storage as a service company through its API. It could also delegate the storage of the message and photo identifier to an in-house timeline software module through its API. How could the facial recognition be handled? Well, that could be delegated to some expert in facial recognition offering their services via … you guessed it … an API.

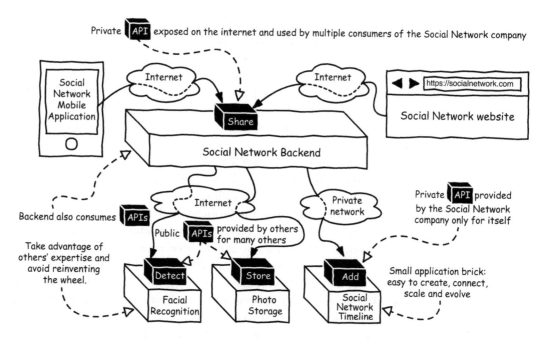

Figure 1.4 A system composed of public and private software LEGO® bricks connected via APIs.

Note that in figure 1.4, each API only exposes one function. This keeps the figure as simple as possible: a single API can expose many functions. The backend can, for example, expose functions such as Add Friend, List Friends, or Get Timeline.

This looks like a software version of the LEGO bricks system; you know, those plastic blocks that you can put together to create new things. (Aristotle was probably playing with some of these when he had the realization that "the whole is greater than the sum of its parts.") The possibilities are endless; the only limit is your imagination.

When I was a child, I used to play with LEGO bricks for endless hours—creating buildings, cars, planes, spaceships, or whatever I wanted. When I was bored with of one of my creations, I could destroy it completely and start something new from scratch, or I could transform it by replacing some parts. I could even put existing structures together to create a massive spaceship, for example. It's the same in the API world: you can decompose huge systems of software bricks that can be easily assembled and even replaced thanks to APIs, but there are some minor differences.

Each software brick can be used at the same time by many others. In our example, the backend API can be used by a mobile application and a web site. An API is usually not made to be consumed by a single consumer but by many. That way, you don't have to redevelop everything all the time.

Each software brick can run anywhere on its own as long as it's connected to a network in order to be accessible via its API. That offers a good way to manage performance and scalability; indeed, a software brick like the Facial Recognition one in figure 1.4 will probably need far more processing resources than the Social Network Timeline one. If the former is run by the Social Network company, it could be installed on a different, dedicated, and more powerful server, while the Social Network Timeline runs on a smaller one. And being accessible via a simple network connection allows any API provided by anyone to be used by anyone.

In the API world, there are two types of bricks exposing two types of APIs: *public APIs* and *private APIs*. The Facial Recognition and Photo Storage software bricks are not built and not even run by the Social Network company but by third parties. The APIs they provide are public ones.

Public APIs are proposed *as a service* or *as a product* by others; you don't build them, you don't install them, you don't run them—you only use them. Public APIs are provided to anyone who needs them and is willing to accept the terms and conditions of the third-party supplier. Depending on the business model of the API providers, such APIs can be free or paid for, just like any other software product. Such public APIs unleash creativity and innovation and can also greatly accelerate the creation of anything you can dream of. To paraphrase Steve Jobs, there's an API for that. Why lose time trying to reinvent a wheel that will, irremediably, not be round enough? In our example, the Social Network company chose to focus on its core expertise, connecting people, and delegated facial recognition to a third party.

But public APIs are only the tip of the API iceberg. The Social Network Backend and Social Network Timeline bricks were created by the Social Network company for its own use. The timeline API is only consumed by applications created by the Social Network company: the mobile Social Network Backend in figure 1.4. The same goes for the mobile backend, which is consumed by the Social Network Mobile Application. These APIs are *private APIs*, and there are billions of them out there. A private API is one you build for yourself: only applications created by you or people inside your team, department, or company use it. In this case, you are your own API provider and API consumer.

> **NOTE**   The public/private question is not a matter of *how* an API is exposed, but *to whom*. Even if it's exposed on the internet, the mobile backend API is still a private one.

There can be various kinds of interactions among *true* private APIs and public ones. For example, you can install commercial off-the-shelf software like a content management system (CMS) or a customer relationship management system (CRM) on your own servers (such an installation is often call *on premise*), and these applications can (even must!) provide APIs. These APIs are private ones, but you do not build those yourself. Still, you can use them as you wish and, especially, to connect more bricks to your bricks. As another example, you can expose some of your APIs to customers or selected partners. Such *almost public* APIs are often called *partner APIs*.

But whatever the situation, APIs basically turn software into reusable software bricks that can be easily assembled by you or by others to create modular systems that can do absolutely anything. That's why APIs are so interesting. But why should their design matter?

1.2 Why API design matters

Even if it is useful, an API seems to be only a technical interface for software. So why should the design of such an interface be important?

APIs are used by software, it's true. But who builds the software that uses them? Developers. People. These people expect these programming interfaces to be helpful and simple, just like any other (well-designed) interface. Think about how you react when faced with a poorly designed website or mobile application UI. How do you feel when faced with a poorly designed everyday thing, such as a remote control or even a door? You may be annoyed, even become angry or rant, and probably want to never use it again. And, in some cases, a poorly designed interface can even be dangerous. That's why the design of any interface matters, and APIs are no exception.

1.2.1 A public or private API is an interface for other developers

You learned in section 1.1.1 that the API consumer can be either the software using the API or the company or individuals developing that software. All these consumers are important, but the first consumer to take into consideration is the developer.

As you've seen, different APIs are involved in the example social networking use case. There is the timeline module that handles data storage and exposes a private API. And there are the public (provided by other companies) facial recognition and photo storage APIs. The backend that calls these three APIs does not pop into the air by itself; it's developed by the Social Network company.

To use the facial recognition API, for example, developers write code in the Social Network software in order to send the photos to have faces detected and to handle the result of the photo processing, just like when using a software library. These developers are not the ones who created the facial recognition API, and they probably don't know each other because they are from different companies. We can also imagine that the mobile application, website, backend, and the data storage module are developed by different teams within the company. Depending on the company's organization, those teams might know each other well or not at all. And even if every developer in the company knows every little secret of every API it has developed, new developers will inevitably arrive.

So, whether public or private, whatever the reason an API is created and whatever the company's organization, it will sooner or later be used by other developers—people who have *not* participated in the creation of the software exposing the API. That is why everything must be done in order to facilitate these newcomers when writing code to use the API. Developers expect APIs to be helpful and simple, just like any interface they have to interact with. That is why API design matters.

> ### Developer experience
>
> An API's *developer experience* (DX) is the experience developers have when they use an API. It encompasses many different topics such as registration (to use the API), documentation (to know what the API does and how to use it), or support (to get help when having trouble). But all effort put into any DX topic is worth nothing if the most important one is not properly handled—API design.

1.2.2   *An API is made to hide the implementation*

API design matters because when people use an API, they want to use it without being bothered by petty details that have absolutely nothing to do with them. And, to do so, the design of an API must conceal implementation details (what actually happens). Let me use a real-life analogy to explain this.

Say you decide to go to a restaurant. What about a French one? When you go to a restaurant, you become a *customer*. As a restaurant's customer, you read its menu to find out what kinds of food you can order. You decide to try the Bordeaux-style lamprey (it's a famous French fish dish from the Gascony region). To order the meal you have chosen, you talk to a (usually very kind and friendly) person called a *waiter* or *waitress*. A while later, the waiter comes back and gives you the meal you have ordered—the Bordeaux-style lamprey—that has been prepared in the *kitchen*. While you eat this delicious meal, may I ask you two questions?

First, do you know how to cook Bordeaux-style lamprey? Probably not, and that may be the reason why you go to a restaurant. And even if you do know how to cook this recipe, you may not want to cook it because it's complex and requires hard-to-find ingredients. You go to a restaurant to eat food you don't know how to cook or don't want to cook.

Second, do you know what happened between the point in time when the waiter took your order and when they brought it back to you? You might guess that the waiter has been to the kitchen to give your order to a cook, who works alone. This cook prepares your meal and notifies the waiter when it is done by ringing a small bell and yelling, "Order for table number 2 is ready." But this scenario could be slightly different.

The waiter might use a smartphone to take your order, which is instantly shown on a touchscreen in the kitchen. In the kitchen, there's not a lonely cook, but a whole kitchen brigade. Once the kitchen brigade prepares your meal, one of them marks your order as Done on the kitchen's touchscreen, and the waiter is notified on the smartphone. Whatever the number of cooks, you are unaware of the recipe and ingredients used to cook your meal. Regardless of the scenario, the meal you've ordered by talking to the waiter has been cooked in the kitchen, and the waiter has delivered it to you. At a restaurant, you only speak to the waiter (or waitress), and you don't need to know what happens in the kitchen. What does all this have to do with APIs? Everything, as shown in figure 1.5.

From the social networking mobile application developer team's perspective, *sharing a photo* using the backend API is exactly the same, however the backend is implemented. The developers don't need to know the recipe and its ingredients; they only provide the photo and a message. They don't care if the photo is passed through image recognition before or after being added to the timeline. They also don't care if the backend is a single application written in Go or Java that handles everything, or relies on other APIs written in NodeJS, Python, or whatever language. When a developer creates a *consumer application* (the customer) that uses a *provider application* (the restaurant) through its API (the waiter or waitress) to do something (like ordering a meal), the developer and the application are only aware of the API; they don't need to know how to *do something* themselves or how the provider software (the kitchen) will actually do it. But hiding the implementation isn't enough. It's important, but it's not what people using APIs really seek.

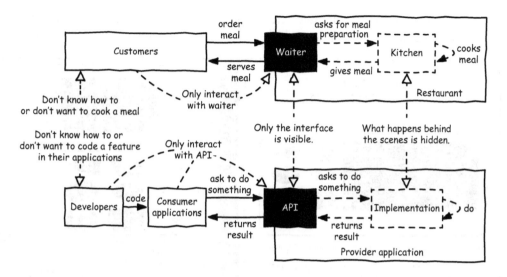

Figure 1.5   The parallels between dining at a restaurant and using an API

1.2.3   *The terrible consequences of poorly designed APIs*

What do you do when you use an everyday thing you've never used before? You take a close look at its interface to determine its purpose and how to use it based on what you can see and your past experience. And this is where design matters.

Let's consider a hypothetical example: a device called the UDRC 1138. What could this device be? What might be its purpose? Well, its name does not really help us to guess it. Maybe its interface can give us more clues. Take a look at figure 1.6.

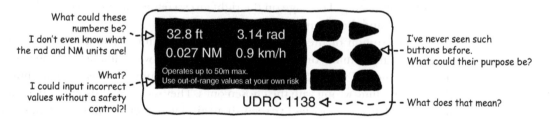

Figure 1.6   The cryptic interface of the UDRC 1138 device

On the right, there are six unlabeled, triangular and rectangular buttons. Could they mean something like start and stop? You know, like media player buttons. The four other buttons have unfamiliar shapes that do not give any hint about their purpose. The LCD display screen shows unlabeled numbers with units such as ft, NM, rad, and km/h. We might guess that *ft* is a distance in feet, and *km/h* is a speed in kilometers per hour, but what might *rad* and *NM* mean? And, at the bottom of the LCD screen, there's also a troublesome warning message telling us that we can input out-of-range values without a safety control.

This interface is definitely hard to decipher and not very intuitive. Let's take a look at the documentation, shown in figure 1.7, to see what it tells us about the device.

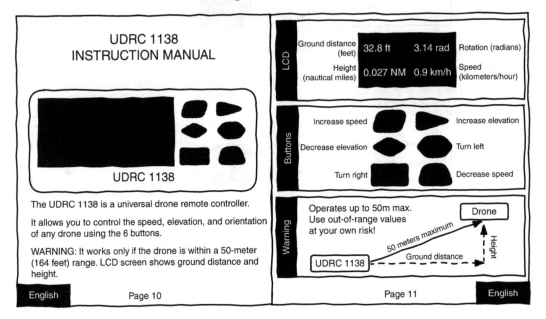

Figure 1.7   The UDRC 1138's documentation

According to the description, this device is a universal drone remote controller—hence the UDRC 1138 name, I suppose—that can be used to control any drone. Well, it sounds interesting. The page on the right gives a few explanations of the LCD screen, the buttons, and the warning message.

The description of the LCD screen is quite puzzling. Ground distance is in feet, height in nautical miles, drone orientation is provided with radians, and speed is in kilometers per hour. I'm not familiar with aeronautical units of measurement, but I sense there's something wrong with the chosen ones. They seem inconsistent. Mixing feet and meters? And in all the movies I've seen about airplanes, feet measure height and nautical miles measure distance, not the inverse. This interface is definitely not intuitive.

Looking at the button's descriptions, we can see that to increase elevation we use the triangular button at the top right, and to decrease it we use the diamond-shaped button in the second row. The connection isn't obvious—why aren't these related controls next to each other? The other controls also use shapes that mean absolutely nothing and seem to be placed randomly. This is insane! How is a user supposed to use the device easily? Why not use good old joysticks or directional pads instead of buttons?

And last, but not least, the explanation of the warning message. It seems that the drone can only be operated withing a 50 meter range—the range being calculated based on the ground distance and height provided by the LCD screen. Wait, what? We have to calculate the distance between the remote controller and the drone using the Pythagorean theorem?! This is total nonsense; the device should do that for us.

Would you buy or even try to use such a device? Probably not. But what if you have no other option than to use this terrible device? Well, I wish you the best of luck; you'll need it to achieve anything with such a poorly designed interface!

You're probably thinking that such a disastrous interface couldn't actually exist in real life. Surely designers couldn't create such a terrible device. And even if they did, surely the quality assurance department would never let it go into production! But let's face the truth. Poorly designed devices—everyday things with poorly designed interfaces—*do* go into production all the time.

Think about how many times you have been puzzled or have grumbled when using a device, a website, or an application because its design was flawed. How many times have you chosen not to buy or not to use something because of its design? How many times were you unable to use something, or to use it correctly or how you wanted to, because its interface was incomprehensible?

A poorly designed product can be misused, underused, or not used at all. It can even be dangerous for its users and for the organization that created it, whose reputation is on the line. And if it's a physical device, once it has gone into production, it's too late to fix it.

Terrible design flaws are not reserved to the interfaces of everyday things. Unfortunately, APIs can also suffer from the disease of poor design. Recall that an API is an interface that developers are supposed to use within their software. Design matters, whatever the type of interface, and APIs are no exception. Poorly designed APIs can be just as frustrating as a device like the UDRC 1138. A poorly designed API can be a real pain to understand and use, and this can have terrible consequences.

How do people choose a public API, an API as a product? Like with an everyday thing, they look at its interface and documentation. They go to the API's developer portal, read the documentation, and analyze the API to understand what it allows them to do and how to use it. They evaluate whether it will let them achieve their purpose effectively and simply. Even the best documentation will not be able to hide design flaws that make an API hard or even dangerous to use. And if they spot such flaws, these potential users, these potential customers, will not choose the API. No customers, no revenue. This could lead to a company going bankrupt.

What if some people decide to use the flawed API anyway? Sometimes, users may simply not detect flaws at first sight. Sometimes, users may have no other choice than using such terrible APIs. This can happen, for example, inside an organization. Most of the time people have no other choice but to use terrible private APIs or terrible APIs provided by commercial off-the-shelf applications.

Whatever the context, design flaws increase the time, effort, and money needed to build software using the API. The API can be misused or underused. The users may need extensive support from the API provider, raising costs on the provider side. These are potentially grave consequences for both private and public APIs. What's more, with public APIs, users can complain publicly or simply stop using them, resulting in fewer customers and less revenue for the API providers.

Flawed API design can also lead to security vulnerabilities in the API, such as exposing sensitive data inadvertently, neglecting access rights and group privileges, or placing too much trust in consumers. What if some people decided to exploit such vulnerabilities? Again, the consequences could be disastrous for the API consumers and providers.

In the API world, it's often possible to fix a poor design after the API goes into production. But there is a cost: it will take time and money for the provider to fix the mess, and it might also seriously bother the API's consumers.

These are only a few examples of harmful impacts. Poorly designed APIs are doomed to fail. What can be done to avoid such a fate? It's simple: *learn how to design APIs properly.*

1.3   *The elements of API design*

Learning to design APIs is about far more than just learning to design programming interfaces. Learning to design APIs requires learning principles, and not only technologies, but also requires knowing all facets of API design. Designing APIs requires one to not only focus on the interfaces themselves, but to also know the whole context surrounding those and to show empathy for all users and the software involved. Designing APIs without principles, totally out of context, and without taking into consideration both sides of the interface—the consumer's side and also the provider's—is the best way to ensure a total failure.

1.3.1   *Learning the principles beyond programming interface design*

When (good) designers put a button in a specific spot, choose a specific form, or decide to add a red LED on an object, there is a reason. Knowing these reasons helps designers to create good interfaces for everyday items that will let people achieve their goals as simply as possible—whether these items are doors, washing machines, mobile applications, or anything else. It's the same for APIs.

The purpose of an API is to let people achieve their goals as simply as possible, whatever the *programming* part. Fashions come and go in software. There have been and there will be many different ways of exposing data and capabilities through software. There have been and there will be many different ways of enabling software communication over a network. You may have heard about RPC, SOAP, REST, gRPC, or GraphQL. You can create APIs with all of these technologies: some are architectural styles, others are protocols or query languages. To make it simpler, let's call them *API styles.*

Each API style can come with some (more or less) common practices that you can follow, but they will not stop you from making mistakes. Without knowing fundamental principles, you can be a bit lost when choosing a so-called common practice; you can struggle to find solutions when facing unusual use cases or contexts not covered by common practices. And if you switch to a new API style, you will have to relearn everything.

Knowing the fundamental principles of API design gives you a solid foundation with which to design APIs of any style and to face any design challenge. But knowing such design principles is only one facet of API design.

1.3.2 *Exploring all facets of API design*

Designing an interface is about far more than placing buttons on the surface of an object. Designing an object such as a drone remote controller requires designers to know what its purpose is and what users want to achieve using it. Such a device is supposed to control the speed, elevation, and direction of a flying object. This is what users want to do, and they don't care if it is done using radio waves or any other technology.

All these actions must be represented by a user interface with buttons, joysticks, sliders, or some other type of control. The purpose of these controls and their representations must make sense, they must be easily usable by users, and most importantly, they must be totally secure. The UDRC 1138's interface is a perfect example of a totally unusable and unsecure interface with its perplexing LCD or buttons and its absence of a safety control.

The design of such a remote control must also take into consideration the whole context. How will it be used? For example, if it is to be used in extreme cold, it would be wise to use controls that can be operated with bulky gloves. Also, the underlying technology may add some constraints on the interface. For example, transmitting an order to the drone cannot be done more than *X* times per second.

Finally, how could such a terrible design be put into production? Maybe the designers involved were not trained sufficiently and did not get enough guidance. Maybe the design never was validated. If only some people, maybe potential users, had reviewed this design, its blatant flaws probably could have been fixed. Maybe the designers created a good model but, in the end, their plan was not respected at all.

Whatever its quality, once people get used to an object and its interface, changes must be made with extreme caution. If a new version of this remote controller were to come out with a totally different button organization, users might not be willing to buy the new version because they would have to relearn how to operate the controller.

As you can see, designing an object's interface requires focusing on more than just buttons. It's the same with API design.

Designing an API is about far more than just designing an easy-to-understand and easy-to-use interface on your own. We must design a totally secure interface—not unduly exposing sensitive data or actions to consumers. We must take the whole context into consideration—what the constraints are, how the API will be used and by whom, how the API is built, and how it could evolve. We have to participate in the whole API lifecycle, from early discussions to development, documentation, evolution, or retirement, and everything in between. And as organizations usually build many APIs, we should work together with all other API designers to ensure that all of the organization's APIs have a similar look and feel in order to build individual APIs that are as consistent as possible, thus ensuring that the sum of all the APIs is as easy to understand and easy to use as each individual one.

Summary

- Web APIs turn software into reusable bricks that can be used over a network with the HTTP protocol.
- APIs are interfaces for developers who build the applications consuming them.
- API design matters for all APIs—public or private.
- Poorly designed APIs can be underused, misused, or not used at all, and even unsecure.
- Designing a good API requires that you take the whole context of the application into consideration, not only the interface itself.

Designing an API
for its users

This chapter covers

- Which perspective to focus on when designing APIs

- Approaching API design like designing a user interface

- How to accurately determine an API's real goals

If you were eager to jump right into the programming interface design battlefield, I'm deeply sorry, but you will have to wait for the next chapter. In this chapter, we look at the API's users' needs.

When you want to build or create something, you need a plan. You need to determine what you want to do before actually doing it. API design is no exception.

An API is not made to blindly expose data and capabilities. An API, like any everyday user interface, is made for its *users* in order to help them achieve *their goals*. For a social networking API, some of these goals could be to share a photo, to add a friend, or to list friends. These goals form the functional blueprint required to design an effective API, and that's why identifying goals is a crucial step in the API design process. These goals—what users can achieve using your API—must make sense for the users, and none should be missed.

Determining a relevant and comprehensive list of goals demands a focus on the *consumer's perspective*: the point of view of the API's users and the software consuming the API. This perspective is the cornerstone of API design, and it is what must guide the API designer throughout the design process. Sticking to this perspective not only requires you to understand it, but you must also be aware of another perspective that can hinder API design—the *provider's perspective* (the organization's point of view and the software exposing the API).

2.1   The right perspective for designing everyday user interfaces

API designers have much to learn from the design of everyday user interfaces, whether they are interfaces of physical or virtual objects. From everyday physical interfaces (doors, kitchen appliances, or TV remote controls) to everyday virtual interfaces (websites or mobile applications), all share common design principles that must be applied to the design of APIs too. Choosing the right point of view, the right perspective, is one of the most crucial aspects of design for all of these interfaces and for APIs.

> **NOTE**   Focus on what happens under the hood and it will end in a total disaster. Focus on what users can do and everything will go smoothly.

When designing APIs, separating these two perspectives and understanding them isn't always easy at first. But transposed into the real world, all this becomes blatantly obvious, and how these two perspectives can affect API design becomes easier to grasp.

2.1.1   Focusing on how things work leads to complicated interfaces

Let me introduce, with fanfare, the Kitchen Radar 3000 (shown in figure 2.1). According to the advertisement, this kitchen appliance brings "state-of-the-art military-grade components into your kitchen so you will never ruin any recipe and will become the fastest cook in town." Whoa, totally thrilling, isn't it? Well, not really.

What on earth is a Kitchen Radar 3000? Its name does not help us to decipher its purpose. Maybe its control panel can give us some clues … or maybe not.

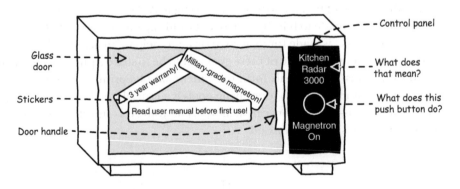

Figure 2.1   The Kitchen Radar 3000

As you can see in figure 2.1, there's a single Magnetron On button. What is a magnetron? What happens when it's turned on? This device is a total mystery.

But look, there's a sticker on the glass door that invites us to read the user manual (figure 2.2). Maybe we will find some useful information there to help us understand this strange kitchen appliance's purpose and how to use it.

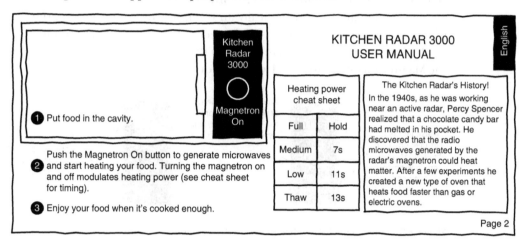

Figure 2.2   The Kitchen Radar 3000's (insane) user manual

OK, according to the user manual, the Kitchen Radar 3000 seems to be a new type of oven that uses radio microwaves, or simply microwaves, to heat food. It was invented by someone who was working on radars, hence the name. What a terrible idea: naming something based on its history and totally hiding its real purpose!

So how does it work? When users push and hold the Magnetron On button, it turns a component called the magnetron on. This component's job is to generate radio microwaves. These microwaves generate heat when they pass through the food put inside the Kitchen Radar 3000's cavity. Once the food is cooked, users can release the button to turn the magnetron off.

This control panel is not really convenient—users have to time themselves while pressing the button! And that's when users want to use the full heating power of the oven. What happens if they want to use only a fraction of that power? They have to press and release the Magnetron On button at a certain pace, corresponding to the desired heating power. Doing so turns the magnetron on and off, generating fewer microwaves and, therefore, less heat than holding the button down continuously. This is totally insane! Who would use such a device willingly? Probably nobody.

Frankly, this device has not really been designed. It's only exposing its inner workings (the magnetron) and history (the radar) to its users. The device's purpose is hard to decipher. Not only do users have to be aware of how a magnetron operates, but the provided control panel is just a nightmare to use. This appears to be a case where the designer, focusing on how things work, created a device that's not only hard to understand but also hard to use. Was this inevitable? Of course not! Let's see how we can fix this design disaster.

2.1.2   Focusing on what users can do leads to simple interfaces

How could we improve the Kitchen Radar 3000 to make it easier to understand and easier to use? Well, if this device was designed by focusing on how it works, what about trying to redesign it by thinking the opposite way? Let's focus on the users' needs and redesign the device's control panel accordingly.

This kitchen appliance is basically an oven, sort of. And what do users want to do when they use an oven regardless of the technology it uses? They want to heat or cook food. We could simply rebrand the Kitchen Radar 3000 as a microwave oven and replace the Magnetron On button label with Heat or Cook, as shown in figure 2.3.

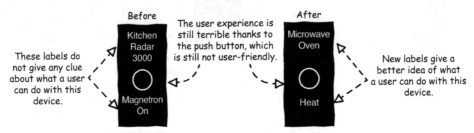

Figure 2.3   Rebranding the Kitchen Radar 3000 as a microwave oven

Well, that's better. By simply changing some labels, we've made it easier for users to understand what this device is for: an oven is obviously made to heat things, and the button obviously starts the heating process.

But this microwave oven still provides a terrible user experience, especially when it comes to heating food at a fraction of the full heating power. Users still have to master the button push/release pace to heat something more slowly. Figure 2.4 shows how we could simplify that.

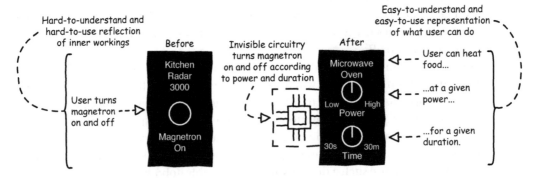

Figure 2.4   Simplifying use by redesigning the control panel

How do people usually heat food using an oven or other cooking device? They heat it for a given *duration* at a given *power*. We could replace the Heat push button with some controls that allow users to provide a duration in seconds and minutes and also specify a low, medium, or high heating power. Some circuitry behind the control panel will handle the magnetron and turn it on and off according to the user's inputs.

This is perfect! This kitchen appliance is now easy to understand and easy to use thanks to this brand-new control panel. This new interface is no longer a cryptic direct access to the device's inner workings. It does not give any hint about what's really happening inside the box; it only focuses on the user's needs. It is a user-friendly representation of what can be achieved with the oven. The details of the inner workings stay hidden inside the circuitry behind the control panel and won't bother the user.

We've just redesigned a kitchen appliance's control panel—so what? What does all this have to do with API design? Everything! We have created an interface that is an easy-to-understand and easy-to-use representation of what users can do with a device, without bothering them with irrelevant inner-working concerns. If you keep this mindset when designing APIs, you will be a great API designer! Why? Because an API is basically a control panel for software and must obey the same rules as any everyday interface.

2.2 Designing software's interfaces

An API is the labels and buttons of software—its control panel. It can be understood at first sight or stay a total mystery, even after days of investigation. It can be a real pleasure to use or a total misery, just like some real-world objects.

Creating an API that is an easy-to-use and easy-to-understand interface requires us to design it while being focused on the good point of view, the right perspective: what users can do. Focus on how the software operates and it will end in a total disaster. Focus on what users can do with it and everything will go smoothly—just like when designing a real-world object.

2.2.1 Viewing an API as software's control panel

When you use a microwave oven, or any other everyday object, you interact with it through its control panel, its interface. You read labels, push buttons, or turn knobs. It's exactly the same when you want to interact programmatically with software: you use its API. As mentioned, an API is software's control panel. But what does this mean, exactly? Let's turn our redesigned Kitchen Radar 3000, our microwave oven, into software (as shown in figure 2.5) to answer this question.

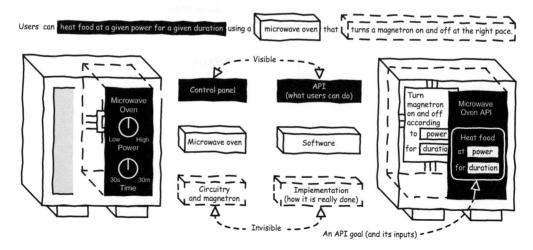

Figure 2.5 Comparing a microwave oven to software

The whole microwave oven becomes the software, the control panel becomes the software's API, and the circuitry behind the control panel becomes the implementation.

The API is what users see; it is a representation of what they can do. The implementation is the code running behind the API. It's how things are really done, but it stays invisible to the user.

An API provides a representation of goals that can be achieved by using it. The microwave oven's API allows its users to heat food. To be achieved, a goal may need some information (inputs). Users have to provide a power setting and a duration to heat their food. The goal's implementation uses the information provided through the API to operate. In this case, the implementation turns the magnetron on and off at a given pace according to the provided power for the provided duration. And when the goal is achieved, it can return some information.

So, an API is a control panel made to interact programmatically with software to achieve goals. But just like with everyday interfaces, those goals might be expressed from the provider's perspective (turn magnetron on) rather than the consumer's (heat food). Is this as big a problem for APIs as it is for everyday interfaces?

2.2.2   *Focusing on the consumer's perspective to create simple APIs*

To understand the consequences of designing an API from the provider's perspective (unduly exposing inner workings), let's compare the pseudocode needed to use the Kitchen Radar 3000 API and the Microwave Oven API.

The Kitchen Radar 3000 API proposes two goals: turn magnetron on and turn magnetron off. The following listing shows how to use these controls to heat food.

Listing 2.1   Using the Kitchen Radar 3000 API

```
if <power> is high           ◄──────┐
  turn magnetron on                  │  No on/off cycle if power is high
  wait for <duration>
  turn magnetron off
else
  if <power> is medium       ◄──────┐
    cycle = 7s                       │  Calculate on/off cycle waiting
  else if <power> is low             │  time based on power
    cycle = 11s
  else if <power> is thaw
    cycle = 13s
  end if                     ┌── Alternating on/off cycle
  for <duration>     ◄───────┘
    turn magnetron on
    wait for <cycle>
    turn magnetron off
  end for
end if
```

If developers want to create a program to heat food using this API, they will have to turn the magnetron on, wait for a given time (duration), then turn the magnetron off. But that's the simple use case when they want to use the full heating power. If they want to heat something at a fraction of full power, they will have to turn the magnetron on and off at a pace that will achieve the desired heating magnitude.

Just like its real-world equivalent, the Kitchen Radar 3000 API is a nightmare to use. Developers need to write complex code in their software in order to use it. They can even make mistakes. There's a bug in the pseudocode, by the way. Did you spot it? The next listing shows how to fix it.

Listing 2.2 Fixing the bug

```
// alternating on/off cycle
for <duration>
  turn magnetron on
  wait for <cycle>
  turn magnetron off
  wait for <cycle>  ◄──────┐  This line was missing.
end for
```

The alternating on/off cycle `for` loop misses a `wait for <cycle>`, which is definitely not the best code, but it works. Let's now see how to do the same thing using the Microwave Oven API, which provides a single `heat food` goal. Heating food with this is simple, as shown in the following listing.

Listing 2.3 Using the Microwave Oven API

```
heat food at <power> for <duration>
```

Developers only need to write a single line of pseudocode; it can't be simpler than that. As a developer who wants to provide software to heat food, which API would you prefer to use: the one that needs complicated, error-prone code, or the one that needs a single error-proof line of code? This is, of course, a rhetorical question.

Just like a control panel, the complexity or simplicity of an API depends above all on the perspective you focus on when designing it. Did you know anything about magnetrons and the microwave oven's invention before reading this book? Probably not. Why? Because a microwave oven's control panel is designed from its users' perspective. It does not expose irrelevant inner workings. It does not require the user to be a magnetron or radar expert to use it. It can be used by anyone who wants to heat food. And did this lack of knowledge interfere with your use of a microwave oven? Absolutely not. Why? Because when you use it, you just want to heat food. You don't care about exactly how it will be done.

This is how any API must be designed. An API must be designed from its consumer's perspective and not its provider's. Figure 2.6 contrasts these two perspectives.

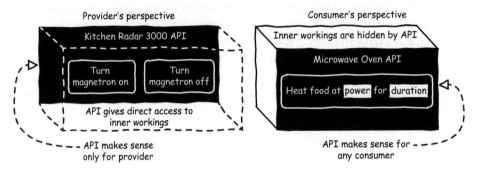

Figure 2.6   The consumer's versus provider's perspective

An API designed from the provider's perspective is only a window showing inner workings and, therefore, presenting goals that make sense only for the provider. As you saw with the Kitchen Radar 3000 API, such an API will unavoidably be complicated to use, and consumers will not be able to do what they want to do simply. In contrast, an API designed from the consumer's perspective is a display screen hiding inner workings. It only shows goals that make sense for any consumer and lets them achieve what they want to do simply. Focusing on this perspective will put an API on the right path to ensure its usability.

OK, when designing an API, we need to think about the consumer first. And, by doing so, it seems important to clearly identify the goals that consumers can achieve when using an API in order to ensure the creation of an easy-to-understand and easy-to-use API. But how do we do that accurately and exhaustively?

2.3   *Identifying an API's goals*

Based on our microwave oven experiment, I hope you are now convinced that the very first step in the API design process is to determine what its users can achieve by using it—to identify the API's real goals. For our Microwave Oven API, it was simply heat food; but, for a social networking API, it could be goals like share a photo, add a friend, or list friends. But such simple descriptions are not precise enough. How does a user add a friend, exactly? What is needed to do that? What does the user get in return? It is fundamental in designing an API to have a deep, accurate, and precise knowledge of

- Who can use the API
- What they can do
- How they do it
- What they need to do it
- What they get in return

These pieces of information are the foundations of your API, and you need those to be able to design an accurate programming interface. The method and the API goals canvas described in this chapter are simple but powerful tools that will help you acquire all the information you need.

The goal of designing software (or anything else) that fulfills users' needs is not something new. It has been a goal as long as software has existed. Numerous methods have been and are still being invented in order to collect users' needs, to get a deep and accurate understanding of them, and finally to create some software that fulfills their goals more or less efficiently and accurately. These methods can all be used to identify an API's goals. Feel free to use the one you are familiar with or adapt the method presented in this book as you see fit, as long as you know who your users are, what they can do, and how they can do it. The following sections describe these principles.

2.3.1 Identifying the whats and the hows

When we redesigned the Kitchen Radar 3000 into a microwave oven, we answered two questions, as shown in figure 2.7. The first question was, "What do people want to do when they use an oven?" The answer was, "They want to heat food." This answer led to a second question: "How do people heat food?" The answer was, "They heat food at a given power for a given duration." This simple questioning helped us identify the information we needed to design a simple and user-friendly heat food goal for the Microwave Oven API—the *whats* and the *hows*. This example shows two of the fundamental questions to ask when determining an API goals list:

- What can users do?
- How do they do it?

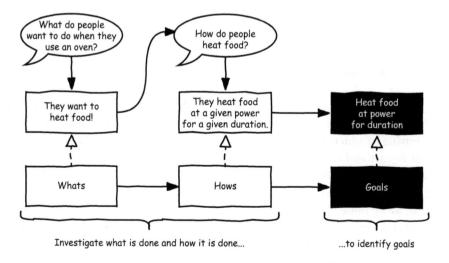

Figure 2.7   How we redesigned the Kitchen Radar 3000's control panel

With these questions, we roughly describe what can be done with the API (the *whats*) and decompose them into steps (the *hows*), with each step becoming a goal of the API.

But, in this example, the whats and the hows are basically the same thing, so do we really need to do this decomposition? Definitely. Unfortunately, the microwave oven example is too simplistic to illustrate that. We need a more complex use case, so let's work on an API for an online shopping website or mobile application. What would be the whats and the hows of a Shopping API? Figure 2.8 shows these.

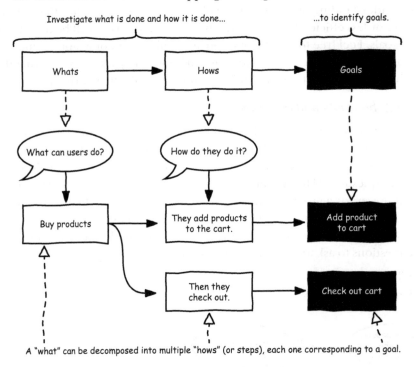

Figure 2.8   The Shopping API whats and hows

What do people do when they shop online? Well, they buy products. And how do they buy these products? They add them to their shopping cart and then check out.

So, buying products is a two-step process that can be represented by these goals: add product to cart and check out cart. Without doing the decomposition, we could have wrongly listed a single buy product goal. That's why we must decompose the whats into hows: if we don't do that, we might miss some goals.

Great, we're done! To identify an API's goals, we just need to roughly list what users can do and decompose these actions into steps by examining how they do them. Each step corresponds to a goal. So, let's take the next step and design the programming interface corresponding to these goals. But wait … I think we missed something.

When we redesigned the microwave oven, we did more than just identify a heat food goal. We implicitly identified the power and duration as the user's inputs. That helped us to redesign the Kitchen Radar 3000's control panel, so it could be interesting to identify goal inputs and outputs.

2.3.2   Identifying inputs and outputs

A goal might need some inputs to be achieved. For our Microwave Oven API, the heat food inputs were the power and duration. These inputs helped us to design the microwave's control panel and API. A goal can even return some outputs when achieved. These outputs also impact the API design. So, let's identify these goals for our Shopping API, as shown in figure 2.9.

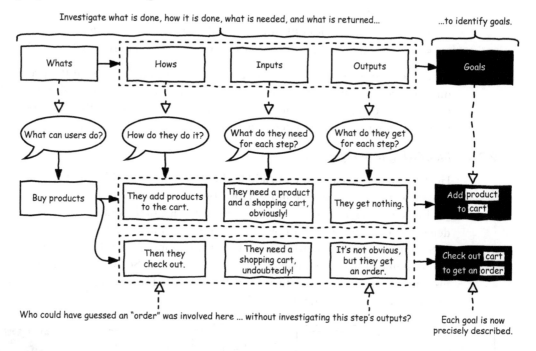

Figure 2.9   The whats, the hows, and their inputs and outputs

What do people do when they shop online? Well, they buy some products. And how do they buy these products? They add them to their shopping cart and then check out. Nothing new for these two first questions. Let's now dig into each step to determine its inputs and outputs.

We'll start with the add products to the cart goal. What do people need to add a product to a cart? They obviously need a product and a cart. Good, and do they get something in return when they add a product to their cart? No. Well, these new questions do not seem to give us any really useful information; the answers are quite obvious. Maybe we will get something more interesting for the check out step

Do people need something to check out a cart? Clearly, a cart. Still an obvious answer. And do they get something in return? Yes, an order confirmation. (This one was not so obvious.)

Could we have guessed that the API would manipulate some orders by just looking at the check out cart goal? Maybe with such a simple API, but maybe not with a more complex one.

To design an accurate software control panel comprising all the needed buttons and labels, we need to have an accurate vision not only of the goals, but also of what we need to achieve them and what we get in return. Identifying an API's goals isn't only about what can be done with it, but also what data can be manipulated through it. This is why we need to add two more questions to our list:

- What can users do?
- How do they do it?
- New question to identify inputs: What do they need to do it?
- New question to identify outputs: What do they get in return?

Great, now we really are done! Let's go to the next step and design the programming interface corresponding to these goals. But wait … we missed something again! How does a user get a product to add to the shopping cart? It seems that this obvious question can be of interest when detecting some missing goals after all.

2.3.3   *Identifying missing goals*

How does a user get a product to add to the shopping cart? This is a mystery. It seems we missed one goal, and maybe more. How could we avoid that? There is no silver bullet, but by examining the sources of the inputs and usage of the outputs, we might be able to detect some missing whats or hows and, therefore, some missing or unidentified goals.

So how do users get a product to add to the shopping cart? They probably search for it by its name or description before adding it to the cart. So, we can add a new search for products step in the buy products *what*. We must not forget to apply our questioning to this new step, as shown in figure 2.10.

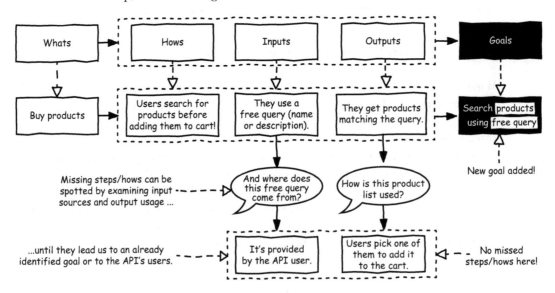

Figure 2.10   Adding a missing how

What do users need to search for a product? Well, it's a free text query; it can be a name or a description, for example. What does this search return? A list of products matching the query. How do users get the search query? They provide the search query themselves. How is the list of products used? Users pick one of them to add to the cart.

We've now dug into all the inputs and outputs until the answers led us to the API's users or an already identified goal. This way, we're sure there are no more missing steps on this path. Great. One problem solved. Let's investigate the next step, check out cart, as shown in figure 2.11.

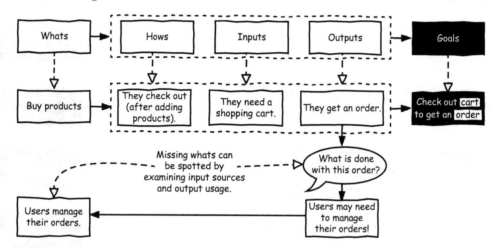

Figure 2.11   Adding a missing what

It needs a cart and returns an order. We will not investigate where the cart comes from (you can do that as an exercise), but what is done with the order? Why do we return it to the user? Maybe so the user can check the order's status? Interesting, but I sense there's more. Users will probably need to manage their orders. I think we have just spotted a missing what! So, let's add a new manage orders answer to our "What can users do?" question and start our investigation.

How do users manage their orders? They should be able to list their orders in chronological order to check their status. So we have two steps to investigate. The resulting Shopping API goals list is shown in figure 2.12.

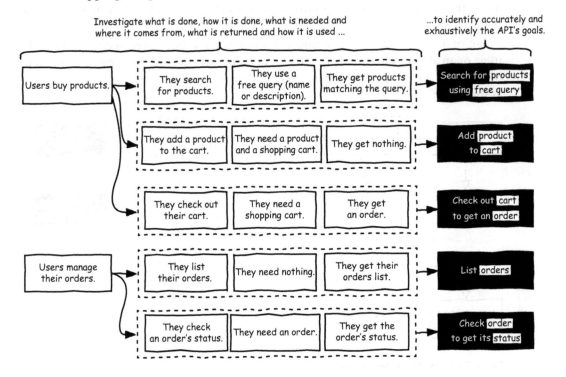

Figure 2.12   Shopping API goals list with the new user's manage their orders what

First, list orders: What input is needed to list orders? Nothing. What is returned? A list of orders. Where do the inputs come from? We don't need any input to list orders, so we don't need to think about where the inputs come from. What is done with the outputs? Users can pick one of the orders in the list to check its status. Now we're done with the first step of managing orders.

The second step, check order status: What input is needed to check an order's status? An order. What is returned? An order status. Where does the order come from? From the check out cart or the list orders step. What is done with the order's status? We want to provide this data to inform users, nothing more.

Fantastic. A new what, two more hows, and goals identified. So let's enhance our questioning with two more questions to identify inputs sources and outputs uses:

- What can users do?
- How do they do it?
- What do they need to do it?
- What do they get in return?
- New question to identify missing goals: Where do the inputs come from?
- New question to identify missing goals: How are the outputs used?

Investigating input sources and output uses definitely helps to spot missing API goals. But we are still not ready to design the programming interface. The goals list is still incomplete because I intentionally made yet another mistake. Do you know what it is? If you apply our questioning to our latest goals list, you should be able to find it. To tell the truth, there are many missing goals; we have only scratched the surface of the Shopping API's goals. But the one I have in mind concerns the products returned by the search for products goal. The next section addresses that answer.

2.3.4 Identifying all users

We've said that users can search for products and add them to their carts, but where do those products come from? They come from the products catalog, of course! But these products don't magically appear by themselves in this catalog. Someone must have put them there. As a customer, you don't add products to the catalog yourself; some admin user does that. You see?

By simply applying our usual line of questioning, we've again spotted a hole in our Shopping API goals list. This is great! But instead of waiting to discover these users by investigating inputs and outputs, we could be more efficient by adding a new dimension in our questioning, as shown in figure 2.13.

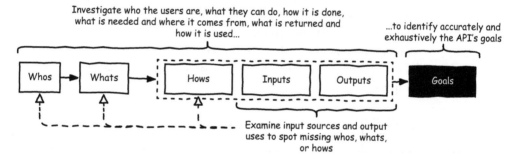

Figure 2.13   Investigating the whos, whats, hows, inputs, and outputs to identify goals

Identifying the different types of users is mandatory when building an exhaustive API goals list. So we must add another inquiry to our line of questioning in order to explicitly identify them all:

- New question to identify all users and avoid missing whats: Who are the users?
- What can they do?
- How do they do it?
- What do they need to do it?
- What do they get in return?
- Where do the inputs come from?
- How are the outputs used?

If we *first* identify the different types of users of our API, we can build a comprehensive goals list more easily. Note that the term *user* is used in a broad sense here; it can be an end user using the application consuming the API, the consumer application itself, or end user's or consumer application's roles or profiles. And remember, we can still rely on examining inputs and outputs to make sure we spot all users.

That makes a lot of questions to handle. Let's see how we can make this questioning easier with an API goals canvas.

2.3.5   *Using the API goals canvas*

Now that we know which questions to ask and why we must ask them in order to identify an API's comprehensive and precise list of goals, let's see how we can handle this investigative process with an API goals canvas, as shown in figure 2.14.

The *API goals canvas* is nothing more than a table composed of six columns, matching the process we have discovered through the previous sections:

- *Whos*—Where you list the API's users (or profiles)
- *Whats*—Where you list what these users can do
- *Hows*—Where you decompose each of the what's into steps
- *Inputs (source)*—Where you list what is needed for each step and where it comes from (to spot missing whos, whats, or hows)
- *Output (usage)*—Where you list what is returned by each step and how it is used (to spot missing whos, whats, or hows)
- *Goals*—Where you explicitly and concisely reformulate each how + inputs + outputs

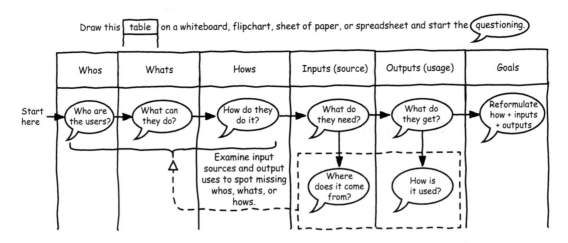

Figure 2.14   The API goals canvas

Whos	Whats	Hows	Inputs (source)	Outputs (usage)	Goals
Customers	Buy products	Search for products	Catalog (manage catalog), free query (provided by user)	Products (add product to cart)	Search for products in catalog using free query
		Add product to cart	Product (search for products), cart (owned by user)		Add product to cart
Admin	Manage catalog	Add product to catalog	Catalog (owned by user), product (provided by user)		Add product to catalog

Figure 2.15 The Shopping API goals canvas (partial view)

Figure 2.15 shows a partial view of the API goals canvas for our Shopping API. The API goals canvas and its underlying questioning method help you envision who uses the API, what they can do with it, how they do it, what they need, and what they get in return. These are the fundamental pieces of information you need to design the programming interface representing the identified goals.

You might have noticed that we did not talk about fine-grained data and errors. We will talk about those later in chapter 3 (section 3.3) for fine-grained data and in chapter 5 (section 5.2) for errors. The API goals canvas is only a high-level view; you should not dive too much into details at this stage.

Be warned that even without diving too much into such details, filling an API's goals can be quite difficult in some complex contexts. There can be many users/profiles or too many whats use cases to deal with. This isn't specific to API design; this happens when designing any software solution. Do not try to cover all use cases in one shot. Instead, focus on a small set of use cases. If a what contains many steps or many branches, focus on the main path and, after that, check if there are variations leading to new goals in other paths. The same goes for users: trying to explore all whats for all users or profiles can be difficult. Focus on the main user or profile, and after that check if there are variations for others.

Listing an API's goals is an iterative process. You have to proceed step by step—not trying to do everything at once. And you will also have to refine and modify this list based on some considerations or constraints like usability, performance, or security. You will discover those throughout the rest of this book.

NOTE Feel free to adapt this method and tool, or use any other one you are familiar with, as long as it enables you to get the information listed in the API goals canvas.

Unfortunately, this method does not guarantee that your API goals list will be defined from the consumer's perspective. Yes, the first question ("Who are the users?") doesn't prevent the provider's perspective from surfacing in your API's goals. To be sure you don't fall into one of its traps while building your API goals list, we need to investigate the various facets of the *treacherous* provider's perspective.

2.4   Avoiding the provider's perspective when designing APIs

Whether you're designing your API from scratch or basing it upon existing systems, the provider's perspective will inevitably show up in every stage of its design. Being aware of its various facets is fundamental for any API designer who hopes to stay on the consumer's perspective path and design easy-to-understand and easy-to-use APIs.

Do you remember our Kitchen Radar 3000 API? Its name laden with history, and its user-unfriendly Turn magnetron on/off goals. Exposing the inner workings was a blatant example of API design heavily influenced by the provider's perspective. Unfortunately, this perspective is not always so obvious, but there's an adage popular among people working in software design that brings into the light the dark corners of the provider's perspective. It is known as *Conway's law*, and it is often quoted to explain how a system's design can be influenced by its inner workings. It states that

> *"Any organization that designs a system (defined broadly) will produce a design whose structure is a copy of the organization's communication structure."*

Mel Conway
"How Do Committees Invent?"
Datamation, April 1968

This adage can be applied to a wide range of systems, from human organizations to software systems and, of course, APIs. It means that an API's design can be influenced by the communication structure of the organization providing it, as shown in figure 2.16.

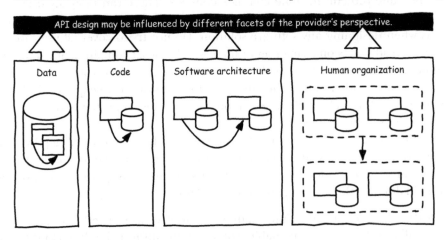

Figure 2.16   The different facets of the provider's perspective

Data, code and business logic, software architecture, and human organization shape the communication structure of a company and, therefore, can influence the design of its APIs.

2.4.1 Avoiding data influences

An API is fundamentally a way to exchange data between two pieces of software—a consumer and a provider. Therefore, it is unfortunately common to see API designs that mirror the underlying data organization. How data is structured or named can influence the design of the API, as shown in figure 2.17.

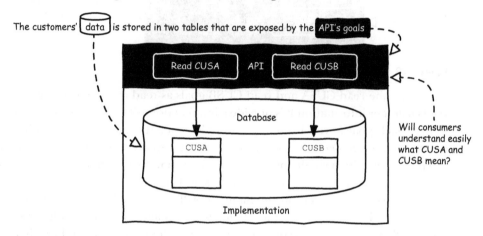

Figure 2.17   Exposing the data organization through the API

Let's say our Shopping API implementation handles customer information in two tables called CUSA and CUSB (don't ask me why!). An API design influenced by such a data structure could bluntly expose two goals: read CUSA and read CUSB. Such an API is hard to understand. What do CUSA and CUSB mean exactly? (I'll also let you imagine the tables' cryptic column names that might be directly exposed to the consumer.) It is also hard to use! Consumers have to use two goals to retrieve all customer data.

> **WARNING**   If your API's goals list and data match your database too closely, whether in structure or name, you might be designing your API from the provider's perspective. In that case, don't hesitate to double check if it's really relevant for the API's users to have access to such details.

Frankly, exposing your database model is more often than not a terrible idea and can lead to an unappealing user experience. Hopefully, figure 2.18 shows how we could fix such a problem.

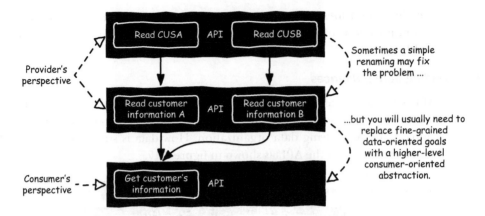

Figure 2.18   Fixing data organization exposure

Renaming the read CUSA and read CUSB goals as read customer information A and read customer information B is one idea, but that doesn't really improve the user experience. Such goals, even if their meaning is easier to understand, are still exposing the provider's perspective. It would be better to replace these two fine-grained, data-oriented goals with a single, higher-level get customer's information goal that is more consumer-oriented and both easy to understand and use.

Mapping data organization and names to API goals and data can make the API hard to understand and use. Using the API goals canvas and focusing on what users can do should allow you to easily avoid such design problems, but they still can happen. So, while you are identifying the API's goals, you should always check that you are not bothering the consumers by unnecessarily exposing your data model through whats, hows, inputs, or outputs.

Exposing the data model is the most obvious sign of the provider's perspective, but this is not the only way it can manifest. How we manipulate the data can also be exposed through an API, and this too is a terrible idea.

2.4.2   *Avoiding code and business logic influences*

The code that manipulates data—the implementation's business logic—can influence API design. Exposing such logic through the API can bother not only the consumer but also the provider. Figure 2.19 shows such an example.

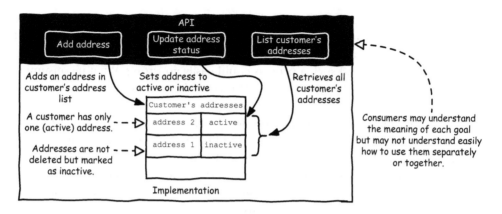

Figure 2.19   Exposing business logic through the API

Let's say that for our Shopping API's implementation, each customer has a single active address. But addresses in the system are never deleted; instead, their *status* is set to *inactive* when the customer moves. An API design influenced by this business logic could provide these provider-oriented goals:

- List customer's addresses (active and inactive)
- Add an address for customer
- Update an address status (to active or inactive)

The words used to describe these goals are understandable, but the overall purpose of the goals might not be obvious to a consumer who doesn't know exactly how the system handles addresses. These goals expose how the data is processed internally; figure 2.20 shows how they have to be used.

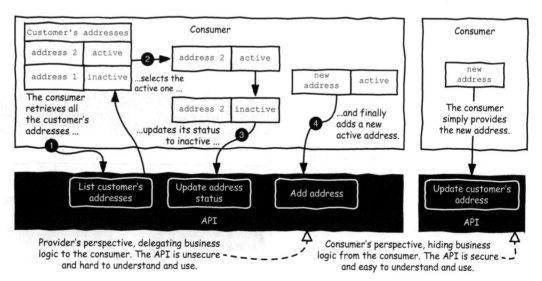

Figure 2.20   Fixing business logic exposure

The left side of figure 2.20 shows how to change a customer's address using this API. Consumers have to list the existing addresses to spot the active one, update it to set its status to inactive, and then add a new active address. Quite simple, no? Not at all! It is awfully complex and such a process could easily go wrong. What if consumers do not set the previous address to inactive? This could be terrible for data integrity—the provider is at risk here.

Thankfully, there is a simple solution shown on the right side of figure 2.20. This whole complex and dangerous mess could be replaced by a simple update customer's address goal. The implementation could do the rest, just like when we let the underlying circuitry handle the magnetron on/off cycle for our Kitchen Radar 3000 API.

Exposing internal business logic can make the API hard for the consumer to use and understand, and can be dangerous for the provider. Again, using the API goals canvas and focusing on what users can do should let you easily avoid such design problems, but they still can happen.

> **TIP** While you are identifying the API's goals, you should always check that you are not inadvertently exposing internal business logic that is not the consumer's business and that could be dangerous for the provider.

We were only dealing with a single software component here. How might things go if we want to build APIs based upon a more complex system involving multiple applications interacting with each other? The provider's perspective is a problem here too.

2.4.3 *Avoiding software architecture influences*

Partly thanks to APIs, it's very common to build systems based on different pieces of software that communicate with each other (remember section 1.1.2 in chapter 1). Such a software architecture can influence API design in the same ways as internal business logic. Figure 2.21 shows such an example.

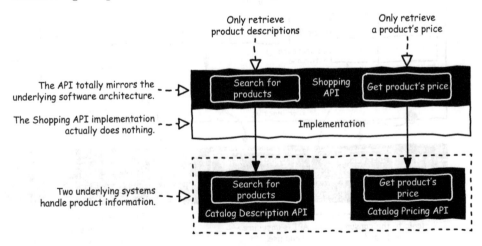

Figure 2.21 Exposing software architecture through the API

Let's say that, for our shopping system, we've decided to handle product descriptions and product pricing in two different backend applications. There are many good (and bad) reasons to do that, but that's not the issue here. Whatever the reasons, it means that product information is hosted in two different systems: Catalog Description and Catalog Pricing. A Shopping API designed from the provider's perspective can bluntly expose those two systems with a search for products goal that only retrieves product descriptions and a get product's price goal that returns a product's price. What does this mean for the consumers? Nothing good. Let's look at that in figure 2.22.

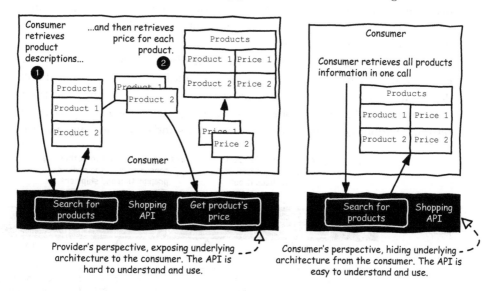

Figure 2.22   Fixing software architecture exposure

The left side shows that in order to search for products and show relevant information to a customer (like description *and* price), a consumer might first have to use the search for products goal to get the descriptions, and then retrieve each found product's price using the get product's price goal to gather all the relevant information. That's not really consumer-friendly.

Consumers don't care about your software architecture choices. What they care about is seeing all the information they need about products when they search for them. It would be better to provide a single search for products goal and let the implementation gather the necessary information from the underlying Catalog Description and Catalog Pricing systems, as shown on the right side of the figure.

Mapping the API design to the underlying software architecture can make the API hard for consumers to understand and use. Once again, using the API goals canvas and focusing on what users can do should allow you to easily avoid such design problems, but they still can happen. So while you are identifying the API's goals, you should always check that your whats and hows are not the result of your underlying software architecture.

We're almost done with our exploration of the different facets of the provider's perspective. After data, code and business logic, and software architecture, there's only one left. It's the most treacherous one: human organization.

2.4.4   *Avoiding human organization influences*

As long as there is more than one person in an organization providing APIs, you will be confronted with the *human organization* aspect of the provider's perspective. This is the fundamental source of Conway's law, mentioned earlier. People are grouped in departments or teams. All these different groups interact and communicate in various ways, using various processes that will inevitably shape all the different systems inside the organization, including APIs.

Let's say our organization that provides the Shopping API is split into three different departments: the Order department that handles customer orders, the Warehouse department that handles the product warehouse and packaging, and the Shipment department that handles the shipment of packages to customers. Figure 2.23 shows the resulting Shopping API designed from provider's and consumer's perspectives.

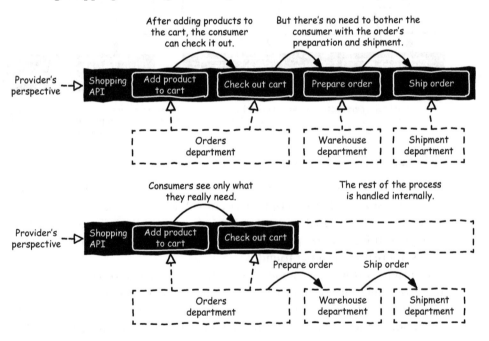

Figure 2.23   Avoiding human organization exposure

If designed from the provider's perspective, our API can expose goals matching this human organization. The problem with these API goals is that they will expose the organization's inner workings in a way that is totally irrelevant to people outside the organization.

If consumers want to order goods for customers, they will have to use the add product to cart, check out cart, prepare order, and ship order goals. We are again exposing things that are not the consumer's business. What reason is there for a consumer to use the goals prepare order and ship order? Absolutely none. From a consumer's point of view, everything should stop at the check out cart goal. When a consumer uses the check out cart goal, the implementation should deal with the Warehouse department to trigger the order's preparation, and the Warehouse department should deal with the Shipment department to trigger the order's shipping. The rest of the process should be handled internally.

Mapping API design to the underlying human organization can make the API hard to understand, hard to use, and even totally irrelevant. Using the API goals canvas and focusing on what users can do should, as before, let you easily avoid such design problems—but they still can happen. So, while you are identifying the API's goals, you should always check if your whats and hows are really the consumer's business.

In the end, all the different aspects of the provider's perspective relate to exposing aspects that are not the consumer's business through the API. Let's see how we can include this matter in our API goals canvas.

2.4.5 Detecting the provider's perspective in the API goals canvas

You have learned that to identify an API's goals, you need to dig into the whos, whats, hows, inputs and their sources, and, finally, outputs and their usage. With this method, you should be able to avoid the most obvious intrusions of the provider's perspective without thinking too much about it. But you also saw that the provider's perspective can be treacherous and not so obvious. Fortunately, our investigations into the provider's perspective showed us its different facets and how it can be spotted by simply considering if what we have identified is really the consumer's business. Figure 2.24 shows a final update to our API goals canvas in order to be fully ready to build a comprehensive and consumer-oriented API goals list.

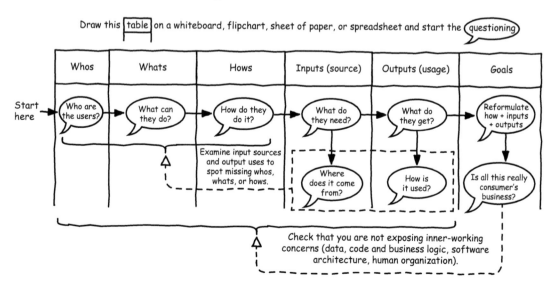

Figure 2.24 The updated API goals canvas

As you can see, all we need to do is add the final question: "Is all this really the consumer's business?" With this question, as you have seen, we will check if any element comes from the provider's perspective (data, code and business logic, software architecture, or human organization). An API goals list established with this canvas will be a strong foundation for the design of the programming interface. In the next chapter, you'll discover how to design such a programming interface based on an API goals list.

Summary

- To be easy for consumers to understand and use, an API must be designed from the consumer's perspective.
- Designing an API from the provider's perspective by bluntly exposing inner workings (data, code and business logic, software architecture, and human organization) inevitably leads to hard-to-understand and hard-to-use APIs.
- A comprehensive and consumer-oriented API goals list is the strongest foundation for an API.
- Identifying users, what they can do, how they do it, what they need to do it, and what they get in return is the key to building a comprehensive API goals list.

Designing a programming interface

3

This chapter covers

- Transposing API goals into a programming interface
- Identifying and mapping REST resources and actions
- Designing API data from concepts
- Differentiating between REST APIs and the REST architectural style
- Why the REST architectural style matters for API design

In the previous chapter, you learned how to identify an API's goals—what users can achieve using it. For a Shopping API, some of these goals could be search for products, get product, add product to cart, check out cart, or list orders. These goals form the API's functional blueprint that we will use to design the actual programming interface that is consumed by its users (developers) and their software. To design this programming interface, we will transpose these goals and their inputs and outputs according to an API style, as shown in figure 3.1.

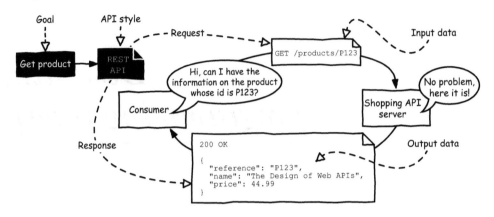

Figure 3.1   REST programming interface for the get product goal

REST stands for Representational State Transfer. Here, the REST API style transposes the get product goal into a programming interface. It is represented by a GET /prod-ucts/{productId} request, where productId is an input parameter (here its value is P123), and a 200 OK is a response with some output data consisting of the reference, name, and price properties. How do we design such a programming interface?

Representing goals using REST or any other type of programming interface requires that you first understand how it works. Indeed, what do these GET, /products/{pro-ductId}, or 200 OK mean, for example? Without knowing that, you will be unable to actually design such a programming interface. Once you have some basic knowledge, you can analyze the goals and represent them according to the chosen API style. You also have to design data exchanged through the API more accurately than what we did when filling in the API goals canvas. The process is similar to what you do when programming.

That sounds quite straightforward, doesn't it? But things are not always that simple. After learning how to transpose basic goals to a programming interface, you might realize that some of your goals cannot be represented easily. In such cases, you have to find a path between user-friendliness and compliance with the chosen API style in order to come up with the best possible representation.

After all this, you may wonder what Representational State Transfer actually means and why it has been chosen as the main example programming interface for this book. To teach API design, why use REST APIs? Why are these APIs better than others? Although they are widely adopted, there's a far more important reason behind this choice: REST APIs are based on the REST architectural style, which relies on solid foundations that are useful to know when designing any type of API. We'll get to that soon, but first things first. Let's talk about some basic REST API principles.

3.1 Introducing REST APIs

To gain sufficient knowledge about REST APIs in order to actually design one, we will analyze the REST API call made by a consumer of the Shopping API to get a product's information, as seen in this chapter's introduction (figure 3.1). We'll take for granted that the REST representation of this goal is GET /products/{productId}, and we will work on the GET /products/P123 example. If you remember section 1.1.1, you should guess that this request has something to do with the HTTP protocol. This analysis will show us how HTTP is actually used by this call. After that, we will be able to dive into the HTTP protocol and the basic principles of REST APIs.

3.1.1 Analyzing a REST API call

What happens when a consumer wants to complete the goal *get product*? Or, more specifically, what happens when they want to get detailed information about a product with the ID P123 from the products catalog using the REST Shopping API? Consumers have to communicate with the server hosting the API using the HTTP protocol, as shown in figure 3.2.

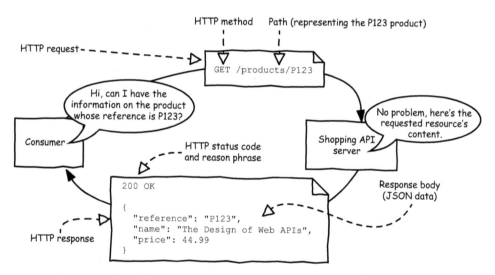

Figure 3.2   A REST API call using the HTTP protocol

Because this goal is represented by GET /products/{productId}, the consumer has to send a GET /products/P123 HTTP request to the Shopping API server. In reply, the server returns an HTTP response containing 200 OK, followed by the requested product's information. (Note that this HTTP exchange has been simplified in order to focus only on the elements that matter to us.)

The request is composed of the GET HTTP method and the /products/P123 path. The *path* is an address identifying a resource on the server; in this case, the P123 product in products. The *HTTP method* indicates what the consumer wants to do with this resource: GET means that they want to retrieve the resource. From a functional perspective, such a request means something like, "Hi, can I have the information on the product whose ID is P123?" But from the HTTP protocol's perspective, it means, "Hi, can I have the resource identified by the /products/P123 path?"

The first part of the response is composed of the 200 HTTP status code and its OK reason phrase. The *HTTP status code* tells us how the processing of the request went. Thanks to the reason phrase, we can guess that the 200 HTTP status code means that everything went OK. The second part of the response is called the *response body*. It contains the content of the resource identified by the path in the request, which, in this case, is the P123 product's information represented as JSON data.

From a functional perspective, the response returned by the API server basically means, "Sure, here's the requested product's information." From the HTTP perspective, it means, "No problem, here's the requested resource's content."

The JSON data format

JSON is a text data format based on how the JavaScript programming language describes data but is, despite its name, completely language-independent (see https://www.json .org/). Using JSON, you can describe objects containing unordered name/value pairs and also arrays or lists containing ordered values, as shown in this figure.

```
{
  "aString": "a string value",
  "aNumber": 1.23,
  "aBoolean": true,
  "aNullValue": null
  "anObject": {
    "name": "value"
  }
}
```

```
[
  { "aString": "one",
    "aNumber": 1 },
  { "aString": "two",
    "aNumber": 2 },
  { "aString": "three",
    "aNumber": 3 }
]
```

A JSON object   A JSON array

Example of JSON documents

An object is delimited by curly braces ({ }). A name is a quoted string ("name") and is separated from its value by a colon (:). A value can be a string like "value", a number like 1.23, a Boolean (true or false), the null value null, an object, or an array. An array is delimited by brackets ([]), and its values are separated by commas (,).

The JSON format is easily parsed using any programming language. It is also relatively easy to read and write. It is widely adopted for many uses such as databases, configuration files, and, of course, APIs.

Now you know how consumers can call the Shopping API to achieve the get product goal. But the HTTP protocol is not made just to retrieve JSON documents.

3.1.2   *Basic principles of HTTP*

HTTP is the foundation of communication for the World Wide Web. It is a programming language-agnostic protocol that is designed to allow the exchange of documents (also called *resources*) between applications over the internet. HTTP is used by a wide range of applications, the best known of which are web browsers.

A web browser uses HTTP to communicate with a web server hosting a website. When you type a URL (such as http://apihandyman.io/about) in the browser's address bar, it sends a GET /about HTTP request to the server hosting apihandyman.io, just like when an API consumer sends a request to a REST API server. The response sent by the server contains a 200 OK HTTP status followed by the HTML page corresponding to the URL.

Browsers use the protocol to retrieve any type of resource (document): HTML pages, CSS files, JavaScript files, images, and any other documents that are needed by the website. But that's not its only use. When you upload a photo to a social networking website, for example, the browser uses the HTTP protocol, but this time to send a document to a server. In this case, the browser sends a POST /photos request with a body containing the image file. The HTTP protocol can therefore also be used to send the content of a resource.

HTTP requests and responses always look the same regardless of what is requested and what is the result of the processing of the request (figure 3.3).

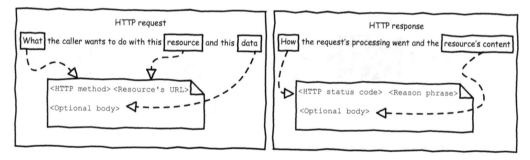

Figure 3.3   The basic structure of an HTTP request and response

Whatever its purpose, a basic HTTP request contains an HTTP method and a resource's path. The *HTTP method* indicates what is to be done with the resource identified by the path. You have already seen two HTTP methods—GET to retrieve a resource and POST to send one—and you will discover more later in this chapter.

This first part of the request can be followed by a body containing the content of the resource that needs to be sent to the server to create, update, or replace a resource, for example. This content can be of any type: a JSON document, a text file, or a photo, for example.

As mentioned previously, the HTTP response returned by the server always contains a status code and explanatory reason phrase. This indicates how the processing of the request went—if it was a success or not. You have so far seen only one HTTP status code, 200 OK, but you'll discover more later in this book (like the well-known 404 NOT FOUND that will be explained in section 5.2.3). This first part of the response can be followed by a body containing the content of the resource that was manipulated by the request. Like the request's body, this content can be of any type.

The HTTP protocol seems quite simple. But are REST APIs that use this protocol that simple?

3.1.3 *Basic principles of REST APIs*

You have seen that using the REST Shopping API for the get product goal, consumers have to send an HTTP request to the server hosting the API. This request uses the GET HTTP method on the /products/{productId} path that identifies the product. If everything is all right, the server returns a response that contains an HTTP status indicating that, along with the product's data. You also saw that if a web browser wants to retrieve a page from my apihandyman.io blog, it sends an HTTP request. This request uses the GET HTTP method on the page's path (/about, for example). If everything is all right, the web server also returns a response containing a 200 OK HTTP status and the page's content. Exactly the same thing happens!

Both the web server and the Shopping API server expose an HTTP interface that respects the HTTP protocol's expected behavior. A basic REST API not only uses the HTTP protocol, it totally relies on it, as shown in figure 3.4.

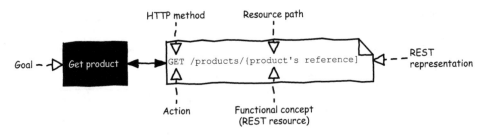

Figure 3.4   Mapping a goal to an HTTP request

To let its consumers achieve their goals, a REST API allows them to manipulate resources identified by paths using standardized HTTP methods. A *resource* is a functional concept. For example, /products/{productId} identifies a specific product in the products catalog. This path identifies a product resource. The GET HTTP method represents the retrieve action that can be applied to this resource to actually get the product.

A REST API call is nothing more than an HTTP call. Let's see now how we get from the get product goal to GET /products/{product's reference}—how we transform goals to HTTP method and path pairs.

3.2   Transposing API goals into a REST API

You have discovered that a REST API represents its goals using the HTTP protocol. Goals are transposed into resource and action pairs. Resources are identified by paths, and actions are represented by HTTP methods. But how do we identify these resources and actions? And how do we represent them using paths and HTTP methods?

We do what has always been done in software design. We analyze our functional needs to identify resources and what happens to them before transposing them into a programmatic representation. There are many software design methods that you could use to identify resources and what you can do with them based on some specifications, like the API goals canvas from the previous chapter. This book, however, shows a very simple method in four steps (see figure 3.5).

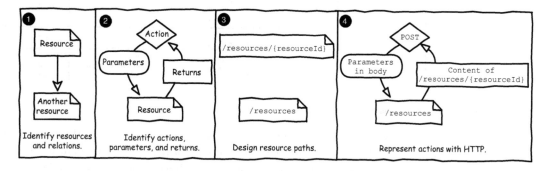

Figure 3.5   From goals to REST API

First, we have to identify resources (functional concepts) and their relationships (how they are organized). Then we have to identify for each resource the available actions and their parameters and returns. Once this is done, we can proceed to the actual HTTP programming interface design by creating resources paths and choosing HTTP methods to represent actions.

In the following sections, we'll walk through this process in more detail. Here, we only talk about the nominal case, when everything is 200 OK. We will talk about error handling in section 5.2.

> **NOTE**   Once you're familiar with the process of mapping goals to resource paths and HTTP methods using this method, feel free to adapt it or use your preferred software design method as long as you achieve the same result.

3.2.1   Identifying resources and their relationships with the API goals canvas

The API goals canvas you discovered in chapter 2 describes who the users are, what they can do, how they do it, what they need to do it, and what they can get in return. We can use this information to identify the API goals that we will transpose into a REST API. To practice on a basic but complete example, I have enhanced the manage catalog part of the Shopping API goals canvas we began working with in chapter 2 (figure 3.6).

- - This table is an API goals canvas (see chapter 2).   *We will transpose these goals into a REST API. - - ⬎*

Whos	Whats	Hows	Inputs (source)	Outputs (usage)	Goals
Admin users	Manage catalog	Add product	Catalog (API), product info (user)	Added product (get, update, delete, replace)	Add product to catalog
		Get product's information	Product (search, add)	Product info (user)	Get product
		Update product's information	Product (get, search, add), updated info (user)		Update product
		Replace product	Product (get, search, add), new product info (user)		Replace product
		Delete product	Product (get, search, add)		Delete product
		Search for products	Catalog (API), free query (user)	Products matching query (get, update, delete, replace)	Search for products in catalog using a free query

Figure 3.6   The API goals canvas for the manage catalog what

As you can see in this figure, when managing the product catalog, admin users can add a product to the catalog. They can also retrieve a product's information and update, replace, or delete it. Finally, it's possible to search for products using a free query. Figure 3.7 shows how we simply analyze the API goals and list all the nouns to which the goals' main verbs apply for identifying resources.

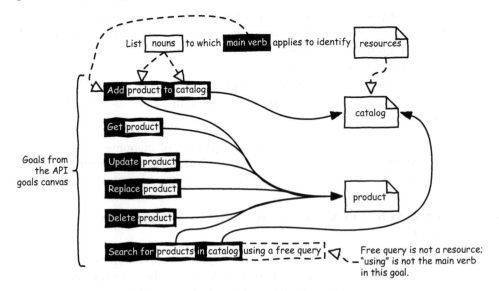

Figure 3.7   Identifying resources

When we add a product to the catalog, the main verb is *add*, and it is applied to both the product and catalog resources. When we get a product, the main verb is *get*, and it is applied to the product only. But when we search for products in the catalog using a free query, *free query* is a noun, not a resource, because the *search* verb does not apply to it directly. Therefore, we can identify two resources: *catalog* and *product*.

Now let's see how these resources are related. To discover the resources' organization, we list goals mentioning more than one resource (see figure 3.8).

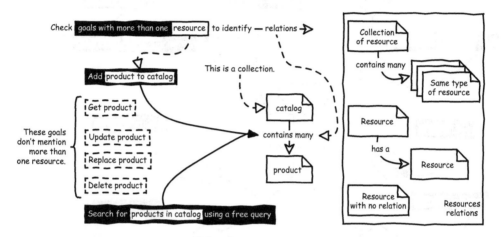

Figure 3.8   Identifying resource relationships

We have two goals dealing with more than one resource. In the first one, we add a product *to* the catalog. In the second one, we search for products *in* the catalog.

Resources may or may not have relationships to other resources, and a resource can contain some other resources of the same type. Such a resource is called a *collection resource* or simply *collection*. In our case, the catalog resource is a collection: it contains product resources. If we were designing an API related to city planning, a city could be a collection resource containing many building resources. A resource can also be linked to other resources; for example, a building resource could be linked to an address resource.

We have identified our catalog and product resources and how they are related. What can we do with them?

3.2.2   *Identifying actions and their parameters and returns with the API goals canvas*

A REST API represents its goals through *actions* on resources. To identify an action, we take the goal's main verb and link it to the resource to which it applies, as shown in figure 3.9.

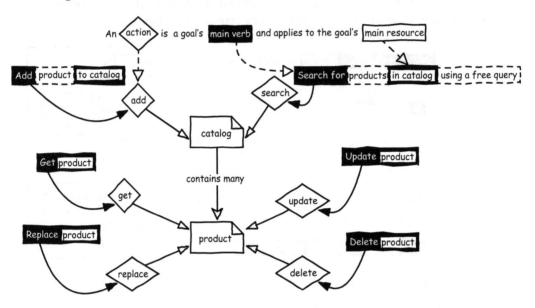

Figure 3.9   Identifying actions

This is straightforward for goals with a single resource, such as get product, where the verb *get* applies to the product resource. But what about the goals add product to catalog and search for products in catalog using a free query? Do we link add and search to product or catalog? We add a product *to* the catalog and we search for products *in* the catalog; in this use case, *add* and *search* are linked to the catalog resource. That means we link the verb to the main resource (catalog) that is used or modified—the other one (product) is only a parameter or a return.

These actions might need some additional parameters and can return some information. Fortunately, we've already identified these parameters and returns; the API goals canvas comes with a complete list of inputs (parameters) and outputs (returns), as shown in figure 3.10.

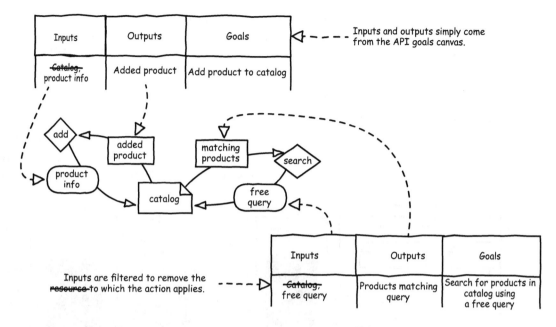

Inputs	Outputs	Goals
~~Catalog,~~ product info	Added product	Add product to catalog

Inputs and outputs simply come from the API goals canvas.

Inputs	Outputs	Goals
~~Catalog,~~ free query	Products matching query	Search for products in catalog using a free query

Inputs are filtered to remove the ~~resource~~ to which the action applies.

Figure 3.10 Identifying action parameters and returns

We just need to filter the inputs because some of them can be resources to which the action is applied. When we apply *add* to the catalog resource, we need some product information as an input; and, in return, we get the newly created product resource. We provide a free query to the *search* action that is applied to the catalog resource, and this action returns the matching product resources. We then do exactly the same thing for actions applied to the product resource, and we're done! We have identified all the resources and their actions, including parameters and returns, by analyzing the API canvas and its goals (figure 3.11).

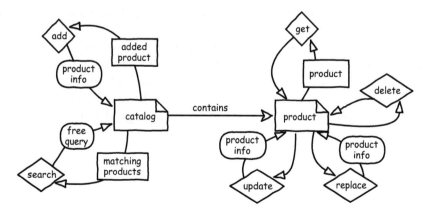

Figure 3.11 All the identified resources and actions

As you can see, this process is not really different from what you do when you design the implementation of software. It takes a long time to describe how to do this in a book, but actually doing it takes only a couple of minutes with the API canvas. Let's now see how we represent all of this with the HTTP protocol. We will start by representing resources with paths.

3.2.3 Representing resources with paths

By analyzing the API goals canvas, we have identified two resources: catalog and product. We also have discovered that the catalog resource is a collection of product resources. How can we design these resources' paths? Figure 3.12 shows how to do so.

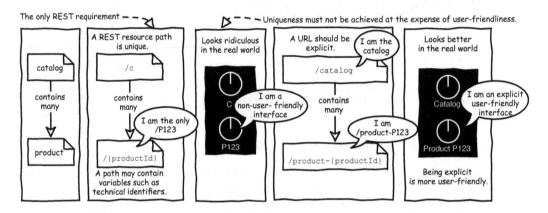

Figure 3.12   A REST resource's path. The only requirement is that it must be unique, but it should also be explicit.

A REST resource's path only needs to be unique. To identify the catalog, we could use a /c path. For products, we could use the product reference or technical ID and build a /{productId} path with it (/P123, for example). Such variables in paths are called *path parameters*. The /c and /{productId} paths are perfectly valid REST paths because they are unique.

But let's be frank. What would you think about such an interface in the real world? This is not really consumer-friendly; and, remember from chapter 2, we should always design an API for its users. It would be better to choose paths that indicate explicitly what they represent. Why not simply use /catalog for the catalog resource and /product-{productId} for the product resource? That sounds good, but these paths are not the only possibilities, as figure 3.13 shows.

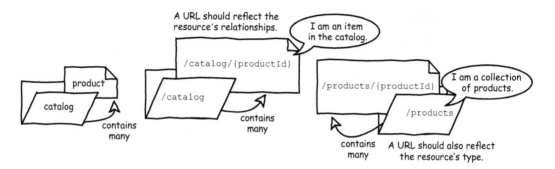

Figure 3.13   A REST resource's path should expose hierarchy and type.

To improve user-friendliness, the relationship between the catalog and product resources could be reflected in the paths like in the folder hierarchy you find on a filesystem. Each product resource is an item in the catalog collection identified by /catalog, so we could choose the path /catalog/{productId} to represent a product. We could also explicitly indicate that a catalog is a collection of product resources by using a /products path, with a product from this collection being represented by the /products/{productId} path. That's a lot of options! Figure 3.14 shows them all.

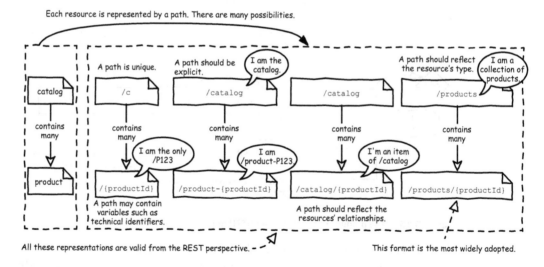

Figure 3.14   Choosing your resource path format

From a pure REST perspective, all of these representations are valid. Even if we've already discarded cryptic paths such as /c and /{productId} because they are obviously not consumer-friendly, we still have many possibilities. A catalog resource could be represented by /catalog or /products and a product resource by /product-{productId}, /catalog/{productId}, or /products/{productId}.

> **NOTE**   You can choose whichever representation you prefer, but keep in mind that your resource paths must be user-friendly. API users must be able to decipher them easily, so the more information you provide in your paths, the better.

Although there are no official REST rules regarding resource path design (apart from uniqueness), the most widely adopted format is /{plural name reflecting collection's item type}/{item id}. Using resource paths exposing resource hierarchy and using plural names for collections to show the collection's item type has become a de facto REST standard.

In our example, a catalog should therefore be identified by /products and a product by /products/{productId}. This structure can be extended to multiple levels as in /resources/{resourceId}/sub-resources/{subResourceId}.

We're almost done! We have identified resources and their actions, and we have designed our resource paths. Here comes the final step, representing actions with the HTTP protocol.

3.2.4 *Representing actions with HTTP*

Let's start with the catalog resource and its add action, as shown in figure 3.15.

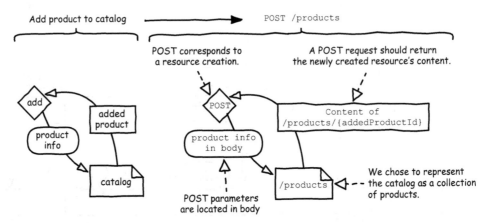

Figure 3.15   Add product to catalog as an HTTP request

The HTTP representation of the goal add product to catalog is POST /products. When we add a product to the catalog resource identified by /products, we actually *create* a product resource using the provided product information. The HTTP method corresponding to the creation of a resource is POST. A POST request's parameters are usually passed in the request body, so the product information parameter goes there. Once the product resource is created, the action should return the newly created resource identified by its path: /products/{addedProductId}.

Now, what is the HTTP representation of the search action of the catalog resource? The HTTP representation of search for products in catalog using a free query is GET /products?free-query={free query}, as shown in figure 3.16.

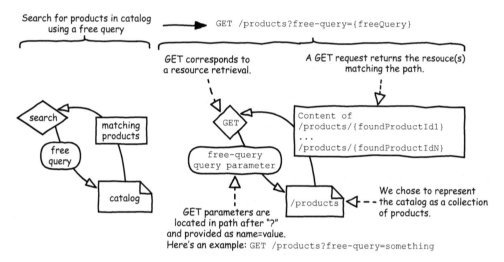

Figure 3.16   Search for products in catalog using a free query as an HTTP request

When we search for products, we want to retrieve them, so we have to use the GET HTTP method on the /products path. To only retrieve products matching some query, like a product name or partial description, we need to pass a parameter to this request. A GET HTTP request's parameters are usually provided as query parameters in the path, as demonstrated in the following listing.

> **Listing 3.1   Query parameter examples**

```
GET /example?param1=value1&param2=value2
GET /products?free-query=something
```

The parameters are located after the ? at the end of the path and provided in name=value format (param1=value1, for example). Multiple query parameters are separated by &. Once the search is done, the GET request returns the resources matching the path (which includes the free-query parameter).

We have represented all of the catalog resource's actions, so let's work on the product resource. We start with get product, which is relatively easy to represent as an HTTP request, as illustrated in figure 3.17.

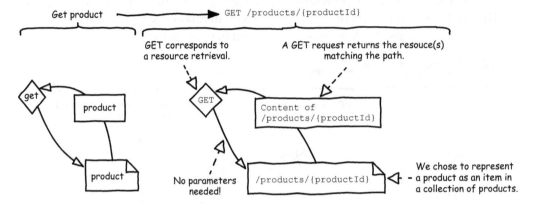

Figure 3.17   Get product as an HTTP request

We want to retrieve the product resource identified by /products/{productId}, so we again use the GET HTTP method. The HTTP representation is therefore GET /products/{productId}. A GET resource always returns the resource corresponding to the provided path, so this action returns the content of this resource.

Now it's time to discover new HTTP methods! How do we represent delete product with the HTTP protocol? The HTTP representation of this goal is simply DELETE /products/{productId}, as shown in figure 3.18.

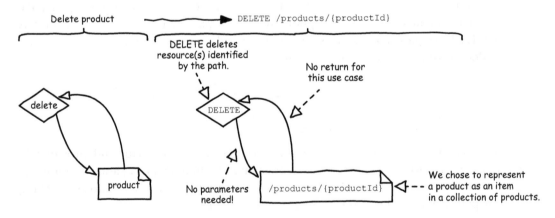

Figure 3.18   Delete product as an HTTP request

The DELETE HTTP method's purpose is obviously to delete the resource matching the provided path. In our use case, this action does not return any information.

Deleting a product was easy. Now can you guess what HTTP method we will use to update a product? There's a trap here—the HTTP representation of update product is PATCH /products/{productId}, not UPDATE /products/{productId}, as shown in figure 3.19.

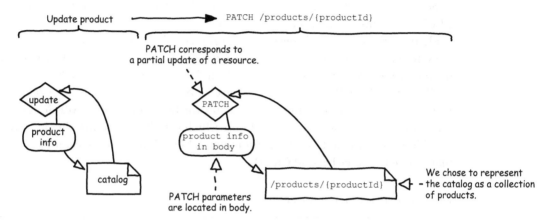

Figure 3.19 Update product as an HTTP request

The PATCH HTTP method can be used to partially update a resource. Like POST, the request parameters are passed in the request's body. For example, if you want to update a product's price, you can use PATCH on the product resource and pass the updated price in the body. In our use case, this action does not return any information.

Our last example illustrates an HTTP method that has two purposes. The HTTP representation of replace product is PUT /products/{productId}, as illustrated in figure 3.20.

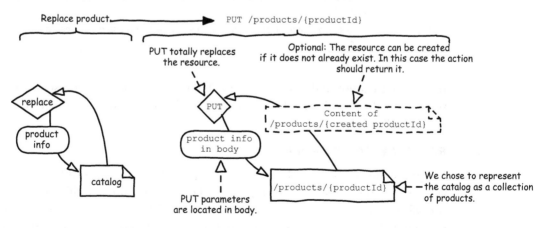

Figure 3.20 Replace product as an HTTP request

The PUT HTTP method can be used to totally replace an existing resource or to create a nonexisting one and provide its identifier. In the latter case, it has the same effect as the add product to catalog action. Like POST, the request parameters are passed in the request's body. In our use case, this action does not return information, but if you use PUT for creating a resource, the created resource should be returned.

So, the POST, GET, PUT, PATCH, and DELETE HTTP methods essentially map the basic CRUD functions (create, read, update, delete). Do not forget that these actions are made from the consumer's perspective; for example, if you DELETE /orders/0123, it does not mean that the order 0123 will actually be deleted from the database containing the orders. Such actions might simply update this order status to CANCELED.

These CRUD HTTP methods also have to be used to represent *more than or not so CRUD* actions. It can sometimes be difficult for beginning REST API designers (and sometimes even seasoned ones) to choose which HTTP method matches an action that doesn't obviously map to a CRUD function. Table 5.3 shows some examples of actions that can help you see beyond CRUD.

Table 3.1   HTTP methods beyond CRUD

HTTP method	Action
POST (and PUT in creation)	Create a customer, add a meal to a menu, order goods, start a timer, save a blog post, send a message to customer service, subscribe to a service, sign a contract, open a bank account, upload a photo, share a status on a social network, and so on
GET	Read a customer, search for a French restaurant, find new friends, retrieve opened accounts for the last 3 months, download a signed contract, filter best selling books, select black-and-white photos, list friends, and so forth
PATCH/PUT	Update a customer, replace goods in an order, switch plane seat, edit an order's delivery method, change an order's currency, modify a debit card limit, temporarily block a credit card, and so on
DELETE	Delete a customer, cancel an order, close a case, terminate a process, stop a timer, and so on

If you really cannot find a resource and HTTP method pair to represent your action, you can use the default POST HTTP method as a last resort. We will talk more about this in section 3.4.

3.2.5   *REST API and HTTP cheat sheet*

Congratulations! You have learned to transpose API goals into REST resources and actions, and represent them using the HTTP protocol. You should now have a good overall view of REST API resources and actions. Let's sum up everything you've learned thus far with a cheat sheet, shown in figure 3.21. That makes a lot of things easier to remember!

Remember, at the beginning of this chapter, you saw that the result of GET /products/ P123 was some data. We now have to design that data!

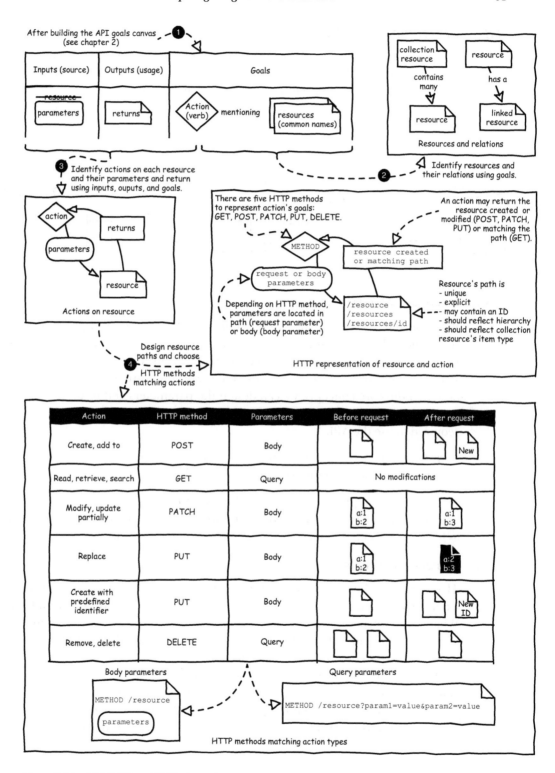

Figure 3.21   REST API and HTTP cheat sheet

3.3 Designing the API's data

You now know how to transpose API goals into REST resources and actions and give them a programmable representation with paths and methods using the HTTP protocol. You have also identified the actions' parameters and returns. But the resources, parameters, and returns you have identified are only vaguely described. How do we design these data items? The design process is outlined in figure 3.22.

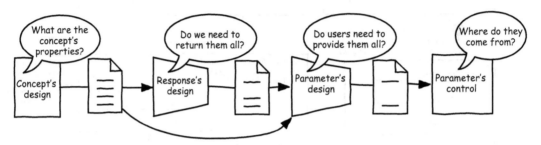

Figure 3.22   Designing API data

Whatever the type of API, we start designing the data just like any programmable representation of a concept—just like a database table, a structure, or an object. We simply list the properties and stay consumer-oriented. Consumers must be able to understand the data, and we must not expose inner workings through its design. Once we've designed the core concepts, we can design the parameters and responses by adapting them. And finally, we must ensure that consumers will be able to provide all the data required to use the API.

> **NOTE**   Some parameters like the free query one used by the search for products in the catalog action may need a simpler design process.

As before, the simplest method shown here is intended to expose the basic concepts. Feel free to adapt it or use a different software design method that you're familiar with, as long as you keep the spirit alive and achieve the same results.

3.3.1 Designing concepts

The concepts that we have identified and turned into REST resources will be exchanged through parameters and responses between the consumer and provider. Whatever its purpose, we must take care in the design of such a data structure to offer a consumer-oriented API, just as we did when designing the API goals. Figure 3.23 illustrates how to design a concept such as a product.

We start by listing the data structure's properties and giving each a name. A product can have `reference`, `name`, and `price` properties, for example. It could also be useful to tell the customer when the product was added to the catalog (`dateAdded`) and let them know whether it's in stock or not (`unavailable`). And what about listing the

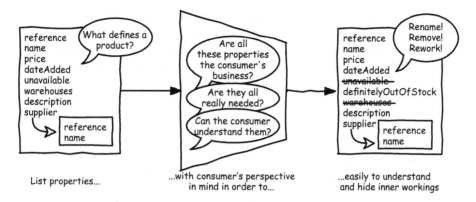

Figure 3.23 Designing a consumer-oriented concept

warehouses where this product can be found and its suppliers? Finally, we might want to return a fuller description of the product.

While listing these properties, you must remember what you learned in chapter 2 about the consumer's and provider's perspectives. We must analyze each one to ensure that our design is focused on the consumer's perspective and does not reflect the provider's. We can do this by asking ourselves if each property can be understood, is really the consumer's business, and is actually useful, as shown in figure 3.23. In our example, the property names seem understandable; we have avoided obviously cryptic names such as r and p for reference and price, for example. But on second thought, the `ware-houses` list isn't really relevant for users, so we'll remove that. We'll also rename the `unavailable` property to `definitelyOutOfStock` to be more explicit.

The most important information about a property is its name. The more self-explanatory the name is, the better. But defining a property only by its name isn't enough when it comes to describing a programming interface, as shown in figure 3.24.

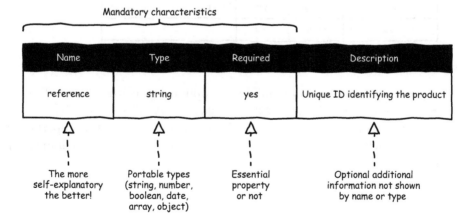

Figure 3.24 Property characteristics

We also need to be clear about each property's type. For example, what is the type of the `reference` property? Is it a `number` or a `string`? In this use case, it's a `string`. Is it an essential property that must always requested or returned? That is the case for this one. And a final question: What exactly is a reference? Its description indicates that it is a unique ID identifying the product.

As figure 3.24 illustrates, for each property, the characteristics we need to gather are

- Its name
- Its type
- If it's required
- An optional description when necessary

Figure 3.25 shows a detailed list of the possible properties of the product resource. It also shows on the right of the properties list an example of a product's JSON document.

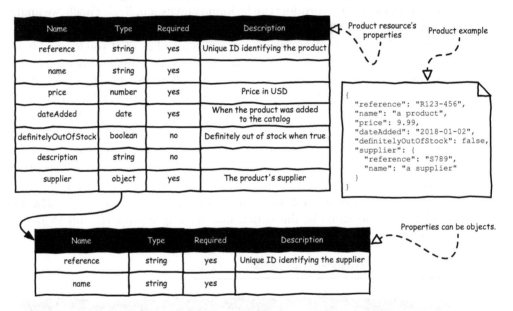

Figure 3.25   The product's resource properties

So, a product is composed of required and optional properties. Some of them (such as `reference`, `price`, `definitelyOutOfStock`, and `dateAdded`) are of basic types (such as `string`, `number`, `boolean`, or `date`). There can also be complex properties, such as `supplier`, which is an object. (A property can also be an `object` containing properties or an `array`.)

A name and a type are the most obvious information to gather about a property when designing a programming interface. An API can be consumed by software written in many different languages.

TIP When choosing a property's type, use only portable basic data types shared by programming languages, such as `string`, `number`, `date`, or `boolean`.

In addition to knowing a property's name and type, we must also know if this property should always be present. Indicating whether a property is required or optional is an often-forgotten aspect of API design, but this information is crucial in both the parameter and response contexts for API designers, consumers, and implementers. Note that the required or optional status of a property can vary depending on the context. For now, we'll set this status to required only if it is an essential property of the concept.

Sometimes, name and type are not sufficient to accurately describe a property. To provide additional information that cannot be obviously reflected by the property's name and type, adding a description can be valuable in such cases. Once we know what our concepts are made of, we can use them as responses or parameters to our goals.

3.3.2 Designing responses from concepts

The same concept can appear in different contexts, as shown in figure 3.26.

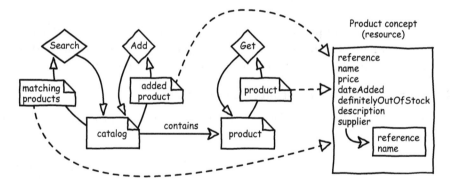

Figure 3.26 Different representations of the same concept in different response contexts

For example, the catalog resource actions add product and search for products both return a product (or, in the latter case, potentially more than one). The product resource action get product returns a product too. These different product representations might not be exactly the same as shown in figure 3.27.

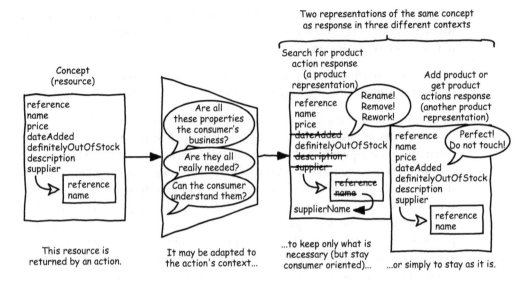

Figure 3.27   Designing different responses from a single concept

While add product and get product should return the complete product, search for products can only return a reference, name, price, and the supplier's name as supplierName.

When we design responses, we should not blindly map the manipulated resource. We must adapt them to the context by removing or renaming properties and also adjust the data structure. But do we design the parameters the same way?

3.3.3   *Designing parameters from concepts or responses*

When we add, update, or replace a product, we pass some product information as a parameter (figure 3.28).

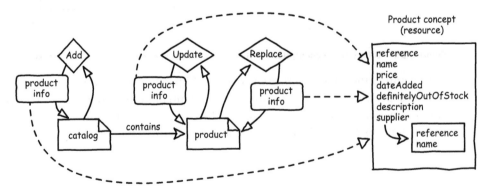

Figure 3.28   Different representations of the same concept in different parameter contexts

But what does this parameter consist of? Or, more precisely, *these* parameters as shown in figure 3.29. The product information parameter passed in these three cases might not be the same; they may not look like the responses we just designed, and they may not exactly reflect our product concept.

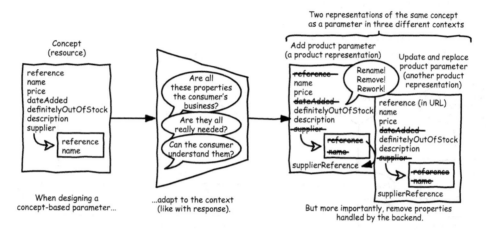

Figure 3.29   Designing different parameters from a single concept

When a product is created, its reference is generated by the backend, so there's no need for the consumer to provide it when adding a product. But we need this reference to update or replace a product (note that the reference will be passed in the path as a path parameter: /products/{reference}). In all these use cases, the consumer does not need to provide the supplier.name property; only its reference is needed; the backend has a way to find a supplier's name based on its reference. To simplify the data organization, we can therefore remove the supplier object and replace it with supplierReference. dateAdded is also generated by the backend when the product is added to the catalog, so we don't need that either. As with responses, the same concept can have different representations in an API's parameters, depending on the context (creation versus updating, for example).

> **NOTE**   A parameter must provide the needed data, but nothing more. It should not include data that is exclusively handled by the backend.

By proceeding this way, we ensure that the product information parameter contains only the data that's absolutely necessary in each context. But are we sure the consumer can provide all this data?

3.3.4   Checking parameter data sources

When adding a product to the catalog, consumers should be able to easily provide data such as name, price, and description. But what about the supplierReference? How can consumers know such a reference? This kind of questioning probably sounds familiar. That's because when identifying the API goals, we verified that consumers could provide all the necessary inputs, either because they already know the information or because they are able to retrieve it from another API goal. But now we are dealing with a more detailed view of these input parameters.

Consumers must be able to provide all of a parameter's data, either because they know the information themselves or because they can retrieve it from the API. If data cannot be provided, it might be a sign of a missing goal or the provider's perspective. Therefore, we must verify again that all the needed data can be provided by the consumer. This verification process, illustrated in figure 3.30, ensures that consumers will always be able to provide parameter data, and that there are no gaps in the API.

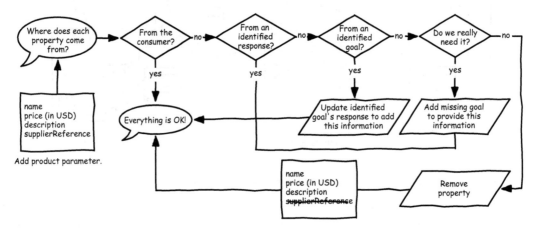

Figure 3.30   Verifying that consumers can provide all the parameter's data

In this case, consumers might already know the `supplierReference` because it is provided on the product's label, or it may come from a response we have already designed. It could also come from another goal; in which case, we just need to update its response to add this information in order to provide it to the consumer. We may also simply have missed a goal. In that case, we will have to add it to the API goals canvas and process it like any other goal, identifying who can use it, defining its inputs and outputs, and designing its programmable representation. Or we might simply realize that we don't really need it.

We will not solve this mystery here—its purpose is to show that parameters must be closely verified and that you can discover some missing features when you get into the details of an API's design. This is totally normal; designing an API is a process of continuing improvement. Step-by-step, the design will be refined to become more accurate, complete, and efficient.

3.3.5   *Designing other parameters*

What about the `free-query` parameter of the search for products goal? It is a string that can contain a partial description, a name, or a reference. This is an optional query parameter; if it is not provided, all available products are returned.

Whatever the parameter is—a query parameter like `free-query` or even a body parameter not based on an identified concept—we do the same thing. We choose a consumer-oriented representation and check that the consumer is able to provide any requested data.

With what you've learned so far, you should be able to design any basic REST API. But sometimes you might encounter challenging design problems and sticking to the chosen API type representation might be hard. Perfection is not always possible in the API design world.

3.4 Striking a balance when facing design challenges

When you choose to use a specific API type, it is important to know that sometimes you can encounter limitations. You might struggle to find a representation of a goal that conforms to the chosen API model. You might also end up with a representation that conforms to the model but is not as user-friendly as you expected. Sometimes the perfect representation does not exist, and therefore, as an API designer, you will have to make some trade-offs.

3.4.1 REST trade-off examples

Mapping actions on resources to HTTP methods and paths is not always straightforward. There are common techniques to circumvent such problems, and often by exploring various solutions, you can finally find one that works with your chosen API model. But sometimes this API style-compliant solution might not be user-friendly.

You might have noticed that I carefully avoided transposing goals that were related to a user buying products and focused on the catalog-related goals. Goals related to catalog management are perfect to show the basics of HTTP and REST APIs. The resources are relatively simple to identify, and goals with actions such as add, get or search, update, and delete (who said CRUD?) are easily mapped to HTTP methods. But things aren't always so simple.

When users buy products, they have the check out cart goal at the end of the process. How can we represent such a goal when it's not obvious how to transpose it into a path and HTTP method couple? When a designer fails to map an action on a REST resource to any HTTP method, a first option is often to create an action resource (figure 3.31).

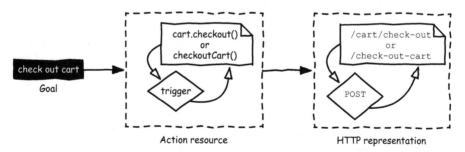

Figure 3.31 Using an action resource

An *action resource* is not a thing represented by a noun, but an action represented by a verb. It is simply a function. An action resource can be seen as a method of a class and, therefore, can be represented as a sub-resource of a resource. If we choose to represent the cart resource by the /cart path, the cart.checkout() method could be represented by the path `/cart/check-out`. But we could also consider it as a stand-alone `checkoutCart()` function and create a `/check-out-cart` action resource accordingly. In both cases, we use the HTTP method `POST` to trigger the action resource.

> **NOTE**   The HTTP method `POST` is the default method to use when no other method fits the use case.

An action resource absolutely does not conform to the REST model, but it works and is totally understandable by consumers. Let's see if we can find a solution that's closer to the REST model. We could, for example, consider that checking out the cart changes some status (figure 3.32).

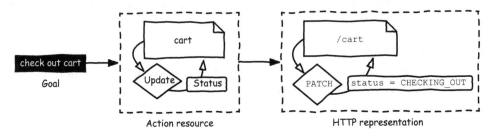

Figure 3.32   **Updating a status**

The cart resource might contain a `status` property. To check out the cart, we can update it with `PATCH` to set its value to `CHECKING_OUT`. This solution is closer to the REST model but less user-friendly than the action resource: the check out cart goal is hidden within an update of the cart resource. If we keep on brainstorming, I'm sure we can find a solution that totally fits the REST API model.

Let's get back to the basics. We must ask ourselves a few questions:

- What are we trying to represent?
- What happens in this use case?
- What happens when we check out a cart?

Well, an order is created that contains all the cart's products. And after that the cart is emptied. That's it! We are creating an order. Therefore, we can use a `POST /orders` request to create an order and check out cart, as shown in figure 3.33.

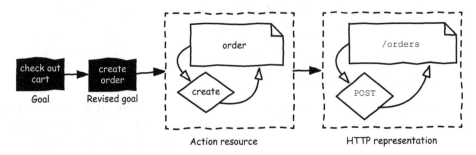

Figure 3.33   **Conforming to the REST API model**

This solution totally conforms to the REST API model, but is it really user-friendly? The purpose of this REST representation might not be obvious to all users.

3.4.2 Balancing user-friendliness and compliance

So which option wins? The totally non-REST but so user-friendly `POST /cart/check-out` or `POST /check-out-cart` action resources? The more REST but a little bit awkward `PATCH /cart`? Or the totally REST but not so user-friendly `POST /orders`? It will be up to you to choose (figure 3.34) or to find a better solution.

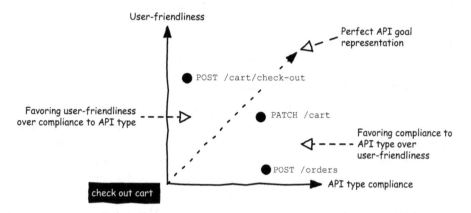

Figure 3.34 A balance between user-friendliness and API type compliance

Sometimes you might not find the perfect API goal representation, even after intense brainstorming and with the help of the entire team. Sometimes you might not be really satisfied or even be a bit disappointed by an API design you are working on. Unfortunately, this is totally normal.

It is important to master the fundamentals behind the chosen programming interface model or API style to be able to find solutions that are as close as possible to the chosen model. But it is also important to be able to make some reasonable trade-offs to keep the API consumer-friendly and not diverge too much from the API model. Skill at this comes through practicing, observing other APIs, and, most importantly, talking to your consumers and other API designers.

Congratulations! You should now be able to transpose any API goal to a REST API. But now that we have covered what a REST API is and how to create one based on an API goals canvas, we should explore REST beyond mapping goals to HTTP method and path pairs. This is important because REST matters for the design of any type of API.

3.5 Understanding why REST matters for the design of any API

As T.S. Eliot said, "The journey, Not the destination matters…." I could have explained all the API design principles presented in this book using the totally outdated Xerox Courier RPC model that was created in the 1970s, the despised SOAP model created at the end of the 20th century, the now widely adopted REST, or the more recent gRPC or GraphQL. And these are only a few examples among many. As explained in chapter 1 (section 1.3), there have been, there are now, and there always will be different styles of programming interfaces allowing software to communicate remotely. Each of them had, has, or will have its own specificities, pros, and cons, and will obviously produce an API with a specific look and feel. But whatever its type, designing an API requires basically the same mindset.

Up to this point, we've been considering REST APIs as APIs that map goals to paths and HTTP methods. But REST is far more than that. REST is a widely adopted API style; but, more importantly, it is based on the solid foundations of the *REST architectural style*, which is crucial to know when creating any type of API. That's why I chose REST as the main example programming interface for this book. Let's see what this REST style is, and what it means not only for API designers but also for API providers.

3.5.1   *Introducing the REST architectural style*

When you type a URL such as http://apihandyman.io/about in a web browser's address bar, it sends a GET /about request to the apihandyman.io web server. It's easy to imagine that the web server will return some static HTML document stored in its filesystem, but that might not be the case. The /about resource's content could be stored in a database. And what happens when a social media web server receives a POST /photos request? Does the server actually store the provided file as a document in a /photos location on the server's filesystem? Maybe. Maybe not. It could also store this image in a database.

Browsers interacting with web servers are left totally unaware of such implementation details. They only see the HTTP interface, which is only an abstraction of what it can do and not an indication of how it is done by the server. And how is it that a web browser can interact with any web server implementing an HTTP interface? It's because all web servers use exactly the same interface.

This is a part of the magic of HTTP. This is a part of the magic of REST.

The REST architectural style was introduced by Roy Fielding in 2000 in his PhD dissertation "Architectural Styles and the Design of Network-based Software Architectures." Fielding developed this architectural style while he was working on version 1.1 of the HTTP protocol. During the HTTP 1.1 standardization process, he had to explain everything—from abstract web notions to HTTP syntax details—to hundreds of developers. That work led to the creation of the REST model.

The aim of the REST architectural style is to facilitate building distributed systems that are efficient, scalable, and reliable. A *distributed system* is composed of pieces of software located on different computers that work together and communicate through a network, like the one shown in figure 3.35.

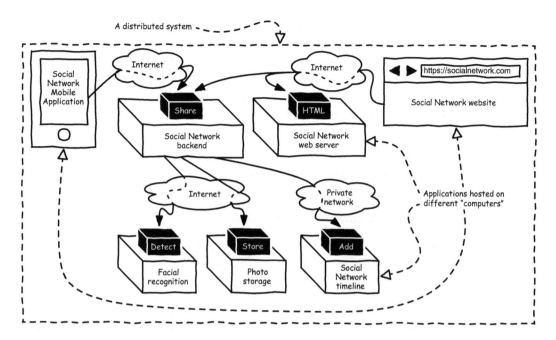

Figure 3.35   A distributed system

This should sound familiar to you because, from the beginning of this book, we have talked about distributed systems. A web browser and a web server comprise such a system, as do a consumer (like a mobile application) and API servers. Such systems must provide for fast network communication and request processing (*efficiency*), be capable of handling more and more requests (*scalability*), and be resistant to failure (*reliability*). The REST architectural style also aims to facilitate portability of components (*reusability*), simplicity, and modifiability. To achieve all this—to be RESTful—a software architecture needs to conform to the six following constraints:

- *Client/server separation*—There must be a clear separation of concerns when components like a mobile application and its API server work and communicate together.
- *Statelessness*—All information needed to execute a request is contained within the request itself. No client context is stored on the server in a session between requests.
- *Cacheability*—A response to a request must indicate if it can be stored (so a client can reuse it instead of making the same call again), and for how long.
- *Layered system*—When a client interacts with a server, it is only aware of the server and not of the infrastructure that hides behind it. The client only sees one layer of the system.
- *Code on demand*—A server can transfer executable code to the client (JavaScript, for example). This constraint is optional.

- *Uniform interface*—All interactions must be guided by the concept of identified resources that are manipulated through representations of resource states and standard methods. Interactions must also provide all metadata required to understand the representations and know what can be done with those resources. This is the most fundamental constraint of REST, and it is the origin of the Representational State Transfer name. Indeed, using a REST interface consists of transferring representations of a resource's states.

That might sound terribly scary and far from API design concerns, but these constraints should be understood by any API provider, in general, and any API designer, in particular.

3.5.2 *The impact of REST constraints on API design*

The REST architectural style was primarily created as a support to describe the World Wide Web and the HTTP protocol, but it can be applied to any other software architecture design with the same needs. A REST API, or RESTful API, is an API (which, in a broad sense, comprises both the interface and its implementation) that conforms (or at least tries to conform) to the REST architectural style constraints. These constraints obviously have a lot of implications for REST APIs but also for any type of API. Some of them can be a little hard to grasp at this time, but we will explore them throughout the book while digging into the various aspects of API design. What if I were to tell you that we've already started to explore three of them, perhaps without you realizing it?

Do you remember the consumer's perspective we talked about in the previous chapter? As shown in figure 3.36, there are two REST constraints underneath this design principle.

When exploring the consumer's perspective, we saw that an API provider must not delegate its job to the API consumer—like turning the magneton on and off on the Kitchen Radar 3000 (see section 2.1). This is an example of the *client/server* constraint.

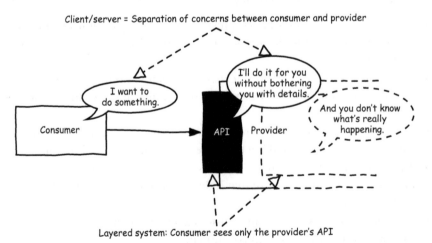

Figure 3.36   REST constraints and the consumer perspective

We also saw that an API consumer is only aware of the provider's API and does not know what's happening beyond this interface—like in the restaurant example where customers order meals without having a clue about what is really happening in the kitchen (see section 1.2.2). This is what the *layered system* constraint means. These two constraints, and focusing on the consumer's perspective in general, will help you build APIs that are easy to understand, use, reuse, and evolve.

We also have started to uncover the *uniform interface* constraint in section 3.2.3 and section 3.2.4 as illustrated by figure 3.37.

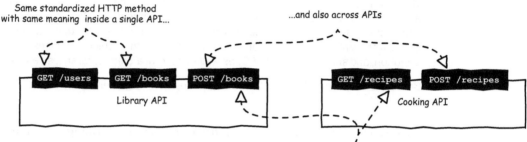

Figure 3.37   Creating APIs with uniform interfaces using HTTP

Each resource is identified by a unique path. Inside a single API and across APIs, POST /resource-A and POST /resource-B have the same meaning: create something. By representing goals with HTTP using unique paths and, most importantly, *standardized* HTTP methods, we are creating a uniform interface, which is consistent with itself and also with other interfaces. In chapter 6, we will get deeper into the other aspects of the uniform interface. We will talk more about REST representation and discover the other constraints (statelessness, cacheability, and code on demand, for example) while learning to design APIs in the next chapters. Table 3.2 gives a recap of all sections describing the REST architectural style constraints.

Table 3.2   REST constraints in *The Design of Web APIs*

REST constraint	Insights in the book
Client/server separation constraint	Chapter 2, section 2.1
Statelessness constraint	Chapter 5, section 5.3.4
Cacheability constraint	Chapter 10, section 10.2.2
Layered system constraint	Chapter 1, section 1.2.2
Code on demand constraint	Chapter 5, section 5.3.2
Uniform interface constraint	This chapter, section 3.2.3 and section 3.2.4, and chapter 6

Digging into REST beyond this book

This book should give you enough information about all these concepts for the purposes of API design, but if you want to dig more deeply into the REST architectural style, there are two documents that you might want to read. The first is Fielding's dissertation, "Architectural Styles and the Design of Network-based Software Architectures," which is publicly available on the University of California, Irvine (UCI) website, https://www.ics .uci.edu/~fielding/pubs/dissertation/top.htm. The first time you read it, you can jump directly to chapter 5, "Representational State Transfer (REST)."

The world has evolved since 2000, however, and REST has been used, misused, and abused since. You might therefore also be interested in reading "Reflections on the REST Architectural Style and 'Principled Design of the Modern Web Architecture,'" by Fielding et al., https://research.google.com/pubs/pub46310.html, which describes the history, evolution, and shortcomings of REST as well as several architectural styles derived from it.

Be forewarned: these documents do not give any specific guidelines regarding API design.

In the next chapter, you will discover a structured way of describing programming interfaces, much like the one we have designed, by discovering why and how to describe an API using an API description format.

Summary

- A REST API represents its goals with actions (HTTP methods) on resources (paths).
- You must use portable data such as `object`, `array`, `string`, `number`, `date`, or `boolean` types when designing data.
- A single API concept can have multiple data representations in different contexts.
- If a parameter contains data that cannot be provided by consumers, you missed something.
- Sometimes you will be frustrated or disappointed when designing APIs and having to strike a balance while facing design challenges—this is totally normal.

Describing an API with an API description format

This chapter covers

- What an API description format is
- How to describe a REST API with the OpenAPI Specification (OAS)

In the previous chapters, we explored how to design a basic programming interface using the information collected in the API goals canvas. We identified the resources, actions, parameters, and responses for our example Shopping API. We also designed the API's data. But we did all of this using box-and-arrow diagrams and some tables.

Such figures and tables are always useful for brainstorming and getting an overall idea of how the API's goals can be transposed into a programming interface. But when it comes to describing precisely a programming interface, and especially its data, it is simpler and more efficient to use a structured tool like an API description format. Being code-like and a standardized description of an API, this offers many advantages:

- It notably facilitates the sharing of your design with anyone involved in your project.
- It can be easily understood by people knowing this format and by any API documentation tools (among many others).

The *OpenAPI Specification* (OAS) is a popular REST API description format. In this chapter, we will walk through its basics in order to uncover the benefits of using such a format.

4.1   What is an API description format?

An *API description format* is a data format whose purpose is to describe an API. Figure 4.1 shows how the programming interface for the add product to catalog goal can be described in a simple text file using such a format.

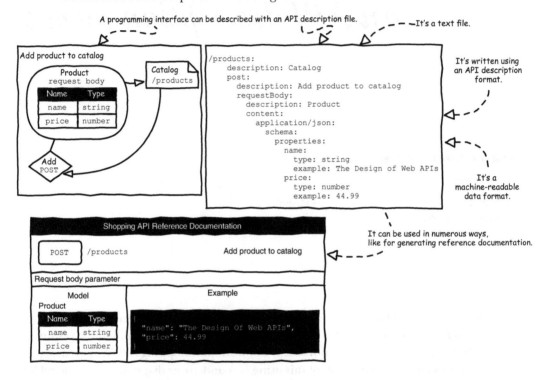

Figure 4.1   Describing a programming interface with an API description format

This text file uses data to tell the same story as our tables and hand-drawn box-and-arrow diagrams. According to the description at the top of the document, the /products resource represents the *catalog*. It contains a POST HTTP method that we can use to add a product to catalog. This POST operation needs a requestBody containing a name and a price. The description even provides additional information, such as example values for the properties. Such a file can be written quickly using a simple text editor. But, most importantly, because this file contains structured data, programs can read it and easily transform it into something else. A basic use is to generate reference documentation that describes all of an API's goals. You can share this with all the people involved in the project so they have a good overview of the design being created.

That sounds interesting, and it's only the tip of the iceberg. This simple text file uses the OAS. Let's take a closer look at this popular REST API description format before discussing the usefulness of such a format and when to use it while designing APIs.

4.1.1 Introducing the OpenAPI Specification (OAS)

The OpenAPI Specification (OAS) is a programming language-agnostic REST API description format. This format is promoted by the OpenAPI Initiative (OAI), which "…was created by a consortium of forward-looking industry experts who recognize the immense value of standardizing on how REST APIs are described. As an open governance structure under the Linux Foundation, the OAI is focused on creating, evolving and promoting a vendor neutral description format." The OAS (https://www.openapis .org) is a community-driven format; anyone can contribute to it through its GitHub repository (https://github.com/OAI/OpenAPI-Specification).

> ### The OAS versus Swagger
>
> Formerly known as the *Swagger Specification*, this format was donated to the OAI in November 2015 and renamed the OpenAPI Specification in January 2016. The latest version (2.0) of the Swagger Specification became the OpenAPI Specification 2.0. It has evolved since and is, at the time of this book's writing, in version 3.0.
>
> The Swagger Specification was originally created by Tony Tam to facilitate automation of API documentation and SDK (Software Development Kit) generation while working on Wordnik's products.[1] This specification was only a part of a whole framework called the Swagger API, comprising tools like code annotations, a code generator, or documentation user interface, all of those taking advantage of the Swagger Specification. The Swagger brand still exists and provides API tools using the OAS, but be aware that you might encounter both names when searching for information about this format.

Figure 4.2 shows a very basic OAS 3.0 document. This OAS document is written using the YAML data format.

---

[1] Wordnik (https://www.wordnik.com/) is a nonprofit organization providing an online English dictionary.

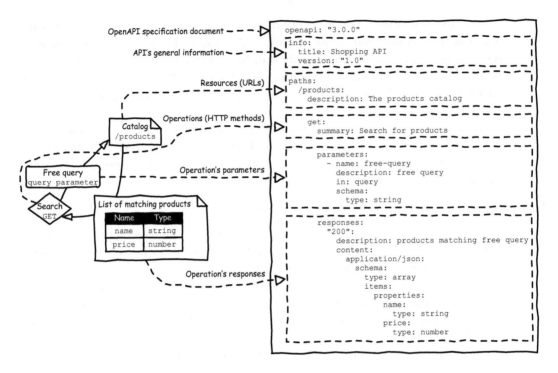

Figure 4.2   An OAS document describing the search for products goal of the Shopping API

YAML

YAML (YAML Ain't Markup Language) is a human-friendly, data serialization format. Like JSON, YAML (http://yaml.org) is a key/value data format. The figure shows a comparison of the two.

YAML

```
simple-property: a simple value

object-property:
  a-property: a value
  another-property: another value

array-property:
  - item-1-property-1: one
    item-1-property-2: 2
  - item-2-property-1: three
    item-2-property-2: 4

# no comment in JSON
```

JSON

```
{
  "simple-property": "a simple value",

  "object-property": {
    "a-property": "a value",
    "another-property": "another value"
  },

  "array-of-objects": [
    { "item-1-property-1": "one",
      "item-1-property-2": 2 },
    { "item-2-property-1": "three",
      "item-2-property-2": 4 }
  ]
}
```

No comments in JSON

YAML versus JSON

Note the following points:

- There are no double quotes (" ") around property names and values in YAML.
- JSON's structural curly braces ({ }) and commas (,) are replaced by newlines and indentation in YAML.
- Array brackets ([]) and commas (,) are replaced by dashes (-) and newlines in YAML.
- Unlike JSON, YAML allows comments beginning with a hash mark (#).

It is relatively easy to convert one of those formats into the other. Be forewarned though, you will lose comments when converting a YAML document to JSON.

Such a basic OAS document provides general information about the API, such as its name and version. It describes the available resources (identified by their paths) and each resource's operations (or actions, as you saw in the previous chapter) identified by HTTP methods, including their parameters and responses.

An OAS document can be written in YAML or JSON, so which one should you use? As you will be writing the documents yourself, I recommend using the YAML format, which is, in my opinion, easier to read and write.

Though this book focuses on OAS, other REST API description formats exist; the most notable OAS competitors are RAML and Blueprint. I choose to focus on OAS, not only because I use it everyday, but also because it is community-driven and widely used. Note, however, that this book is not called *OpenAPI Specification in Action*.

OAS and its ecosystem offer many features and, while we will discover some of them throughout this book, it won't be possible to cover them all. Once you are familiar with what is presented in this book, I recommend you read the OAS documentation (https://github.com/OAI/OpenAPI-Specification/tree/master/versions) and use the OpenAPI Map (https://openapi-map.apihandyman.io), a tool I created to help you find your way through the specification.

You've seen that an API description format such as the OAS lets you describe an API using a text file containing some kind of structured data. But you could also use a word processor or spreadsheet document to do the same thing. I urge you to avoid doing so; let's see why.

4.1.2 *Why use an API description format?*

Indeed, you could describe a programming interface using a word processor or spreadsheet document. You could also easily share such a document with others. But can you version it easily? Can you generate documentation from it? Can you generate code from it? Can you configure API-related tools with it? Can you … ? I could probably cover an entire page with such questions. Using an API description format has benefits throughout the API lifecycle, and especially during the design phase. It benefits not only the API providers but also API consumers.

DESCRIBING APIs EFFICIENTLY IS LIKE WRITING CODE

An OAS document is a simple text file that can be easily stored in a version control system such as Git, just like code. It is therefore simple to version it and track modifications while iterating on the API design.

An OAS document has a structure that helps to describe a programming interface more efficiently. You have to describe resources, operations, parameters, and responses. You can define reusable components (such as a data model, for example), avoiding the painful and risky art of maintaining copy/pasted pieces of API descriptions.

Speaking of writing an OAS document, you can use your favorite text editor, but I recommend using an editor that specifically handles this format. You can use the online Swagger Editor (http://editor.swagger.io) shown in figure 4.3.

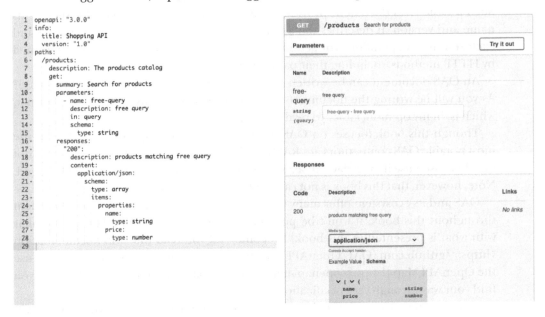

Figure 4.3   The Swagger Editor, an online OAS editor

Because OAS is a machine-readable format, this editor offers features like autocompletion and document validation, and the right-hand panel shows a useful rendering of the edited OAS document. To see a human-friendly representation of the data structures used as parameters or responses, the Model and Example Value views are especially useful. This editor is an open source project, and its source code is available on GitHub (https://github.com/swagger-api/swagger-editor).

This online editor is great because you only need a browser to run it, but it can be cumbersome to constantly download or copy and paste the edited file to actually save or open it. I personally use the Microsoft Visual Studio Code editor along with the Swagger Viewer extension (https://marketplace.visualstudio.com/items?itemName=Arjun .swagger-viewer), which supplies a SwaggerUI-based preview panel, and the openapi-lint extension (https://marketplace.visualstudio.com/items?itemName=mermade.openapi-lint), which provides autocompletion and validation. This configuration provides the same experience as the online editor, and you work directly with your files.

Note that there are API design tools that let you describe a programming interface without writing any code. Some of them propose interesting features like collaborative working. If you want to use such a tool, that's fine; just check that your work can be exported to a known and used API description format. But even though such tools exist, it's still worthwhile to know how to write an OAS document. You need almost nothing to use such a format, and one day you might want to build your own tooling around this format.

SHARING API DESCRIPTIONS AND DOCUMENTING APIS EASILY

An OAS document can be easily shared with others even outside your team or company to get feedback on your design. Unlike a specific internal format known only by a few, the OAS format is widely adopted. People can import the document into the online Swagger Editor or many other API tools. Alternatively, to avoid bothering them with the OAS document itself, you can provide access to a ready-to-use, human-friendly rendering. An OAS document can be used to generate API reference documentation that shows all the available resources and operations. You can use the Swagger UI (https://github.com/swagger-api/swagger-ui) for this, which shows the OAS document as in the right-hand pane of the Swagger Editor.

There are non-Swagger OpenAPI tools, too. For example, as an alternative to Swagger UI, you can use a tool such as ReDoc (https://github.com/Rebilly/ReDoc), which is also open source. Figure 4.4 shows the ReDoc OpenAPI tool.

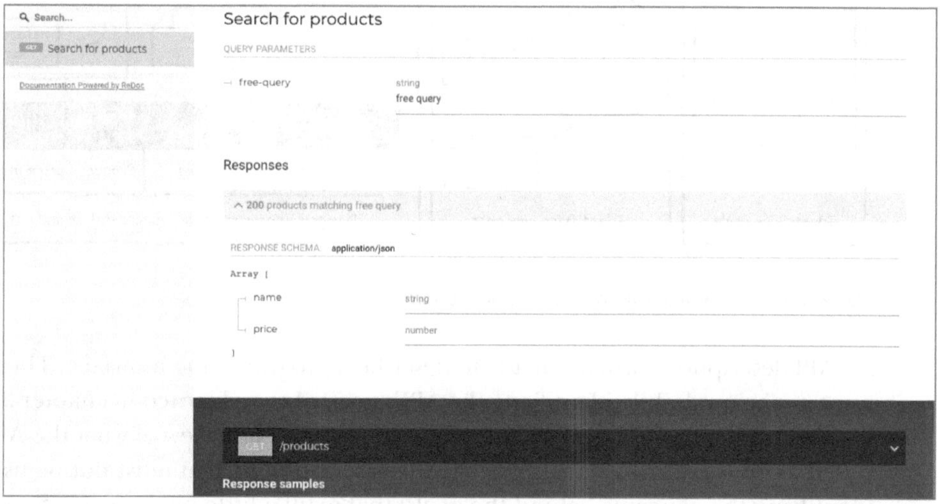

Figure 4.4   An OAS document rendered in ReDoc

And one final note: to create API documentation, you will discover advanced uses of OAS in chapter 12.

GENERATING CODE AND BEYOND

Once an API is described with an API description format, the implementation code can be partially generated from it. You will get an empty skeleton of source code that you can also use to generate a working mockup. Consumers can also take advantage of such machine-readable API descriptions to generate code to consume the API. And such a format can also be used by API testing or security tools, and many other API-related tools. For example, most API *gateway solutions* (proxies made to expose and secure APIs) can be configured using an API description file such as an OAS document.

TIP Check the https://openapi.tools/ website that lists a selection of OAS-based tools to get a glimpse of the OAS ecosystem.

These examples alone show how an API description format is more efficient than a word processor or spreadsheet document. And OAS documents can be used in many other ways.

4.1.3 *When to use an API description format*

Before starting to describe an API using an API description format, however, you must be sure you're doing so at the right time, as shown in figure 4.5.

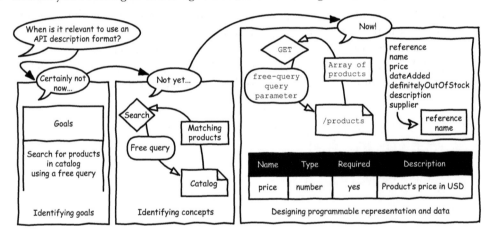

Figure 4.5   When to use an API description format

An API description format is made to describe a programming interface. Therefore, it must not be used while identifying the API's goals. As you learned in chapter 3, designing the programming interface first without having a clear view of what the API is supposed to do is a terrible idea! And an API description format must not be used while identifying the concepts behind the goals; that's still a little bit too early. Sure, it's the first step of designing the programming interface, but during this phase you are still not dealing with a real programming interface. An API description format definitely *must* be used, however, when designing the programmable representation of goals and concepts, and the data.

When you design a REST API, you can start to use the OAS when you design the resource paths and choose the HTTP methods describing actions. It is possible to create a minimal file containing only these elements. Once that is done, you can complete the document by describing the API's data. As you will discover in the following section, describing all of this will be far simpler and more efficient using an API description format than drawing tables, arrows, and boxes. But do not forget that all people involved in the project and who need to actually see the API design might not be familiar with a code-like format such as the OAS, so always provide a way to get a human-friendly representation of the file you are working on. With that in mind, let's see how we can describe REST API resources and actions using the OAS.

4.2 Describing API resources and actions with OAS

As shown in figure 4.6, when we transposed API goals into a programming interface in chapter 3, we identified resources and actions and represented them with paths and HTTP methods.

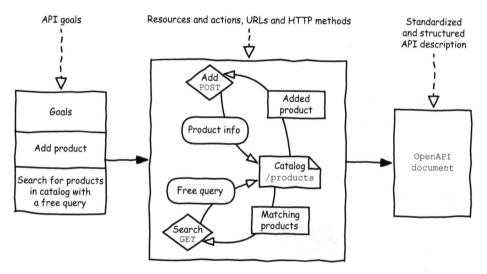

Figure 4.6 From figure to OAS document

We used boxes and arrows to describe this programming interface, but this can also be done in a more structured way using the OAS. The resulting document will contain exactly the same information as the corresponding figure, but this time the information will be presented as data in a structured document. Let's get started now on our document describing the Shopping API.

4.2.1 Creating an OAS document

The following listing shows a minimal but valid OAS document. This document is written using OAS version 3.0.0. It describes an API named Shopping API in its 1.0 version.

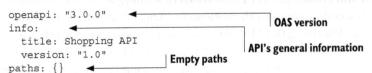

```
openapi: "3.0.0"                              OAS version
info:
  title: Shopping API                         API's general information
  version: "1.0"
paths: {}                    Empty paths
```

The structure of OAS documents can evolve from one version to another, so parsers use the openapi version to adapt their parsing accordingly. Note that both the specification (openapi) and API (info.version) version numbers must be surrounded by quotes. Otherwise, OAS parsers will consider these as numbers and document validation will fail because these two properties are supposed to be strings.

The listing shows the paths property only to make the document valid. (If it's not present, the parser reports an error.) The paths property contains the resources available to this API. We can set its value to {} for now—this is how you describe an empty object in YAML. A nonempty object (like info) does not need the curly braces. Next, we will start to fill the paths property by adding a resource.

4.2.2   *Describing a resource*

As shown in figure 4.7, while working on the goals search for products and add product to catalog, we identified a catalog resource. We chose to represent it with the /products path.

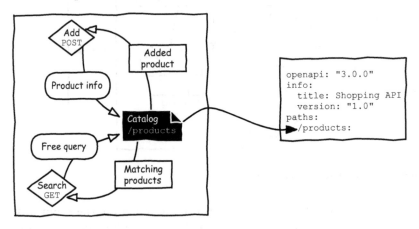

Figure 4.7   Adding a resource to the OAS document

In order to describe this resource in the OAS document, we must add the /products path into the paths property as shown in figure 4.7 (don't forget to remove the empty curly braces!). We'll also describe what this resource is (The products catalog) using the description property of the resource, as shown in the following listing.

Listing 4.2 Describing a resource

```
openapi: "3.0.0"
info:
  title: Shopping API
  version: "1.0"
paths:                          ◄──────| API's resources          Resource's path
  /products:        ◄──────────────────────────────────|
    description: The products catalog    ◄──────────────| Resource's description
```

The `description` is not mandatory, but providing descriptions of your API's resources will be useful throughout the API lifecycle. It's like when you code: the code can be understandable on its own, but comments or JavaDoc, PHPDoc, JSDoc, or <your favorite language>Doc annotations about its use will always be welcomed by other people who read your code or the documentation generated from it.

Because an API by definition will be used by others, it is really important to take advantage of the documentation possibilities of API description formats. During this design phase it is especially useful to keep a link between your earlier work, like the API goals canvas or concept identification, and the programmable representation. It might also help people with whom you share this design to understand it more easily (/products being a catalog might not be obvious to everyone).

A resource described within an OAS document must contain some operations. Otherwise, the document is not valid. The catalog resource is used by two goals: search for products and add product. Let's see how we can describe them as operations in the OAS document.

4.2.3 Describing operations on a resource

We can add to our document in order to provide all the information for each goal we identified by the end of section 3.2. For each one, we know which HTTP method it uses, and we have a textual description of its inputs and outputs, as shown on the left side of figure 4.8.

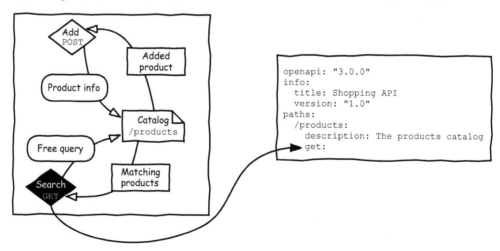

Figure 4.8   Adding an action to a resource

To represent search for products, we chose to use the GET HTTP method on the catalog resource represented by the /products path. This action uses a *free query* parameter and returns products matching the query. To add this action to the /products resource, we use a get property. We can also use documentation features to provide more information about this GET /products operation. We'll set the summary property to Search for products and the description to Search for products in catalog using a free query parameter, as shown in the following listing.

Listing 4.3   Describing an action on a resource

```
openapi: "3.0.0"
info:
  title: Shopping API
  version: "1.0"                  Resource
paths:
  /products:
    description: The products catalog          Action's HTTP method
    get:
      summary: Search for products             Action's short description
      description: |
        Search for products in catalog
        using a free query parameter           Action's long description
```

The summary property is a short description of the action, without details. The goal defined in the API goals canvas is usually perfect to use here. There is also a description property, which can be used to provide a more detailed description of the action. Here we use it to indicate that this action is using a free query parameter. Note that the description property is multiline. This is a YAML feature: to be multiline, a string property must start with a pipe (|) character.

In an OAS document, an operation must describe at least one response in its responses property, as shown in listing 4.4. For now, we will use this mandatory response to provide an informal description of the output of the search for products action. We'll add a responses property containing a "200" response (for HTTP status code 200 OK), whose description is Products matching free query parameter.

Listing 4.4   Describing an action's responses

```
openapi: "3.0.0"
info:
  title: Shopping API
  version: "1.0"
paths:
  /products:
    description: The products catalog
    get:
      summary: Search for products
      description: |
        Search for products in catalog           Action's response list
        using a free query parameter
      responses:
```

```
"200":                  ◄─────────────────────  | 200 OK HTTP status response
  description:  |  ◄─────────────────────
    Products matching free query parameter   | Response's description
```

As mentioned, an action's possible responses are described in its responses property. Each response is identified by its HTTP status code and *must* contain a description property. The "200" property stands for the 200 OK HTTP status, which tells the consumer that everything went fine. (Did you notice the quotes around the status code? They are needed because YAML property names must be strings and 200 is a number.) The response's description property states that if everything went OK, the Products matching free query parameter are returned. We will explore the possible responses and HTTP status codes returned by an action in more depth in chapter 5.

Now that we have added this action to the /products resource, our OAS document is valid. But we're not done yet. There is a second action on this resource: add product. We chose the HTTP method POST to represent the add product action on the catalog resource. It takes some product information and returns the product added to the catalog (see figure 4.9).

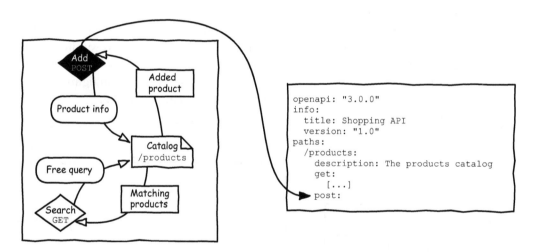

Figure 4.9　Adding another action to a resource

To add this action, we proceed exactly like we did previously. The following listing shows how to do this.

Listing 4.5　Describing another action

```
openapi: "3.0.0"
info:
  title: Shopping API
  version: "1.0"
paths:                          ┌─ Resource
  /products:          ◄────────┘
    description: The products catalog
```

```
get:
  summary: Search for products
  description: |
    Search for products in catalog
    using a free query parameter
  responses:
    "200":
      description: |
        Products matching free query parameter
post:
  summary: Add product
  description: |
    Add product (described in product info
    parameter) to catalog
  responses:
    "200":
      description: |
        Product added to catalog
```

Action's HTTP method

Action's short description

Action's long description

Action's response list

200 OK response

200 OK response's description

We add a post property inside the object describing the catalog resource identified by the /products path. We set its summary property to Add product and its description to Add product (described in product info parameter) to catalog. We add a "200" property inside responses and set its description to Product added to catalog.

The /products resource's post operation is now described within the OAS document. Anyone looking at this document can tell what this operation does by reading its summary, description, and response description. As shown in figure 4.10, this document contains the same information we identified in section 3.2.

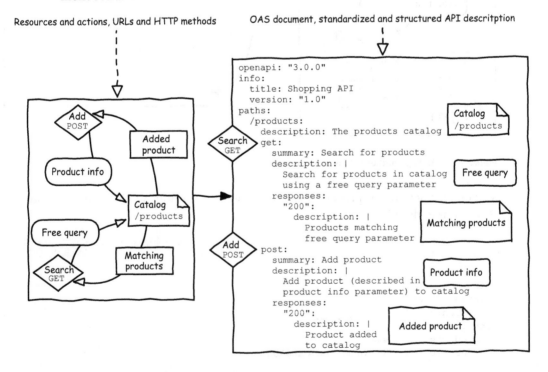

Figure 4.10   OAS document corresponding to the initial figure

Congratulations! You now know the basics of how to describe a resource and its actions using the OAS. Even if it is not yet complete, such a description already provides interesting information about the API. We have a formal and structured description of the resource's path and HTTP methods, and we are able to determine which goal corresponds to which action and how they work, thanks to the `description` properties.

But this document only provides a vague description of each operation's inputs and outputs. In the previous chapter, we designed these inputs and outputs in detail. Let's see now how to complete this document by describing those.

4.3 Describing API data with OpenAPI and JSON Schema

In the previous chapter, when we designed the programming interface matching the identified goals, we did not stop after designing the resource paths and choosing the HTTP methods. In section 3.3, we fully described the actions' parameters and responses, including descriptions of the data organization and properties (figure 4.11).

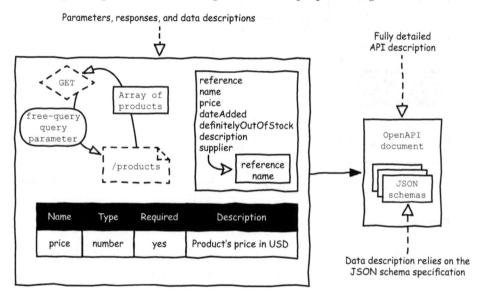

Figure 4.11 From figures and tables to a detailed OAS document

The OAS relies on the JSON Schema specification (http://json-schema.org) to describe all data—query parameters, body parameters, or response bodies, for example. JSON Schema aims to describe data formats in a clear human-readable and machine-readable way. It can also be used to validate JSON documents against a JSON *schema*, a data description made with JSON Schema. This format can be used independently from OAS to describe and validate any type of JSON data.

> **NOTE** OAS uses an adapted subset of JSON Schema. It does not use all JSON Schema features, and some specific OAS features have been added to this subset.

In this chapter, *JSON Schema* refers to the JSON Schema specification, whereas a *JSON schema* is an actual schema, a description of data. Note the difference in capitalization. Let's see how we can describe API data using the OAS and JSON Schema. We'll start with the search for products query parameter.

4.3.1 Describing query parameters

To search for products, API users have to provide a *free query* parameter to indicate what they are looking for (figure 4.12). In the previous chapter, we decided that this parameter would be a query parameter named `free-query`. To search for products using the API, a consumer would issue a `GET /products?free-query={free query}` request (for example, `GET /products?free-query=book`).

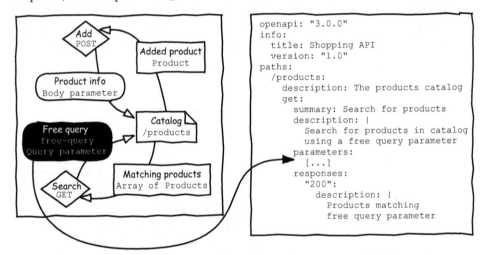

Figure 4.12   The search for products free query parameter

To describe this parameter, we add a `parameters` property inside the `get` operation of the `/products` resource, as shown in the following listing.

Listing 4.6   Describing parameters

```
openapi: "3.0.0"
info:
  title: Shopping API
  version: "1.0"
paths:                          Resource
  /products:        ◄──────
    get:                         Action
      summary: Search for products
      description: |
        Search for products in catalog
        using a free query parameter
      parameters:        ◄─────     Action's parameters list (except body)
        [...]
```

```
responses:
  "200":
    description: |
      Products matching free query parameter
```

When an action on a resource needs parameters other than body parameters, they are described in the action's `parameters` property. In this case, to describe the parameter, we set its `name` to `free-query`, as shown in the following listing.

Listing 4.7　Describing a query parameter

```
parameters:
  - name: free-query          ◄──── │ Parameter's name │   │ Parameter's description │
    description: |            ◄──────────────────────────────┘
      A product's name, reference, or   │ Parameter's location │
      partial description
    in: query                ◄─────────────────────┘   │ Whether a parameter is mandatory │
    required: false          ◄──────────────────────────┘   │ Parameter's data structure description │
    schema:                  ◄──────────────────────────────────┘
      type: string           ◄────────────────────────────────────┘ Parameter's type (string)
```

We indicate that the parameter is located `in` the `query` but is not `required`, and that its data structure is described in `schema`. This schema simply indicates that this parameter's type is `string`. We also provide some additional information in its `description` to tell that its value could be `A product's name, reference, or partial description`.

The `parameters` property is a list or array. In YAML, each element of a list or array starts with a dash (`-`). To describe a parameter, we need at least three properties: `name`, `in`, and `schema`. This parameter's description also contains two optional properties: `required` and `description`.

The parameter's name is the name that will be shown in the path (`/products?free-query={free query}`). The `in` property indicates the location of the parameter. Here, it's a query parameter, so it's located after a `?` in the path.

The `required` property, which indicates if the parameter must be provided, is not mandatory. If `required` is not set, its default value is `false`, indicating that the parameter is optional. You are under no obligation to set it unless you need to define a parameter as `required`. But even though the parameter is optional, it's always better to explicitly specify `required: false`. This way, you are sure that you've considered whether each parameter is mandatory or not.

> **TIP**　Even though `description` is optional, I recommend that you always provide one. The parameter's name alone is more often than not insufficient to describe what is expected.

The parameter's data structure described in the `schema` property is a JSON schema. As mentioned earlier, JSON Schema is used in an OAS document to describe the API's data—from a simple `string` query parameters to more complex structures used as body parameters and responses. Using JSON Schema, let's see how we can describe a product, such as the one designed in section 3.3.1.

4.3.2 Describing data with JSON Schema

We'll start with a very basic version of the product, as shown in figure 4.13. It's composed of a reference, a name, and a price. The reference and name properties are of type string and price is a number.

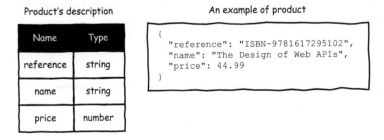

Figure 4.13   A basic product description

Earlier, to describe a simple string query parameter with JSON Schema, we used type: string. Now, to describe such a product object, we have to use the type object and list its properties. Each property is identified by its name and type, as seen in the following listing.

> **Listing 4.8   Describing a very basic product with JSON Schema**

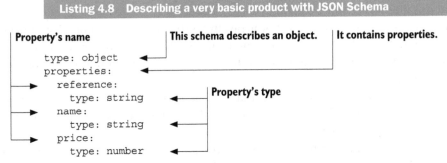

But when we discussed designing the API's data in the previous chapter, you learned that we must also identify which properties are required. Because the reference, name, and price properties are all mandatory, we'll add an optional description for the sake of example (see figure 4.14).

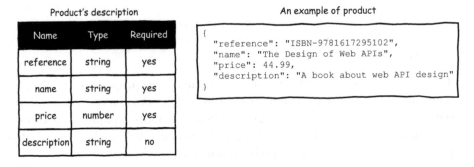

Figure 4.14   A product description with required flags

Now the product is composed of mandatory `reference`, `name`, and `price` properties and an optional `description`. To indicate that in the corresponding JSON Schema, we add `reference`, `name`, and `price` entries into the object's `required` properties list, as shown in the following listing.

Listing 4.9   Required and optional properties for product

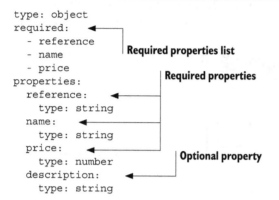

```
type: object
required:
  - reference
  - name
  - price
properties:
  reference:
    type: string
  name:
    type: string
  price:
    type: number
  description:
    type: string
```

Required properties list

Required properties

Optional property

The JSON Schema allows us to indicate which properties are required in an object with its `required` list. Any property whose name is included in this list is mandatory. Any property whose name is not in this list is considered optional. In this case, `description` is the only optional property.

Our schema is getting pretty accurate, but when we designed the product resource, we found that we sometimes needed to add some descriptions because the property names were not sufficient to explain their nature. Let's add a description to the object to show that it describes `A product`. We can also add a description to explain what a `reference` is. We can even add an example to show what a product's reference looks like. The next listing shows this.

Listing 4.10   Documenting a JSON schema

```
type: object
description: A product
required:
  - reference
  - name
  - price
properties:
  reference:
    type: string
    description: Product's unique identifier
    example: ISBN-9781617295102
  name:
    type: string
    example: The Design of Web APIs
  price:
    type: number
    example: 44.99
```

Object's description

Property's description

Property's value example

```
description:
  type: string
  example: A book about API design    ◄────┐ Property's value example
```

Just like the OAS, the JSON Schema comes with useful documentation features. An object and all of its properties can be described, and an example value can be provided for each property.

We're still missing something, though. The product resource we designed in the previous chapter didn't only have literal properties (strings or numbers), as shown in figure 4.15.

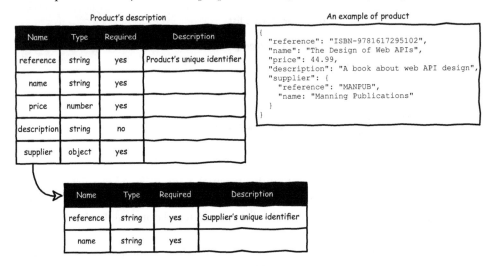

Figure 4.15   A product with supplier description

Indeed, it also had a complex `supplier` property, which is mandatory. A supplier is defined by its `reference` and its `name`, which are both required. The following listing shows the updated JSON schema.

Listing 4.11   Describing a complex property with the JSON Schema

```
type: object
description: A product
required:
  - reference
  - name
  - price
  - supplier    ◄────┐ The supplier is required.
  - supplier
properties:
  reference:
    type: string
    description: Product's unique identifier
    example: ISBN-9781617295102
```

```
name:
  type: string
  example: The Design of Web APIs
price:
  type: number
  example: 44.99
description:
  type: string
  example: A book about API design        ──────  The supplier object property
supplier:                              ◄──────────┘
  type: object
  description: Product's supplier        ──────  The supplier's required properties
  required:                           ◄──────────┘
    - reference          ──────  The supplier property descriptions
    - name            ◄──────────┘
  properties:
    reference:
      type: string
      description: Supplier's unique identifier
      example: MANPUB
    name:
      type: string
      example: Manning Publications
```

To add the `supplier` property to the product JSON schema, we add it to the `proper-ties` list and set its `type` to `object`. We supply a description for the property and a list of its required properties (`reference` and `name`); then we describe those properties. For the `reference` property, we supply a `type`, `description`, and `example`. For the `name` property, we only set a `type` and `example`. Finally, we add the `supplier` property to the product's `required` list.

As you can see, describing data using the JSON Schema is simple; you can describe any data structure using this format. Unfortunately, this book does not cover all of its features. To learn more, I recommend you read the Schema Object description in the OAS (https://github.com/OAI/OpenAPI-Specification/tree/master/versions), and then the JSON Schema specification (http://json-schema.org/specification.html). Now that you know how to describe data structures using the JSON Schema, let's describe the search for products response.

4.3.3   Describing responses

When users search for products, they are supposed to get the products matching the provided free query (figure 4.16). The corresponding GET /products?free-query= {free query} API request returns a 200 OK HTTP response whose body will contain an array of products.

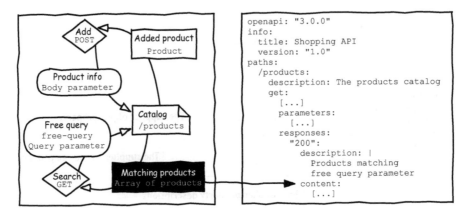

Figure 4.16   Describing the search for products response

In an OAS document, the data returned by an operation in the body of an HTTP response is defined in its content property, as shown in listing 4.12. When describing the content of a response, you have to indicate the media type of the document contained in the response's body. The media type is provided in the HTTP response. For now, as stated earlier, we'll take it for granted that our API returns JSON documents, so we indicate application/json in the response. (We talk about this HTTP feature later in chapter 6.)

Listing 4.12   Describing the response's data

```
openapi: "3.0.0"
info:
  title: Shopping API
  version: "1.0"
paths:
  /products:
      get:
        summary: Search for products
        description: |
          Search using a free query (query parameter)
        parameters:
        [...]
        responses:
          "200":
            description: Products matching free query
            content:
              application/json:
                schema:
                  [...]
```

Response body's definition →
Response body's media type →
Response body's JSON schema →

Once that is done, we can describe the schema of the returned JSON document using the JSON Schema, as shown in listing 4.13. The GET /products action returns an array of products. We already know how to describe a product using the JSON Schema, but how do we describe an array of products? As you can see in the next listing, an array is described using the array type. The items property contains the schema of the array's elements. This array contains some products; you should recognize the product JSON Schema we created earlier.

Listing 4.13 Describing an array of products

```
responses:
  "200":
    description: Products matching free query
    content:
      application/json:
        schema:
          type: array
          description: Array of products
          items:
            type: object
            description: A product
            required:
              - reference
              - name
              - price
              - supplier
            properties:
              reference:
                description: Unique ID identifying a product
                type: string
              name:
                type: string
              price:
                description: Price in USD
                type: number
              description:
                type: string
              supplier:
                type: object
                description: Product's supplier
                required:
                  - reference
                  - name
                properties:
                  reference:
                    type: string
                  name:
                    type: string
```

Response body's media type → `application/json:`

Response body's JSON schema → `schema:`

Response type is an array → `type: array`

Array's items schema → `items:`

The next listing contains an example of a JSON document returned in the response's body corresponding to the JSON Schema.

Listing 4.14 Array of products JSON example

```
[
  {
    "reference": "123-456",
    "name": "a product",
    "price": 9.99,
    "supplier": {
      "reference": "S789",
      "name": "a supplier"
```

```
    }
  },
  {
    "reference": "234-567",
    "name": "another product",
    "price": 19.99,
    "supplier": {
      "reference": "S456",
      "name": "another supplier"
    }
  }
]
```

As you can see, describing the response's data is pretty simple. And you know what? Describing body parameters is just as easy.

4.3.4 *Describing body parameters*

Let's take a look at the add product action. To add a product to the catalog, the API user has to provide some product information in the body of their request, as illustrated in figure 4.17.

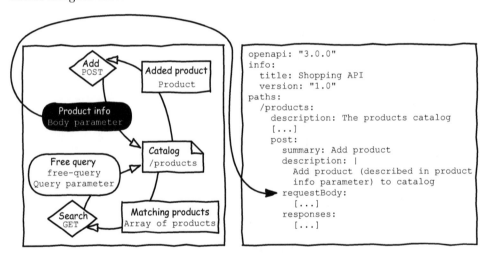

Figure 4.17   Describing the add product body parameter

Describing the body parameter of add product is done almost the same way as describing the response of search for products, as you can see in the following listing.

Listing 4.15   Describing an action's body parameter

```
openapi: "3.0.0"
info:
  title: Shopping API
  version: "1.0"
paths:
  /products:
```

```
                description: The products catalog
                [...]
                post:
                  summary: Add product
                  description: Add product to catalog
                  requestBody:
                    description: Product's information
                    application/json:
                      schema:
                        [...]
                  responses:
                    "200":
                      description: Product added to catalog
```

Body parameter's description → (points to `description: Product's information`)

Body parameter's definition ← (points to `requestBody:`)

Body parameter's media type ← (points to `application/json:`)

Body parameter's schema ← (points to `schema:`)

The body parameter of an HTTP request is described in its `requestBody` property. Like a response's body, a body parameter has a media type (`application/json`), and its content is described with a JSON Schema. The complete description of this parameter is shown in the following listing.

Listing 4.16 Body parameter's complete description

```
requestBody:
  description: Product's information
  content:
    application/json:
      schema:
        required:
          - name
          - price
          - supplierReference
        properties:
          name:
            type: string
          price:
            type: number
          description:
            type: string
          supplierReference:
            type: string
```

Body parameter's schema ← (points to `schema:`)

The body parameter's schema (or request body's schema) is described like any other data in OAS using the JSON Schema. As previously designed, the mandatory information needed to add a product to the catalog is its `name`, `price`, and `supplierReference`. The `description` is optional. The following listing shows what the JSON document might look like.

Listing 4.17 Product information JSON example

```
{
  "name": "a product",
  "price": 9.99,
  "supplierReference": "S789"
}
```

See? It was as easy as anticipated. Why? Because describing the request's and response's body is done the same way. Providing a common way of doing different things is a basic principle of design. This approach can be used when creating anything, from a door to an API description format, to make it user-friendly. We will investigate this from the API design perspective later in chapter 6.

We only need to describe add product's response to finish the catalog resource's description. We have learned all we need to do that. We know how to describe an action's response and its data. And, fortunately, search for products and add product return the same type of data, a product, so we already have the JSON Schema describing the response's data. But if we do that as we have learned, we will duplicate the product JSON Schema in the OAS document. Let's see how we can handle this more efficiently.

4.4   Describing an API efficiently with OAS

It's always useful to dig into an API description format's documentation to learn all its tips and tricks, just like you would do when learning a programming language. There are two basic things that you need to know when writing OAS documents:

- How to reuse components such as JSON schemas, parameters, or responses
- How to define path parameters efficiently

4.4.1   Reusing components

Both search for products and add product return product resources. It would be a pity to describe the same thing twice. Fortunately, OAS allows us to describe reusable components such as schemas, parameters, responses, and many others, and use them where needed using a *reference* (figure 4.18).

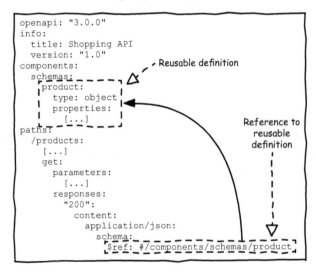

Figure 4.18   Reusable components in the OAS document

All we have to do to avoid describing a product JSON Schema twice is to declare it as a *reusable schema*. Reusable components are described in the `components` section that's at the root of the OAS document. Within this section, reusable schemas are defined in `schemas`; each reusable schema's name is defined as a property of `schemas`. This property contains the reusable component, a JSON Schema. In the following listing, `product` contains the product JSON Schema we created earlier.

Listing 4.18 Declaring a reusable schema

```
openapi: "3.0.0"
[...]                         Reusable components
components:          ◄─────┐
  schemas:          ◄──────── Reusable schemas
    product:        ◄─────────────── Reusable schema's name
      type: object  ◄───────────┐
      description: A product     │
      required:                  │ JSON Schema
        - reference
        - name
        - price
        - supplier
      properties:
        reference:
          description: |
              Unique ID identifying
              a product
          type: string
        name:
          type: string
        price:
          description: Price in USD
          type: number
        description:
          type: string
        supplier:
          type: object
          description: Product's supplier
          required:
            - reference
            - name
          properties:
            reference:
              type: string
            name:
              type: string
```

Now, instead of redefining the product JSON Schema, we can use a JSON reference to access this predefined schema when we need it. A *JSON reference* is a property whose name is `$ref` and whose content is a URL. This URL can point to any component inside the document, or even in other documents. Because we are only referencing local components, we use a local URL containing only a fragment describing the path to the needed element, as shown in figure 4.19. Here, `product` is located in `schemas`, which is located in `components` at the root of the document.

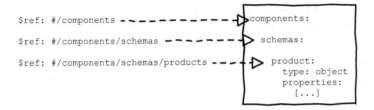

Figure 4.19   JSON references to local components

The following listing shows how we can use a reference for the POST /products response.

Listing 4.19   Using a predefined component with its reference

```
post:
  summary: Add product
  description: Add product to catalog
  [...]
  responses:
    "200":
      description: Product added to catalog
      content:
        application/json:                    Response's schema
          schema:                                              Reference to predefined schema
            $ref: "#/components/schemas/product"
```

When users add a product to the catalog, they get the created product in return. So when defining the response schema, instead of redescribing the product JSON Schema, we can just use a $ref property whose value is a reference to the predefined schema. We can do the same for search for product, which returns an array of products, as shown in the next listing.

Listing 4.20   Using a predefined component in an array with its reference

```
get:
  summary: Search for products
  description: |
    Search using a free query (query parameter)
  parameters:
    [...]
  responses:
    "200":
      description: Products matching free query
      content:
        application/json:
          schema:
            type: array
            items:
              $ref: "#/components/schemas/product"
```

Response's schema — Reference to predefined schema — An array — Array's items schema

The schema we have predefined only describes a product, not an array of products, so here we use the predefined schema to describe the array's items schema. To do that, as before, we simply replace the schema with a reference ($ref) to the predefined schema. This means that we can combine inline and predefined definitions. Note that we can also use multiple predefined definitions when needed.

We're now done with the catalog resource identified by the `/products` path and its two actions, `get` and `post`. These elements are fully and efficiently described thanks to the OAS and JSON Schema. There is one last thing to investigate with the OAS in order to be able to fully describe a basic REST API—how to describe a resource with a variable path.

4.4.2 Describing path parameters

The product resource, which can be deleted, updated, or replaced, is identified by a variable path (figure 4.20). Note that the get, update, and replace actions return the same product and also that the update and replace actions use the same parameter. Note also the `/products/{productId}` path contains a `productId` variable, which is called a *path parameter*.

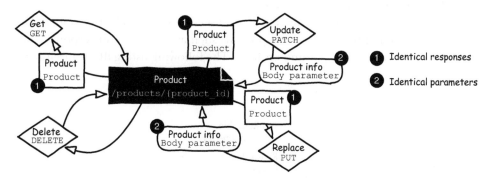

Figure 4.20　The product resource and its actions

You already learned how to define parameters on the action level with `GET /prod-ucts?free-query={free query}`, so let's do this again with `DELETE /products/{pro-ductId}`. The following listing shows how we can define this in our OAS document for the delete action.

> **Listing 4.21　Deleting a product**

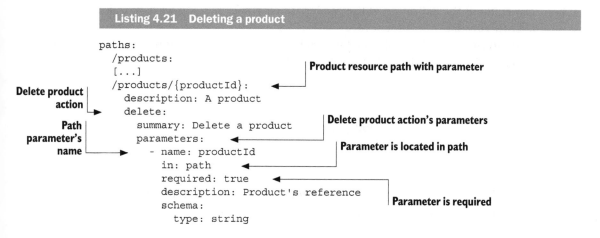

First we add a new /products/{productId} path to define the product resource. As you can see, the path parameter is identified with curly braces ({productId}) in paths. Then, we define this path parameter in the delete action's parameters list. It is defined almost like any other parameter that goes in the parameters section: we need to set its name, location, and schema. The name must match the name inside the curly braces in the path, so we set it to productId. The location (in) is obviously path, and this parameter's type, defined in its schema, is string.

We're almost done, but there is one last thing we must not forget to do: because it is a path parameter, we also have to make this parameter mandatory by setting required to true. If we don't do that, the parser throws an error.

That wasn't so different from defining a query parameter. Now, what if we wanted to describe the product's update and replace actions? We could describe the path parameter the same way, but that would mean duplicating this description in each new action. How can we do that more efficiently?

Earlier, we discovered the components section of the OAS document. This section allows us to define reusable components such as schemas and responses, and we can also describe reusable parameters here. The following listing illustrates how we do this.

> **Listing 4.22   Describing a reusable parameter**

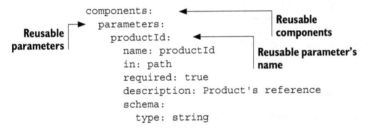

```
components:
  parameters:              ◀──────  Reusable
    productId:     ◀──────           components
      name: productId
      in: path                      Reusable parameter's
      required: true                name
      description: Product's reference
      schema:
        type: string
```

Reusable parameters

To define a reusable parameter, we do exactly what we did for our reusable schema. In the components section at the root of the OAS document, each reusable parameter is defined as a property of parameters and identified by name. The productId property contains the definition of the productId path parameter as we have defined it for DELETE /products/{productId}.

Pretty simple, isn't it? Like the JSON Schema, we use this predefined parameter with a JSON reference, as shown in the following listing.

> **Listing 4.23   Using a predefined parameter**

```
components:
    parameters:              Path parameter definition
      productId:     ◀──────
        [...]
paths:
  /products:
    [...]                    Product resource's path with parameter
  /products/{productId}:  ◀──────
```

```
delete:
  parameters:
    - $ref: #/components/parameters/productId
  [...]
put:
  parameters:
    - $ref: #/components/parameters/productId
  [...]
patch:
  parameters:
    - $ref: #/components/parameters/productId
  [...]
```

Reference to predefined parameter

Instead of defining the same parameter three times, we simply use a $ref property pointing to the unique and reusable productId definition.

That's much better! The productId parameter is defined once and used in three different places. But do you know what? We can do even better. Strictly speaking, the productId parameter is not an action's parameter; it's a resource's parameter.

In an OAS document, parameters can be defined not only at the action level but also at the resource level, again in a parameters section. The structure of this section is exactly the same as at the action level. All parameters defined on the resource level are applied to all actions on the resource. Therefore, as the next listing demonstrates, to simplify our document even more, we can simply define the productId path parameter in the parameters section of the /products/{productId} path.

Listing 4.24 Resource-level parameters

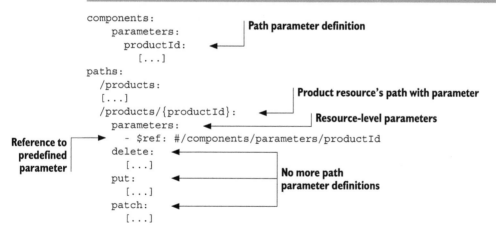

```
components:
    parameters:
      productId:
        [...]
paths:
  /products:
    [...]
  /products/{productId}:
    parameters:
      - $ref: #/components/parameters/productId
    delete:
      [...]
    put:
      [...]
    patch:
      [...]
```

Congratulations! With all that you have now discovered about OAS, you should be able to finish the descriptions of the product resource's actions. But more importantly, you will now be able to create a formal description of any basic REST API using OAS and share it with all the people involved in your project. Don't hesitate to dig into the OAS documentation (https://github.com/OAI/OpenAPI-Specification/tree/master/versions), use my OpenAPI Map (https://openapi-map.apihandyman.io), and experiment to discover other features.

This chapter concludes the first part of this book. You have acquired a basic set of API design skills, and you now know

- What an API really is
- How to identify its goals from the consumer's perspective
- How to transpose them into a programmable representation
- How to formally describe this programmable representation using OAS

In the next part, we will improve on these skills so you can create APIs that anybody can use easily, without even thinking about it. In the next chapter, we dig into the API's usability by investigating how to design straightforward APIs.

Summary

- An API description format is a simple and structured way to describe and share a programming interface.
- An API description document is a machine-readable document that can be used in numerous ways, including to generate API reference documentation.
- You use an API description format only when designing the API's programmable representation and data, and not before.
- Always take advantage of an API description format's documentation features. Explore the API description format's documentation in depth so you can use it efficiently and, especially, to define reusable components where possible.

Part 2

Usable API design

Now that you have finished the first part of this book, you are able to identify an API's real goals and represent them as a programming interface, all while having the consumer's perspective in mind and avoiding the provider's. This is a solid basis for designing an API that does the job—but people expect more from APIs than just *doing the job*. An API is worth nothing if it is not usable. The more usable an API is, the less effort is required to work with it, and the more people may choose to use it. They even may love to use it. *Usability* is what distinguishes awesome APIs from mediocre or passable ones.

Usability is vital for any API, as for any everyday object. Do you remember the Kitchen Radar 3000? Its interface was terrible because it simply exposed inner workings. Unfortunately, such a terrible design can be achieved when creating APIs, even when avoiding the dreaded provider's perspective! Fortunately, fundamental principles of usability can be learned by observing everyday things.

When people use an everyday object, they want to achieve their goals without being overwhelmed by an abundant but fuzzy set of functions. And they love to think that they are smart because they can discover everything about an object by themselves. It is the same for APIs.

Consumers don't want to have to think when they use APIs; they want APIs with a straightforward design that lets them achieve their objectives instantly, without having to lose time understanding data, goals, or error feedback. They also want concise and organized sets of goals, not an overwhelming, gigantic, motley API. And, most importantly, they want to feel at home when they use an API; they want to have a feeling of déjà-vu because the API tells them everything, and its design also conforms to standards or common practices.

Designing a straightforward API

This chapter covers

- Crafting straightforward representations of concepts
- Identifying relevant error and success feedback
- Designing efficient usage flows

Now that you have learned to design APIs that actually let consumers achieve their goals, you have a solid foundation in API design. Unfortunately, only relying on the basics does not mean that consumers will actually be able to use the "APIs that do the job." Remember the UDRC 1138 shown in figure 5.1? It *is* possible to design a terrible interface that does the job.

Figure 5.1   A terrible interface that does the job

When faced with an unfamiliar everyday object, what do you do? You observe it. You analyze its form, labels, icons, buttons, or other controls in order to get an understanding of its purpose, its current status, and how to operate it. To achieve your goal using this object, you might need to chain various interactions, providing inputs and receiving feedback. When you do all that, you don't want uncertainties; everything must be crystal-clear. You don't want to waste time, so everything must go swiftly and efficiently. You want your experience using any everyday object to be as straightforward as possible. You definitely don't want to face another interface like the UDRC 1138. That is the basis of *usability*. And it's exactly the same with APIs.

People expect APIs to be usable. They expect straightforward representations, straightforward interactions, and straightforward flows. We will uncover some fundamental principles of usability by observing everyday things in various situations, then transpose those principles to API design. We will work for now, and for the rest of this book, on an imaginary retail Banking API provided by the fictitious Banking Company. This API could be the one used, for example, by a mobile banking application to get information about current accounts, such as balance and transactions, and transfer money from one account to another. Let's start by learning to craft representations that fit this bill.

5.1   Designing straightforward representations

How a designer chooses to represent concepts and information can greatly enhance or undermine usability. Avoiding the provider's perspective and focusing on the consumer's, as you learned to do in chapter 2, is the obvious first step toward usability—but we also need to take care of a few other aspects to ensure that we design straightforward representations. Let's work on a simple alarm clock to discover these aspects.

Figure 5.2 shows how we can modify an alarm clock's appearance. It shows how we can modify the representations used in order to make it the least usable possible.

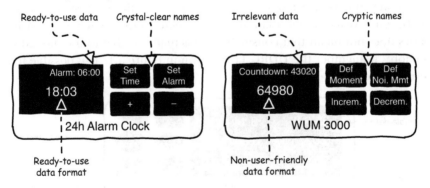

Figure 5.2   Transforming an alarm clock into a less usable device

First, we can use more cryptic labels. The 24h Alarm Clock becomes the WUM 3000 (Wake Up Machine 3000). The Set Time, Set Alarm, and + and – buttons are replaced by Def Moment (Define Moment), Def Noi. Mmt (Define Noise Moment), Increm. (Increment), and Decrem. (Decrement). We can also use a less user-friendly format for the current time and replace it with the number of seconds elapsed since midnight, so 18:03 becomes 64,980. And finally, we can replace the alarm time with closely related but less useful information: a countdown to the alarm time in seconds, for example. If the current time is 18:03, the 06:00 alarm time then becomes 43,020 (and counting).

Just like the 24h Alarm Clock, the WUM 3000 does not expose inner complexity. Both are made to show time and, more importantly, make some awful noise at a given moment. But the representations used are slightly different, and this affects usability. The 24h Alarm Clock is usable because a user can understand what this device is, what its current status is, and how to use it by just reading the labels, buttons, and display screen. On the other hand, the WUM 3000 is far less usable because these elements are quite cryptic and confusing.

It's exactly the same with APIs. The choices you make with regard to names, data formats, and data can greatly enhance or undermine an API's usability. You already know how to design these things; you just have to consider whether the chosen representations make sense and are easily understandable for the consumer, focusing on the consumer's perspective and designing with the user in mind. Let's explore these topics a bit more closely, though, to fully uncover how to craft straightforward representations.

5.1.1 Choosing crystal-clear names

It's impossible to determine what a WUM 3000 is and how to use it based solely on its name or its Def Moment and Def Noi. Mmt buttons, while a 24h Alarm Clock is obviously ... an alarm clock. Code names, awkward vocabulary, and cryptic abbreviations can make an everyday object totally confusing. The same goes for APIs.

When you analyze needs with the API goals canvas, you have to name inputs and outputs. These inputs and outputs have to be represented as resources, responses, or parameters, all of which have names. These elements can contain properties, which have names too. When representing these with a tool such as the OpenAPI Specification (OAS), you might have to choose names for reusable JSON schemas. Depending on the chosen API style, goals can be represented as functions, which also have names. Names are everywhere. So how do you choose those?

In section 2.2.2, you discovered the consumer's and provider's perspectives. We already know that we must choose names that mean something for the consumers. But even knowing that, we must be careful when crafting those names.

Let's say the Banking Company's current accounts come with an optional overdraft protection feature. If the overdraft protection is active, the bank will not apply any fees in the event of the customer's withdrawal exceeding the available balance. It could be interesting to know if this option is active or not when retrieving information about a bank account with the Banking API provided by this company. Figure 5.3 shows how it could be represented in the API.

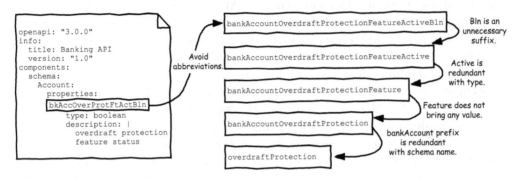

Figure 5.3   Choosing a property name

The first idea is to use a `boolean` property named `bkAccOverProtFtActBln`, which is `true` when the feature is activated and `false` otherwise. But while using the Boolean type totally makes sense, this `bkAccOverProtFtActBln` property name is not totally user-friendly, to say the least. Using abbreviations is usually not a good idea because it makes them harder to understand. (Note that abbreviations like *max* or *min* are acceptable because they are commonly used; we'll talk more about that in section 6.1.3.)

With fewer abbreviations, this property name becomes `bankAccountOverdraft-ProtectionFeatureActiveBln`; that's a descriptive and readable name. But while it's clear, it's awfully long. Let's see how we can find a better but still easily understandable alternative.

The `Bln` suffix states that this property is a Boolean. Some coding conventions can promote the use of prefixes or suffixes like `bln`, `dto`, `sz`, `o`, `m_`, and so on to explain the technical nature of a property, class, or structure. Because you are aware of the provider's perspective, you've probably already guessed that exposing internal coding conventions in this way might not be wise. But even if we set aside the provider's perspective, do such technical details matter to consumers? Not at all.

Consumers will have access to the API's documentation, which describes this property as a Boolean. And when testing the API, developers will see that the property is a Boolean because its value is `true` or `false`. So, we can shorten the name to `bankAccountOverdraftProtectionFeatureActive`.

Because the API's consumers can see that this property is a Boolean, we can also get rid of the `Active` suffix. This word is redundant with the Boolean type and, therefore, has absolutely no informative value. So, we can shorten the name to `bankAccountOverdraftProtectionFeature`.

Speaking of informative value, does the word *Feature* have any interest? Not really. From a functional point of view, it simply states that this is a property/service of the bank account. This could be explained in the property's documentation. So, we can also get rid of this word and shorten the property's name to `bankAccountOverdraftProtection`.

And finally, this property belongs to a *bank account*, so there's no need to state the obvious in its name. Therefore, the property can simply be named `overdraftProtection`. We have gone from seven words to two.

> **TIP** I recommend that you try to use no more than three words to craft names (whatever their purpose).

Basically, what we did in crafting this name is to use words that consumers can understand easily, and we took advantage of the context surrounding what we are naming to find a short but still clearly understandable name. We also have avoided abbreviations and exposing internal code conventions. This is all you have to do if you want to find crystal-clear names for resources, parameters, properties, JSON schemas, or anything else that needs a name.

Some of the names we choose when designing APIs are meant to identify data. And as we saw with the `overdraftProtection` Boolean property, choosing adequate data types can greatly facilitate understanding.

5.1.2 Choosing easy-to-use data types and formats

The WUM 3000 showed us that inadequate data representation can ruin usability. A value such as 64,980 is not obviously a time, and even if users know it is, they still have to do some calculations to decipher its true meaning: 18:03. Lacking context, the wrong data type or format can hinder understanding and usage.

But that's for an everyday object used by human beings. With APIs, data is simply processed by the software consuming the API, and it can perfectly interpret complex formats. It can even transform the data before showing it to an end user if necessary. So why should we care about data types and formats when designing an API?

We must never lose sight of the fact that an API is *a user interface*. Developers rely not only on names to understand and use the API, but also on its data. It's common for developers to analyze sample requests and responses, call the API manually, or analyze returned data in their code for learning, testing, or debugging purposes. They might also need to manipulate specific values in their code. To do all that, they need to be able to understand the data. If the API only uses complex or cryptic data formats, such an exercise will be quite difficult. So just like names that must be understood at first sight, the meaning of an API's raw data must always be crystal-clear for developers.

> **TIP** Choosing appropriate data formats when designing an API is as important as choosing appropriate names in order to provide a straightforward representation in your API.

As seen in section 3.3.1, APIs typically use basic portable data types such as `string`, `number`, or `boolean`. It can be relatively straightforward to choose a type for a property. If we go on designing the bank account concept we started in the previous section, adding the account's name and balance is quite simple. Indeed, a bank account's name should obviously be a `string` and its balance a `number`. But, in some cases, you have to be careful when choosing data types and formats to ensure that what you are designing is understandable by a human being, as shown in figure 5.4. The figure shows examples of a bank account's data in two different versions: on the left side, the data is not easy-to-use; it is the opposite on the right side.

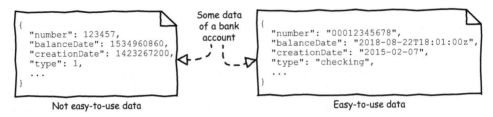

Some data
of a bank
account

```
{
    "number": 123457,
    "balanceDate": 1534960860,
    "creationDate": 1423267200,
    "type": 1,
    ...
}
```
Not easy-to-use data

```
{
    "number": "00012345678",
    "balanceDate": "2018-08-22T18:01:00z",
    "creationDate": "2015-02-07",
    "type": "checking",
    ...
}
```
Easy-to-use data

Figure 5.4   Impacts of data types and format on usability

Thanks to the `Date` suffix and the `1534960860` value, seasoned developers should be able to understand that `balanceDate` is a UNIX timestamp. But will they be able to decipher this value just by reading it? Probably not. Its ISO 8601 string counterpart, `"2018-08-22T18:01:00z"`, is far more user-friendly and can be understood by anyone without any context and without effort (well, almost without effort, once you know that it's `"YEAR-MONTH-DAY"` and not `"YEAR-DAY-MONTH"`).

The same goes for the `creationDate`, whose left-side value is `1423267200`. But note that its ISO 8601 value shows only the date without a time: `"2015-02-07"`. To lessen the risk of time zone mishandling, I recommend not providing a time value when it's not needed.

The `type` property is supposed to tell if an account is a checking or savings account. While on the not easy-to-use side, its value is a cryptic number, `1`; its easy-to-use one is a more explicit string value, `checking`. Using numerical codes is usually a bad idea; they are not people-friendly, so developers will have to constantly refer to the documentation or learn your nomenclature to be able to understand such data. Therefore, if you can, it is better to use data types or formats that can be understood by just reading them.

And finally, a tricky case: if the account number is provided as a number (`1234567`), consumers have to be careful and may have to add missing leading zeros themselves. The string value `"00012345678"` is easier to use and is not corrupted.

So when choosing data types and format, you must be human-friendly and, most importantly, always provide accurate representation. When using a complex format, try to provide just enough information. And, if possible, try to stay understandable without context.

OK, we know now how to choose names and data types or formats. But the usability of a representation also depends on which data we choose to use.

5.1.3   *Choosing ready-to-use data*

The WUM 3000 showed us how providing the wrong data can affect usability. When we design APIs, we must take care to provide relevant and helpful data, going beyond just the basic data that we learned to identify in section 3.3. The more an API is able to provide data that will aid understanding and avoid work on the consumer side, the better. Figure 5.5 shows some ways to achieve that when designing the REST API representation of the read account goal.

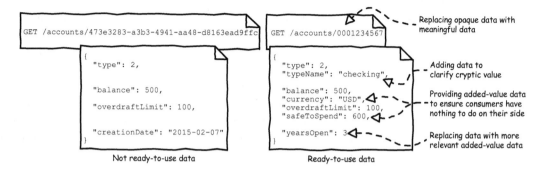

Figure 5.5   Simplify consumers work with ready-to-use data

In the previous section, you saw that it would be a better idea to provide a human-readable type like checking. But what if, for some reason, we have to use a numerical nomenclature? In that case, a savings account's type is 1 and a checking account's is 2. To clarify such numerical values, we can provide an additional typeName property. Its content could be savings or checking. That way the consumers will have all the information they need to understand what kind of bank account they are working with, without having to learn a nomenclature or refer to the API's documentation. Providing additional information definitely helps to clarify cryptic data.

The overdraft protection feature has some limits. If the bank account's balance goes into a negative value beyond a certain limit ($100, for example), fees will be applied. This means that if the balance is $500, the account's owner can spend $600. We can provide a ready-to-use safeToSpend property in order to avoid the consumer having to do this calculation. We can also provide information about the account's currency so consumers know that balance, overdraftLimit, and safeToSpend amounts are in US dollars. Providing static or precalculated added value data ensures that consumers have almost nothing to do or guess on their side.

It's also a good idea to replace basic data with related but more relevant data. For example, the account's creationDate might not really be of interest because the consumer will likely only want to know how many years the account has been open. In that case, we could provide this information directly instead of the account's creation date. This way the consumer only gets relevant and ready-to-use data.

When we design REST APIs, each resource must be identified by a unique path (see section 3.2.3). Such URLs are usually built around resource collection names and resource identifiers. To identify a bank account, we could use the URL /accounts/{accountId}. A bank account is an item identified by an accountId in a collection named accounts. But what could this accountId be? It could be a technical ID such as 473e3283-a3b3-4941-aa48-d8163ead9ffc. This is known as a *universal unique identifier* (UUID). These IDs are randomly generated, and the probability of generating the same ID twice is close to zero. This way we're sure that the /accounts/473e3283-a3b3-4941-aa48-d8163ead9ffc path is unique, but we cannot identify which bank account this URL represents by just reading it!

Maybe we could use a more user-friendly value such as the bank account number, which is also unique. That way, the URL to identify a bank account becomes /accounts/{accountNumber}. The /accounts/0001234567 path is still unique and now has a clearer meaning. Doing so is not reserved to the path parameter—providing meaningful data eases use and understanding for any value.

As you can see, once you know which aspects you must take care of, designing straightforward representations is relatively straightforward. But APIs are not only about static data: people interact with them to achieve their goals. And each one of these interactions must be straightforward too.

5.2   *Designing straightforward interactions*

To interact with an object or an API, users have to provide inputs to explain what they want to do. In return, they get some feedback telling them how it went. Depending on how the designer took care of the design of an interaction, these users can be completely frustrated or totally delighted. Washing machines are a perfect example of both cases.

Let's say that you've just gotten back from a vacation and it's laundry time. If you are lucky enough to have a straightforward washing machine, like the one shown on the left in figure 5.6, your task is quite simple.

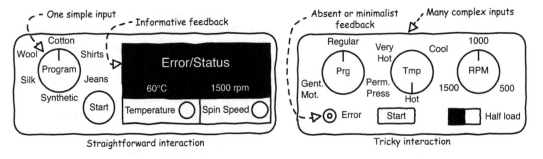

Figure 5.6   Straightforward versus tricky washing machine

You open the door, put your laundry in, add some soap, and then choose the washing program. To do that, you turn a big knob—obviously named Program—to select the type of laundry using labels with obvious names like Wool, Silk, Cotton, Jeans, Shirts, or Synthetic. The machine will choose the appropriate clean/rinse cycles, water temperature, and spin speed according to the laundry type. It will also choose the water level according to the laundry weight given by a weight sensor. If desired, you can adjust parameters such as temperature and spin speed yourself, using the obviously named Temperature and Spin Speed buttons or knobs. But this is usually not necessary because the automatically selected parameters are accurate in 95% of all cases.

When everything is OK, you push the start button. Unfortunately, the machine does not start. It makes some alerting beeps, and the LCD screen displays a "Door still open" message. You close the door, but the machine still refuses to start; it beeps again and the LCD screen now displays a "No water" message. You forgot that you shut off the water before going on vacation! After reopening your home's main water valve, you push the start button again. The machine now starts, and the LCD screen displays the remaining time in hours and minutes. We can even imagine that this straightforward washing machine reports the two problems in one shot to let you solve both problems at once.

Unfortunately, doing laundry is not always that simple. As shown on the right in figure 5.6, some washing machines are trickier to use.

With a not-so-straightforward washing machine, you might have to provide more information in a less user-friendly way. The programs available via the Prg knob have quite mysterious names such as Regular, Perm. Press (for permanent press), or Gent. Mot. (for gentler motion). There might be no weight sensor, and you might have to push a Half load button to indicate that the machine is not full of laundry. You might have to select the temperature and spin speed yourself using the Tmp and RPM knobs. And good luck choosing the correct temperature—from Cool to Very Hot. Once you've provided all the inputs, the error and success feedback might not be as informative as with the more user-friendly machine. In case of a problem such as "Door still open" or "No water," the washing machine might simply not start. If you're lucky, a red LED might light up, but without further explanation. And if you succeed in determining and solving all the problems, the machine might eventually start without telling you how long the wash cycle will take.

So, which type of interaction do you prefer? The straightforward one requiring minimal, understandable, and easy-to-provide inputs and showing helpful error feedback and informative success feedback? Or the tricky one requiring multiple obscure inputs and giving absolutely no clue about what is happening? This is, of course, a purely rhetorical question. Let's see how we can transpose this idea of straightforward interactions to the design of a money transfer's inputs and feedback for our Banking API.

Remember that in chapters 2 and 3, you learned how to design goals, parameters, and responses from the consumer's perspective, avoiding the provider's one. We will not discuss that matter again here.

5.2.1 Requesting straightforward inputs

The first step of an interaction belongs to the users. It's up to them to provide some inputs to say what they want to do. As API designers, we can give them a hand by designing straightforward inputs like those on the easy-to-use washing machine, using what we learned earlier in this chapter.

In our Banking API, a money transfer consists of sending an amount of money from a source account to a destination account. The transfer can be immediate, delayed, or recurring. An *immediate* transfer is obviously executed immediately, while a *delayed* one is executed at a future date. A *recurring* transfer is executed multiple times, from a start date to an end date, at a set frequency (say, weekly or monthly). Figure 5.7 shows how we can apply what we have learned so far to design straightforward inputs for a money transfer. The names should be clear, avoiding obscure abbreviations; the data types and formats, easy to understand; and the data, easy to provide.

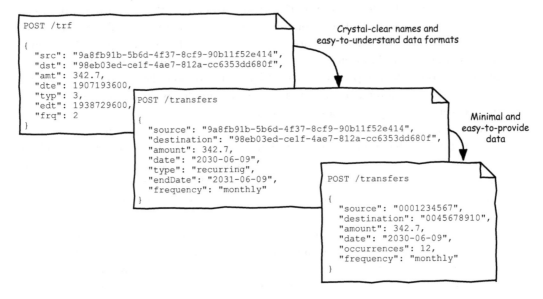

Figure 5.7   Designing straightforward inputs

The first of our rules for designing straightforward representations is to use crystal-clear names. The transfer money goal is therefore represented by a POST /transfers REST operation (which creates a transfer resource) instead of POST /trf (an abbreviation). We also use obvious property names like source and destination instead of src or dst, for example.

The next rule is to use easy-to-understand data formats. We will avoid the use of UNIX timestamps (1528502400, for example) and use ISO 8601 dates (2018-06-09, for example) for all date properties, such as the date that represents the delayed execution date or the first occurrence date of a recurring transfer. We also avoid using numerical codes for properties such as frequency and type, preferring instead human-readable values such as weekly or monthly and immediate, delayed, or recurring.

We can make this input even more straightforward by following the third rule and requesting easy-to-provide data. It's better to use meaningful values such as account numbers for source and destination instead of obscure UUIDs. It also might be simpler to provide the number of money transfer occurrences instead of calculating an endDate for a recurring transfer. And finally, we can get rid of the type property that tells us if the transfer is immediate, delayed, or recurring because the backend receiving the request can guess its value based on the other properties.

This way, we end up with inputs that are totally straightforward. The user should find everything easy to understand when reading the documentation or looking at an example. And, most importantly, this API goal is dead simple to trigger. But what happens once the user has provided these straightforward inputs? Let's explore the second part of the interaction: the feedback.

5.2.2 Identifying all possible error feedbacks

The first response we got when using the washing machine was an error feedback. What does that mean for API design? Unlike what we have seen in previous chapters, an API interaction is not always successful, and we must identify all possible errors for each goal. The transfer money goal can also trigger such error feedback, shown in figure 5.8.

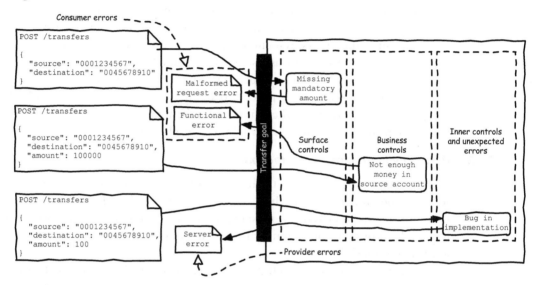

Figure 5.8   Malformed request and functional errors

Consumers can get error feedback if they do not provide a mandatory property such as amount. They can also get an error if they provide the wrong data type or format, such as using a UNIX timestamp instead of an ISO 8601 string for the date property. Such errors are known as *malformed request errors.*

But even if the server is able to interpret the request, that does not guarantee the response will be a successful one. The money transfer's amount might exceed the safe-to-spend value or the maximum amount the user is allowed to transfer in one day, or it might be forbidden to transfer money to an external account from certain internal accounts. Such errors are *functional errors,* triggered by the implementation's business rules.

These malformed request and functional errors are caused by the consumers, but the provider can also trigger some even if the request is completely valid. Indeed, a down database server or a bug in the implementation can cause a *server error.*

That's three different types of error—malformed, function, and server. You must identify, for each goal, all possible errors for each error type. Note that we will explore other types of errors in chapters 8 and 10.

Malformed request errors can occur when the server is unable to interpret a request. Because consumers must send requests to use the API, such errors can happen in any interaction. These errors can usually be identified just after designing the programming interface. At that point, we have a detailed view of the request that a consumer needs to send and every part of the request that might be the cause of such an error.

Functional errors mostly occur when consumers try to create, update, or delete data or trigger actions. They can typically be identified once the API goals canvas is filled in because each goal is fully described from a functional point of view. There's no magic method to identify these potential errors; it's up to you, helped by people who know the business rules at work behind a goal, to anticipate them. And server errors can happen on each goal. From the consumer's perspective, identifying a single server error is usually sufficient.

When listing the errors, remember that you must always focus on the consumer's perspective. For each of them, as discussed in section 2.4, you must check if it is the consumer's business or not. For example, on server errors, consumers just need to know that their request could not be processed and that it is not their fault. That's why a single generic server error is sufficient. But identifying possible errors is not enough; we must design an informative representation for each of them.

5.2.3   *Returning informative error feedback*

The problems encountered with the two washing machines were more or less easily solved, depending on how each error was represented. An API's error feedback must be as informative as possible. It must explicitly tell consumers what the problem is and, if possible, provide information that consumers can use to solve it using a straightforward representation.

You saw in section 3.3.1 that a REST API that relies on the HTTP protocol uses an HTTP status code to signify if the request was a success or not, as shown in figure 5.9.

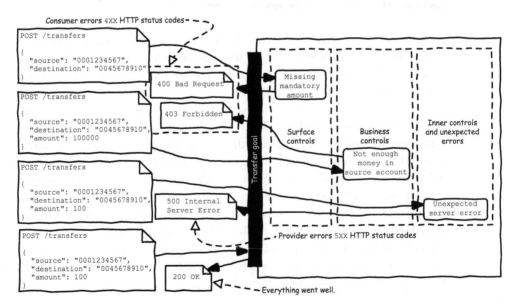

Figure 5.9   Choosing accurate HTTP status codes

You already saw that a `200 OK` HTTP status obviously means that the processing of the request went well. If the mandatory amount is missing in the request, a `400 Bad Request` status code is returned. If the amount is too high, that's a `403 Forbidden`. And if the server miserably crashed, a `500 Internal Server Error` is returned.

The `200 OK` set aside, how did the three other HTTP status codes come about? According to RFC 7231, which describes the "Hypertext Transfer Protocol (HTTP/1.1): Semantics and Content," (https://tools.ietf.org/html/rfc7231#section-6), we must use 4XX-class HTTP status codes for errors caused by the consumers and 5XX-class for errors caused by the provider.

> **RFC** An RFC (Request For Comments) is a type of publication from the technology community used to describe internet standards, but it can also convey simple information and even experimental new concepts (which can become standard).

Each class of codes contains a basic X00 code; for example, the `500 Internal Server Error` is the main status of the 5XX class and is perfect to signify any type of server error in a generic way. We could use a `400 Bad Request` status for all the identified errors caused by the consumers. But in that case, consumers will only know that their request is invalid without any other hint about the problem. Being able to differentiate between a "Missing mandatory amount" and "Not enough money in source account" would be quite interesting. Fortunately, the HTTP protocol comes with many 4XX codes that can be more accurate than a basic `400 Bad Request` one.

We can keep the basic `400 Bad Request` when there's a missing mandatory property or an incorrect data type. To notify the user that we're refusing to execute a transfer that exceeds the amount that's safe to spend, or that they've requested a transfer they aren't authorized to execute, we can use the `403 Forbidden` status. This code means that the request is formally valid but cannot be executed.

There is another 4XX status code that you will use a lot: it is the well-known `404 Not Found`, which can be used to signify that a resource is not found. For example, it could be returned on a `GET /accounts/123` request if the account 123 does not exist.

There are many different HTTP status codes. You should always check which one is most accurate when designing error feedback. Table 5.1 shows how some of these can be used.

Table 5.1 Malformed request and functional error HTTP status codes

Use case	Example	HTTP status code
Wrong path parameter	Reading a non-existing account with a `GET /accounts/123` request	404 Not Found
Missing mandatory property	`amount` not provided	400 Bad Request
Wrong data type	`"startDate":1423332060`	400 Bad Request
Functional error	`amount` exceeds safe to spend limit	403 Forbidden
Functional error	Transfer from `source` to `destination` is forbidden	403 Forbidden

Table 5.1   Malformed request and functional error HTTP status codes *(continued)*

Use case	Example	HTTP status code
Functional error	An identical money transfer has already been executed in the last 5 minutes	409 Conflict
Unexpected server error	Bug in implementation	500 Internal Server Error

When consumers get one of these HTTP status codes as error feedback, they will know that the problem is on their side if the status code is a 4XX one, but they will have a better idea about the source of the problem. If the error is a 404, they will know that the provided URL does not match any existing resource and probably contains an invalid path parameter. If they get a 403, they will know that their request is formally valid but has been rejected due to some business rules. If they get a 409, they will know their request is in conflict with a previous one. And if they get a 400, they will know that their request contains invalid data or is missing a mandatory property.

That's a good start, but an HTTP status code—even an accurate one—is not enough. The HTTP status alone does not provide enough information to help solve the problem. We should therefore also provide an explicit error message in the response body, as demonstrated in the following listing.

Listing 5.1   A basic error response body

```
{
    "message": "Amount is mandatory"
}
```

A consumer who receives a 400 Bad Request status code along with an object containing an Amount is mandatory message will be able to fix the problem easily. Well, a human consumer will be able to interpret this message easily, but what about a machine?

Let's say our Banking API is used in a mobile application. Obviously, bluntly showing an Amount is mandatory message to an end user is better than just showing a Bad Request message. But wouldn't it be preferable to highlight the amount field to help the end user fix the problem? How can the mobile application know which value has caused the problem? It might parse the error message string, but that would be pretty dirty. It would be better to provide a way to programmatically identify the property causing the error, as shown in the next listing.

Listing 5.2   A detailed error response

```
{
    "source": "amount",
    "type": "AMOUNT_OVER_SAFE",
    "message": "Amount exceeds safe to spend"
}
```

Along with the error message, we could provide a source property that contains the path to the property causing the problem. In this case, its value would be amount. This would enable the program to determine which value is causing the problem in the case of a malformed request. But in the event of a functional error, the mobile application still won't know the exact type of error. Therefore, we could also add a type property containing some code. Its value for an amount exceeding what is safe for the customer to spend, for example, could be AMOUNT_OVER_SAFE. The corresponding message for the customer could be Amount exceeds safe to spend. Proceeding in this way would enable both humans and programs consuming the API to be able to accurately interpret any errors that arise.

As you can see, we have again applied the principles of straightforward representation to design these errors. Note that you don't have to define a specific type for each error; you can define generic types as shown in the next listing. For example, the MISSING_ MANDATORY_PROPERTY type can be used in any error for any missing mandatory property.

Listing 5.3   A detailed error response using a generic type

```
{
  "source": "amount",
  "type": "MISSING_MANDATORY_PROPERTY",
  "message": "Amount is mandatory"
}
```

These are only a few examples of information you can provide for errors. You are free to provide as much data as necessary in order to help consumers solve the problems themselves. You could, for instance, provide a regular expression describing the expected data format in case of a BAD_FORMAT error.

More complex error handling

Note that if the input is more complex, a simple source might not be enough. For example, if we wanted to create a bank account with multiple owners, the input parameters might contain an owners list. This listing shows how we could handle an error in one of this list's items.

Listing 5.4   A detailed error response indicating an error source

```
{
  "source": "firstname",
  "path": "$.owners[0].firstname",
  "type": "MISSING_MANDATORY_PROPERTY",
  "message": "Firstname is mandatory"
}
```

We could add a path property containing a JSON path to be more accurate. A *JSON path* (https://goessner.net/articles/JsonPath/) lets you represent a node's address in a JSON document. If a mandatory firstname is missing on the first owner in the list, the path value would be $.owners[0].firstname.

Providing informative and efficient feedback requires us to describe the problem and provide all needed information in both human- and machine-readable format in order to help the consumer solve the problem themselves (if they can). When designing a REST API, this can be done by using the appropriate HTTP status code and a straightforward response body. That works for reporting only one error at a time. But what if there are multiple problems?

5.2.4 *Returning exhaustive error feedback*

In the best possible scenario, the straightforward washing machine reports the two problems (door open and no water) together. This is definitely a must-have feature if you want to build usable APIs. For example, a transfer money request can present multiple malformed request errors. Suppose a customer submits a request that is missing values for the source and destination. They will first get error feedback telling them that the mandatory source property is missing. After fixing this error, they'll do another call and get another error telling them that the destination property is missing. This is a great way to frustrate consumers. All this information could have been given in the initial error feedback!

To avoid too many request/error cycles, and the wrath of consumers, it's best to return error feedback that is as exhaustive as possible, as shown in the next listing.

Listing 5.5   Returning multiple errors

```
{
  "message": "Invalid request",
  "errors": [
    {
      "source": "source",
      "type": "MISSING_MANDATORY_PROPERTY",
      "message": "Source is mandatory"},
    {
      "source": "destination",
      "type": "MISSING_MANDATORY_PROPERTY"},
      "message": "Destination is mandatory"}
  ]
}
```

We should therefore return in one shot a list of errors containing the two malformed request errors. Each error can be described as you saw previously in listing 5.3. The same also applies if the request is not malformed but contains multiple functional errors.

What happens if there are both types of errors? Figure 5.10 shows what might happen in that case.

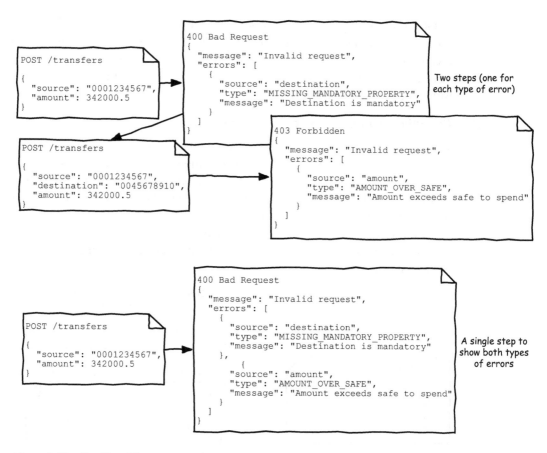

Figure 5.10 Handling different types of errors

In this example, the request contains a valid `source` account but is missing the `desti-nation` account and includes an `amount` exceeding what is safe for the user to spend. When designing single errors, we chose to use `400 Bad Request` for this type of malformed request error and `403 Forbidden` for the functional ones. We could choose to keep these two types of errors separated, and return error feedback to report the missing `destination` first, followed by a second message to report the functional error ("Amount exceeds safe to spend"). But does that make sense for consumers? Do they really care about the distinction? Probably not, at least in the specific use case where we provide all the necessary information to determine the kind of error.

I would recommend returning a generic `400 Bad Request` containing all malformed request and functional errors. Note that this solution might not be the silver bullet, however. You will have to analyze your particular situation in order to make the best choice when it comes to keeping error categories separated or not.

Grouping multiple errors in one feedback message simplifies an interaction by reducing the number of request/error cycles. But if you are designing a REST API, it means using a generic HTTP status and relying on the response data to provide detailed information about each error. Once all problems are solved, the interaction should end with a success feedback.

5.2.5   *Returning informative success feedback*

With the washing machine use case, we saw that providing informative success feedback can be really helpful for users. It is, indeed, really helpful to known when the washing will end. Similarly, an API's success feedback must provide useful information to the consumers beyond a simple acknowledgment. How do we achieve this? By applying what we have learned in this chapter so far!

When using the REST API style, informative success feedback can rely on the same things as error feedback: an accurate HTTP status code and a straightforward response body, as shown in figure 5.11.

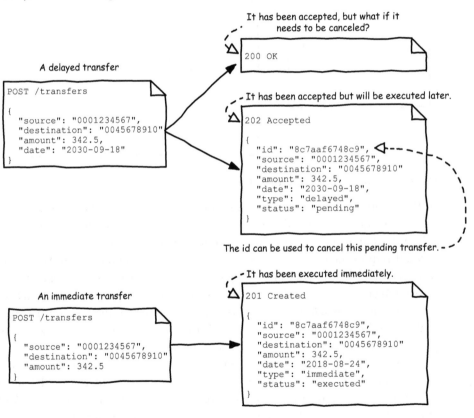

Figure 5.11   Fully informative success feedback

As stated by RFC 7231 (https://tools.ietf.org/html/rfc7231#section-6.3), "…the 2xx (Successful) class of status code indicates that the client's request was successfully received, understood, and accepted." Therefore, we could return a 200 OK for all successes. But as with the 4XX class, there are many 2XX codes that can more accurately describe what has happened in some use cases.

If the money transfer is an *immediate* one, we could return a 201 Created HTTP status code, which means that the transfer has been created. For a *delayed* transfer, we could return a 202 Accepted response, indicating that the money transfer request has been accepted but not yet executed. In this case, it is implied that it will be executed at the requested date. The same goes for a *recurring* transfer: we could use 202 Accepted to tell the consumers that the transfers will be executed when they should. But again, an HTTP status is not enough; a straightforward and informative feedback message is far more useful.

Such a response should contain every piece of the created resource's information, as you have learned in previous chapters. Returning properties calculated by the server (like the transfer type or its status) is interesting, just like the time at which the washing is supposed to end on the washing machine. The ID is especially interesting for consumers that might need to cancel a specific delayed transfer they have just created. Without it, they simply won't be able to do so.

So basically, informative success feedbacks provide information about what has happened and also give information that can help during the next steps. Let's summarize the rules we've identified for designing straightforward interactions:

- Inputs and outputs must be straightforward.
- All possible errors must be identified.
- Error feedback must explain what the problem is and should help the consumers to solve it themselves.
- Reporting multiple errors one by one should be avoided.
- Success feedback should provide information about what was done and give information to help for the next steps.

We are now able to design individual interactions that are straightforward. But will these straightforward interactions form a simple flow when used together?

5.3 Designing straightforward flows

To use an object or an API, a user might have to chain multiple interactions. Usability heavily depends on the simplicity of this flow of interactions.

If you are on the 5th floor of a building and you want to go to the 16th, you might want to use one of the four elevator cabins. Figure 5.12 shows different possible versions of your elevator journey.

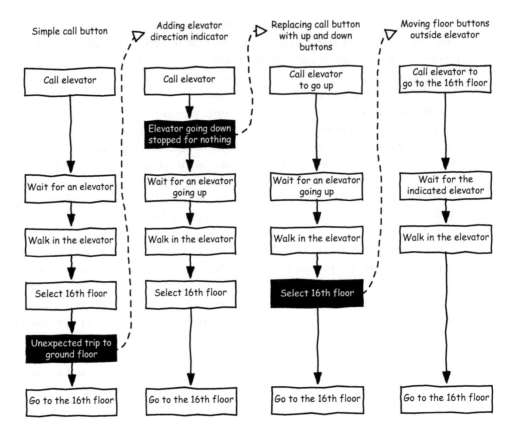

Figure 5.12   Improving elevator usage flows

If the system is basic, there's a single call button on the wall for all cabins. It lights up when you push it. Then you wait, not knowing which one of the elevator cabins will come. A bell rings when one of them has arrived. You walk in and push the button for the 16th floor. Unfortunately, this elevator was going down to ground floor. So you go down to the ground floor and, after that, go up to the 16th.

Walking into an elevator cabin without knowing its direction of travel can be annoying. Fortunately, elevator manufacturers have enhanced their systems to avoid such a situation by adding some light signal or an LCD screen outside each elevator cabin to show if it's going up or down. That's better, but why stop an elevator that's going down for someone who wants to go up? It's really frustrating for users who are waiting for an elevator cabin, and also for the ones who are inside the cabin. This pain point can be removed by replacing the single call button with two buttons: up and down. You can now call an elevator to go up or down, and only cabins going in that direction will stop on your floor.

But when you walk into the elevator cabin, you still have to push a second button to tell it which floor you want to go to. In some systems, the up and down buttons have been replaced by the floor buttons you encounter inside the elevator cabin. Now when you want to call an elevator to go to the 16th floor, you simply push the button for that floor, and an LCD screen tells you which elevator cabin to use.

As you can see, the interaction flow to go to the 16th floor has been simplified by improving feedback, improving inputs, preventing errors, and even aggregating actions. This interaction flow has become totally straightforward. Let's see how we can apply these principles to create a straightforward API interaction flow when transferring money with the Banking API.

5.3.1 Building a straightforward goal chain

We've seen how improving inputs and feedback by adding a direction indicator and replacing the call button with up and down buttons helped to improve the chain of actions needed to go to a building's 16th floor. By taking care of inputs and feedback in a similar way in our API, we can build a straightforward goal chain.

A chain exists only if its links are connected. When consumers use an API for a specific goal, they must have all the data needed to execute it. Such data may be known by the consumers themselves or can be provided by previous goal outputs. This is what you learned in section 2.3. The partial API goals canvas shown in figure 5.13 provides such information.

Whos	Whats	Hows	Inputs (source)	Outputs (usage)	Goals
Consumers	Transfer money from an account to an owned or external account	List accounts		Accounts list (money transfer)	List accounts
		List pre-registered beneficiaries		Pre-registered beneficiaries list (money transfer)	List beneficiaries
		Transfer money	Source (list accounts), destination (list accounts, list beneficiaries), amount (consumer)	Transfer report	Transfer money

Figure 5.13 The Banking API goals canvas

This canvas tells us that to make an immediate money transfer, consumers need to provide an `amount`, a `source` account, and a `destination` account. Consumers obviously know how much money they want to transfer. The source account must be one of the accounts consumers can retrieve with the list accounts goal. If the API is used by a mobile banking application, these accounts are the ones belonging to the person using the application. The destination account must be one of these accounts (for example, to transfer money from a current account to a savings account) or a pre-registered external beneficiary (for example, to send money to a friend or pay the apartment rent).

If you wonder why the Banking Company forces its customers to pre-register beneficiaries, it is for both security and usability purposes. A two-factor authentication using a regular password and a confirmation SMS, email, or security token generating random passwords is required to register an external beneficiary, thereby ensuring that only the actual customer can do so. And once the beneficiary is registered, the money transfer is quite simple: no need to remember and carefully type the destination account number and no need for two-factor authentication. Consumers can use the list account and list beneficiaries goals in order to get possible sources and destinations before they transfer money to one. So, we have a chain.

But a chain is only as strong as its weakest link. Each interaction participating in a flow must be a straightforward one. This is what you learned earlier in section 5.2. Figure 5.14 shows the transfer money flow.

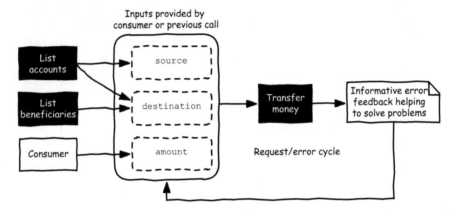

Figure 5.14   The transfer money flow

The list accounts and list beneficiaries goals are pretty straightforward because they do not need inputs and return no errors. The inputs to the transfer money goal are straightforward, but this goal can return many different errors. If we were to only return a 400 Bad Request error message, consumers might have a hard time successfully executing a money transfer. But thanks to what you have learned in this chapter, you know now that you must provide informative and exhaustive error feedback in order to help consumers solve the problems they encounter. This will greatly reduce the number of request/error cycles and avoid artificially extending the API call chain length.

So the first step toward a straightforward API goal chain is to request simple inputs that can be provided by consumers or another goal in the chain, and return exhaustive and informative error feedback to limit request/error cycles. With what we've learned, we should be able to a build a straightforward goal chain. But couldn't we make it shorter and more fluid by preventing errors?

5.3.2   *Preventing errors*

In the elevator example, adding a direction indicator helped to prevent an unexpected trip to the ground floor. Preventing errors is a good way to smooth and shorten the API goals flow. But how can we prevent errors? By applying one of the principles of straightforward representations—providing ready-to-use data. We have to analyze each error in order to determine if it can be prevented by providing some data prior to this goal.

The money transfer goal can trigger various functional errors:

- Amount exceeds safe to spend limit
- Amount exceeds cumulative daily transfer limit
- Source account cannot be used as source for transfer
- This destination cannot be used with this source

Let's try to prevent the `Source account cannot be used as source for transfer` error. We could add a `forbiddenTransfer` Boolean property to each account retrieved by the list accounts goal. That way the consumer will only be able to provide a source account with this property set to `false` when requesting a money transfer. But it means that the consumer will have to do some filtering on its side. Figure 5.15 shows a better alternative.

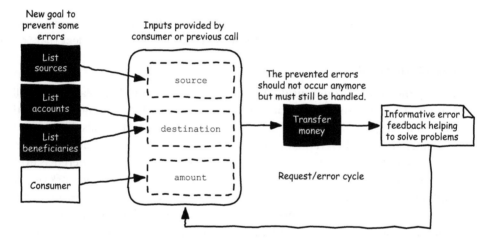

Figure 5.15   Preventing errors in the money transfer flow

Here, a new list sources goal returning only accounts that can be used as a source for a money transfer has been added. This goal could also return with each account the maximum allowable amount for a transfer, based on the safe-to-spend and cumulative daily transfer limits, in order to prevent the corresponding errors. The consumer can use these ready-to-use values to implement surface controls on its side.

That's quite good. With this new goal, we can prevent three of the four errors! But note that whatever error is prevented must still be handled by the transfer money goal. Some consumers cannot implement surface controls or directly call this goal without providing the proper parameters.

As you can see, preventing errors can make the goal flow more fluid. Remember that you can do this by

- Analyzing possible errors to determine added value data that could prevent them
- Enhancing the success feedback of existing goals to provide such data
- Creating new goals to provide such data

REST constraints: Code on demand

On a website, the code-on-demand constraint is fulfilled when a web server provides JavaScript files that contain code that is executed in the browser. You could try to do that with APIs too, but that would mean that you provide code that can be understood by all consumers whatever the programming language these are built with. Such a scenario seems quite unrealistic, but you can achieve a "sort-of code on demand" by providing adequate data through dedicated helper goals or regular goals as we have just done for the money transfer. Many business rules can be represented with more or less complex data that consumers will be able to use like code.

Indeed, the goal flow has been improved. But is it efficient and consumer-oriented to have to call list accounts and list beneficiaries to know all the possible destination values?

5.3.3   Aggregating goals

Putting the floor buttons outside the elevator cabin permitted replacing the call an elevator and select 16th floor actions with a single one: call an elevator to go to the 16th floor. Such aggregations can be useful for optimizing the API goals flow.

It might have bothered you that the destination value could come from either the list accounts or the list beneficiaries goal. Such a design could be considered as evidence of the provider's perspective because it requires consumers to do some work on their side. And if we take into account that some source/destination associations are forbidden, it becomes clear that this is a perfect example of the provider's perspective. As shown in figure 5.16, we can fix that problem by creating a list destinations for source goal that replaces list accounts and list beneficiaries as the source for the destination property.

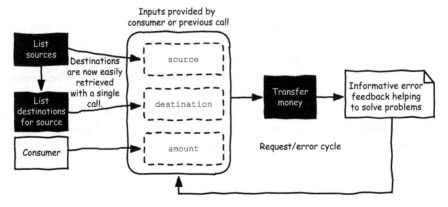

Figure 5.16   A single call is needed to list destinations from the selected source.

This new *aggregated* goal returns only the destinations possible for a given source, with the source being retrieved with list sources. This new goal will simplify the goal flow, and there's a bonus! It also prevents the `This destination cannot be used with this source` error. Now consumers have fewer goals to use, and they have access to everything they need to avoid error feedback from the transfer money goal.

Is that all we can do? Figure 5.17 shows one last optimization.

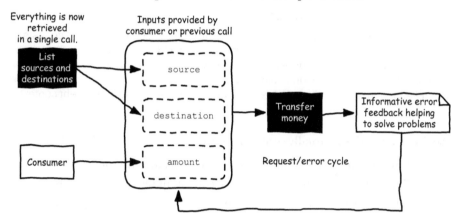

Figure 5.17   A single call provides all the data needed to select the source and destination.

Because the number of possible source/destination combinations is relatively limited, we can provide all the possible source/destination associations with a single list sources and destinations goal that aggregates list sources and list destinations for source. It's not mandatory, but it's a possibility.

Be warned that such aggregations must only be done if the resulting goals really make sense for the consumer from a functional perspective. Also be warned that such aggregations can give rise to performance issues; we will talk about this subject in chapters 10 and 11. For now, there is one last thing we have to talk about to create fully straightforward flows.

5.3.4   Designing stateless flows

This topic is not present in the elevator real life example; it comes from the REST constraints you saw in section 3.5.2.

Let's imagine, the following workflow to trigger a money transfer:

1 List source.
2 List destination for a selected source (the source is stored in session on the server side).
3 Transfer $USD to destination (the source used is the one stored in session on the server).

Such flow is *stateful* and this is definitely not a good idea; it must never be designed nor implemented. Indeed, the transfer goal cannot be used alone as it relies on data stored in session thanks to previous calls. Some consumers might perfectly be able to choose source and destination on their own without using the list destination goal. Each goal must be usable without the others and all needed inputs must be explicitly declared.

REST constraints: Statelessness

Statelessness is achieved by storing no context on the server between requests (using a session) and only relying on the information provided along with a request to process it. That ensures that any request can be processed by any instance of an API implementation instead of a specific one holding the session data. And that also favors the use of the API goals independently and, therefore, facilitates their reuse in different contexts.

So, in order to design totally straightforward flows, you must follow these rules:

- Ensure that each goal provides a straightforward interaction.
- Ensure that outputs and inputs are consistent between goal calls.
- When possible, prevent errors by adding data to existing goals to create new goals.
- When possible, aggregate goals but only if it make sense for the consumer from a functional perspective.
- Each goal of the chain must be stateless.

And that's all for straightforward API design! In the next chapter, we will continue digging into usability to learn how to design predictable APIs that can be used instinctively.

Summary

- Any representation must be easily understandable by people and programs.
- Any representation must be as informative as possible.
- Error feedback must provide enough elements to understand and maybe fix the problem.
- Success feedback must describe what has been done.
- Goal flows can be optimized by adding data or goals to prevent errors.
- Goal flows can be simplified by aggregating goals, but only if that makes sense from a functional perspective.

Designing a predictable API

This chapter covers

- Being consistent to create intuitive APIs
- Adding features to simplify use and adapt to users
- Adding metadata and metagoals to guide users

In the previous chapter, we started our journey to learn how to build usable APIs and discovered fundamental principles we can use to create straightforward APIs that are easy to understand and easy to use. This is good—we now know how to design a decent API. But we can do better. What about designing an *awesome* API? What about designing an API that users will be able to use instinctively without thinking about it, even if it is the very first time they're using it? How can we do that?

Have you ever felt tremendous pleasure when using an unfamiliar object or application for the first time? You know, when everything is so intuitive and easy that you feel outrageously smart as you discover on your own all of its possibilities? This is possible not only because you are actually outrageously smart, but also because the thing you are using has been designed to make it totally predictable. Of course, not everything is capable of providing such a tremendous feeling, but every day you might encounter situations where predictability gives you a hand without you realizing it.

137

Why do you know how to open a door in a building you've never been to? Because it looks like the doors you have encountered before. How can you use an ATM in a country using a language you don't understand? Because it adapts its interface to you. How can you find your way in a huge and labyrinthine subway station? Because there are signs telling you where to go.

Can we really design such intuitive APIs? Yes, we can! Just like any object, an API can be predictable because it shares similarities that other users have encountered before, because it can adapt to the users' will, or because it provides information to guide them.

6.1   *Being consistent*

If you encounter a washing machine like the one shown in figure 6.1, with a button showing a triangle icon oriented from left to right, you can guess this button's purpose easily. Why? Because you've already seen this icon on various media players.

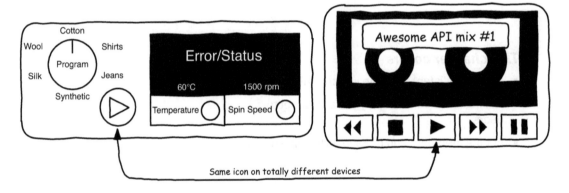

Figure 6.1   A washing machine and cassette player sharing the same icon

Since the mid-1960s, all media players have used such an icon. From obscure DCC (Digital Compact Cassette) players to compact disc players and software media players, each one of these devices uses the same triangle icon for the Start Play button. Therefore, you can guess that this button starts the washing machine.

> **NOTE** A *consistent* design is free from variation or contradiction; it helps to make an interface intuitive by taking advantage of users' previous experiences.

I'm sure you know what the standard Pause button looks like too. What if a media player does not use this standard icon for its Pause button? Users will be puzzled and will have to make an effort to understand how to pause the audio or video that's playing.

> **NOTE** An *inconsistent* design introduces variations or contradictions that make an interface harder to understand and use.

Again, what is true for real-world human interfaces is also true for APIs. It is essential to keep the design of an API consistent—to make it predictable. This can be done with a little bit of discipline by ensuring consistency of data and goals inside and across all

APIs, using and meeting prescribed standards, and by shamelessly copying others. But if consistency can lead to an awesome API design, it must never be used at the expense of *usability*.

6.1.1 Designing consistent data

Data is at the core of APIs—resources, parameters, responses, and their properties shape an API. And all of their meanings, names, types, formats, and organization must be consistent in order to help consumers understand these easily. So, designing consistent APIs starts with choosing consistent names, as shown in figure 6.2.

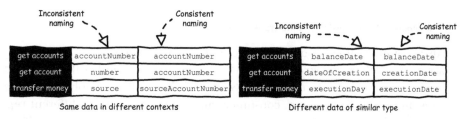

Figure 6.2   Inconsistent and consistent naming

In a poorly designed Banking API, an account number could be represented as an `accountNumber` property for the get accounts goal's result, as a `number` property for get account, and as a `source` property for the money transfer goal's input. Here, the same piece of information in three different contexts is represented with totally different names. Users will not make the connection between them easily.

Once users have seen an account number represented as `accountNumber`, they expect to see that piece of information always represented by `accountNumber`. People are used to uniformity in design. So, whether this property is part of a fully detailed account listing, a summary of the account list, or used as a path parameter, an account number must be called an `accountNumber`.

When choosing names for various representations of the same concept, take care to use similar ones. When used for a money transfer to identify the source account, the original name should remain recognizable but can be altered in order to provide more information about the nature of the property; we might call it `sourceAccountNumber`, for example. Now consumers are able to make a connection between these properties and guess that they represent the same concept.

That also works for unrelated data of a similar type or for representing similar concepts. For example, `balanceDate`, `dateOfCreation`, and `executionDay` all represent a date, but the first one uses the suffix `Date`; the second one, the prefix `dateOf`; and the third, the suffix `Day`. Using a *generic* suffix or prefix in a name to provide additional information about the nature of what is named is a good practice, as long as it is done consistently. Here (figure 6.2), the good design uses the same `Date` suffix for all dates, but you can choose another solution as long as you remain consistent. But even correctly named, a property, for example, can still be subject to inconsistency, as shown in figure 6.3.

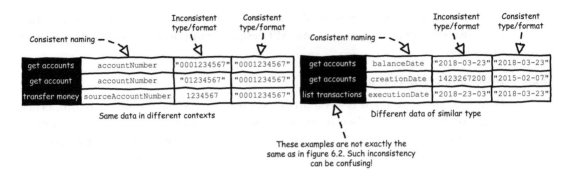

Figure 6.3   Inconsistent and consistent data types and formats

An account number could be represented as the string `"0001234567"` in the get accounts result, as the string `"01234567"` for get account, and as the number `1234567` for the money transfer goal's input. Such variations will inevitably cause bugs on the consumer side. To fix them, consumers must standardize these different representations and know when to convert one type or format to another to use it in a given context.

People and software don't like to be surprised with such inconsistencies. Once consumers have seen the first `accountNumber` property as a string with a specific format, they expect all other account number representations to be strings with the same format. Even if they have different names, different representations of the same concept should use the same type and format.

Choosing a data type or format can also have an overall impact on the API. How do you think consumers will react if they see the `balanceDate` of a bank account as an ISO 8601 string (such as `2018-03-23`), the `creationDate` of an account represented by a UNIX timestamp (such as `1423267200`), and the `executionDate` of a transfer as YYYY-DD-MM date (such as `2018-23-03`)? They won't like it because it's inconsistent.

People seek global uniformity in design. Once consumers have seen one date and time property represented by an ISO 8601 string, they expect all date and time properties be ISO 8601 strings. Once a data format has been chosen for a type of data, it should be used for *all* representations of the same data type.

Consumers seek global uniformity in all aspects of the API, however, not just data types and formats. What is the problem with a URL's `/accounts/{accountNumber}`, which represents an account, or `/transfer/{transferId}`, which represents a money transfer? It's `/accounts` versus `/transfer`—plural versus singular. Once consumers are familiar with the use of plural names for collections, they expect to see all collections with plural names. You can use a singular for collections if you want, but whatever your choice, stick to it! And this doesn't only apply to URLs: it concerns every single name and value you choose.

NOTE Naming conventions can be defined for property names, query parameter names, codes, JSON Schema models in an OpenAPI file, and more. Once you choose a naming convention, strictly follow it.

Now, what's the problem with the two URLs and the two data structures shown in figure 6.4? Their data organizations are inconsistent.

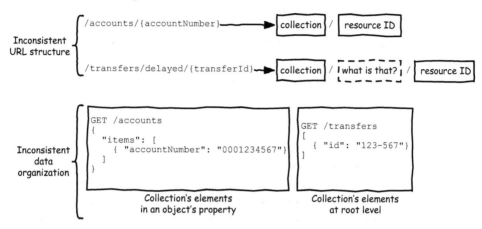

Figure 6.4 Inconsistent organization

The /accounts/{accountNumber} and /transfers/delayed/{transferId} URLs don't have the same organization. The /transfers/delayed/{transferId} URL introduces an unexpected level between the collection name and resource ID, making the URL harder to understand. We could use /delayed-transfers/{transferId} instead, for example.

Each level of a URL should always have the same meaning. Once consumers are used to a data organizational pattern, they expect to see it used everywhere. Again, this doesn't only apply to URLs; data organization in inputs and outputs can present patterns too. In the bottom part of figure 6.4, the elements of two collections are represented in two different ways. If every collection resource you have designed so far is represented by an object containing a property called items, which is an array, do not dare to design one as a simple array. Why? Because consumers will be surprised by this variation.

Once data organization conventions have been chosen, follow those strictly. Basically, every bit of an API's data must be consistent. But APIs are not only made of static data; they are made to do things, and all of an API's behaviors must be consistent too.

6.1.2 *Designing consistent goals*

An API behavior is determined by its goals: these await inputs and return success or error feedbacks, and all these goals can be used to form various flows. Obviously, all of this must be consistent.

What's the problem with the read account and get user information goals? These two goal names are inconsistent—they represent the same type of action but use different verbs. It would be wiser to name them *read account* and *read user information,* especially if they have to be represented as functions in code, like readAccount() and readUser-Information(). Hopefully, for REST APIs, the programmatic representation of these goals will magically be consistent, thanks to the use of the HTTP protocol. Indeed, both of these goals will be represented by a GET /resource-path request using the same HTTP method (on different paths).

As you saw in section 6.1.1, data must be consistent, and so must a goal's inputs. For example, it could be helpful when listing an account's transactions with a GET /accounts/{accountId}/transactions request to be able to retrieve only the ones that occurred between two dates. Query parameters such as fromDate=1423267200 and untilDay=2015-03-17 can do the job but are obviously inconsistent. It would be better to use fromDate=2015-02-07 and toDate=2015-03-17. You must use consistent names, data types, formats, and organization when designing a goal's inputs.

The same goes for the feedback returned in case of success or error. If all goals leading to the creation of something return a 200 OK status code without taking advantage of codes such as 201 Created or 202 Accepted, it would be wise to avoid introducing new goals returning different success HTTP status codes instead of the usual 200 OK. Indeed, you are free to use only a small subset of all existing HTTP status codes; that can make sense in some contexts. But even if consumers are supposed to treat any unexpected 2XX status as a 200 OK, such inconsistency might surprise some of them.

Consistency matters for error messages too. You must obviously return consistent HTTP status codes to signify errors, but the informative data returned must also be consistent. You learned to design such data in section 5.2, and if you have defined generic codes like MISSING_MANDATORY_PROPERTY to signify that a mandatory property is missing, always use this code across your API.

Finally, consistency concerns not only how the API looks, but also how it behaves. If all previously designed sensitive actions (like a money transfer) consist of a control <action> and a do <action> goal—the first one doing all possible verifications without executing the action, and the second one actually executing the action—any new sensitive actions must be represented with goals having the same behavior. When designing APIs, you must also take care to create consistent goal flows.

So every single aspect of the interface contract, every behavior of an API, must be consistent. But we only talked about being consistent *within* an API; indeed, this is only the first level of consistency in API design.

6.1.3   *The four levels of consistency*

When you look at the buttons of a TV remote, you can see that these are consistent; the number buttons, for example, all have the same shape. If you look at a TV remote and a Blu-Ray or a DVD player from the same manufacturer, these may have little differences, but they are mostly consistent as they usually share common features (the same number buttons, for example). If you look at any media device or media player, these too are consistent, presenting the same controls, especially the play button. There may be some little differences again, but you still feel comfortable switching from one to the other. And finally, if you encounter a play button on a washing machine, you know what its purpose is because you probably have seen it before, perhaps on different media players. These examples show four levels of consistency that can be applied to the design of APIs:

- *Level 1*—Consistency within an API
- *Level 2*—Consistency across an organization/company/team's APIs
- *Level 3*—Consistency with the domain(s) of an API
- *Level 4*—Consistency with the rest of the world

We have just seen the first level, how an API must be consistent with itself—proposing consistent data, goals, and behaviors. Every time you make a design choice, you must ensure that it will not introduce a variation in the API, or worse, a contradiction. When looking at the API as a whole, consumers must see a regular interface. When they jump from one part to another, they must have the feeling that this new part is familiar. They must be able to guess how this new part works even if they have never used it before.

Just as consistency is important within an API, it is also important across the APIs that an organization provides. This is the second level of consistency. An organization might have one team with a single API designer or multiple teams with many designers, and everything in between. The consumers of an organization's APIs do not care if these APIs were designed by one or many designers. What they care about is that the APIs share common features so they can understand and use any part of the API easily, once they have learned to work with one.

Just as different goals within an API must share common features, different APIs within an organization must also share common features. Sharing common features (such as data organization, data types, or formats) enhance interoperability between APIs. It's easier to take data from an API and feed it to another if the features are consistent.

The third level is about being consistent with the domain(s) of or used by an API. For example, representing an address is not done in the same way if you just want to get some customers' addresses compared to if you want to provide formatted addresses to be printed on envelopes. If you have to calculate distances in an API for marine navigation, you will use nautical miles and not miles or kilometers. There usually are standard or at least common practices that you must follow when working on a specific domain.

And the fourth and last level: APIs have to be consistent with the rest of the world. There are common practices—standards, if you will—that you can use. Not only does following these make your APIs predictable for people who have never used any of your APIs before, thereby enhancing your APIs interoperability with the rest of the world, but it also makes your API designer's job easier. Let's see how this is possible.

6.1.4 *Copying others: Following common practices and meeting standards*

Why reinvent the wheel when someone has already done that? There are thousands of standards that you can use in your API; there are thousands of APIs whose designers design using common practices, and there are some reference APIs that you can shamelessly copy. You know the meaning of the play and pause symbols shown in figure 6.5 because you have seen them on various devices.

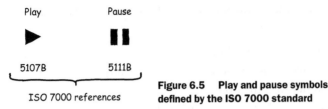

Figure 6.5   Play and pause symbols defined by the ISO 7000 standard

You might have learned their meaning by reading the user manual of the first device using them that you encountered, but after that, every time you saw these symbols, you were able to guess what they meant. On each device using these symbols, their purpose is the same.

The look and meaning of the play and pause symbols are defined by the ISO 7000 standard (https://www.iso.org/obp/ui/#iso:pub:PUB400008:en). Once users have encountered these symbols on one device, they are able to guess their purpose on any other device. They are able to use a new device without prior experience with it because they have experience with other devices using the same standards. Any designer willing to create a start/pause-something button will probably use these symbols instead of reinventing new ones. Like any real-world device, an API can take advantage of standards (in a broad sense) to be easier to understand.

Our Banking API might have to provide information about amounts in various currencies. Creating our own currency classification and always using it in all of our banking-related APIs is a good thing. That way, we are at least consistent within our organization. But it would be better to use the ISO 4217 international standard (https://www.iso.org/iso-4217-currency-codes.html), which lets you represent currencies by a three-letter code (USD, EUR) or a three-digit code (840, 978). Using such a standard, we can be consistent with the entire world! Anyone who has ever used the ISO 4217 standard elsewhere will understand the meaning of the ISO 4217 currency codes without having to learn a nonstandard classification. Similarly, the ISO 8601 standard we saw earlier to represent date and time values is not only a human-friendly format, but is also widely adopted in the software industry.

> **NOTE**   Using standards facilitates understanding because consumers might already be familiar with the meanings. It also enhances your API's interoperability because its data will be easily usable by other APIs using the same standards.

There are standards for data formats, data naming and organization, and even processes. And not all of them are defined by the ISO; there are many other organizations defining standards and recommendations that you could use in your API design. Use your favorite search engine and look for something like "<some data> standard" or "<some data> format," and you will probably find a format that you can use to represent "<some data>." Try to find out how to represent phone numbers, for example.[1]

---

[1]   You should find the E.164 format, which is recommended by the ITU-T (the ITU Telecommunication Standardization Sector).

But being *standard* does not always mean following ISO's or another organization's specifications. If our Banking API represents a delayed transfer with `/delayed-trans-fers/{transferId}` URL, you might guess that using the HTTP method `DELETE` would cancel a delayed transfer. If you get a `410 Gone` response, you might guess that the delayed transfer was executed or canceled before you tried to delete it. How can you guess that? Because you expect the Banking API, which claims to be a REST API, to strictly follow the HTTP protocol, which is defined by RFC 7231 (https://tools.ietf.org/html/rfc7231).

The `DELETE` HTTP method can be used on a resource to delete, undo, or cancel the concept represented by a URL. The `410 Gone` response is quite explicit; according to the standard, it "… indicates that the resource requested is no longer available and will not be available again." And further, it "… should be used when a resource has been intentionally removed and the resource should be purged."

So, REST APIs can be consistent by simply applying the HTTP protocol's rules to the letter. That way, anyone can quickly get started using any REST API.

REST constraints: Uniform interface

The REST architectural style states that "… all interactions must be guided by the concept of identified resources which are manipulated through representations of resource states and standard methods." The *standard method* part is indeed a powerful concept that helps to ensure consistency. Basically, the whole HTTP protocol (especially HTTP methods, but also HTTP status codes) provide a consistent framework for REST APIs, making them totally predictable.

In the API design world, there are common practices that can be followed, such as the one shown in figure 6.6.

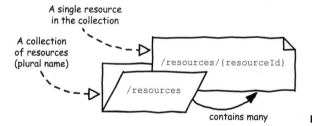

Figure 6.6   A common URL pattern

As you saw in section 3.2.3, while there are no standard rules for the URL structure of REST APIs, many of these use the `/resources/{resourceId}` pattern. Here, `resources` is a collection identified by a plural noun. It contains elements of type `resource`.

Even if not everything is standardized in the API design world, there are common practices that are very close to being standards. It is wise to follow them in order to ensure that your API will be easily understood by consumers based on their experience with other popular APIs.

And finally, in many cases, you can simply copy what others have done. Why bother rethinking pagination parameters from the ground up when this problem has been dealt with by so many other API designers? You can look at some well-known APIs and reuse the design you prefer. Doing this will simplify your life as an API designer, and if your users have used those APIs, they will feel at home when using yours for the first time. Everybody wins.

Here's a scenario to practice this topic. Let's say you have to design an API that processes images to create a matching color palette for web developers. Free-tier users can request up to 10 palettes per month; if they want more they have to purchase a subscription. Both free and paid users can send a maximum of one request per second. Sent images cannot be larger than 10 MB. Consider the following questions:

- How would you represent colors in a standard way that fits web developers' needs?
- Which explicit HTTP status codes could you use to tell
  - Free-tier users they have to pay to get more?
  - Any users they have exceeded their requests-per-second quota?
  - Any users that an image is too large?
- Which RFC (Request For Comments) could you use to provide straightforward error feedback?
- Bonus: fully design and describe this API using the OpenAPI Specification.

As this section has demonstrated, being consistent within and across APIs is a good thing. It lessens the need for practicing with our APIs to use them effectively—all we need to do is follow commonly used standards or practices and even (shamelessly or not) copy others. It also makes our APIs interoperable, especially when using conventional standards. And as icing on the cake, it makes our job as API designers easier so that we don't lose time reinventing the wheel. Consistency *seems* to simplify everything; but unfortunately, that's not always true.

6.1.5   *Being consistent is hard and must be done wisely*

You must be aware of two things about consistency: it's hard to be consistent, and consistency must not be applied blindly. Being consistent across APIs simply requires following the same conventions when designing different APIs. It also requires knowing which APIs actually exist. That is surprisingly hard and requires discipline.

You must formally define your design with rules in a document called the "API Design Guidelines" or the "API Design Style Guide." Even if you are the only API designer in your organization, such guidelines are important because over time we tend to forget what we have done previously (even in a single API). Defining such guidelines not only facilitates standardizing the overall organization's API surface, it also facilitates the API designer's job. You will learn in chapter 13 how to create such guidelines.

You'll also need access to existing API designs in order to stay consistent with your organization's APIs. Once you have your API design cheat sheet and your API directory, you can concentrate on solving real problems and not waste your time reinventing the wheel you created a few months ago.

Consistency is good but not at the cost of usability or common sense. Sometimes you will realize that if you push consistency too far it will ruin flexibility and make the process of design outrageously complicated, leading to consistent but totally unusable APIs. The important thing is to understand that sometimes you can be inconsistent because of a given context for the sake of usability (as we saw in section 3.4 when talking about design trade-offs). You will discover also in chapter 11 that there is not a single way of creating APIs: designing APIs requires us to adapt to the context.

So being consistent is a great way of being predictable, and doing so helps consumers intuitively use your API. But you can also cheat and let people choose what they want to get out of using your API, which makes it even more predictable.

6.2 Being adaptable

When you buy a book from an online retailer, you can often buy it in different versions. It might be sold as a printed book, an e-book, or an audio book. It can also be presented in various languages, like the French translation of this book, *Le Design des APIs Web*, that I hope to do one day. All these versions are different representations of the same book; it's up to you to indicate which version you want when you add the book to your shopping cart.

And when you read the ordered book, you usually do not read it all at once. You read it page by page, and when you stop, you mark the last page you read. When you continue reading, you jump directly to the last page read without rereading the book from the beginning. When you read some kinds of books, especially technical ones, you might jump directly to a specific chapter or section and, hence, a specific page, so you might not read the chapters in their natural order. You might also only read the parts concerning a specific topic.

Managing different representations of the same concept and providing a partial, selected, or adapted representation of some content is not reserved for books; we can do that with APIs too. We can create such an *adaptable* API design that helps to make the API predictable and also satisfy different types of users. If consumers can specify what they want, they can predict what they will get.

Here we discuss three common ways of making an API design adaptable: providing and accepting different formats; internationalizing and localizing; and providing filtering, pagination, and sorting features. This is not an exhaustive list of options—you can find others and even create your own when needed.

6.2.1 Providing and accepting different formats

JSON is the obvious way of representing an account's transactions list in our Banking API. As shown on the left side of figure 6.7, a list of transactions could be an array of JSON objects, each composed of three properties: a date, a label, and an amount.

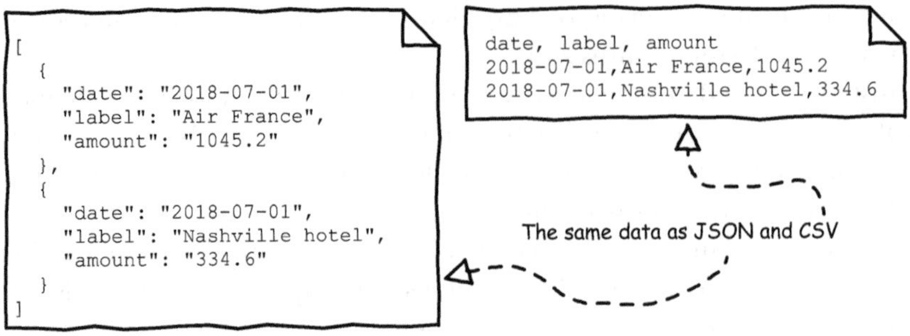

```
[
  {
    "date": "2018-07-01",
    "label": "Air France",
    "amount": "1045.2"
  },
  {
    "date": "2018-07-01",
    "label": "Nashville hotel",
    "amount": "334.6"
  }
]
```

```
date, label, amount
2018-07-01,Air France,1045.2
2018-07-01,Nashville hotel,334.6
```

The same data as JSON and CSV

Figure 6.7   A list of transactions as JSON and CSV

But JSON is not the only option. The right side of the figure shows the same data represented in a *comma-separated values* (CSV) format. In this case, a list of transactions is represented by lines of text. Each line representing a transaction is composed of three values separated by commas (,): the first one is the date, the second one the label, and the third one the amount. This transactions list could also be represented by a PDF file. You can also allow consumers to choose among different formats, depending on their needs. The only limit is your imagination.

REST constraints: Uniform interfaces

The REST architectural style states that all interactions must be guided by the concept of identified resources that are manipulated through *representations* of resource states and standard methods and provide all metadata required to understand the representations and know what can be done with those resources.[a] A single resource can be provided by a consumer and returned by a provider in many different formats using different representations like JSON or CSV, for example. This provides a powerful mechanism that allows the REST API to adapt to their consumers and, therefore, to be predictable. The headers returned also provide information about the actual format of the returned representation.

---

2   Roy Thomas Fielding, "Architectural Styles and the Design of Network-based Software Architectures," 2000 (https://www.ics.uci.edu/~fielding/pubs/dissertation/rest_arch_style.htm#sec_5_2).

But if the get account's transactions goal can return a list in various formats, how can consumers tell which format is needed? Figure 6.8 shows two different ways to do so.

As shown on the left in figure 6.8, we could add a `format` parameter to this goal in order to let consumers specify if they want the transactions list in JSON, CSV, or PDF format. To get the list as a CSV document, for example, consumers could send a GET request that specifies `format=CSV` like so:

```
GET /accounts/{accountId}/transactions?format=CSV
```

That's a possibility, but because the Banking API is a REST API, we could also take advantage of the HTTP protocol and use *content negotiation*. When sending the

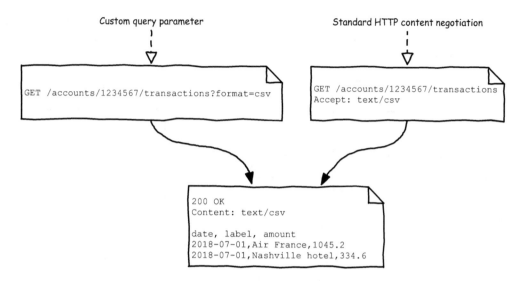

Figure 6.8 Two options to request the transactions list as a CSV document

GET /accounts/{accountId}/transactions request to the API server, consumers can add an Accept: text/csv HTTP header after the HTTP method and URL to indicate that they want this transactions list as CSV data. (This approach is shown on the right in figure 6.8.) If everything is OK, the API server responds with a 200 OK HTTP status code followed by a Content-type: text/csv header and the list of transactions as a CSV document.

Consumers can also send Accept: application/json or Accept: application/pdf to get JSON data or a PDF file, respectively, with the server returning a response with a Content-type: application/json or Content-type: application/pdf header followed by the document in the appropriate format. This example has introduced two new features of the HTTP protocol: HTTP headers and content negotiation. Let's take a closer look at these.

HTTP headers are colon-separated name/value pairs. They can be used in both requests and responses to provide some additional information. In a request, these headers are located after the request line containing the HTTP method and URL. In a response, they are located after the status line containing the HTTP status code and reason phrase. There are around 200 different standard HTTP headers, and you can even create your own if needed. They are used for various purposes, one of which is content negotiation.

Content negotiation is an HTTP mechanism that allows the exchange of different representations of a single resource. When an HTTP server (hence a REST API server) responds to a request, it must indicate the media type of the returned document. This is done in the Content-type response header. Most REST APIs use the application/json media type because the documents these return are JSON documents. But consumers can provide an `Accept` request header containing the media type they want to get. As shown in figure 6.9, in the Banking API, the three possible media types for the account's transactions list are `application/json`, `application/pdf`, and `text/csv`.

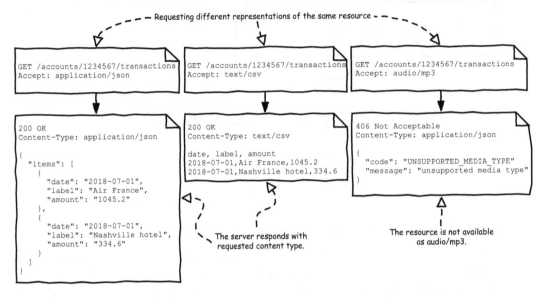

Figure 6.9   **Requesting three different representations of an account's transactions list**

If the consumer requests a media type like `audio/mp3` that the provider does not handle, the server will respond with a `406 Not Acceptable` error. Note that a request without an `Accept` header implies that the consumer will accept any media type. In that case, the server will return a default representation—JSON data, for example.

That also works when the consumer has to provide data in the body of the request. In section 5.2.1 in the last chapter, you saw that to create a transfer, consumers have to send a `POST /transfers` request, whose body contains a source account, a destination account, and an amount. This body was expected to be a JSON document, but it could also be of another media type. For example, a consumer might send an XML document containing the information needed to create a transfer.[2] To do that, they must provide the `Content-type: application/xml` header. If the API server is unable to understand XML, it returns a `415 Unsupported Media Type` error. If the consumers also want to get the result as an XML document instead of a JSON one, they must provide the `Accept: application/xml` header along with the `Content-type` header. This tells the server, "I am sending you XML and I would like you to respond using XML too."

---

[2] XML (eXtensible Markup Language) is a markup language that is supposed to be both human- and machine-readable. This was the de facto standard for API and web services before JSON. In XML, a property such as the amount would be represented as `<amount>123.4</amount>`.

That's great—content negotiation, whether provided by the protocol used or handled manually, lets consumers choose the format they want to use when communicating with an API, as long as it is supported. But we can do more than that.

6.2.2 *Internationalizing and localizing*

Even translated into French, the *Le Design des APIs Web* e-book is only another representation of the same book. How can we apply this concept to the Banking API example?

Back in section 5.2.3, you learned to design straightforward error feedback. When the customer attempts a money transfer, for example, the API can return an error with the message Amount exceeds safe to spend. Such a message could be shown to all end users—but what if they do not understand English? The developers building the application or website using the Banking API will have to manage translation of this message on their side. From a technical point of view, this is possible because the error is identified with a clearly identifiable AMOUNT_OVER_SAFE type. But maybe we, the API designers, can give a hand to developers using our API and propose a way to get error messages in languages other than English.

We could add a language parameter to all the Banking API goals, with its value being an ISO 639 language code (http://www.loc.gov/standards/iso639-2/php/code_list.php). For example, the ISO 639 code fr stands for French, and en stands for English. In section 6.1.4, you learned that using standards is good in order to ensure that a value will be easily understandable and interoperable. But wait—en simply means *English*. UK English and US English can be considered different languages, just like French and French Canadian. So, ISO 639 isn't a good idea; it would be better to use a more accurate standard to identify the language.

RFC 5646 (https://tools.ietf.org/html/rfc5646), which defines language tags, is the standard we're looking for. This format uses ISO 639 language codes and ISO 3166 country codes: US English is en-US, UK English is en-UK, French is fr-FR, and French Canadian is fr-CA.

As you can see, choosing a standard might not be straightforward. You have to be careful when choosing one and be sure that it really fulfills your needs.

Now that we've found the right standard, we can create translations of all our error messages in all the languages we want to support. For example, when using the transfer money goal with the language parameter set to fr-FR, the AMOUNT_OVER_SAFE human-readable error message might be Le montant dépasse le seuil autorisé. Note that any text returned by the API, not only error messages, can be returned in the language indicated in the language parameter. It can also be represented as a query parameter, but because the Banking API is a REST API, we can take advantage of the HTTP protocol to provide it instead.

> **WARNING** I do not recommend using automatic translations; the result can be far from accurate and totally ruin your attempt of being consumer and end-user friendly.

Content negotiation not only applies to data formats, but also to languages. Just as consumers can use the Accept and Content-type HTTP headers to specify a media type, they can also use the Accept-Language and Content-Language headers to indicate which language they are speaking, as shown in figure 6.10.

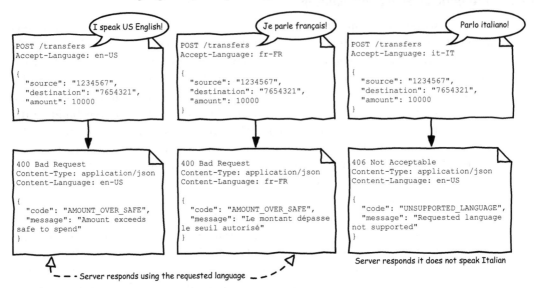

Figure 6.10   Negotiating content language with an API

When using POST /transfers to transfer money, if consumers provide no headers, the API server can return a response with a Content-Language: en-US header to indicate that any textual content is in US English. If, however, consumers provide an Accept-Language: fr-FR HTTP header with their requests to indicate that they want to get textual content in French, the API server responds with a Content-Language: fr-FR header, and any textual data will be translated into French. If the requested language—Italian (it-IT), for example—is not supported, the server returns a 406 Not Acceptable HTTP status code. Because this status code can also be returned when the consumer requests a media type that is not supported, it's also a good idea to provide straightforward error feedback with a clear error code like UNSUPPORTED_LANGUAGE and a message like Requested language not supported.

Adapting data values to developers, their applications, and their end users isn't only about language translation, though. In the US, for example, people use the imperial system of measurement, while in France they use the metric system. People in the US and France do not use the same units, the same date and number formats, or the same paper sizes. Being able to adapt to all these variations is possible if your API supports internationalization and localization (often called i18n and l10n, with the numbers indicating the number of characters between the first and last letter of the word).

For our REST Banking API, *internationalization* means being able to understand that an `Accept-Language: fr-FR` header means that the consumer wants a localized response using French language and conventions. On the server side, it means that if the requested localization is supported, the content will be returned localized along with a `Content-Language: fr-FR` header. If it's not supported, the server returns a `406 Not Acceptable` status code.

For the Banking API, *localization* means being actually able to handle the `fr-FR` locale. The data returned should be in French, using the metric system, and a PDF should be generated using the A4 size and not the US letter size, for example. This topic is not specific to APIs; these issues apply to all areas of software development.

> **NOTE** Internationalization (i18n) is the mechanism that allows software, an application, or an API to do localization. Localization (l10n) is about being able to handle the adaptations to a locale, which is basically composed of a language and a region or country.

But as API designers and providers, should we really care about internationalization and localization? This is a totally legitimate question that must be answered sooner or later when designing an API. It depends on the nature of your API and the targeted consumers and/or their end users. If you're lucky, the data exchanged through your API might not be impacted at all by localization concerns, so you might be able to bypass it. If you do not target people in different locales, you might not need to handle internationalization. Be cautious, though, because sometimes people can use different locales in the same country (the `en-US` or `es-US` locales in the US, for example).

If you don't think you need them, you can start without internationalization features and update your API later if needed. But be aware that while adding internationalization features to an existing API can be done easily and transparently from the consumer's point of view, modifying an implementation that was not built with internationalization in mind might be trickier.

Note that there are other aspects of content negotiation, like priorities when requesting multiple variants of a resource and content encoding, that we will not explore in this book. You can read more about this in RFC 7231 (https://tools.ietf.org/html/rfc7231).

We've seen that consumers can specify not only the data format they want to use but also the language and units, for example. Is it possible to provide an even more customizable API in order to be even more predictable? Yes, it is!

6.2.3 *Filtering, paginating, and sorting*

A bank account that has been open for many years can have thousands of transactions in its history. A customer who wants to get an account's transactions using the Banking API probably does not want to see all of these transactions at once and would prefer to get a subset. Maybe they want to see the 10 most recent ones and then possibly go deeper into the list. As shown in figure 6.11, this could be done by adding some optional parameters to this goal, such as `pageSize` and `page`.

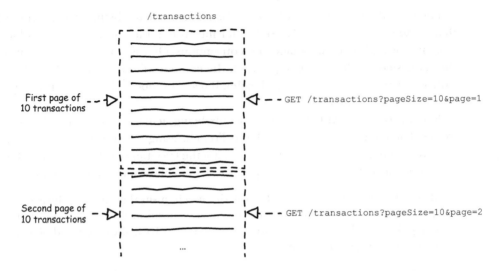

Figure 6.11   Simple pagination

On the server, the transactions list is split virtually into pages, with each page containing pageSize transactions. If pageSize is not provided, the server uses a default value, and if page is not provided, the server returns the first page by default. To get the first page of 10 transactions, consumers would have to provide pageSize=10 and page=1. To get the second page of 10 transactions, they would provide pageSize=10 and page=2.

In our REST Banking API, these *pagination* parameters could be passed as query parameters, as in GET /accounts/1234567/transactions?pageSize=10&page=1. But we could also take advantage of the HTTP protocol and use the Range HTTP header. To get the first page of 10 transactions, this header would be Range: items=0-9. To get the next page, the header is Range: items=10-19.

The Range header was created to allow a web browser to retrieve a portion of a binary file. The value of a request's Range header is <unit>=<first>-<last>. A standard unit is bytes, so bytes=0-500 would return the first 500 bytes of a binary file.

We can use a custom unit like items. Sending a Range header with the items=10-19 value tells the server, "I want the collection's items from indexes 10 to 19." I could have chosen another unit name, such as transactions, but that would mean that if we wanted to paginate the /accounts collection resource, the unit would be accounts. The unit name used to paginate can be guessed from the collection name, but I prefer to favor the generic name items. That way, there's no need to guess the unit for paginating collections: it is always the same.

If consumers want a subset of transactions, however, they might like to have more control over this subset. Maybe they only want to see transactions that have been categorized as *restaurant* transactions. To get these specific transactions, the consumer might send a GET /accounts/1234567/transactions?category=restaurant request. The category query parameter is used here to filter the transactions and only return the ones categorized as restaurant.

This filtering example is a really basic one. If you want to practice, here's a problem you will have to solve sooner or later as an API designer: filtering a collection on numerical values. Let's say you're designing an API dealing with secondhand cars. Users should be able to list available cars having a mileage between two values using a `GET /cars` request and one or more query parameters. Using a natural language, such a query would be something like, "List cars with mileage between 15,000 and 30,000 miles." Try the following exercises:

- Find a way of designing such a filter.
- Find at least two other ways of doing the same thing by searching through existing APIs (or API design guidelines).
- Decide which one you prefer.
- Bonus: for all these different ways, describe the request and its parameter(s) using the OpenAPI Specification.

By default, transactions are ordered from latest to oldest; when consumers request transactions, they get the latest first. Consumers might also want to get the transactions sorted by descending amounts (higher amounts first) and in chronological order (from oldest to latest). To get such a list, they might send a request like this:

```
GET /accounts/1234567/transactions?sort=-amount,+date
```

The `sort` query parameter defines how the transactions list should be sorted. It contains a list of direction and property couples. The direction + is for ascending and - is for descending. The `-amount` and `+date` values tell the server to sort the transactions by amount in descending order and by date in ascending order. Note that this is only one way of providing sorting parameters; it can be done in other ways too.

These pagination, filtering, and sorting features can be used together. Using the `category=restaurant&sort=-amount,+date&page=3` query parameters in a `GET /accounts/1234567/transactions` request returns the third page of the restaurant transactions, ordered by descending amount and ascending date.

As this section has demonstrated, besides making our API look familiar, a good way of making it predictable is to let consumers say what they want and give it to them. A third way of making an API predictable is by giving consumers some clues about what they can do with it.

6.3 *Being discoverable*

In most books, you know which page you are reading because its number is printed on it. Sometimes, the current chapter or section is also indicated at the top or bottom of the page. Earlier, we saw that when you read some books, you can jump directly to a specific chapter or section. This is possible because the book comes with a handy table of contents (TOC) listing the chapters and sections and on which pages they start. When you read a book, therefore, you read its content, but you also have access to additional information about the content itself. You could read the book without using this extra information; if all of it were removed, the content would be unaffected. But reading the book would be far less convenient.

If the book is a novel, not having a TOC (or even page numbers) isn't really a problem. A novel is more interesting read page after page, without being spoiled by a too-explicit preview of the contents (like "Chapter XI: The character you have become so attached to dies"). But if the book is a practical one, like the one you are reading now, you might want to scan the TOC before you begin reading to get a better idea of what the book is about in order to be sure it is relevant for you. You might also want to jump to a specific section because you have a specific problem to solve. Without a TOC and page numbers, it would not be easy to find what you are looking for. This additional information makes a book *discoverable*. It's not mandatory, but it greatly improves the reading experience.

Like books, APIs can be designed in order to be discoverable. This is done by providing additional data in various ways, but discoverability can also be improved by taking advantage of the protocol used. REST APIs have the discoverable feature in their genes because they use URLs and the HTTP protocol.

6.3.1   *Providing metadata*

In section 6.2.3, you discovered the pagination feature. When accessing an account's transactions list, consumers of the Banking API can indicate which page of transactions they want. But how do they know that there are multiple pages available?

For now, the server's response when consumers request an account's transactions list consists only of an object containing an `items` property, which is an array of transactions. Sounds like a book without page numbers and a TOC. This response could be improved by adding some data about pagination, as shown in figure 6.12.

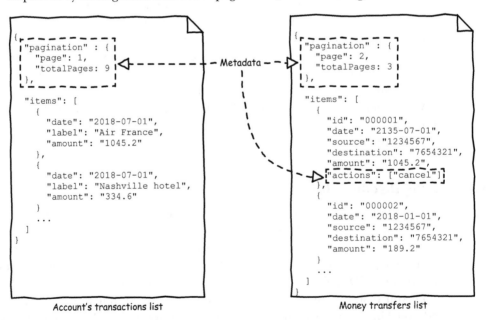

Figure 6.12   Providing metadata to explain "Where am I and what can I do"

If a first call to the get account's transactions goal is made without pagination parameters, the server could return the items array along with the current page's number (page, whose value is 1) and the total number of pages (totalPages, whose value could be 9). This will tell consumers that there are eight more pages of transactions ahead.

Thanks to the additional data, the transactions list is now discoverable. In computer science such data is called *metadata*; it's data about data. Metadata can be used to tell consumers where they are and what they can do.

Let's look at another example, just to show that metadata is not limited to pagination. Using the Banking API, consumers can transfer money from one account to another immediately or on a predefined date. When listing past transfer requests, the server can return both executed and postponed requests. An already executed request cannot be canceled, but a postponed one that has not yet been executed can be. As shown in figure 6.12, we could add some metadata describing the possible actions on each transfer request. For an already executed money transfer, the actions list would be empty. For a postponed one, it could contain a cancel element. This will tell consumers which ones they can use the cancel money transfer goal on.

As you can see, an API can return metadata along with data in order to help consumers discover where they are and what they can do. The API can be used without this extra information, but metadata greatly facilitates its use. By adding metadata, we are basically applying what we learned in section 5.1—we are providing ready-to-use data. This can be done with any type of API. Depending on the API in question, you can rely on other mechanisms to provide such information, especially by taking advantage of some of your chosen protocol's features.

6.3.2 *Creating hypermedia APIs*

Using the REST Banking API, consumers can retrieve a list of accounts by calling GET / accounts. Each account comes with a unique id that can be used to build its URL (/accounts/{accountId}) and to retrieve detailed information about it using the GET HTTP method. This id can also be used to retrieve an account's transactions with GET / accounts/{accountId}/transactions. Thanks to the pagination metadata we have just added, consumers will know if there are more transactions than the ones returned by their first call. In that case, they can use GET /accounts/{accountId}/transactions?page=2 to get the next page of transactions. They can even jump directly to the last page of transactions. They just have to take the lastPage value and use it to GET / accounts/{accountId}/transactions?page={lastPage value}.

Sounds like a well-designed API with crystal-clear URLs and even metadata that helps consumers, right? Now, let's imagine a situation where you're browsing a bank's website and all the hypermedia links have been removed. Would you be happy as a customer to have to read a user's manual to learn what all the available URLs are? If you wanted to see detailed information about one of your accounts, would you be happy about having to construct the page's URL yourself by copying and pasting the account number? The World Wide Web without its hypermedia links would be quite terrible to use.

Fortunately, this isn't how it works. Once on a website, you can discover its content simply by clicking links and going from one page to another. REST APIs rely on World Wide Web principles, so why not take advantage of these? As shown in figure 6.13, a *hypermedia* Banking API would provide an `href` property for each account returned by `GET /accounts`.

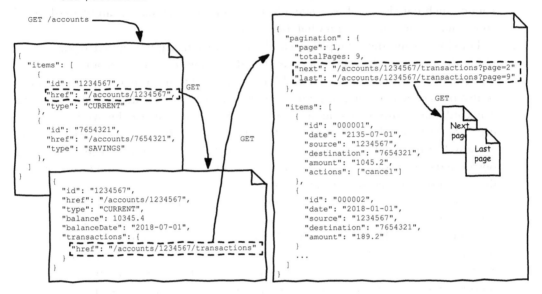

Figure 6.13   Hypermedia Banking API

For the `1234567` account, its value would be `/accounts/1234567`. Consumers wanting to get access to this account's detailed information would then just have to `GET` this ready-to-use relative URL without needing to construct it themselves. And the response to this request would have a `transactions` property, whose value could be an object containing an `href` property with a value of `/accounts/1234567/transactions`.

Again, consumers would just have to `GET` this `href` value to get the account's transactions list. And of course, the pagination metadata would provide URLs like next and last using properties whose values could be `/accounts/1234567/transactions?page=2` and `/accounts/1234567/transactions?page=9`, respectively. Consumers would then be able to browse the API without the need to know its available URLs and their structures.

REST APIs provide links just like web pages. This facilitates API discovery and, as you will see later in this book, API updating. There is no standard way to provide this hypermedia metadata, but there are common practices, mostly based on how links are represented in HTML pages and the HTTP protocol.

Hypermedia metadata usually uses names such as `href`, `links`, or `_links`. Although there is no standard, several hypermedia formats have been defined. The best-known ones are HAL, Collection+JSON, JSON API, JSON-LD, Hydra, and Siren. These formats come with differing constraints regarding the data structure.

HAL (http://stateless.co/hal_specification.html) is relatively simple. A basic HAL document has a `links` property containing the available links. Each link is an object identified by its relationship (or `_rel`) with the current resource. The `self` relationship is used for the resource's link. The link object contains at least an `href` property with the full URL or relative URL. For a bank account resource, the link to its transactions would be located there as `transactions` as the following listing shows.

Listing 6.1 A bank account as a HAL document

```
{
  "_links" : {
    "self": {
      "href": "/accounts/1234567"          ◄──── Link to the bank account resource itself
    },
    "transactions": {
      "href":"/accounts/1234567/transactions"    ◄──── Link to the bank
    }                                                   account's transactions
  }
  "id": "1234567",
  "type": "CURRENT",
  "balance": 10345.4
  "balanceDate": "2018-07-01"
}
```

The concept of link relationship is not specific to HAL; it is defined by RFC 5988 (https://tools.ietf.org/html/rfc5988). Hypermedia APIs do not only provide available URLs; they can also provide available HTTP methods. For example, with the Siren hypermedia format (https://github.com/kevinswiber/siren), we can describe the `cancel` action on a postponed money transfer. Siren also comes with constraints regarding the data structure: the properties are grouped in `properties`, links to other resources are located in `links`, and actions are in `actions`. The next listing shows an example of a Siren document.

Listing 6.2 A money transfer as a Siren document

```
{
  "properties" : {          ◄──── Groups a resource's properties
    "id": "000001",                under properties
    "date": "2135-07-01",
    "source": "1234567",
    "destination": "7654321",
    "amount": "1045.2"
  },                        ◄──── Equivalent to HAL's _links
  links: [                  ◄────
    { "rel": ["self"],
      "href": "/transfers/000001" }
  ],                        ◄──── Describes an action with a
  actions: [                      name, URL, and HTTP method
    { "name": "cancel",
      "href": "/transfers/000001",
      "method": "DELETE" }
  ],
}
```

> ### REST constraints: Uniform interface
>
> The REST architectural style states that all interactions must be guided by the concept of identified resources that are manipulated through representations of resource states and standard methods and provides all metadata required to understand the representations and know what can be done with those resources.[a] REST APIs are hypermedia APIs that provide all the metadata needed to help consumers navigate through them like a website to facilitate their discovery. Metadata can be used to describe not only link relationships between resources but also among available operations. This part of the REST architectural style uniform interface constraint is called *hypermedia as the engine of the application state* (often worded as the unpronounceable *HATEOAS*).
>
> ---
>
> [a] Roy Thomas Fielding, Architectural Styles and the Design of Network-based Software Architectures, 2000 (https://www.ics.uci.edu/~fielding/pubs/dissertation/rest_arch_style.htm#sec_5_2).

Providing hypermedia metadata is the most common way of taking advantage of the web roots of REST APIs to create predictable APIs, but the HTTP protocol provides features that can be used to make REST APIs even more predictable.

6.3.3   *Taking advantage of the HTTP protocol*

So far, we have used GET, POST, PUT, DELETE, and PATCH HTTP methods. The following listing shows that an OPTIONS /transfers/000001 request can be used to identify the available HTTP methods on a resource.

Listing 6.3   Using the OPTIONS HTTP method

```
OPTIONS /transfers/000001

200 OK
Allow: GET, DELETE
```

If the API server supports this HTTP method and the resource exists, it can return a 200 OK response along with an Allow: GET, DELETE header. The response clearly states that GET and DELETE HTTP methods can be used on /transfers/000001. Like metadata that can provide information about the data (section 6.3.1), such *metagoals* can provide information about API goals.

Earlier in this chapter, you saw that an account's transactions list could be returned as a JSON, CSV, or PDF document. The following listing shows that when responding to a GET /accounts/1234567/transactions request, an API server can indicate other available formats with a Link header.

Listing 6.4   A response indicating other available formats with the Link header

```
200 OK
Allow: GET
Content-type: application/json        ◄──    The transactions list returns
Link: </accounts/1234567/transactions>;       as a JSON document.
        type=application/pdf,                  It is also available in PDF
    </accounts/1234567/transactions>;          and CSV formats. (Note that
        type=text/csv                          it is actually a single line.)
```

```
{
  "items" : [
    ...
  ]
}
```

Note that such use of the HTTP protocol by REST APIs cannot be widespread. Like choosing a standard, you should check if such features are really useful to consumers. If so, you might have to explain them in detail in your documentation for people who are not HTTP protocol experts.

> **TIP** Always check the possibilities of the protocol used by your API, but be careful not to confuse users with sparsely used features. You can use such features, but they will have to be carefully documented.

If you want to practice the lessons from this section, you can try updating the Shopping API we were working with in chapters 3 and 4, using the OpenAPI Specification as follows:

- Add hypermedia features using HAL (or Siren) to represent links between resources.
- Add pagination, filtering, and sorting features with relevant metadata and hypermedia controls.
- Add a content negotiation feature to support the CSV format.
- Add the OPTIONS HTTP method where necessary.

In the next and final chapter about usability, you will learn to organize and size your APIs in order to keep them usable.

Summary

- To create APIs whose operations can be guessed, consistently define conventions and follow common practices and standards.
- Being consistent in your design not only makes your API easier to use, but also makes its design simpler.
- Always check if your API needs to provide different representation and/or localization and internationalization features.
- For each goal dealing with lists, consider whether paging, filtering, and sorting features will facilitate its use.
- In order to guide consumers, provide as much as metadata as possible (like hypermedia links, for example).
- Always check the underlying protocol and use its available features to make your API predictable, while taking care not to confuse users with complex or totally unused features.

Designing a concise and well-organized API

Now that you know how to design straightforward and predictable APIs, we have one last thing to cover in order to be sure we're designing *usable* APIs. TV remote controls sometimes look intimidating with their numerous and not always well-organized buttons. Some microwave ovens or washing machines offer far too many functions for mere mortals. Overwhelming, disorganized, indistinct, or motley everyday interfaces, at best, puzzle their users and, at worst, frighten them.

"Less is more" and "a place for everything and everything in its place" are two adages that every API designer should apply. Organizing and sizing an API's data, feedback, and goals is important in order to provide an API that can be easily understood and will not overwhelm users. If this is not done, all that we have learned about creating straightforward and predictable APIs is worth nothing.

7.1 Organizing an API

If you have ever used a TV remote control, you should be able to understand the meaning of any button on the four examples shown in figure 7.1. All of them propose exactly the same functions, using 15 buttons; but, depending on the buttons' organization, the usability goes from terrible to perfect.

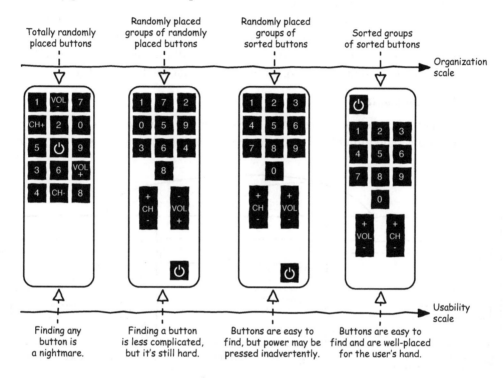

Figure 7.1 The organization of a TV remote control's buttons affects its usability.

On the first remote control (on the left), the buttons are randomly placed, making it difficult to find any given one. On the second remote control, buttons are grouped by type, making those easier to find. If users are looking for the 7 button, for example, they know they can find it in the group of number buttons. The channel (CH) + and - buttons and volume (VOL) + and - buttons are also grouped together.

But just grouping buttons is not sufficient. On the third remote control, the buttons in each group have been sorted. The 7 button is now easier to find thanks to the ascending sorting in the numbers group. Putting the volume + button on top of its group is also better for two reasons:

- +/- are usually placed that way to mimic what they represent: up/down.
- The channel + button is on top of its group, so this change means the two groups are consistent.

Finally, the fourth remote control's button groups are rearranged to make it even easier to use. The power button is placed at the top to prevent it from being pressed inadvertently while the user is holding the remote control. The channel and volume button groups are also switched to match common practice on remote controls. Now that the buttons are placed intuitively, you can easily use the remote control—maybe even in the dark while watching a movie.

As this example shows, it's easier to find a specific element in a set and understand its purpose if elements are logically grouped and sorted. It's the same for APIs—organization matters. Just like an everyday object, an API can be either unusable or perfectly intuitive, depending on the organization of its data, feedback, and goals.

7.1.1   Organizing data

Designing a well-organized API starts with the data, so let's look at a concrete example. The initial bank account representation shown in figure 7.2 (a) contains

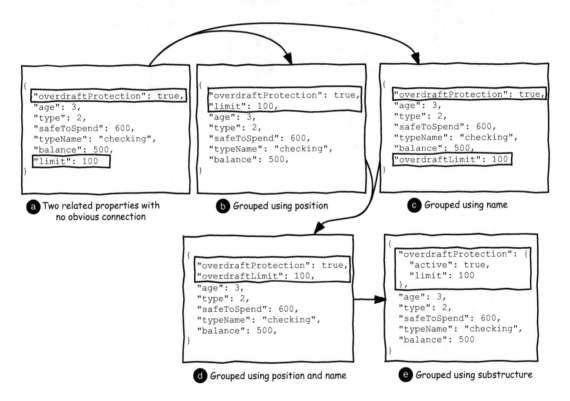

Figure 7.2   Grouping data in the bank account's representation

two highlighted properties: `overdraftProtection` and `limit`. The `overdraft-Protection` property indicates whether overdraft protection is active on the account, and `limit` tells how much overdraft protection is available. Here its value is `100`, meaning that any transaction that causes the account to go more than $100 over its balance will be blocked. These two properties are related, but nothing explicitly tells us that in the design.

We can make some changes to make this relationship more obvious. A first idea would be to move the two properties closer to each other (b), but it's still not clear that they're related. Renaming `limit` to `overdraftLimit` gives a better result (c), but combining these two techniques is better still (d). This way, we create a virtual boundary around those. We could also create a more solid boundary by putting these two properties into an `overdraftProtection` substructure (e).

Grouping data is the first step, but it's not enough. Having to constantly scroll up and down through the API's response to find the most important data can be terribly annoying. *Sorting* data can enhance readability for human beings (programs do not care at all about this).

As shown in figure 7.3, two other groups can be created by moving `type` and `typeName` and also `safeToSpend` and `balance` closer together. In each group, properties are sorted from more important (on top) to less important (on the bottom). All the groups are also sorted by importance.

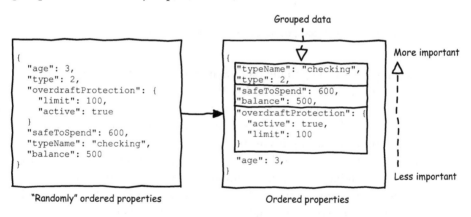

Figure 7.3 Sorting data in the bank account's representation

This organization will also be visible in the documentation or code generated from the specification of your API. Grouping properties in a dedicated structure can also help to provide a better vision of what is required or not, as shown in figure 7.4.

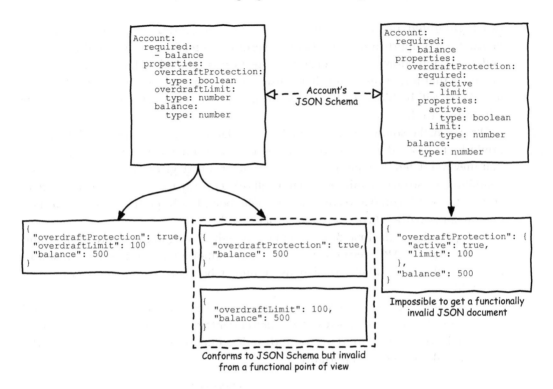

Figure 7.4   Grouping data to manage an optional group of required properties

In this example, according to the JSON Schema on the left, both `overdraftProtection` and `overdraftLimit` are optional. But from a functional point of view, if `overdraft-Protection` is `true`, then `overdraftLimit` is mandatory. Grouping these two properties in an optional `overdraftProtection` object containing two mandatory `active` and `limit` properties solves this problem.

Not that such a strategy is basically exposing the provider's perspective—here, a JSON Schema limitation that does not allow one to describe the required/optional properties' combinations. But it is always good to know this trick; sometimes it can be of great help in order to provide a highly accurate JSON Schema.

To design usable data, you must organize it by creating data groups—moving related properties closer together, using common prefixes, or creating substructures—and sorting the data in those groups and the groups themselves from more important to less important.

7.1.2 Organizing feedback

A well-organized API provides well-organized feedback. In section 5.2, you learned how we can use HTTP status codes to provide informative feedback. As a reminder, table 7.1 shows some of the use cases you've seen.

Table 7.1 HTTP status code examples

Use case	HTTP status code	Class	Meaning
Creating a money transfer	`201 Created`	2XX	Immediate money transfer created
Creating a money transfer	`202 Accepted`	2XX	Delayed money transfer created
Creating a money transfer	`400 Bad Request`	4XX	Missing mandatory property or wrong data type
Getting a bank account	`200 OK`	2XX	Requested bank account returned
Getting a bank account	`404 Not Found`	4XX	Requested bank account does not exist

HTTP status codes are grouped into *classes*. A response in the 2XX class means that everything went OK, while a 4XX response means that there's a problem with the request and the consumer should fix it. Grouping HTTP status codes this way makes these easier to understand.

If an API returns a 413 status code to your request, you know that the problem is on your side, even if you've never seen this status code before.[1] Why? Because it's a 4XX-class code. This unknown 4XX should be treated the same way as a 400 status code (see section 5.2.3).[2]

Organizing feedback isn't just about status codes, though. You can also organize more specific or custom feedback. In section 5.2.4, you saw that when returning multiple errors it can be helpful to categorize them. Figure 7.5 shows a response to a delayed money transfer creation request that specifies an `amount` exceeding the safe-to-spend limit, that's missing the `destination` account, and that provides the execution `date` as a UNIX timestamp.

---

[1] This code actually means that your request is larger than the server is willing or able to process (https://tools.ietf.org/html/rfc7231#section-6.5.11).

[2] RFC7231 states that, "… a client MUST understand the class of any status code, as indicated by the first digit, and treat an unrecognized status code as being equivalent to the x00 status code of that class …" (https://tools.ietf.org/html/rfc7231#section-6).

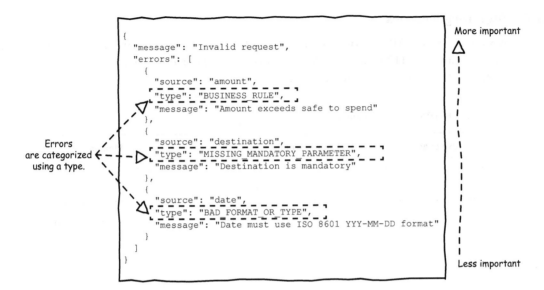

Figure 7.5   Grouped and sorted errors

As you can see, each error has a type, which gives us a clue about the source of the problem. The first error from the BUSINESS_RULE group has obviously triggered a business control. The MISSING_MANDATORY_PARAMETER error obviously concerns a missing mandatory parameter. And the obvious BAD_FORMAT_OR_TYPE error tells us that the property's value does not conform to the expected type or format. The errors are also sorted from most- to least-critical: the Amount exceeds safe to spend error is the most serious one, followed by Destination is mandatory, and the less-critical Date must use ISO 8601 YYY-MM-DD format.

When designing an API, you must organize feedback to facilitate its interpretation by taking advantage of the organization of the underlying protocol's feedback, creating your own feedback organization, and sorting multiple errors from most-to-least critical.

7.1.3   Organizing goals

Last but not least, goals also deserve to be well-organized. If you are familiar with object-oriented programming, you can compare this to organizing methods in classes. An API's goals can be organized both virtually and physically. As shown in figure 7.6, the OpenAPI Specification you discovered in chapter 4 can be used to organize an API's goals *virtually*.

On the left in figure 7.6 is a totally disorganized Banking API definition. On the right, the goals have been grouped into two categories, Account and Transfer, by adding a tags property on each operation.

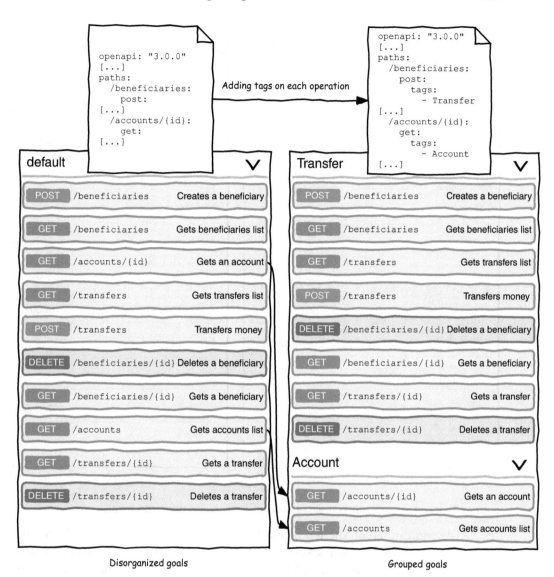

Figure 7.6   Grouping goals with tags in an OpenAPI Specification document

NOTE   An operation can belong to multiple categories if necessary.

But how did we choose each goal's group? There's no magic recipe, but the idea is to group together goals that are related from a functional point of view. If you're designing a REST API, you must not be fooled by the paths when doing that; you must focus on the functionality of the goals and not their representations, as shown in figure 7.7.

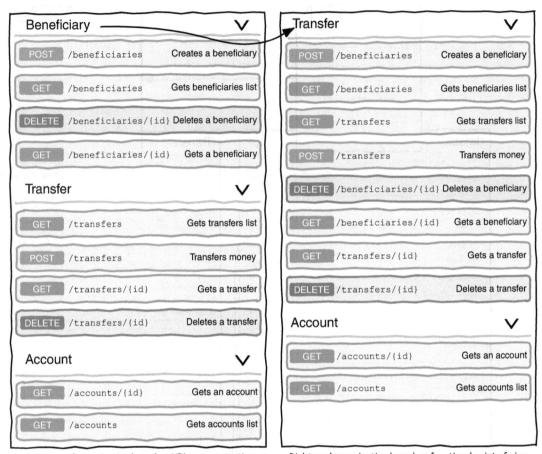

Figure 7.7 **Grouping goals with tags based on functionality versus URL representation**

As you can see on the left of this figure, if we were to focus on paths, we might end up with three categories: Beneficiary (for the /beneficiaries paths), Transfer (for the /transfers paths), and Account (for the /accounts paths). But it doesn't make sense to separate the goals represented by the /transfers and /beneficiaries paths because they cannot exist without each other.

On the right, we've organized the goals into two categories. This is better, but having the Transfer category before Account does not really reflect how people will use the API. Users are likely to first be interested in operations related to the account domain before trying to use the API to transfer money. As shown in figure 7.8, we can sort the categories by adding a tags definition on the root level. The tags property is a list in which each item contains a tag's name and its description.

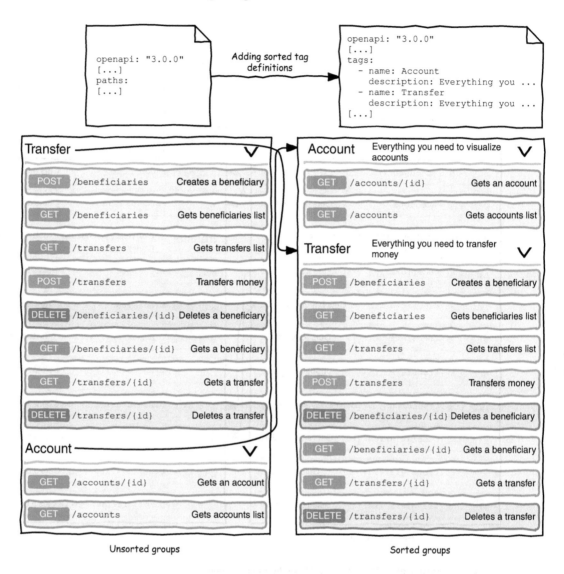

Figure 7.8 Sorting goal groups by adding sorted tags definitions

All we need to do to sort our `Account` and `Transfer` tags as we want is to sort the tag definitions in this `tags` list. Then we can add a `description` for each tag (or each category). Now that the groups are sorted, we should also sort the operations within the groups, as shown in figure 7.9.

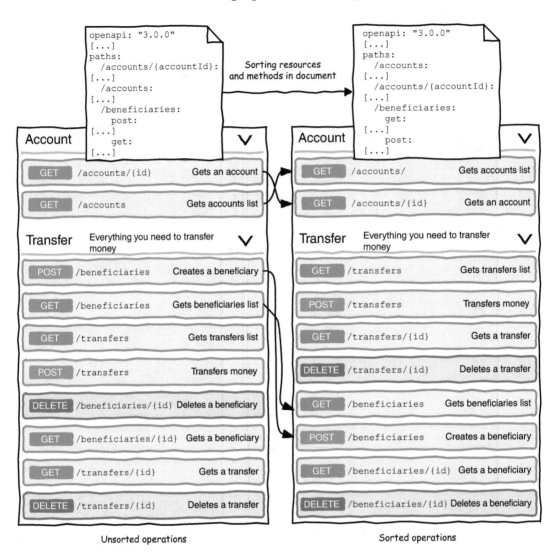

Figure 7.9   Sorting goals in the OpenAPI Specification document

This can only be done by sorting the goals by order of importance in the specification document itself (this is how it should have been done from the beginning, by the way). Here GET /accounts is more important than GET /accounts/{id} because consumers will usually list accounts before accessing an account's detailed information. Note also that the order of the HTTP methods is the same for all resources: GET, POST, DELETE; POST and GET in /beneficiaries have been swapped. Remember what you learned about consistency in section 6.1? Choose one way to sort the HTTP methods and stick to it for all resources! But this is only a *virtual* organization that is not exposed in the API design itself. We could add /account and /transfer root paths to the resource paths to actually group those as shown in figure 7.10.

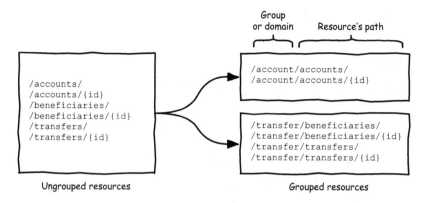

Figure 7.10 Grouping resources by paths

Users would then be able to make connections between resources by just looking at their paths. Be warned, however, that this could make the paths less simple to guess in some cases.

Now it's your turn. Suppose the goals shown in figure 7.11 belong to the API of a famous image-sharing social network called Imagebook. How would you organize those using what you've learned so far?

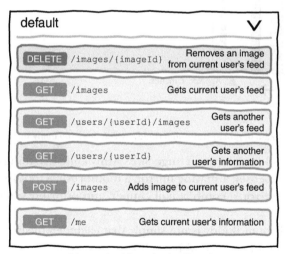

Disorganized Imagebook API goals

Figure 7.11 How would you organize these goals?

Organizing an API's goals virtually or physically facilitates understanding. This can be done by sorting goals in the definition document and taking advantage of the API specification format. And you can possibly add an organization level when designing the programming interface (add a level in the path for the REST HTTP method, for example).

We now know how to design a well-organized API. But as API designers, we must ensure that our APIs are *concise* too.

7.2   *Sizing an API*

In Joe Dante's 1984 movie, *Gremlins*, Randall Peltzer, the main protagonist's father, tries to sell the "invention of the century": the Bathroom Buddy (shown in figure 7.12).

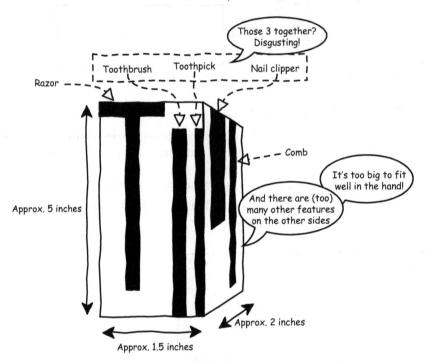

Figure 7.12   The not-so-handy (and kind of gross) Bathroom Buddy, which does too many things

It's an all-in-one device for travelers. Imagine a huge Swiss Army knife-like thing including a razor, a shaving cream dispenser, a shaving mirror, a toothbrush, a toothpaste dispenser, a toothpick, a dental mirror, a comb, a nail clipper, and probably some other more or less useful features.

The problem with the Bathroom Buddy is not simply that each demonstration fails miserably, ending with the inventor covered with toothpaste or shaving cream. The real problem is that it wants to do too many things, and it doesn't really look that handy. It's too big to fit well in hand, and using each function seems to be quite a challenge. Finding where the comb is hidden might not be easy the first few times, and the idea of using the same device to brush my teeth and clip my toenails is quite disgusting, to say the least. A separate toothbrush and nail clipper are far more convenient (and appealing) to use!

> **NOTE**   Objects providing too many functions, too many controls, or too much information are usually not really usable. These tend to be bulky, inconvenient, and intimidating.

And sizing doesn't only matter for everyday objects. What is the right size for a database table? A class? A method? A function? An application? These are questions that come up constantly when you're working with software—and APIs are no exception. Each aspect of an API, including its data and its goals, should be sized wisely. Sometimes you'll find that what you'd considered as a single API can be worth splitting into different ones, just like the the Bathroom Buddy's toothbrush and nail clipper.

7.2.1 Choosing data granularity

The bank account's JSON representation in figure 7.13 contains 32 properties and has a maximum depth of 4.

```
{
  "balance": 123.78,
  "type": {
    "code": "CURRENT",
    "label": "Current Account"
  },
  "holders": [
    { "firstName": "John",
      "lastName": "Doe",
      "birthDate": "1975-05-25",
      "addresses": [
      { "type": "main",
        "street": "123",
        "zip": "",
        "city": "",
        "country": ""}
      ]}
  ],
  "cards": [
    { "type": "DEBIT",
      "number": "XXXXXXXXX5412",
      "holder": {
      "firstName": "John",
      "lastName": "Doe",
      "birthDate": "1975-05-25",
      "addresses": [
        { "type": "main",
          "street": "123",
          "zip": "",
          "city": "",
          "country": ""}
        ]}
    }
  ],
  "transactions": [
    { "date": "2019-09-15",
      "amount": "45.2",
      "label": "Restaurant API Food",
      "category": "restaurant"}
  ]
}
```

32 properties ⟶

Maximum depth 4 ⟶

Figure 7.13 **Number of properties and maximum depth of a bank account representation**

Holding 32 properties seems reasonable; but, depending on the context, it can be too much. What if this representation is used in a list? In that case, it might not be relevant to provide *all* of an account's information when users might need only a summary. Also, if we take a closer look, we can see at least one potential problem: this bank account contains a transactions list. This representation might be trying to do too many things at once, and it might not be easy to manipulate the transactions list from within the bank account. These representations should be separated.

And regarding the maximum depth of 4, it is also quite reasonable, if slightly above the recommended level. This depth is a direct result of grouping using substructures to keep the data readable. As shown in figure 7.14, data granularity has two dimensions: the number of properties and the depth.

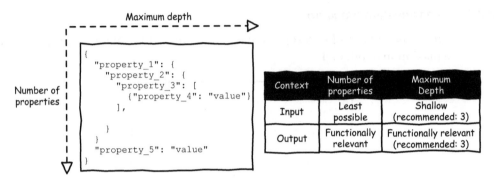

Figure 7.14   Choosing the number of properties and maximum depth

The number of properties that's reasonable for an API to return in a data structure is a matter of functional relevance; the provided properties must all be functionally appropriate in the context in which they are used. The more data an API returns, however, the more the designer must be careful about its organization (remember section 7.1.1) and relevance because, even though these are all pertinent, having a high number of properties does not facilitate usage.

In my experience, I would say that above 20 properties, you should definitely think about organizing those and possibly challenge each one. But this is not a silver bullet; there are fields where it could make sense to have so many properties. Try to define your own rules based on your domain. Recall also that, as we saw in section 5.2.1, we must request the minimum data possible to ensure usability. The number of properties is quite critical in this context.

Regarding the depth, we also have the same input/output duality; but for both contexts, it is recommended to try not to go beyond three levels of depth. Having more than three levels of depth makes manipulating the raw data, coding, and reading the documentation more complicated. Again, this rule might need to be adapted to your context.

Organizing data also helps to make your API easier to understand, so you will have to find a balance. Keep an eye on data granularity, but remember that it is mainly a matter of functional context and not a matter of numbers. But granularity doesn't only matter for data—it also matters for goals.

7.2.2   *Choosing goal granularity*

Take another look at figure 7.15. Is it a good idea to have the transactions included in the bank account representation? Probably not.

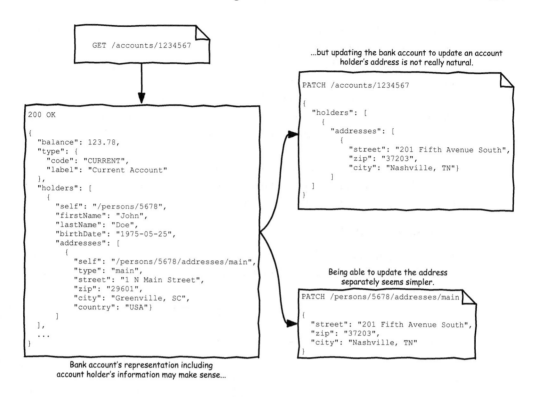

Figure 7.15 **Different goal granularity when reading and modifying data**

If the get bank account goal returns the account *and* its transactions list, we'll have to deal with managing a potentially large number of transactions. Always returning all the transactions can be cumbersome, and managing transaction pagination can be complex (as you learned in chapter 6). A `GET /accounts/{id}?page=2` or `GET /accounts/{id}?transactionPage=2` REST API request seems quite awkward. It is better to provide a separate goal to get a bank account's transactions (`GET /accounts/{id}/transactions`).

Choosing the right granularity for your goals is about ensuring that a goal is not doing two (or more) quite different things. Note also that the granularity of goals is not always consistent. As shown in figure 7.15, it can differ when reading or modifying data, for example.

The Banking API currently allows us to modify an account holder's addresses by updating the bank account resource. While it might be useful for this resource to provide information about the account holder, including their addresses, updating an address by updating the bank account resource is not really natural. Doing the update that way hides the update address goal within another one.

There are two issues here. First, it might not be obvious at first sight that you can update an address by updating a bank account. Second, the account holder's data is independent of a specific bank account. The same account holder might own multiple accounts, so updating the address through an account seems quite awkward. And what if there are other properties of the bank account that can be updated through this resource, such as the overdraft feature?

Requesting minimal inputs and managing errors for the update bank account goal could become quite complex for both designers and consumers because this goal would encompass several subgoals. It would be wiser to provide an independent update address goal as seen at the bottom right in figure 7.15, but it is totally acceptable to give access to the address information through the bank account if it makes sense from a functional point of view.

Remember that a goal's granularity should be determined by context and usability. We'll talk more about goal granularity in chapter 8, but first, if granularity matters for data and goals, it matters, of course, for APIs as well.

7.2.3   *Choosing API granularity*

When we organized the Banking API goals in section 7.1.3, borders appeared around the goals. As shown in figure 7.16, we have grouped the goals into `Account` and `Transfer` categories.

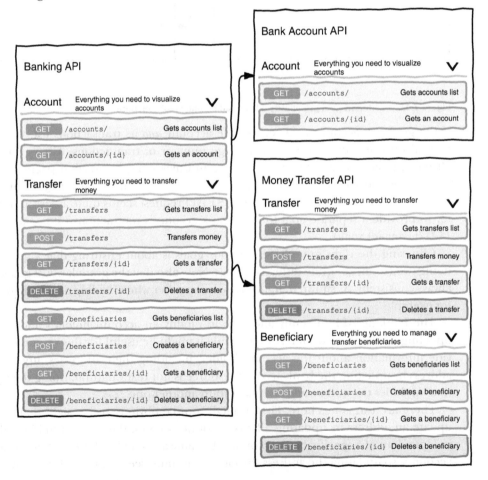

Figure 7.16   From one Banking API to separate Bank Account and Money Transfer APIs

But these are more than just simple categories. Each group of goals could be totally independent. Therefore, why don't we split the Banking API into two smaller but functionally useful APIs? These smaller Money Transfer Bank Account APIs will be easier to manage and can be reused independently in different contexts. Note that in the Money Transfer API, goals have been grouped in the initial Transfer and Beneficiary categories. It now makes sense to organize them into smaller groups.

We have been working with the programming interface representation, but organizing and splitting an API's goals can be done during the first design steps when identifying goals. Try to apply what you have learned here to the Shopping API we designed in chapters 3 and 4. How would you organize and split the goals list shown in table 7.2 into independent, smaller APIs? It's up to you to fill in the Category and API columns; try to come up with at least two different versions. (Hint: thinking about who the users are can help you to find one version.)

Table 7.2 How would you organize and split this Shopping API goals list?

Goal	Category	API
Create user		
Search for products		
Get product's information		
Add product to shopping cart		
Remove product from cart		
Check out cart		
Get cart detail		
List orders		
Add product to catalog		
Update a product		
Replace a product		
Delete a product		
Get an order's status		
Update user		
Delete user		

Remember that once an API is organized into groups of goals while identifying goals or designing the programming interface, it can be split into smaller but functionally significant APIs that can be used independently.

This concludes part 2 of this book; you now know how to design usable APIs. That is already great, but we won't stop here: there is still a lot of ground to cover. In the third part of this book, you will learn to design APIs while taking care of the whole context around them.

Summary

- Organize data properties by sorting them, naming them using patterns, or grouping them in data structures.
- Categorize feedback and sort it by its importance.
- Group goals by focusing on functionality and not representations; you can use API description format features or naming patterns (OpenAPI tags and URL prefixes for REST APIs).
- Keep the number of properties and depth levels as low as possible in data structures.
- Avoid creating *does-it-all* goals.
- Split data structures, goals, and even APIs into smaller but functionally significant elements when possible.

Part 3

Contextual API design

Reading the first two parts of this book, you have learned to design APIs that make sense for consumers—ones that are easy to understand and easy to use without even thinking about it. Is that all you need to design APIs? Absolutely not. Thinking that an API designer's job ends here would even be a terrible mistake. Stopping here would inevitably result in the creation of unfit and even dangerous APIs. Indeed, we designed APIs without much consideration to the whole context surrounding them:

- Is our design totally secure given the intended functions of the API and how it will be exposed to users?
- Will it actually be usable by, let's say, a mobile application on a poor quality 3G network?
- Is our design actually the best one for our targeted consumers?
- Is it actually implementable upon our existing systems?
- Is our design so good that it does not need any documentation?
- Is our design totally consistent with all our other APIs?
- What if we want to update it once it has been pushed into production—can that be easily done?

All these questions must be answered. As API designers, we must take the whole context surrounding an API into account when designing it. Hopefully, you will learn to do so in the following chapters.

We'll talk about security first. API security is not an afterthought delegated to someone else after design. An API must be secure *by design* to ensure that consumers, end users, and anyone or anything between them cannot do or see more than they are supposed to. This requires API designers to understand API security mechanisms, to know how to partition an API to facilitate access control, to include security concerns when designing from the consumers perspective, and, most importantly, to know how to handle sensitive material.

Then we'll see that an API is a living thing; it will irremediably evolve. Designing API modifications requires extra care in order to avoid introducing breaking changes that will force all consumers to update their code to be able to use the updated API. Knowing how to do so is a key skill for API designers, but knowing how to design APIs that are evolvable from the ground up and lessening the risk of breaking changes when modified is even more important.

After that, we'll talk about network constraints. A mobile application running on a smartphone over a 3G network doesn't have the same constraints as an application running on a server on a local network. API designers must ensure that their design will actually be usable for the targeted consumers in their environment. They also must ensure that the design is actually efficient for all use cases, including edge cases which can, for example, imply more data or more calls.

We'll also see that if network efficiency is a major constraint, it is only one among many. Designing APIs requires us to be aware of all constraints from both the consumer's and also the provider's side in order to create APIs that are totally usable and actually implementable.

In the last two chapters, you will discover that API designers have more to do than just designing APIs. We'll talk about documentation. No matter how good a design, it must be documented in order to help not only consumers but also stakeholders understand it. An API must also be documented so the people in charge of its implementation can build it accurately. Just like security, API documentation should not be an afterthought. It is not something that can be completely delegated to someone else after the design; API designers must participate in it.

And finally, we'll see how API designers can contribute to the growth of the organization's API surface. By reviewing API design at various stages from various perspectives, the whole team can ensure that the resulting API will actually be what is expected. API designers have to participate in these reviews, even for APIs they are *not* working on. It is also fairly common to have many API designers working on many APIs in the same organization. This requires that all of them share what they do and how they do it—by creating design guidelines and building a community—in order to ensure a certain consistency and avoid everyone losing time reinventing the wheel.

Designing a secure API

This chapter covers

- The intersection between API security and API design

- Defining user-friendly scopes for access control

- Adapting API design to meet access control needs

- Adapting API design to handle sensitive material

Designing APIs that make sense for their users and are usable is definitely important, but this must not be done without considering security. API security is not an afterthought that you can assume will be handled later (whenever that is) by the security people (whoever they are). Indeed, design and security are inextricably linked when creating an API or anything else.

Regularly, there is some news about a company having been "hacked" through their APIs, especially private ones used for mobile applications. I put quotation marks around hacked because sometimes such hacking is at a kindergarten level. Indeed, in some cases, hackers simply inspect the API responses and discover sensitive data that should have never left the depth of the provider's systems. There is also the classic "What happens if I change the user ID in a request?" … "I get other users' data!"

This is not because an API is *private* or for partners and only used by trusted consumers, so it can expose anything without us giving thought to security. Public API security is usually treated more seriously as long as the people involved actually know what API security means. Security matters for *all* types of APIs; and, as an API designer, you have a part to play in API security.

You must at least have a basic understanding of API security in order to design secure APIs and communicate efficiently with the people involved in their creation. An entire book, if not several, could be written about this topic; the aim of this chapter is only to give an overview without providing details about the actual implementation of API security. Books such as *OAuth 2 in Action*, written by Justin Richer and Antonio Sanso, or *API Security in Action*, written by Neil Madden, both published by Manning (https://www.manning.com/books/oauth-2-in-action and https://www.manning.com/books/api-security-in-action, respectively), provide more detailed information about this topic. While this discussion will obviously be far from complete, it should be sufficient to help you understand how API designers can create APIs that are *secure by design*. Figure 8.1 zooms in on an API call from a security perspective to illustrate where API security and API design collide.

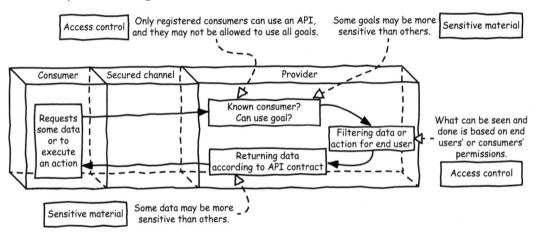

Figure 8.1   Zooming in on an API call from the security perspective

When the Banking API's provider receives API calls, it must do some high-level access control in order to be sure that the consumers are known and allowed to use the requested API goal. Then the provider proceeds with some lower-level access control measures to ensure, for example, that the end users only see their own accounts.

In certain cases, the request and response can contain sensitive personal data that should be handled carefully. The goal itself could also be a sensitive one, such as transferring money, and require extra care. *Access control* and *sensitive material* are the primary areas where API security and API design intersect. We will dive into both of these, but first, we need to dig a little deeper into API security.

8.1 An overview of API security

In order to design secure APIs, you must know some basic API security principles. It is important to also understand what these principles mean, not only for the developers of both API consumers and providers, but also for the end users. We will explore all of this by walking through the three steps of a first API call: registering a consumer, getting credentials allowing consumption of the API, and making the API call. Besides providing a glimpse of an API ecosystem, what follows gives a very simplified and partial vision of the OAuth 2.0 authorization framework defined by RFC 6749 (https:// tools.ietf.org/html/rfc6749). Although it is not the only option, it is commonly used to secure web APIs.

8.1.1 Registering a consumer

Secure APIs only allow known consumers to use them. When developers want to use an API in their consumer applications, whether they are mobile applications or back-end ones, they must first register them. To do so, they can use the API provider's *developer portal.*

An ideal developer portal is a website offering documentation, tutorials, FAQs, forums, support, and any other useful resources and tools that developers can take advantage of to understand what the API does and how to use it. It also provides information about API consumption; developers can check how their consumers use the API and can also have access to logs of the API calls. Developers have to register themselves (and perhaps provide payment information if the API is not a free one). Once that is done, they can register their consumers. Figure 8.2 shows a basic consumer application registration process for the Banking API.

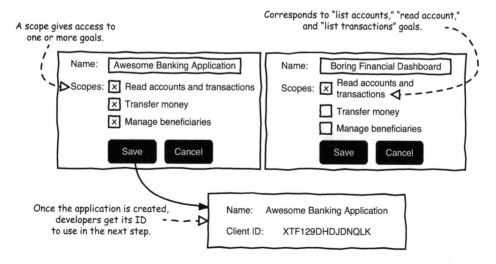

Figure 8.2   Registering a consumer to select which part of the API will be used and to get credentials

Each consumer is given a name. Here we have an Awesome Banking Application and a Boring Financial Dashboard. Then developers have to select which scopes of the API their consumers will use. A *scope* corresponds to one or more goals of the API. The Boring Financial Dashboard uses only the read accounts and transactions scope, which corresponds to the list accounts, read account, and list transactions goals. Therefore, this consumer will only be allowed to use these three goals. The Awesome Banking Application uses all scopes and will, therefore, be allowed to use all of the API's goals. Once this configuration is done, developers can retrieve a *client ID* for their applications, which will be used in the next step.

Not all APIs, especially private ones, come with a developer portal. The same configuration can be done by storing (securely, of course) the application name, scopes, and credentials in a database, for example. Whatever the means, once the consumers are registered, the developers can proceed to the next step: getting the credentials that allow consumers to use the API. Let's see what this means for the Awesome Banking Application.

8.1.2   *Getting credentials to consume the API*

If you've ever used a Sign Up with Google/Twitter/GitHub/Facebook button, what you'll see now should look familiar. The Awesome Banking Application is a third-party application created by the Awesome Company. Its end users are customers of the Banking Company that provides the Banking API. The Awesome Banking Application and its end users must be authenticated in order to get a *token*, which contains the credentials allowing the application to consume the Banking API.

Figure 8.3 shows the roles played by the different parties involved. (This is a simplified and partial view of the OAuth 2.0 implicit flow, which is one way, among others, of getting credentials to allow consumption of an API. Its intent is only to be a support example; it is not a prescription. Security measures must be chosen by security experts. Do not use this specific method without knowing what you are doing.)

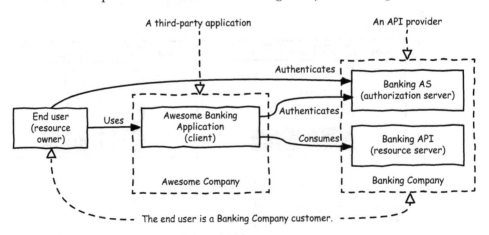

Figure 8.3   Roles involved in the OAuth 2.0 implicit flow

The *resource server* is the application providing the Banking API. The *client* is the third-party Awesome Banking Application that consumes the Banking API. The *resource owner* is the end user using the Awesome Banking Application. And last but not least, the *authorization server* is the application that verifies the identity of the consumer and the end user. Figure 8.4 shows how these parties work together.

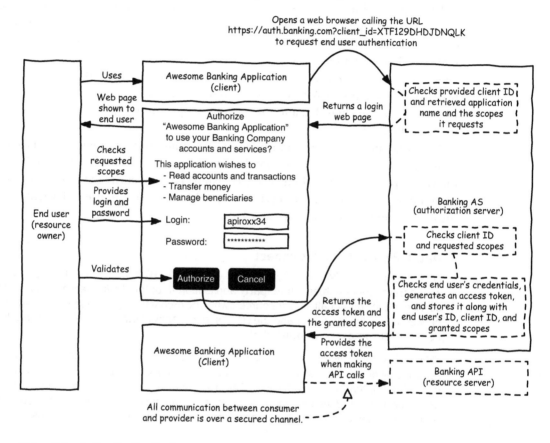

Figure 8.4 Authenticating the Awesome Banking Application and its end users, which provides an access token allowing them to consume the Banking API

To retrieve the credentials, the Awesome Banking Application first contacts the Banking Company's authorization server to request the end user's authentication. This is usually done by opening a web browser window pointing to the authorization server's URL and including the client ID in a query parameter (https://auth.banking.com?client_id=XTF129DHDJDNQLK, for example).

When the authorization server receives this request, it checks that the provided client ID corresponds to a known consumer. If so, it retrieves the consumer's name (Awesome

Banking Application) and the scopes it requests (read accounts and transactions, transfer money, and manage beneficiaries), according to the configuration in figure 8.2. Then it returns a login web page including this information. End users have to check that what the application wants to do (the requested scopes) is appropriate. If so, they provide their login and password and then click the Authorize button.

Clicking this button sends the user's login and password, along with the list of scopes, to the authorization server. It checks that the requested scopes match the ones defined in the client's (the Awesome Banking Application) configuration. And it checks that the end user's login and password are valid. If everything is in order, it generates an *access token*, the credential that allows the Awesome Banking Application to consume the Banking API. The authorization server stores this token along with the end user's ID, the client ID, and the granted scopes; and, finally, it returns the access token to the application.

Note that any communication between consumer and provider takes place over a secured channel, ensuring that nobody can intercept the exchanged data. When using the HTTP protocol, this is done using Transport Layer Security (TLS) encryption (formerly known as the Secure Sockets Layer, or SSL). If you've ever used a URL of the form https://example.com, you have used TLS.

OAuth 2.0 and OpenID Connect

According to RFC 6749 (https://tools.ietf.org/html/rfc6749), "The OAuth 2.0 authorization framework enables a third-party application to obtain limited access to an HTTP service, either on behalf of a resource owner by orchestrating an approval interaction between the resource owner and the HTTP service, or by allowing the third-party application to obtain access on its own behalf."

This framework provides various flows in order to obtain access to an API on behalf of a resource owner. Each flow has its pros and cons and must be used in the right context. It is only an *authorization* framework; OAuth 2.0 does not provide any information about *how* users are authenticated (identified). OpenID Connect (https://openid.net/connect/) is an authentication protocol based on OAuth 2.0, which provides these features.

Now that the Awesome Banking Application has its access token, it can start to consume the Banking API. We look at that in the next section.

8.1.3   *Making an API call*

As a first call to the Banking API, the Awesome Banking Application can request to list the user's accounts, as shown in figure 8.5.

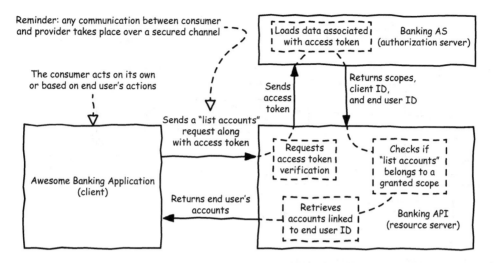

Figure 8.5   The Awesome Banking Application requests to list accounts.

To do so, it sends a list accounts request to the Banking API (over a secured channel, of course). This request also contains the access token retrieved previously. When the Banking API receives this request, it contacts the authorization server to check if the access token is valid. If it is a valid token, the authorization server can return the data attached to it, such as the end user's ID, the client ID, and the granted scopes.

The Banking API's implementation first checks that the list accounts goal belongs to one of the scopes granted to the Awesome Banking Application. Because the read accounts and transactions scope was granted to the end user, as described in the previous section, the implementation proceeds to the next step.

The consumer requests the list accounts goal without further explanation. Should the implementation return *all* the available accounts? Certainly not! The consumer's request is made in the context defined by the data attached to the access token. The end user's ID is attached to the access token, and the implementation uses it to filter the accounts. That way, it returns only the accounts that should be returned to the user making the request.

We've now been through all the steps of our first API call. We understand the mechanics, but let's see what all this means from the API designer's perspective.

8.1.4   *Envisioning API design from the perspective of security*

Figure 8.6 sums up the basic security principles you have seen so far and which of these have an impact on API design.

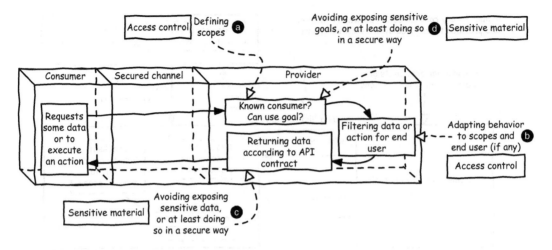

Figure 8.6   How API security and API collide

You have seen that all communication between consumer and provider should take place over a secured channel, ensuring that no data can be intercepted. This has nothing to do with API design, but it's always good to know that the communications are secure. You have also seen that only registered consumers should be allowed to consume an API. These consumers should only be allowed to use the parts of the API they really need and to which end users have requested access.

On the other side, the implementation needs to know which consumer is requesting a goal in order to verify that it is actually allowed to use this goal. Defining scopes (a), partitioning the API in order to grant access to only selected goals, cannot be done without input from the API designers because these groups of goals must make sense for developers as well as end users. Besides knowing if a consumer is allowed to use a goal, the implementation (b) also needs to know on whose behalf a request is being made in order to adapt its behavior to the specific end user's rights. If end users are actually involved, that is not always the case. That matter is the implementation's job, but API designers should keep this in mind because it can impact the design of the API.

Is that all? Do API designers just have to think about access control to design secure APIs? No. There is another, far less obvious aspect of API security that matters for API designers.

The Awesome Banking Application can list accounts over a secure connection only if it provides a valid access token, and the scopes attached to that token encompass this goal. The returned accounts are only the ones owned by the end user attached to the access token. That sounds totally secure, doesn't it? But what if for each account, the data returned contains a list of all the debit cards attached to it? And what if for each card, the provided data includes its number, security code, expiration date, and the account holder's full name? That would be a huge problem because this data is highly sensitive.

Should the Banking API provide such data? Probably not. Thinking about API design from the perspective of security is not only a matter of access control; it also involves asking the question, "Should we really expose this data (c) through our API?" And this question matters not only for data but also for goals (d).

So, to create APIs that are secure by design, API designers must take care of application access control, end user access control, and sensitive material. Let's see how we can do that.

8.2 Partitioning an API to facilitate access control

Let's start with one of the most obvious aspects of secure API design: how to partition an API to facilitate access control. But first, let's talk about why we must group goals in scopes in order to grant consumers access to only selected goals, and why we must take care with the design of these groups.

In the real world, a hotel is often seen as a whole entity (especially by its guests). Besides rooms, hotels can provide services such as a swimming pool, fitness center, sauna, or spa. These services are usually offered to all guests; they are included in the room price. But sometimes, some of these services are optional. Guests have to tell the hotel staff they want to use them and pay for them in addition to their room price. Some of the services can even be accessible to people who are not staying at the hotel. These customers pay to use only these services without using the rest of the hotel's features. This means that, from the hotel guest and non-guest customer's perspectives, the hotel is but a business providing multiple services that can be accessed independently. At the hotel's reception desk, customers can request access to all or some of these services. The customers then will only be able to use the services they have been granted access to.

This can, even *must*, happen in the API world too. As we saw in section 8.1.1, two different consumers might not use the same goals. Figure 8.7 shows the different goals used by the Awesome Banking Application and the Boring Financial Dashboard.

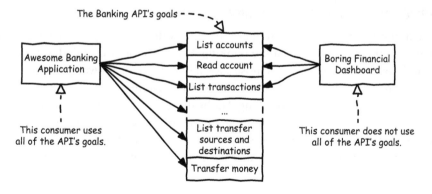

Figure 8.7   Different consumers with different needs do not use the same goals.

The Awesome Banking Application uses all the available goals, while the Boring Financial Dashboard only uses the list accounts, read account, and list transactions goals without ever needing to use the others. But does that mean that this consumer should *not* be allowed to use those other goals? Why would we implement such access controls on an API? The Open Web Application Security Project (OWASP; https://www .owasp.org), a worldwide not-for-profit charitable organization focused on improving the security of software, states that

> *"Every feature that is added to an application adds a certain amount of risk to the overall application. The aim for secure development is to reduce the overall risk by reducing the attack surface area."*

> *OWASP*

By limiting consumers' access to only the goals they really need, you reduce the likelihood of an attack. This is the principle of *least privilege*, which can also be applied to data. Because web APIs can be exposed on the internet, the fewer open doors there are, the better. And as with hotels, some of your API's features can require different paid subscriptions, so you would not want to see consumers who haven't paid the fee using those freely. Enabling access controls eases the process of granting access to different areas of your API to selected consumers only. That's two good reasons for designing scopes. But we must also take care in *how* we design these in order to provide the best developer and end user experiences possible.

When developers register their consumers to use an API, they have to select the appropriate scopes. The same goes for end users: when they allow a third-party application to access an API on their behalf, they have to check the requested scopes and possibly select these by themselves. So an API's goals should be partitioned into various groups, called *scopes*, in order to enable access control mechanisms, and these scopes should be carefully designed. Let's see how we can do that.

8.2.1   Defining flexible but complex fine-grained scopes

A first, a simple way of defining scopes is to bluntly define a scope for each goal. While configuring their consumers via the Banking API's developer portal, developers might see configuration screens such as those shown in figure 8.8, allowing them to select the scopes (or goals, in this case) they need for each consumer.

Configuring the Awesome Banking Application, which provides full access to all of the Banking API's services, requires selecting all of the scopes. Only the list accounts, read account, and list transactions scopes are selected for the Boring Financial Dashboard, which focuses on account activity analysis. Configuring the PayFriend App,

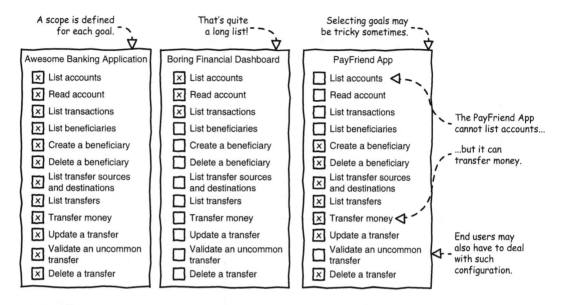

Figure 8.8   Controlling access with fine-grained, goal-based scopes

which proposes to allow its users to easily send money to friends, is trickier. The money transfer-related goals have to be selected carefully. The validate an uncommon transfer scope is unselected for this application because it is meant to be used only by bank advisors to validate certain money transfers that are judged to be unusual, based on their destination or amount. Once the configuration is done, each of these consumers will only be able to use the goals corresponding to the scopes selected for them. For example, the PayFriend App cannot list accounts but can trigger a money transfer.

With 12 scopes corresponding to the 12 goals of the Banking API, the access control configuration is quite flexible, but it can be considered complex. Each scope has to be carefully selected. What if there are more goals and, therefore, more scopes to deal with? The complexity increases. And what if we allow third-party applications to use the API on the behalf of their end users? Those end users will have to deal with this complex configuration too. Both developers and end users can feel overwhelmed or annoyed by the process of carefully selecting a few scopes from a lengthy list.

Maybe we can define less fine-grained and more user-friendly scopes by basing these on concepts and actions. If you have been designing your API using the method described in section 3.2, this should be quite simple because you've already done something like that. Figure 8.9 shows how to define such scopes for our Banking API.

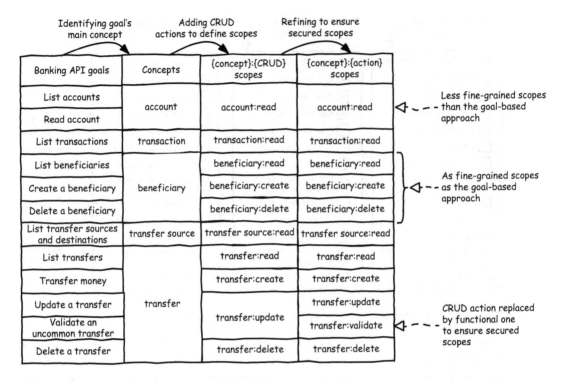

Figure 8.9   Defining fine-grained scopes based on concepts and actions

The first step consists of identifying the main concept (or resource) for each goal. You begin by identifying the main noun in the goal. For example, both the list accounts and read account goals deal with the concept of an *account*. Then you identify the CRUD (Create, Read, Update, Delete) action that best represents the goal's main verb. For these two goals, it is Read; therefore, these fall under the `account:read` scope. Note that the scope-naming convention `{concept}:{action}` is quite common but might not be too user-friendly. Such scope names are usually accompanied by a helpful description, such as

```
"account:read": list accounts and access detailed information about those
```

Unfortunately, this technique does not always reduce the number of scopes. For the beneficiary-related goals, we still end up with three scopes matching the list beneficiaries, create a beneficiary, and delete a beneficiary goals. In some cases, this can even cause problems.

The update a transfer and validate an uncommon transfer goals both update a money transfer and, therefore, could be grouped under the `transfer:update` scope. But that would not be very secure! By allowing a consumer to update a money transfer, we would also allow them to use the far more critical validate an uncommon transfer goal. In this case, it would be wiser to keep this goal under a specific `transfer:validate` scope that uses a custom action instead of a CRUD one.

Partitioning based on concepts and actions can produce scopes that are still flexible, but a little less fine-grained and complex. This must be done carefully, however, to avoid inadvertently granting undue access to critical goals, and the improvement is fairly minimal. Let's think back to what we learned in chapter 7 about designing a concise and well-organized API. Can we use those concepts to try to organize the goals into coarser scopes and provide a more usable solution?

8.2.2 Defining simple but less flexible coarse-grained scopes

In section 7.1.3, you learned how to organize goals into categories. Why not use them as scopes? Figure 8.10 shows what these category-based scopes would look like for the Banking API.

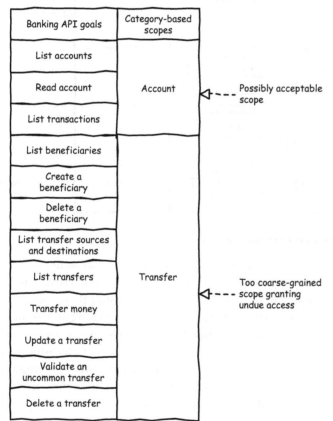

Figure 8.10 Defining category-based scopes is usually not a good idea.

The account scope seems acceptable, but the transfer one is too broad; it might grant undue access to beneficiary-related goals and the critical validate an uncommon transfer. Categories, therefore, are usually not fit to be taken as a basis for scopes because they have different purposes:

- *Categories*—Organize goals from a functional perspective and help consumers understand how to use the API
- *Scopes*—Ensure that consumers are only granted access to the goals they really need

If categories do not work well, how are we supposed to organize our goals into meaningful but secure groups? We can try to base them on what the users can achieve using the API. Such scopes correspond more or less to the whats we identified when filling in the API goals canvas (see section 2.3). Figure 8.11 shows a partial API goals canvas for the Banking API focusing on transfers.

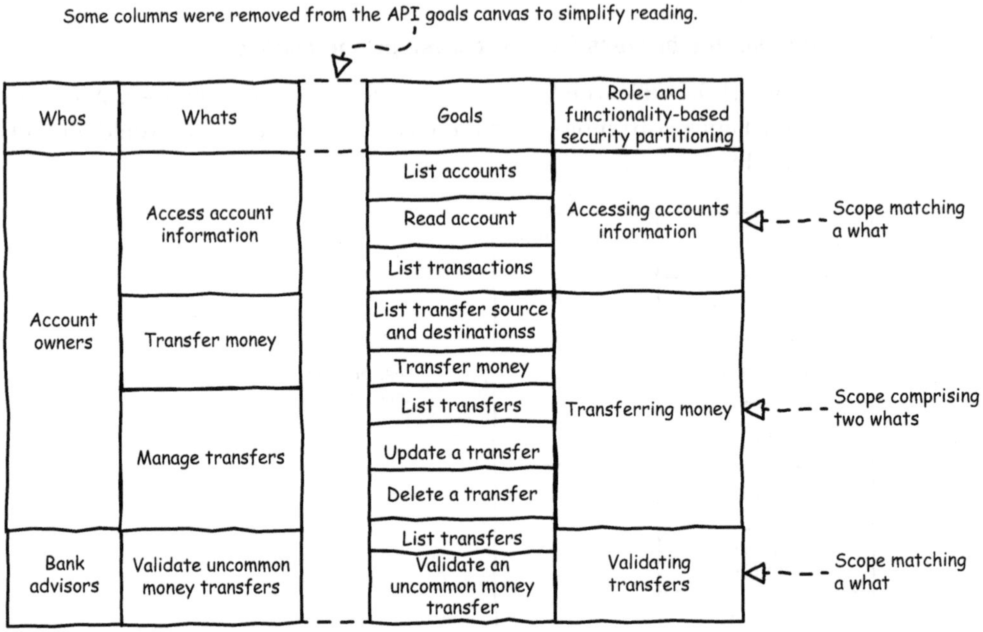

Some columns were removed from the API goals canvas to simplify reading.

Whos	Whats	Goals	Role- and functionality-based security partitioning	
Account owners	Access account information	List accounts	Accessing accounts information	Scope matching a what
		Read account		
		List transactions		
	Transfer money	List transfer source and destinationss	Transferring money	Scope comprising two whats
		Transfer money		
	Manage transfers	List transfers		
		Update a transfer		
		Delete a transfer		
Bank advisors	Validate uncommon money transfers	List transfers	Validating transfers	Scope matching a what
		Validate an uncommon money transfer		

Figure 8.11   Defining role- and functionality-based scopes

This canvas tells us that to access account information, account owners list accounts, read an account, and list its transactions. Therefore, we could create an accessing account information scope matching this what and comprising these three goals. The same goes for bank advisors, who are responsible for validating uncommon transfers. The corresponding goals can be grouped under a validating transfers scope. We could proceed the same way for the transfer money and manage transfers whats, but it might not really make sense to separate these. For example, after creating recurring transfers, consumers might want to be able to delete those once they aren't needed anymore. Therefore, maybe we should create a transferring money scope comprising these two what's.

To practice, I'll let you complete the API goals canvas with the other goals and define the scopes accordingly. As you can see, this way we end up with fewer, less flexible, but more user-friendly scopes. Such coarse-grained scopes can be seen as a kind of shortcut to grant consumers access to several goals at once.

NOTE   Such a role- and functionality-based scope definition strategy should help you avoid inadvertently granting access to critical goals, but you should always double-check this just in case.

You can also create totally *arbitrary* scopes. In some use cases, this might make sense. For example, you could define administrator-level scopes on each resource: a `beneficiary:admin` scope granting access to all goals related to beneficiaries, and so on. You'll have to be careful when defining such scopes, however, because they could allow undue access if granted to applications without the appropriate care.

You've now seen a few different ways of defining scopes. Which one should you use?

8.2.3   Choosing scope strategies

Which strategy is the best when it comes to defining scopes to enable access control on an API? The flexible but complex fine-grained strategy or the less flexible but more user-friendly coarse-grained one? And within each strategy, which approach should you adopt? Unfortunately, there is no one right answer. Depending on the API's consumers, developers, and end users, the most suitable approach can vary. But there's good news: you might not have to choose a single one!

Beyond creating coarse-grained and user-friendly scopes, the whats-based strategy shows something interesting about scopes. In figure 8.12, you can see the goals covered by two of the scopes we just defined.

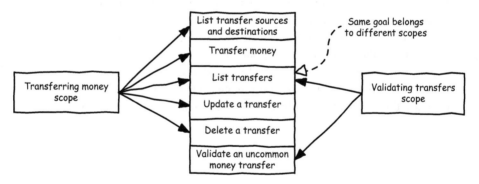

Figure 8.12   The same goals can belong to different scopes.

The list transfers goal belongs to two scopes! This is the good news: it means that there can be some overlap between scopes. This allows us to define different *levels* of scopes.

We could, for example, use a concepts- and actions-based approach, having scopes such as `beneficiary:read` and `beneficiary:delete` along with an arbitrary one, where all goals covered by these scopes would also be covered by a `beneficiary:admin` scope. We could even add a more user-friendly third level of scope using the whats-based strategy for third-party integrations involving end users. We are under no obligation to show or allow all of our API scopes to all of our consumers; we can provide different views of the available scopes when necessary. And, as we've done before, we can take advantage of the API description format to define these scopes.

8.2.4   *Defining scopes with the API description format*

If the API you're designing is associated with an API description format, be sure to check if it allows you to describe scopes. As illustrated in the following listing, the OpenAPI Specification 3.0 allows this.

Listing 8.1   Describing scopes

```
components:
  securitySchemes:
    BankingAPIScopes:          ◄──── Reusable scopes are defined in
                                      components.securitySchemes.
      type: oauth2
      flows:                         You can put in a dummy URL during the
        implicit:                    design phase if needed. (Note: URL
          authorizationUrl:    ◄──── should be on the same line.)
            "https://auth.bankingcompany.com/authorize"
          scopes:
            "beneficiary:create": Create beneficiaries
            "beneficiary:read": List beneficiaries
            "beneficiary:delete": Delete beneficiaries
            "beneficiary:manage": Create, list, and delete beneficiaries
```

A security scheme can contain more than one scope. (annotation pointing to scopes)

The scope definition is done in the `components.securitySchemes` section of the OpenAPI document. The `BankingAPIScopes` scheme defines all the flows and scopes that can be used in the Banking API when using the `oauth2` security type. For now, only the `implicit` flow is available, and when this flow is used, only the scopes related to the beneficiaries are allowed.

There are four scopes defined in this listing. Each scope definition comes with a description. The first three are goal-based ones: `beneficiary:create`, `beneficiary:read`, and `beneficiary:delete`. The fourth one, `beneficiary:manage`, is an arbitrary scope encompassing the three beneficiary-related goals. Defining these scopes is not enough, though. They must be linked to goals, as shown in the next listing.

Listing 8.2   Linking a goal to scopes

```
paths:
  /beneficiaries:
    get:
      tags:
        - Transfer
      description: Gets beneficiaries list
      security:
        - BankingAPIScopes:        ◄──── References a security scheme from
            - "beneficiary:read"          components.securityScheme and lists
            - "beneficiary:manage"        scopes needed to use this goal
      responses:
        "200":
          description: The beneficiaries list
```

Lists the security schemes used (annotation pointing to security)

The list beneficiaries goal is represented by GET `/beneficiaries`. It is covered by the `beneficiary:read` and `beneficiary:manage` scopes of the `BankingAPIScopes` security scheme we defined in listing 8.1. This means that only consumers that have been granted access to at least one of these two scopes can use this goal.

If an API uses two types of scopes, it can be useful to make a distinction between them in the API description. This could be done simply to provide clearer documentation or to enable showing only specific types of scopes, depending on who is using the API, for example. The following listing shows how to organize scopes in different groups.

Listing 8.3   Grouping scopes

```
components:
  securitySchemes:
    ConceptActionBasedSecurity:          ◄──  Contains only
                                              goal-based scopes
      type: oauth2
      flows:
        implicit:
          authorizationUrl: "https://auth.bankingcompany.com/authorize"
          scopes:
            "beneficiary:create": Create beneficiaries
            "beneficiary:read": List beneficiaries
            "beneficiary:delete": Delete beneficiaries
    ArbitraryBasedSecurity:          ◄──  Contains the
                                          higher-level scope
      type: oauth2
      flows:
        implicit:
          authorizationUrl: "https://auth.bankingcompany.com/authorize"
          scopes:
            "beneficiary:manage": Create, list, and delete beneficiaries
```

Again, we apply what you discovered in chapter 7: in designing a concise and well-organized API, we organize the API components to ease understanding and use. The BankingAPIScopes security scheme has been split into two new security schemes, each containing a given type of scope. The following listing shows how to use these new security schemes.

Listing 8.4   Linking a goal to scopes from different groups

```
paths:
  /beneficiaries:
    get:
      tags:
        - Transfer
      description: Gets beneficiaries list
      security:          ◄──  The security section can contain
                              references to different security schemes.
        - ConceptActionBasedSecurity:
          - "beneficiary:read"
        - ArbitraryBasedSecurity:
          - "beneficiary:manage"
      responses:
        "200":
          description: The beneficiaries list
```

The security section now contains references to the ConceptActionBasedSecurity and ArbitraryBasedSecurity security schemes, each of which lists the scope that's used, just like in listing 8.2.

To practice, you can expand this example by adding the other Banking API goals and three levels of scopes (goal-based, arbitrary, and action-based). You could also add another type of OAuth flow, such as the client credential one (hint: look for the "OAuth Flows Object" description in the OpenAPI Specification documentation at https://github.com/OAI/OpenAPI-Specification).

Now that you've seen how to define scopes, let's look at how the API's interface contract can be impacted by lower-level access control matters.

8.3   *Designing with access control in mind*

These days, hotel guests are usually given access cards instead of good old keys. They can use these cards in elevators to gain access to the floors where their rooms are located; and, of course, they can use them to open the doors to their rooms. And, obviously, they cannot use their cards to open the doors of other guests' rooms.

The hotel staff members also have cards, which they can use to access staff-reserved floors or guests' rooms. Different staff members can have access to all of the hotel's rooms, or only the ones located on a given floor. Both guests and staff members have access to the hotel's floors and rooms, but they don't all have the same level of access.

In the API world, low-level, fine-grained access control of this sort exists too. It is mostly handled by the implementation, but API designers also have a role to play here. To ensure that everything goes smoothly, API designers must know what data is needed to actually implement the access controls and adapt their designs if necessary.

8.3.1   *Knowing what data is needed to control access*

Just because the Awesome Banking Application is allowed to list accounts doesn't mean it should be allowed to list *all* accounts. It can only retrieve the ones belonging to its end users, the Banking Company's customers. Now, what if the Banking Company creates a Bank Advisors App using the Banking API for its bank advisors managing the customers' accounts? What should the list accounts goal return for this consumer? Should it return all the customers' accounts or only the ones related to customers managed by the bank advisors? Whatever the answer, list accounts will not have the same behavior when it is triggered for a customer or for an advisor. As shown in figure 8.13, each consumer has a different view of the bank accounts accessible via the list accounts goal.

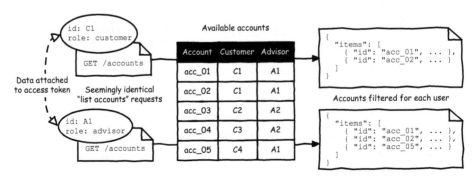

Figure 8.13   Two seemingly identical requests giving different results

In this example, the design of the API does not seem to be affected. In both cases, the representation of the list accounts goal is the same: as a REST API, it would be something like GET /accounts—without any parameters. Its behavior will be modified according to the identity of the end user; but there is no endUserId parameter in the GET /accounts request, so how do we know who this end user is? Actually, this parameter does exist, but it is somewhat hidden.

As you saw in section 8.1.3, consumers must send an access token with their request to make an API call, just like hotel guests have to use their access card to open doors. When this token has been created, it is stored somewhere, along with some minimal security data. This data is a hidden part of the API interface contract. As an API designer, you must know about it in order to be sure that what you design actually works and is secure.

Such data is relatively standard; it usually consists of the consumer ID, the granted scopes, the end user's ID, and possibly the end user's role (the type of user) or permissions (what this specific user is allowed to do). When the implementation receives the request along with the token, it can retrieve the security data and do all necessary access control directly, based on the request's data or based on some other retrieved data.

For example, if the Awesome Banking Application sends a GET /accounts/1234567 request, the implementation must check that the end user whose ID is attached to the access token sent along with the request is referenced as one of the 1234567 account's holders. To be sure about this, however, you'll need to check with those in charge of implementation or, more precisely, those in charge of the security layer. In our case, it's quite simple, but be warned that the access control mechanism is not always so transparent. Also, a goal might need slightly different representations for different end users or roles.

8.3.2 *Adapting the design when necessary*

In section 5.2, we focused on the transfer money goal, which transfers a sum of money from a source account to a destination account. A money transfer is always initiated by a customer's request. The source account belongs to this customer. The destination account is an account also belonging to this customer or to a beneficiary registered beforehand by the customer. The REST representation of this goal consists of a POST /transfers request, whose body contains the three properties amount, source, and destination.

If this goal is used by the Awesome Banking App, which is used by Banking Company customers, a customer's ID is attached to the token sent along with the request. Therefore, the implementation can easily check that everything is in order. It checks that the source account belongs to the customer and also that the destination account belongs to the same customer or a beneficiary registered by this customer.

But what if this transfer money goal is used by the Bank Advisor App? This application is not used by customers, only by bank advisors. Customers, however, can call their bank advisors to request a money transfer. In this case, the user ID attached to the token is the advisor's ID and not the customer's.

The controls in the implementation are less simple but still feasible. The implementation checks that the source account belongs to a customer managed by the advisor. The destination account should belong to the customer owning the account or a beneficiary registered by the same customer. Everything seems to be OK, but there's a problem. The system needs to trace which customer requested the money transfer.

If the bank account belongs to a single customer, it is easy to find the customer's ID because it's the one attached to the bank account, and only the owner of the account can request a transfer. But if the account is a joint one belonging to more than one customer, this doesn't work. The goal needs to be modified in order to convey the correct customer ID to the implementation.

We could add an optional `customerId` property into the `POST /transfers` request's body. We could also create a new representation of the `transfer` resource and use the `POST` method on it like this:

```
POST /customers/{customerId}/transfers
```

The second option seems to make more sense if we step back and look at the API from a higher level. A bank advisor might need to list a customer's transfers, so a

```
GET /customers/{customerId}/transfers
```

using the same resource path could be useful. Whatever the chosen solution, the implementation will now be able to check that, when the transfer money goal is made on the behalf of advisors, it can only do that for customers for whom they have the rights to do so.

Actually, if you use the API goals canvas and the method described in section 2.3, which was to identify all users, what they do, how they do it, and especially what they need to do it, you should be able to deal easily and almost seamlessly with API design versus API security questions. As a reminder, this method is shown again in figure 8.14.

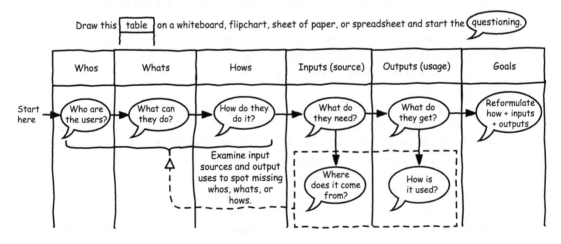

Figure 8.14   The API goals canvas

Working with scopes has shown that even though API designers should avoid the provider's perspective in their designs, they sometimes need to know what's happening in the implementation after all.

There is one last API security topic to work on, and this is probably the most important one from the API designer's point of view. An API exposes data or capabilities. It's therefore up to the API designer to check if these are sensitive, if they should really be exposed, and, if so, to choose the most secure way to include them in the API.

8.4 Handling sensitive material

When people stay in a hotel, they usually do not bring all of their belongings with them. It would not make sense to bring valuable or sensitive items like one's income tax return, a great-great-great-grandmother's jewelry, or a precious and rare Samba de Amigo Maracas set (needed to play the Sega Dreamcast video game of the same name). They probably won't be needed, and they could be either lost or stolen. But there are other valuable items (ID cards, passports, phones, or cameras, for example) that people do need to bring. If these belongings have to be left in the hotel room, they can be secured in the room's safety deposit box. Cash and credit cards can also be secured the same way.

In the API world, as in the software world in general, we must always check whether what can be requested, provided, or done through an API involves sensitive material. If so, we must ensure that it is really needed and then create the most secure design possible. This can be done either by tuning how sensitive material is represented or by choosing adapted access control mechanisms. This matter primarily concerns the API's data, goals, and feedback, but we must also take care with the underlying protocol and architecture used by the API.

8.4.1 Handling sensitive data

When consumers use the read account goal, they get detailed information about an account. This can consist of the account's number, its balance, and the list of debit cards linked to it. In the Banking Company's systems, the basic information linked to a card consists of its holder's name, its number (also called the Primary Account Number, or PAN), its expiration date, and its CVV (Card Verification Value, located on the card's back). Cards provided by the Banking Company can be blocked (useful when you think your card might be lost or stolen). And if customers want to, they can also define a monthly ceiling (they receive an alert by SMS, email, or via a notification when their total monthly payments exceed this level). The data returned might look like what is shown on the left in figure 8.15. But even if this data is sent over a secured connection (see section 8.1.3), is it really wise to return *all* the available data?

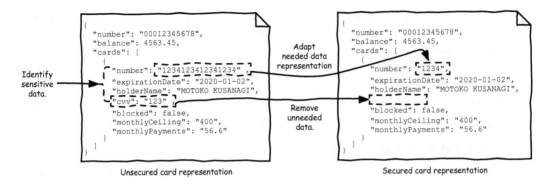

Figure 8.15   **Designing a secure representation of a banking card**

The monthly ceiling, monthly payments to date, and blocked flag are non-sensitive data; no harm can be done with them. On the other hand, the card's number, CVV, holder's name, and expiration date are quite sensitive; this information can be used to make payments online or by phone. Maybe we should think twice before returning all this information.

The CVV is only used for online payments, and it is written on the card itself, so we can remove it. The card number is useful to identify a card, but we could keep only the last four digits; these are sufficient to identify a card in the context of a bank account. We can keep the expiration date and the card holder's name because this is relevant information. Now that we have removed the CVV and chosen a secured representation of the card number, nobody can take advantage of this data to do harm. As you can see, by identifying sensitive data items and choosing to remove some and adapt the representation of others, we're able to design a secure representation of a debit card that remains meaningful and relevant.

So the first step of secure API design is to identify the sensitive data that will be requested and provided via the API. The problem is that the term *sensitive data* covers a wide range of data and can be different, depending on your domain or industry. Identifying sensitive data is sometimes quite simple, as in the debit card example, because what should be considered sensitive is pretty obvious. Similarly, nobody would expose sensitive data such as customers' usernames and passwords. But sometimes, it's not that obvious.

There are many country-specific, domain-specific, and international regulations, standards, or best practices that affect whether and how you can manipulate data. When any system deals with bank cards, it has to comply with the global Payment Card Industry Data Security Standard (PCI DSS). In the US, the Health Insurance Portability and Accountability Act (HIPAA) is a set of standards created to secure protected health information (PHI) by regulating healthcare providers. The General Data Protection Regulation (GDPR) is a European Union regulation impacting any company dealing with European citizens' data.

Whatever the reason why such regulations or standards exist, they can impact the data manipulated through your API. And this is not only a functional matter; there are best practices on the technical side as well, which API designers and implementers should follow. For example, usually it is not recommended to return sequential database keys that would give hints about critical data like how many customers your company has; such sequential data could be used to try to access data belonging to others (although, if your implementation handles access control perfectly, that shouldn't be a problem).

> **NOTE** Always check with your CISO (Chief Information Security Officer), DPO (Data Protection Officer), CDO (Chief Data Officer), or legal department to be sure about which data should be considered *sensitive*.

Once you know which data is sensitive, the second step consists of choosing appropriate representations for that data. As a reminder, doing such adaptations *is* designing the API. Therefore, it requires us to focus on what the consumers can do using the API and not on the data itself.

How the representations will be adapted highly depends on how the data will be used. In the debit card use case, the goal was only to provide detailed information about an account and its linked cards, not to allow users to execute a payment. In that case, it makes sense to not provide the full card number and its CVV. Having this goal-oriented mindset will simplify the adaptation. Figure 8.16 shows four techniques that you can use to create secure representations.

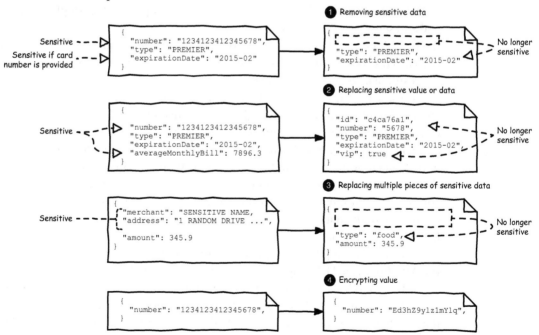

Figure 8.16   Adapting representations of sensitive data to make it non-sensitive

The first technique is simple: you remove any sensitive data that is not required (1). This can have a nice side effect: some sensitive data related to the data that's removed can become non-sensitive. In figure 8.16, for example, removing the sensitive `number` property (a card number) makes the `expirationDate` property non-sensitive.

If sensitive data cannot be removed, you might be able to replace it with a non-sensitive adaptation, as we did with the card number (2). Here, the value of `number` is truncated to make it non-sensitive. Also, the sensitive `averageMonthlyBill` is replaced by a non-sensitive `vip` flag, whose value is the result of `someFunction(averageMonthly-Bill)`. In this case, a goal-oriented design process would probably have solved this problem from the start.

Sometimes it can be useful to combine value and data replacement. For example, if the sensitive data is used as an identifier, it might be more practical to simply create a new non-meaningful identifier to identify a resource instead of using a meaningful but sensitive one. The truncated number, such as `5678`, can be useful to show to end users but not to use as a resource identifier. A `/cards/5678` resource path will probably be unique in the context of a customer, but perhaps not in the wider context of an advisor. Therefore, the card representation might benefit from a totally new `id` containing an opaque ID such as `c4ca76a1`. The resulting `/cards/c4ca76a1` resource path would be unique in both contexts; and, depending on your needs, this new ID could be a replacement of `number` or an addition to the card representation. Note that like removing sensitive data, replacing sensitive data can make other sensitive data non-sensitive. Here, the sensitive `expirationDate` becomes non-sensitive once `number` is replaced.

Data replacement can be applied to multiple properties (3). Replacing a set of precise and sensitive values by a more fuzzy but still meaningful one can also do the trick. In the technique illustrated in figure 8.16, the sensitive `merchant` and `address` properties of a card transaction are combined in a new non-sensitive `type` property, whose value is the result of `someFunction(merchant, address)`.

As a last resort, if sensitive data is really needed as is and if the communication channel's encryption is not enough, the sensitive values can be encrypted (4). In the example in figure 8.16, the value of `number`, which is `1234123412345678`, is encrypted as `Ed3hZ9ylz1mYlq`. But this technique has some downsides. Notably, consumers will have to decrypt the encrypted data to use it. When it comes down to this, it might be simpler and more effective to encrypt the entire messages exchanged over a secured connection established between the consumer and provider. The safest option would be to encrypt the data specifically for each consumer and provide each with the correct key to decrypt the data.

All of this is the job of the people managing the security layer and implementing the API. But as an API designer, you must ensure that all this security stuff is consumer-friendly. By talking to the security people and using the techniques you have learned about how to design APIs, you should be able to design secure representations. But the data exchanged via an API is not the API's only sensitive material—some API goals can be sensitive too.

8.4.2 Handling sensitive goals

There are two kind of sensitive goals: those that manipulate sensitive data and those that trigger actions with sensitive consequences. As with sensitive data, whatever the reason a goal is considered sensitive, the first question you ask yourself must be, "Is this goal really needed?" If not, to keep the API design secure, not including it in the API is the simplest way to deal with it. But that is not always possible.

Let's say that, for a very good reason, the Banking API must provide a card's sensitive information (such as number, CVV, expiration date, and holder's name) to some consumers or end users. It would be wise to ensure that the access to this data is tightly controlled. As shown in figure 8.17, this matter could be handled in four different ways.

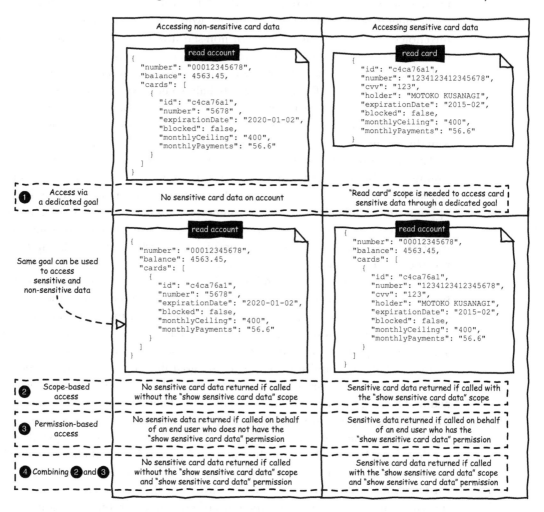

Figure 8.17   Controlling access to goals exposing sensitive data

A first option (1) could be to create a dedicated read card goal providing access to the card's sensitive data. This new goal could be protected by a specific read card scope granted only to the consumers that really need it. The read account goal could stay as it is and still provide the non-sensitive version of the card data.

A second option (2) could be to use a scope to trigger the return of sensitive data. The read account goal would return non-sensitive representations of the card data by default, except for consumers who have been granted the show sensitive card data scope. The implementation of these goals would return the raw sensitive card data instead of the adapted non-sensitive data.

In the first two options, if end users are involved, they will be able to see the sensitive data when using a consumer with the right scope. That might not fit some security requirements. Therefore, a third option (3) would be to do the same thing, but handle the choice of returning the sensitive or non-sensitive representation based on the permissions or roles of the end user attached to the access token.

But using end user permissions only would mean that *any* consumer that has been authorized to use the API on the users' behalf would have access to the sensitive data. If that is a problem, a fourth option (4) could be to combine consumer and end user access control to ensure that access to sensitive data is possible only when an end user with the adequate permissions uses a consumer with the required scope.

The choice of options and which is appropriate to use depends on security constraints and also developer experience. As with designing secure data representations, you will have to talk to the security people in your organization in order to know which options are possible. Also, from a consumer experience perspective, if there's a wide gap between the sensitive and non-sensitive versions of the data, it would be better to provide dedicated goals to access sensitive data instead of modulating the version returned, based on scopes or permissions.

But goals can be sensitive even if they do not manipulate sensitive data. Let's take it for granted that in our Banking API, we're working on a secure representation of the card data and none of its properties are considered sensitive. Besides the basic card data, this representation contains the `blocked` flag and the `monthlyCeiling` amount. These two properties could be updated by end users or, more precisely, by consumers on their behalf. We could add an update card goal allowing this data to be updated. But even if updating the threshold of payments above which an alert is sent is not a sensitive action, blocking the card is quite a sensitive one. Therefore, it would be wise to ensure that blocking a card is done only by end users or consumers allowed to to so.

We can use exactly the same options for this that we used with the goal dealing with sensitive data. We could rely on the end users' permissions and check the implementation to see if the user is allowed to update the `blocked` flag when using the update card goal. We could also rely on a block card scope that would allow a consumer to do the same thing when using this update card goal. And obviously, we could mix these two options. All this would work, but mingling sensitive and non-sensitive data updates in the same goal can make the API complex, especially if the update of sensitive data requires additional security measures like multifactor authentication of end users. In that case, the `monthlyCeiling` property can be updated at once, but the `blocked` property only when the user validates it. It would probably be better to create a dedicated block card goal to handle this update. If we step back and think more about what the API can do and less about the data itself, such a goal makes sense.

So handling sensitive goals requires us to identify whether these manipulate sensitive data or trigger sensitive actions. Once that's done, and we're really sure we need these, we can rely on scopes or permissions to ensure that only authorized consumers and end users can access those goals. But using only scopes or permissions might not be sufficient.

It is sometimes better to adapt the interface contract to provide dedicated, clearly identified, and fine-grained goals handling the sensitive parts (data or actions). Such design adaptation facilitates access control and keeps the API easy to understand and use. But what happens when consumers try to do something they are not allowed to do? What kind of feedback do they get? And should API designers also be concerned about security when designing other kinds of feedback?

8.4.3 Designing secure error feedback

In section 5.2, you learned how to design exhaustive and informative error feedback that helps consumers to solve problems themselves. There we identified two types of errors: those due to a malformed request and those caused by contravening a business rule. Here we need a new security error type to clearly signify security-related errors. The feedback for these errors could use the same kind of representation—a message and a code. What might happen when a consumer triggers a security-related error when calling the Banking API, say, by sending a `GET /cards/c4ca76a1` request?

If a consumer sends a request without providing a token or provides an invalid one, the Banking API server can return a `401 Unauthorized` response. This response might contain a body with a message such as `Missing or invalid token`. If the same consumer retries its request with a valid token but that consumer has not been granted access to the read card scope, the server can return a `403 Forbidden` response accompanied by a `Consumer has not been granted the "read card" scope` message and a `SCOPE` code. And if the consumer tries again after the developer has updated the configuration to add the missing scope, the server can return another `403 Forbidden` response with an `End user is not allowed to access this card` message and a `PERMISSIONS` code. This last response obviously means that the end user does not have permission to read this specific card.

In some circumstances, this last error could be considered an *information leak*. Indeed, explicitly mentioning that the user is not allowed to access the `c4ca76a1` card implicitly confirms that this card actually exists. To avoid such a leak, the Banking API server can instead say that the card does not exist in the context of the end user. It can do that by returning a `404 Not Found` response with a `Card does not exist` message, just like it would do when a consumer requests a card that actually does not exist.

You should also keep the risk of information leaks in mind when designing mal-formed request or functional error feedback. For example, a consumer might try to update a card with a `PATCH /cards/c4ca76a1` request that uses a secure card ID. If the consumer provides an invalid `monthlyCeiling` value to update this card, it would be a terrible idea to return a message containing sensitive information, such as the full card number, as in `Impossible to update the 123412341234124 card`.

And there is another type of error that we did not discuss yet and that is prone to a crit-ical information leak: the unexpected ones; for example, a good old `java.lang.Null-PointerException` (trying to `something.do()` when `something` is `null` in Java) or the quite annoying `Unable to extend table in tablespace` (when there's not enough disk space to extend an on-premise database table to add some data). Obviously such errors *never* happen because everything is fully tested, monitored, and automated ... until they happen, usually at the worst possible moment.

When using the HTTP protocol, such errors are represented by a 5XX class status code, usually the `500 Internal Server Error`. While a 4XX status means it's the con-sumer's fault, a 5XX means it's the provider's. When such unexpected server errors occur, the implementation must never provide detailed information about the tech-nical stack behind the API. You can provide an error ID for further investigation, but be careful not to provide any information that can give a hint about what is actually running behind the interface. So no stack trace and detailed error-describing software versions, server addresses, or the like can appear in such errors. Table 8.1 sums up the various error types you have seen so far.

Table 8.1   Error feedback use cases

Error type	Use case	HTTP status code
Security	Missing or invalid credentials	`401 Unauthorized`
Security	Invalid scopes	`403 Forbidden`
Security	Invalid permissions	`403 Forbidden` or `404 Not Found`
Malformed request	Unknown resource (wrong path parameter)	`404 Not Found`
Malformed request	Missing mandatory parameter or invalid parameter	`400 Bad Request`
Functional	Infringing business rule	`400 Bad Request` or `403 Forbidden`
Technical	Unexpected server error	`500 Internal Server`

As you can see, security error feedback resembles the feedback for other types of errors. When designing a REST API, you just have to use the appropriate HTTP status for these errors, such as 401 or 403. But don't forget that you must be careful about what kind of information you provide with security or technical error feedback (and any other type of feedback) to avoid inadvertently providing access to sensitive information. We're almost done, but there's one last topic to be aware of to be sure that your API handles sensitive material appropriately.

8.4.4 Identifying architecture and protocol issues

How much should we trust the architecture and protocol that will support the APIs we're designing? Not much if we don't know much about them. Figure 8.18 shows a basic (and flawed) API architecture that might be used for the REST Banking API. This example highlights that the secure connection between consumer and provider might not always be as secure as we think.

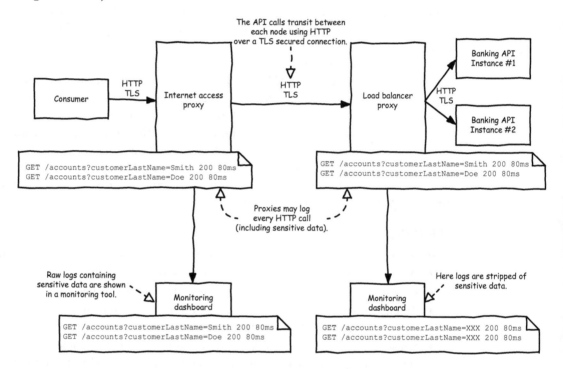

Figure 8.18 A not-so-secure connection between consumer and provider

In this basic architecture, the consumer passes through a proxy to access the internet and make HTTP calls to the Banking API. The Banking API is not exposed directly on the internet; there is another proxy, an HTTP load balancer, that distributes the requests to various instances of the Banking API server application. The communication between nodes is secured using TLS.

Everything seems to be totally secure, but if we take a closer look, we can see that the load balancer logs some data (the HTTP method; URL, including query parameters; an HTTP status code; and response time). The content of these log files is sent to a monitoring tool that can be used to create shiny, useful dashboards showing how the Banking API is used and behaves. That means that anyone who has access to the load balancer's logs or the monitoring tool can see the data contained in a resource path and its query parameters.

Of course, the Banking Company is very strict when it comes to security. All these logs are stripped of sensitive data. The Banking Company, however, does not control what happens on the proxy used by the consumer, which can also log the HTTP calls. Obviously, it is up to the consumer to secure that. But the Banking API can be designed to ensure that if URLs are logged, they do not contain any sensitive information.

For example, if the list of accounts can be filtered by customer name using a request like GET /accounts?customerLastName=Smith, that's a problem. A name is sensitive information, and the customerLastName query parameter will be traced in every HTTP log on the wire between the consumer and the provider. To avoid this potential data leak, it would be safest to propose a POST /accounts/search request, whose body contains the search parameters.

If you are designing a REST HTTP API, take care not to put any sensitive information in path parameters or query parameters because they can be logged. And, for the protocol used to communicate and the architecture built for the API, always check if there are any possible data leaks. If there are potential leaks that could expose sensitive data, you must adapt the API's design accordingly to prevent this.

In the next chapter, you will learn how designing an API's evolution requires extra care to avoid provoking errors on the consumer side and how to minimize this risk from the ground up when designing an API.

Summary

- API designers contribute heavily to API security by minimizing the attack surface.
- An API should only expose and request what is really needed.
- Consumers should only be allowed to use what they really need.
- To ensure security, the design of an API must be done from the user's perspective, keeping in mind what data is needed to control access.
- Sensitive data and goals cover a wide range; exactly what should be considered sensitive might not be obvious and should be identified with the help of technical, security, business, and legal experts.
- API designers must be aware of potential leaks due to the underlying protocol or architecture in order to fully secure the API design.

Evolving an API design

In the previous chapters, you learned how to design APIs that provide features or goals that make sense for their users. You also learned how to design user-friendly and secure representations of these goals. Once all that work is done, is that the end of the API designer's job? Not at all! It's a new beginning.

An API is a living thing that will inevitably evolve, perhaps to provide new features or enhancements to existing ones. To design for such evolutions, you can reuse the same skills you have learned up to this point—but designing evolutions requires some extra care.

Over the years, I've bought several Ikea Billy bookcases to store books, comic books, CDs, LPs, and many other things. A standard Billy bookcase comes with four movable shelves that you can place as you want, thanks to the many holes drilled on both of the internal sides. You just have to place four pegs at the desired height, place the shelf on them, and you're done. If a bookcase is used to store small items like CDs or paperback books, using only four movable shelves can leave a lot of empty space. Fortunately, additional shelves can be bought independently, allowing you to use the empty space to store more small items. But the last time I bought extra shelves for a Billy I'd owned for quite a long time, I had an unpleasant surprise—the pegs were too small to fit well in the holes of my good old Billy.

The 2.0 Billy system uses pegs with a smaller diameter, which are incompatible with the holes of the previous version. I wasn't aware of this until I tried to use these new pegs; it wasn't indicated anywhere when I bought my extra shelves. This was a real bummer. Such *breaking changes* can happen when evolving an API too.

What might happen if the Banking API's provider decided that the balance's currency must now be returned with the bank account's information in order to support various currencies? Figure 9.1 shows how evolving the Banking API in this way could lead to a scenario equivalent to the Billy's peg diameter modification.

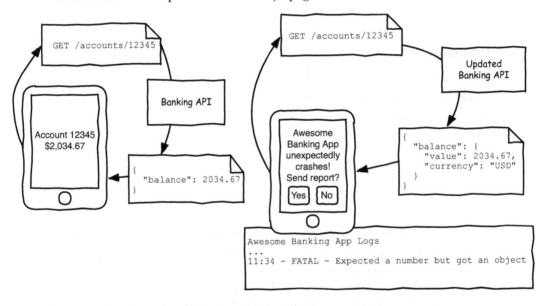

Figure 9.1   A consumer encountering a breaking change after updating the Banking API

In this scenario, the `balance` property, which was a number, is now an object containing a value (the former balance) and its currency (an ISO 4217 currency code string). Although using an ISO 4217 currency code is clever (as you learned in section 6.1.4), modifying the balance this way is definitely not a good idea. Indeed, the Awesome Banking App crashes when parsing the returned data because it expects the `balance` to be a number, not an object. The developers in charge of coding this consumer would usually catch such errors, avoiding crashes like this, but the errors will still prevent the consumer application from functioning properly. To fix this problem, the mobile application needs to be updated.

A *breaking change* is a change that will cause problems for consumers if they do not update their code. Most of the time you cannot synchronize an API update with all of its consumers' updates, so trying to avoid such breaking changes or at least being aware of them when designing an API's evolutions is definitely important. We can carefully design our evolutions in order to avoid introducing some problematic changes. We can even design APIs from the ground up in order to prevent them. But regardless of how carefully we design our APIs and their evolutions, sooner or later, a breaking change is inevitable.

As API designers, we must also be aware of the invisible side of the API contract—all observable behaviors that are not explicitly described in the interface contract that can silently evolve and provoke totally unexpected breaking changes.

To deal with these situations when they come up, it is wise to know how to version our APIs. We'll explore all of these topics in this chapter. We'll start by learning how to (carefully) design evolutions.

9.1 Designing API evolutions

The Banking API evolution described in this chapter's introduction illustrated a possible way of introducing a breaking change. The consumer crashed because of a modified data structure that became impossible to parse (a number became an object). But that's not the only way of introducing a breaking change. Although some are pretty obvious, like this data structure modification, others are more insidious, like modifying the possible values of a property. Also, the consequences might not always be that obvious because the changes might not cause a visible error on the consumer's side. A breaking change could even have impacts on the provider's side. I'll let you imagine what the consequences could be for both consumers and the provider if amount values in dollars were replaced by values in cents in the Banking API, especially for the transfer money goal.

Any modification of the interface contract of an API that can be described formally using an API description format or via textual API documentation can introduce a breaking change. This applies to output data, input data, parameters, response statuses or errors, goals and flows, and security. Knowing how to avoid breaking changes when possible and handling them gracefully when not is, therefore, critical for an API designer.

9.1.1 Avoiding breaking changes in output data

The Banking API proposes a list transactions goal that returns a list of transactions for an account number. The left part of figure 9.2 shows the data returned for each transaction. The right part shows a redesigned version that illustrates various ways of introducing breaking changes that will cause problems to consumers when retrieving an account's transactions list.

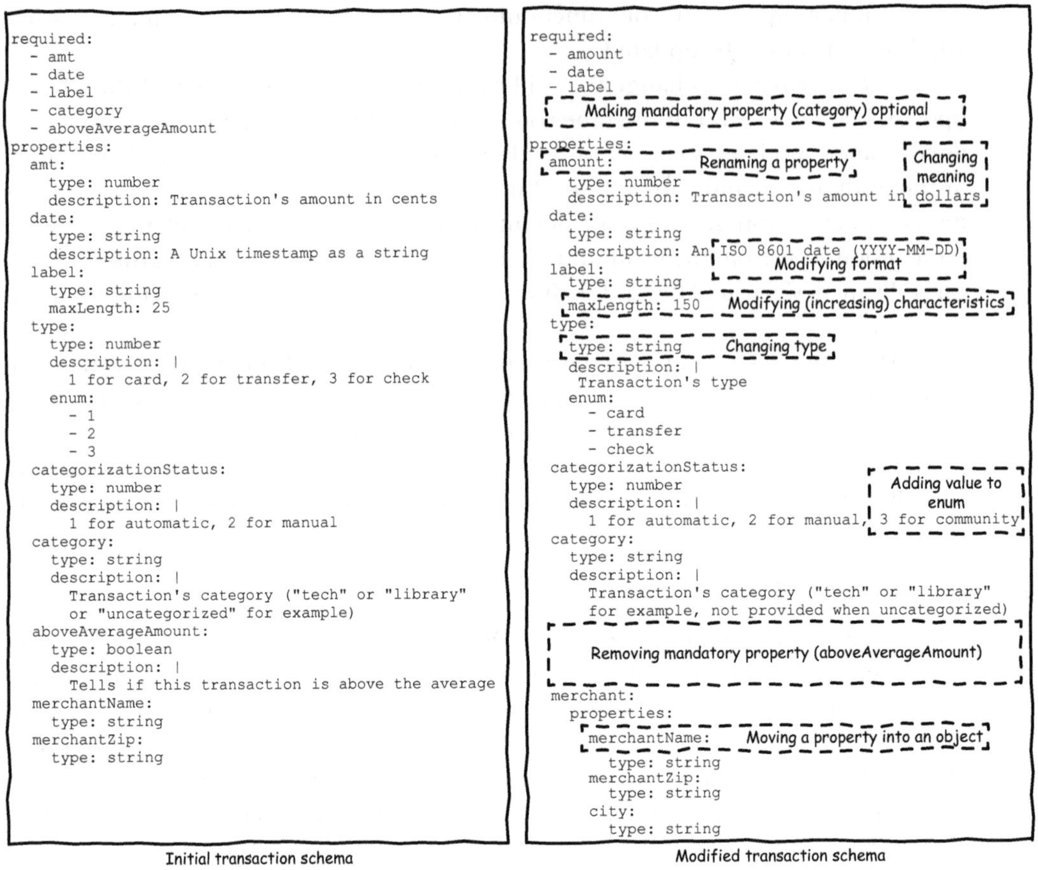

```
required:
 - amt
 - date
 - label
 - category
 - aboveAverageAmount
properties:
 amt:
   type: number
   description: Transaction's amount in cents
 date:
   type: string
   description: A Unix timestamp as a string
 label:
   type: string
   maxLength: 25
 type:
   type: number
   description: |
    1 for card, 2 for transfer, 3 for check
   enum:
    - 1
    - 2
    - 3
 categorizationStatus:
   type: number
   description: |
    1 for automatic, 2 for manual
 category:
   type: string
   description: |
    Transaction's category ("tech" or "library"
    or "uncategorized" for example)
 aboveAverageAmount:
   type: boolean
   description: |
    Tells if this transaction is above the average
 merchantName:
   type: string
 merchantZip:
   type: string
```

Initial transaction schema

```
required:
 - amount
 - date
 - label
        Making mandatory property (category) optional
properties:
 amount:              Renaming a property        Changing
   type: number                                   meaning
   description: Transaction's amount in dollars
 date:
   type: string
   description: An ISO 8601 date (YYYY-MM-DD)
 label:                        Modifying format
   type: string
   maxLength: 150  Modifying (increasing) characteristics
 type:
   type: string      Changing type
   description: |
    Transaction's type
   enum:
    - card
    - transfer
    - check
 categorizationStatus:
   type: number                Adding value to
   description: |                  enum
    1 for automatic, 2 for manual, 3 for community
 category:
   type: string
   description: |
    Transaction's category ("tech" or "library"
    for example, not provided when uncategorized)

    Removing mandatory property (aboveAverageAmount)

 merchant:
   properties:
    merchantName:    Moving a property into an object
      type: string
    merchantZip:
      type: string
    city:
      type: string
```

Modified transaction schema

Figure 9.2   How to introduce breaking changes in the list transactions goal's output

The new designer has renamed the amt property amount, to make its meaning clearer. Based on what you have learned, this is good design, but this change can have a significant impact on the consumer side. The Android version of the Awesome Banking App, which is not as well coded, can crash with the famous java.lang.NullPointer-Exception. The iOS version might just show the transactions without amounts, leaving its end users quite annoyed. A more complex Financial Statistics consumer that does some calculations based on the transaction amounts might consider that each transaction's amount is 0, and this could corrupt its data. Also, moving the merchantName and merchantZip properties into a new merchant structure (because a property for the merchant city has been added, and the designer has presumably read section 7.1.1 of this book) are also examples of breaking changes causing a parsing exception.

What about the `aboveAverageAmount` property that was removed, perhaps because this information was not considered important? Is this a problem too? Definitely, because this property is mandatory. In the initial version of this transaction, it was supposed to always be provided, so removing it could cause the same sorts of problems as renaming `amt` or moving `merchantName`.

Another issue is with the transaction's `type`, which was a number, indicating if it was a card (1), transfer (2), or check transaction (3). It is now a string (because the new designer knows that human-readable codes are usually better than cryptic ones). Although benevolent, such a change will probably cause a parsing error on the consumer side; and even if it doesn't, interpretation of the new values will likely be impossible.

Renaming, moving, or removing properties and changing their types are obvious ways of introducing breaking changes in output data. But some other modifications are more insidious.

The `category` property was mandatory, but it has been made optional. Consumers used to always get it, and now, if they don't, they could face the same problems described in the `amt` renaming case. The `date` property was a string, and it still is, but its format has changed. It was a UNIX timestamp with a string format. While it was usually represented by a number, now it's an ISO 8601 date (the new designer decided to fix this awkward design). Again, this change is benevolent, but it will cause parsing errors on the consumer side.

The modification to the `label` property can also be a breaking change. Its maximum length has been changed from 25 to 150, perhaps because the core banking system behind the Banking API has been updated in order to manage full labels and to stop truncating these. If, on the consumer side, this value is stored in a good old relational database, where its column's size is defined as 25, it will be impossible to store the longer values. These are insidious breaking changes, but there are even less obvious ones.

Look more closely at the descriptions. In the original version, the `amt` description states that the transaction's amount is in cents; but, in the new one, the value is in dollars. When receiving an `amt` value such as 3034 (cents), consumers understood it to be $30.34. Now, they will receive an `amount` value of 30.34 in dollars and will understand it as $0.3034. This might provoke some panic on the consumer side.

Less critically, the `categorizationStatus` was a numerical code indicating how the transaction has been categorized: 1 for automatic and 2 for manual. In the new version, a new code value has been added. The consumers will not be able to interpret the value 3 without being updated. And even if this code had been a human-readable one, such a modification might have been a problem because the application consuming the API might not have been able to interpret it.

That's a lot of different ways of introducing breaking changes. Table 9.1 sums up the various types of modifications and their consequences.

Table 9.1   Breaking changes to output data and their consequences

Modification	Consequences
Renaming a property	Varies, depending on implementation (missing data in UI, data corruption, crash, and so forth)
Moving a property	Varies, depending on implementation (missing data in UI, data corruption, crash, and so forth)
Removing a mandatory property	Varies, depending on implementation (missing data in UI, data corruption, crash, and so forth
Making a mandatory property optional	Varies, depending on implementation (missing data in UI, data corruption, crash, and so forth)
Modifying a property's type	Parsing error
Modifying a property's format	Parsing error
Modifying a property's characteristics (increasing string length, number range, or array items count)	Varies, depending on implementation (database errors, and so forth)
Modifying a property's meaning	Expect the worst
Adding values to enums	Varies, depending on implementation (missing data in UI, data corruption, crash, and so forth)

This list might not be 100% complete, but you get the idea. As you can see, modifying existing elements in the output data can cause more or less obvious breaking changes with more or less significant consequences.

Now that we know how to introduce breaking changes in output data, let's see what kinds of modifications can be done safely. Figure 9.3 shows a backward-compatible evolution of the transaction's schema.

The merchant city information has simply been added as `merchantCity` without modifying the existing merchant properties. The new categorization status, which was supposed to indicate that the categorization was automatic, although based on other customers' data, is handled with the new `communityCategorization` Boolean flag. And replacing the transaction type code numbers with human-readable ones is handled by adding a new `typeLabel` property. Consumers will not be bothered by these new elements.

Another change is to the `type` property, which was optional and now has become mandatory. Instead of *sometimes* getting this property, consumers will *always* get it. Unlike making a mandatory property optional, this is a nonbreaking change. Is it necessary to make such a change? Probably not. It's not really critical. Consumers can go on using the API without being notified of the transaction type.

The label's format has also been changed in a backward-compatible way (purely for the purposes of illustration): its maximum length is now 25 instead of 100. As another example of a nonbreaking change, the optional `categorizationStatus` property could be removed. Depending on how the data is serialized (not all APIs use JSON), that could cause some problems, so it would be better to keep it and always return a `null` value instead.

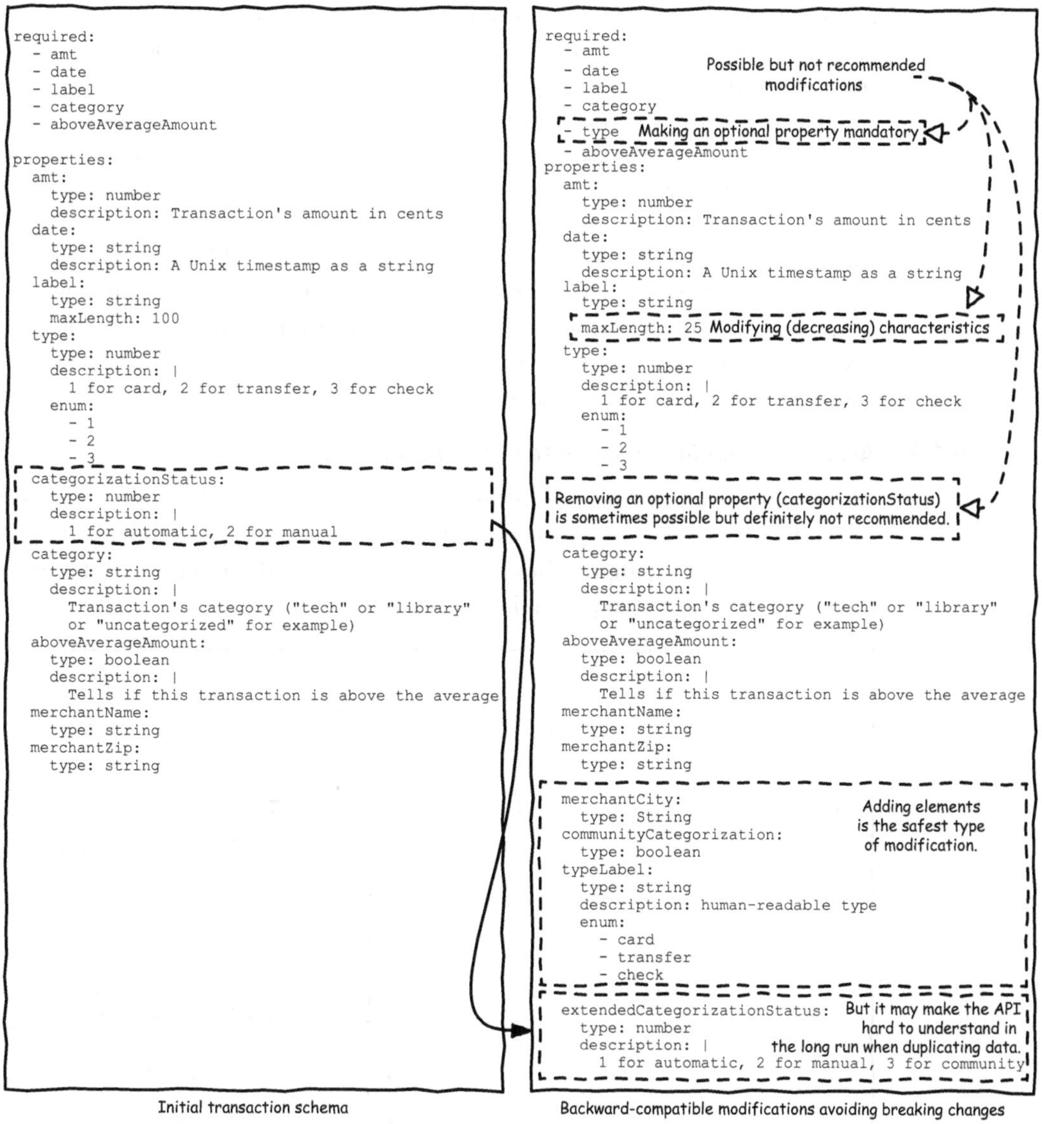

```
required:                          required:
  - amt                              - amt            Possible but not recommended
  - date                             - date                  modifications
  - label                            - label
  - category                         - category
  - aboveAverageAmount               - type   Making an optional property mandatory
                                     - aboveAverageAmount
properties:                        properties:
  amt:                               amt:
    type: number                       type: number
    description: Transaction's amount in cents    description: Transaction's amount in cents
  date:                              date:
    type: string                       type: string
    description: A Unix timestamp as a string    description: A Unix timestamp as a string
  label:                             label:
    type: string                       type: string
    maxLength: 100                     maxLength: 25  Modifying (decreasing) characteristics
  type:                              type:
    type: number                       type: number
    description: |                      description: |
      1 for card, 2 for transfer, 3 for check      1 for card, 2 for transfer, 3 for check
    enum:                              enum:
      - 1                                - 1
      - 2                                - 2
      - 3                                - 3
  categorizationStatus:
    type: number                   Removing an optional property (categorizationStatus)
    description: |                  is sometimes possible but definitely not recommended.
      1 for automatic, 2 for manual
  category:                          category:
    type: string                       type: string
    description: |                      description: |
      Transaction's category ("tech" or "library"      Transaction's category ("tech" or "library"
      or "uncategorized" for example)      or "uncategorized" for example)
  aboveAverageAmount:                aboveAverageAmount:
    type: boolean                      type: boolean
    description: |                      description: |
      Tells if this transaction is above the average      Tells if this transaction is above the average
  merchantName:                      merchantName:
    type: string                       type: string
  merchantZip:                       merchantZip:
    type: string                       type: string

                                     merchantCity:
                                       type: String         Adding elements
                                     communityCategorization:  is the safest type
                                       type: boolean        of modification.
                                     typeLabel:
                                       type: string
                                       description: human-readable type
                                       enum:
                                         - card
                                         - transfer
                                         - check
                                     extendedCategorizationStatus:  But it may make the API
                                       type: number               hard to understand in
                                       description: |           the long run when duplicating data.
                                         1 for automatic, 2 for manual, 3 for community
```

Initial transaction schema   Backward-compatible modifications avoiding breaking changes

Figure 9.3   Designing backward-compatible modifications to the output data

Notice that some of the modifications that were supposed to fix bad design, like changing the `amt` property's name, couldn't be made. This is something that API designers have to live with. Once consumers start to use a poorly designed API, it is impossible to fix it completely most of the time without introducing breaking changes.

The final result might not be the best design, but at least it lets the new designer introduce new features and partially fix some early design mistakes without breaking consumers' code. To be frank, the safest way to modify output data is purely and simply to add new elements. For new features (like `merchantCity`), that's quite simple: just add the new required data. But when it comes to slightly modifying existing ones (like the categorization status value), it is trickier to find a solution. There's no magic recipe, but you can try two approaches, as shown in figure 9.3.

First, you can treat this new value as a flag, as was done in figure 9.3 by adding the communityCategorization Boolean. Second, you can add a new property (say, extendedCategoryStatus) that shows the same data as categorizationStatus plus the new status. If this were done multiple times, however, the resulting design, comprising duplication of data, could be awkward and make the API difficult to understand.

Now, what about when modifying input data and parameters? Does it work the same way? Almost. And this subtle difference is important to know. Let's introduce some breaking changes in the transfer money goal's input data to contrast this with what you've learned about output data modifications.

9.1.2   *Avoiding breaking changes to input data and parameters*

The input shown on the left in figure 9.4 has been slightly modified from what we worked with in previous chapters to illustrate different (possible) breaking changes. The right part of the figure shows various ways a new designer evolving the API might introduce breaking changes in the input data.

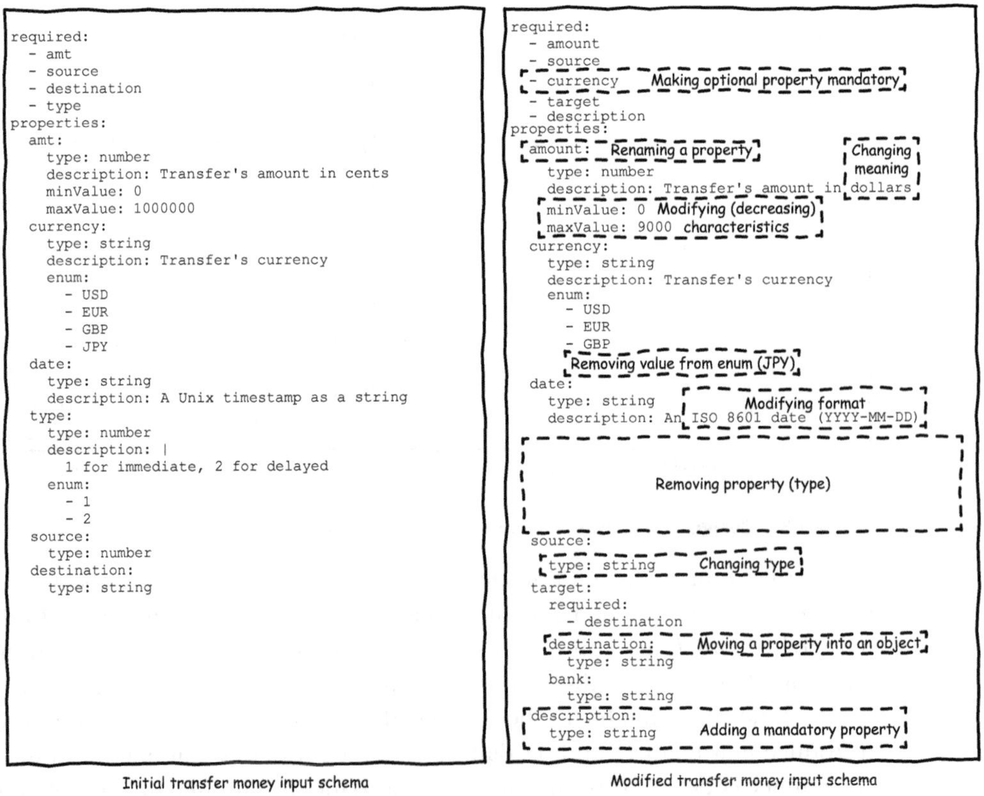

```
required:
  - amt
  - source
  - destination
  - type
properties:
  amt:
    type: number
    description: Transfer's amount in cents
    minValue: 0
    maxValue: 1000000
  currency:
    type: string
    description: Transfer's currency
    enum:
      - USD
      - EUR
      - GBP
      - JPY
  date:
    type: string
    description: A Unix timestamp as a string
  type:
    type: number
    description: |
      1 for immediate, 2 for delayed
    enum:
      - 1
      - 2
  source:
    type: number
  destination:
    type: string
```

Initial transfer money input schema

```
required:
  - amount
  - source
  - currency          Making optional property mandatory
  - target
  - description
properties:
  amount:             Renaming a property          Changing
    type: number                                   meaning
    description: Transfer's amount in dollars
    minValue: 0 Modifying (decreasing)
    maxValue: 9000  characteristics
  currency:
    type: string
    description: Transfer's currency
    enum:
      - USD
      - EUR
      - GBP
                Removing value from enum (JPY)
  date:
    type: string              Modifying format
    description: An ISO 8601 date (YYYY-MM-DD)

                  Removing property (type)


  source:
    type: string     Changing type
  target:
    required:
      - destination
    destination:          Moving a property into an object
      type: string
    bank:
      type: string
  description:
    type: string    Adding a mandatory property
```

Modified transfer money input schema

Figure 9.4   How to introduce breaking changes in the transfer money goal's input data

If the designer renames `amt` to `amount`, a non-updated consumer sending a transfer money request using `amt` will get an error. Depending on how the implementation is done, this error could be because `amt` is now an *unexpected* property or because the new `amount` property is *mandatory*. For a REST API that would mean that it would return a `400 Bad Request` response status.

The same goes for moving a property (here, moving `destination` inside `target`), modifying a property's type (changing `source` from a number to a string), and modifying formats in general (changing the format of `date` and the range of `amount`).

As with the output use case, modifying a property's meaning is a *silent* breaking change. The amount was previously in cents and is now in dollars; therefore, a consumer sending a money transfer of 8,000 cents will instead trigger a transfer of 8,000 dollars. That's a terrible side effect, and it will be up to the bank providing the API to get the money back because the error is on its side.

These breaking changes have a similar effect in both the input and output data use cases, but this is not the case for removing a mandatory property, making a mandatory property optional, or adding values to enums. Removing the mandatory `type` property is a breaking change that will cause an `unexpected property` error. It would be exactly the same if `type` were optional. Making a mandatory property optional has absolutely no consequences for the provider or consumers, but making an optional one (such as `currency`) mandatory will cause missing mandatory property errors. Adding values to enums also has no consequences, but removing values will cause invalid value errors.

So does this mean that, like in the output data case, adding data is the safest way of modifying input data? Not quite. Adding a mandatory property has the same consequences as turning an optional one into a mandatory one: the API will return a `missing mandatory property` error.

Breaking changes are slightly different when it comes to inputs and outputs. Table 9.2 sums up the possible types of breaking changes to input data and their effects, and compares them to the effects of the same or similar changes to output data.

Table 9.2 Breaking changes to input data and their consequences

Modification	Consequences	Effects on input vs. output
Renaming a property	API error	Identical
Moving a property	API error	Identical
Removing a mandatory or optional property	API error	Identical
Making an optional property mandatory	API error	Opposite (same as making a mandatory property optional)
Modifying a property's type	API error	Identical
Modifying a property's format	API error	Identical
Modifying a property's characteristics (decreasing string length, number range, or array items count)	API error	Opposite (same as increasing)

Table 9.2   Breaking changes to input data and their consequences *(continued)*

Modification	Consequences	Effects on input vs. output
Modifying a property's meaning	Expect the worst (impacts mostly provider)	Opposite (impacts mostly consumer)
Removing values from enums	API error	Opposite (same as adding values)
Adding a mandatory property	API error	No error (not a breaking change)

So how can we modify input data in a backward-compatible way? Let's analyze figure 9.5 to find out.

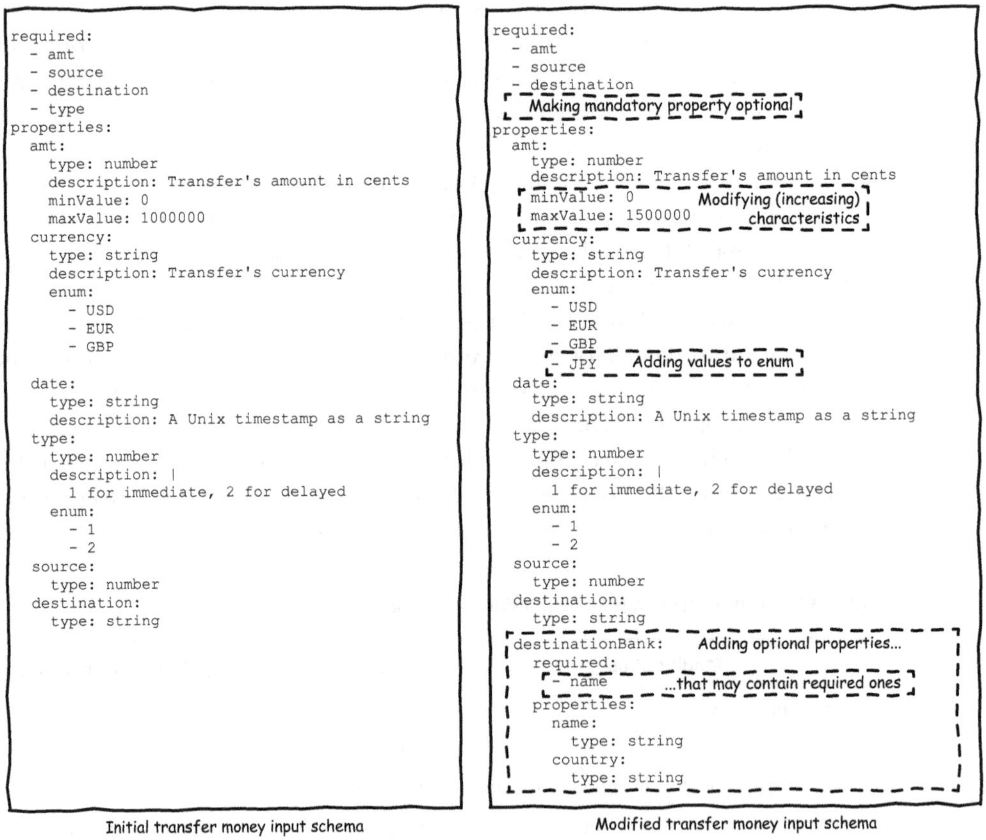

```
required:
  - amt
  - source
  - destination
  - type
properties:
  amt:
    type: number
    description: Transfer's amount in cents
    minValue: 0
    maxValue: 1000000
  currency:
    type: string
    description: Transfer's currency
    enum:
      - USD
      - EUR
      - GBP

  date:
    type: string
    description: A Unix timestamp as a string
  type:
    type: number
    description: |
      1 for immediate, 2 for delayed
    enum:
      - 1
      - 2
  source:
    type: number
  destination:
    type: string
```

Initial transfer money input schema

```
required:
  - amt
  - source
  - destination
                Making mandatory property optional
properties:
  amt:
    type: number
    description: Transfer's amount in cents
    minValue: 0        Modifying (increasing)
    maxValue: 1500000      characteristics
  currency:
    type: string
    description: Transfer's currency
    enum:
      - USD
      - EUR
      - GBP
      - JPY      Adding values to enum
  date:
    type: string
    description: A Unix timestamp as a string
  type:
    type: number
    description: |
      1 for immediate, 2 for delayed
    enum:
      - 1
      - 2
  source:
    type: number
  destination:
    type: string
  destinationBank:      Adding optional properties...
    required:
      - name      ...that may contain required ones
    properties:
      name:
        type: string
      country:
        type: string
```

Modified transfer money input schema

Figure 9.5   Designing backward-compatible modifications to the input data

You might have already guessed that the safest way is to only add optional properties. The destinationBank property is optional, so if consumers don't provide it in their requests, it will not cause an error. But note that the name property inside destination-Bank is mandatory. Indeed, if the added properties are objects, it doesn't matter if their properties are mandatory or optional.

We can also do two other types of modifications safely: a preexisting mandatory property like `type` can be turned into an optional one, and we can slightly modify a property's characteristics. For example, the range of `amt` (in cents) could be modified from `0` to `1000000` to a broader `0` to `1500000`. It is also possible to increase a requested string's maximum length or the number of items in an array. Note that for REST APIs, all of this also applies to query parameters and HTTP request headers.

We have seen that carelessly modifying a goal's input parameters or data can cause errors. These can be subject to breaking changes too. From a broader perspective, modifying how an API provides feedback, whether on success or error, is prone to introduce breaking changes.

9.1.3 Avoiding breaking changes in success and error feedback

Depending on the protocol used, feedback about how the processing of a request went can vary, but it is usually based on a combination of the data returned as a response to a request and some of the protocol's features. We'll talk about the data first.

For both success and error feedback, the data returned can be safely modified based on what you learned in section 9.1.1. There, you saw how to modify success feedback, so let's try to modify an existing error response.

As shown in figure 9.6, we could change the error feedback of the transfer money goal in order to introduce some breaking changes. In the modified version, the `items` property has been renamed `errors`. Consumers will not be able to get the detailed error information required to fix a problem now because they expect to find it in `items`. The same goes for the `type` property's values `MISSING_SOURCE` and `MISSING_DESTINA-TION`, which have been replaced by a generic `MISSING_MANDATORY`. The consumers will not be able to interpret the new error type.

From a pure data perspective, this means that error and success feedback data should be treated equally when it comes to modifying them in order to *avoid* breaking changes. From a functional perspective, the second breaking change means that we cannot introduce new types of errors into existing goals or change existing ones.

This example shows us an interesting thing about breaking changes, and, more specifically, about the scope of their consequences. Modifying the `type` value has an impact that is local to the goal itself, but renaming `items` to `errors` has a more global impact.

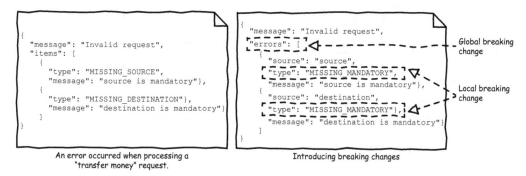

An error occurred when processing a "transfer money" request.

Introducing breaking changes

Figure 9.6 Introducing breaking changes in error feedback

Indeed, because the error message data structure is probably the same across the whole API, this renaming might have been done not only for the transfer money goal but for all goals. That means that not a single consumer will be able to interpret the error feedback of any goal without updating its code. That's quite a breaking change.

Breaking changes with such wide impact are not limited to errors, but can happen when modifying any common feature of an API. For example, changing naming conventions for resource IDs to comply with better guidelines is a global breaking change affecting inputs and outputs. So it's better to look twice at such modifications and apply what you learn in this chapter about avoiding breaking changes. And regarding protocol features, let's see what could happen if we modify HTTP status codes (figure 9.7).

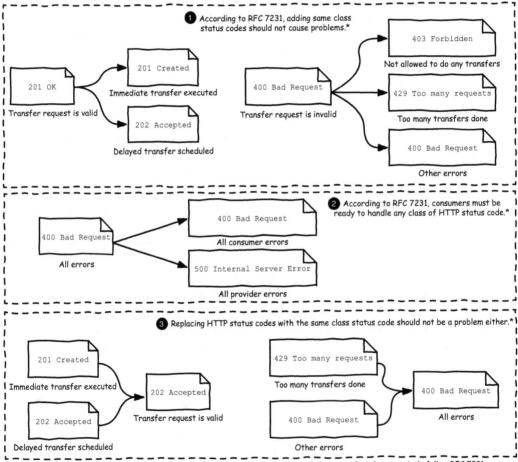

Figure 9.7   Modifying HTTP status codes

The RFC 7231, which describes the HTTP 1.1 protocol, states

> *"HTTP clients are not required to understand the meaning of all registered status codes, though such understanding is obviously desirable. However, a client MUST understand the class of any status code, as indicated by the first digit, and treat an unrecognized status code as being equivalent to the x00 status code of that class...."*

RFC 7231

That means that adding new status codes should not be a problem at all. Indeed, a HTTP client must treat an unrecognized status code as being equivalent to the x00 status code of that class. So when using the transfer money goal, a consumer receiving an unknown (until now) 201 Created must treat it like they would treat a 200 OK. The same goes when receiving a new 429 Too many requests; consumers should treat it as a basic 400 Bad Request.

It also means that returning a new class like 5XX on errors should not be a problem at all. Indeed, "a client MUST understand the class of any status code." Therefore, even if the transfer money goal was not known to return a 500 Internal Server Error according to its documentation, consumers must be ready to handle it. And replacing status codes with codes of the same class should not cause too many problems either: a 201 Created is a success, just like a 202 Accepted. Indeed, the same class code means the same type of error. And, obviously, replacing a 429 Too many requests by a more generic 400 Bad Request makes the feedback less accurate.

This is all well and good, but that's true only if we live in an ideal world—and we do not. Some consumers can only be implemented based on what the documentation says and not strictly following RFC 7231. So an unexpected 500 Internal Server Error will likely cause an unexpected consumer error. Some consumers might follow too strictly your functional interface contract. If a delayed money transfer is acknowledged with a 201 Created status, returning a 202 Accepted will likely cause bugs on some of them, even if you provide generic and self-descriptive feedback, because consumers only expect a 201 Created and nothing else. So you have to hope that consumers strictly implement RFC 7231 and do not follow your functional interface contract too rigidly. That is quite tricky if you do not work closely with them.

The only nonbreaking change that could be done safely would be to remove an HTTP status code because the underlying error will never happen due to some modifications in the implementation. All other modifications, even if they are supposed to be accepted according to RFC 7231, should not be done without extreme caution. Never trust consumers if you don't know how they are actually coded. Of course, this is for the HTTP protocol. If your API relies on another protocol, you will have to check how that protocol works to determine how best to handle feedback modifications based on what you have learned here.

9.1.4 Avoiding breaking changes to goals and flows

Breaking changes can also occur at a higher level when modifying goals and flows. Regarding goals, we already know that modifying inputs, outputs, or feedback is likely to cause breaking changes, but that's not all.

There are two other obvious ways to introduce breaking changes: by renaming or removing goals. For example, the Banking API proposes the goals transfer money and list transfers. These goals are represented by POST /transfers and GET /transfers, respectively. If we decided to rename the transfer resource as money-transfers, consumers using these two goals would get a 404 Not Found response. You could take advantage of the 301 Moved Permanently HTTP status code to redirect all calls on /transfers to /money-transfers. But that works only if consumers understand and actually follow the redirection, as shown in the next listing.

> **Listing 9.1 Activating a redirects flag on a Java HttpUrlConnection**

```
URL obj = new URL("https://api.bankingcompany.com/transfers");
HttpURLConnection conn = (HttpURLConnection) obj.openConnection();
conn.setInstanceFollowRedirects(true);
HttpURLConnection.setFollowRedirects(true);    ◄─── No redirection will be made
                                                    without setting a flag explicitly.
```

Such a configuration might simply be unknown (not all people are HTTP experts), and it can also be deactivated purposely for security reasons. Some consumers might not want to get their request sent to somewhere else without their approval and, more than likely, would prefer to get an error in their code.

Another obvious breaking change would be to remove a goal. Indeed, if we decided to remove the GET method on the transfer resource, consumers using the list transfers goal would get a 405 Method Not Allowed response. Clearly it's better not to remove or rename goals, but does that mean that we can add goals as we please?

Let's say that, for security reasons, the Banking API's designers decide that every money transfer must be validated by the source account owner using a one-time password (OTP) received by SMS. One way to handle this modification would be to add a new validate transfer goal, which must be called after transfer money. It could expect a transfer ID and this OTP, which is sent upon receipt of the transfer money request. The transfer money goal's interface is not changed at all, but because non-updated consumers will never call the new validate transfer goal, they will not be able to trigger money transfers anymore. Even worse, because there is no error, they won't be aware of the problem—it's a *silent* breaking change.

Adding a new transfer money securely goal would not break anything, but it would not secure anything either because consumers would still be able to call the original nonsecure transfer money goal. Introducing a new mandatory step in the existing flow is a breaking change, as is modifying the behavior of existing goals. All you can do at the goal/flow level is add entirely new goals that consumers do not need to use for existing flows. But when doing that, you must pay attention to security.

9.1.5 *Avoiding security breaches and breaking changes*

Modifying an API can introduce breaking changes that affect security and open up the risk of security breaches; therefore, all API modifications must be made with security in mind. Basically, you must apply everything you learned in chapter 8 when modifying an API in any way. For example, for any data added to existing goals' responses, you must ensure that this data will not be provided to consumers that are not supposed to get it.

You must also be careful when modifying scopes. Some modifications could lead to security breaches or breaking changes, as shown in figure 9.8.

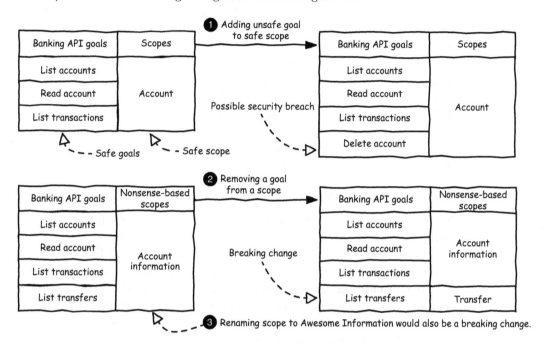

Figure 9.8 Introducing security breaches and breaking changes when modifying scopes

First, depending on the chosen security partitioning strategy (see section 8.2), introducing a delete account goal represented by a `DELETE /accounts/{accountId}` request, for example, could be problematic. If the partitioning is resource-based, any consumer with access to the `/accounts` resource would get access to this quite sensible but dangerous goal.

Second, if adding a new goal to an existing scope is subject to caution, what about removing one? Let's say the access account information scope comprises the list accounts, read account, list transactions, and list transfers goals. Based on what you learned in section 8.2, we know that such a security partitioning, covering different topics, is quite awkward. Maybe we should remove the list transfers goal from this scope to make it more understandable. But that would mean existing consumers with the access account information scope will not be able to use it anymore. So removing a goal from a scope introduces a breaking change. And finally, renaming or removing a scope will have the same effect: consumers will lose access to all goals that were covered by it.

It's not usually up to the API designers to decide how an API is actually secured, but you should know that modifying security aspects of an API can introduce breaking changes. Before reading what follows, think about what you learned in chapter 8 and try to figure out other ways security modifications could introduce breaking changes or security breaches. I'll be back in a minute. When you are done, you can read what follows.

Based on what you have learned so far, you should understand that changing how tokens are acquired (replacing an OAuth 2.0 flow by another, for example) will irremediably cause breaking changes on the consumer's side. Modifying how they should be passed in a request (changing data) is also a breaking change. And last, but not least, as the application/system handling identification can be independent from the API, it could be modified without the knowledge of the people in charge of the API's implementation. Modifying the security data attached to tokens in this way could have terrible consequences on the implementation.

For example, removing the end user ID from the data attached to the access token will, at best, cause unexpected server errors and, at worst, security breaches; the implementation thinking that, as there is no end user involved, the consumer is of an admin type. It is always good to be aware of this, and to remind other people working on the API about the impacts of such modifications.

9.1.6 *Being aware of the invisible interface contract*

So far, what you have seen concerns the visible part of the interface contract: everything that can be described using an API description format or documentation. But some consumers might also rely on the *invisible* parts of the API's interface contract.

For example, an account owner might have different addresses. These addresses are returned in a list, and each one has a `type` property indicating if it is a home, office, or temporary address. Let's say some shrewd developers have spotted that the addresses are always ordered `home`, then `office`, then `temporary`. So when they want to get the home address, they use its index (`0`) instead of scanning the list seeking an address with a `type` of `home`. We all agree that this is total nonsense; consumers must not do that. But if they do, and if this order changes, these consumers will break in a silent way and show the wrong address.

Another example of this invisible interface contract is that consumers might decide that a transaction label, which is just described as a string without any other details, cannot be longer than 50 characters based on the data they have retrieved so far. We already know what can happen if the length of these labels is extended: probably some database errors. As you can see, consumers can rely on parts of the API that are not explicitly described. Indeed, Hyrum's law states that

> *"With a sufficient number of users of an API, it does not matter what you promise in the contract: all observable behaviors of your system will be depended on by somebody."*
>
> Hyrum's law (Hyrum Wright)

What could happen if the transfer money goal was modified from a purely internal perspective (without introducing any modification in the visible interface contract) to add new controls that slightly extend the goal's response time? Some consumers that have tuned their timeouts according to the actual response time can break because the new version of the goal takes longer than their timeout value. These considerations might not be obvious, but any API designer (or anyone working on APIs) must be aware of the invisible parts of the interface contract in order to properly evaluate the importance of any change made to an API.

We have covered many different ways of introducing the dreaded breaking changes. But should we always be afraid of them?

9.1.7 Introducing a breaking change is not always a problem

A *breaking change* is a change that will cause problems for consumers if they do not update their code. As you've seen, these problems can also have repercussions on the provider's side. If the Banking API's consumers are third-party applications developed by other companies, introducing breaking changes to the API is definitely not an option. The consumers will break, and their developers will get upset, lose confidence in the Banking API, and possibly choose to use a competing API instead. Therefore, the Banking Company can lose money—if not worse.

But not all APIs are public ones, consumed by thousands of third-party consumers. If the Banking API were a private one, acting as a simple backend for a single-page application (SPA) as well as a mobile application built by the Banking Company itself, introducing breaking changes would be practicable. All that is required in this case is to update the SPA on the Banking Company's web server hosting the SPA files and force an update of the mobile application, provided that this application includes a force update feature.

As you can see, depending on the context, introducing a breaking change might not be a problem as long as all consumers can be updated synchronously with the API. But to be frank, doing so might not be an easy task. The most secure option if a breaking change is inevitable is to version the API.

9.2 Versioning an API

The day has arrived! The Banking Company has decided to launch version 2 of its famous Banking API. Figure 9.9 shows a possible scenario, among many others, to handle such a change.

The new version of the Banking API is available at apiv2.bankingcompany.com. Consumers switching to this new version get awesome new features, such as the ability

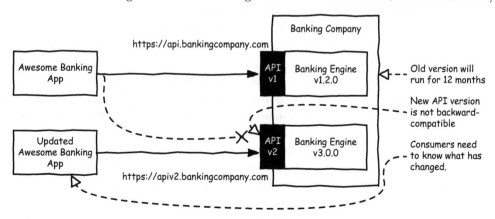

Figure 9.9   The Banking Company has updated its Banking API to version 2.

to make international money transfers in any currency, thanks to the brand-new 3.0.0 banking engine written in Go that has replaced the good old 1.2.0 COBOL one. But, unfortunately, it is not fully backward-compatible.

When switching to this new version, consumers will also need to update their code because some goals, such as the list transactions goal, have been modified in a non-backward-compatible way to make them consistent with the new features. The Banking Company has also announced that it will support version 1 (exposed at api.banking-company.com) for 12 months. This means consumers have 12 months to upgrade, even if they do not use the modified features or intend to use the new ones. It also means that the Banking Company will have to run two versions of its backend for 12 months.

In this case, from the API designer's perspective, the versioning work lies in the non-backward-compatible design—introducing breaking changes and changing the domain name to differentiate the two versions of the API. But API versioning is a subject that goes beyond just API design, and API designers, like any other person working on an API, must be aware of all of its implications.

Besides design, API versioning has impacts on implementation and product management. Indeed, choosing a versioning strategy affects not only how you design an API but also how you implement it (the Banking Company provides the two versions of the API using two separate backends). Also, just because you provide a new version of your product (your API) doesn't mean consumers will be willing to switch to it; many of them might prefer to stick with the previous version. Before we explore the various ways of representing API versioning and its impacts, however, let's clarify what API versioning is and differentiate it from implementation versioning.

9.2.1 *Contrasting API and implementation versioning*

The initial version of the Banking API only provided access to account information, but it quickly evolved to offer more features. Figure 9.10 shows the evolution of this API and its implementation.

Right after its launch, the API was updated to provide the capability of making money transfers. The implementation obviously had to be updated to provide the new transfer-related goals. After this update, the API and the implementation shared the same 1.1 version number. Unfortunately, the first version of the transfer implementation was not really effective. Each money transfer was processed synchronously on each API call. This resulted in long response times, especially when there were more than 100 transfer requests per second. It was then decided to modify the implementation in order to put money transfer requests in a message queue and process them asynchronously without impacting the API.

The new 1.2 implementation was far more effective, while still exposing the same 1.1 API. After that, the Banking Company's CTO became fond of Go and decided to get rid of COBOL. The first attempt was to automatically convert the COBOL code into Go code. Although the Banking API used a completely different programming language, version 2.0 of the implementation was able to expose version 1.1, so consumers did not notice this change at all. Unfortunately, before going live in production, the generated code was revealed to be inefficient and poorly written. So a full manual rewrite was done, and long-awaited new features were also added. But the most important change was that the oldest

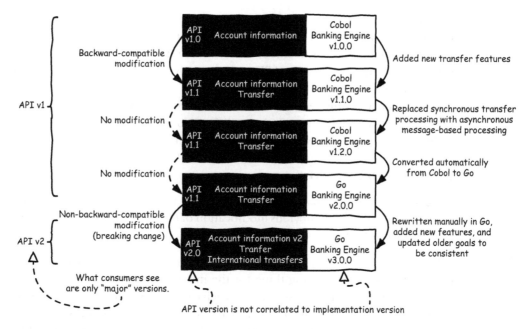

Figure 9.10   **The evolution of the Banking API and its implementation**

goals of the API, the account-information-related ones, were modified to match the API design rules introduced with the transfer features in version 1.1. This breaking change forced the Banking Company to update the API to a non-backward-compatible 2.0 version.

As you can see, an API has a version, like any software component, but it is not correlated to the version of its implementation. The version of an API evolves based on the changes made to the interface contract (the changes that are visible from the consumers' perspective) and not on how the implementation evolves. Two completely different implementations can expose exactly the same version of an API. In this example, the API and implementation version names, like v1.1 or v3.0.0, are based on a well-known and clever system of using numbers to name a software component version—*semantic versioning* (https://semver.org/). It consists of using three digits in this format: *MAJOR.MINOR.PATCH*. Each is incremented in specific situations:

- The MAJOR digit is incremented only on breaking changes, such as adding a new mandatory parameter (see section 9.1).
- The MINOR digit is incremented when new features are added in a backward-compatible manner, like adding new HTTP methods or resource paths in a REST API.
- The PATCH digit is incremented when the modifications made involve backward-compatible bug fixes.

This makes sense for an implementation, but not for an API. Semantic versioning applied to APIs consist of just two digits: *BREAKING.NONBREAKING*. This two-level versioning is interesting from the provider's perspective; it helps to keep track of all the different backward-compatible and non-backward-compatible versions of an API. But consumers don't really care about all those details.

Consumers who were using the account-information-related goals of version 1.0 of the API can seamlessly switch to version 1.1 (NONBREAKING) as if nothing has changed. And even if they decide to use the new transfer features added to v1.1, they're still simply using "the Banking API" without really caring (or knowing) about its exact version number.

Consumers will only really notice changes in the API when the Banking Company introduces version 2.0. Indeed, they will have to actually modify some parts of their code to use it. From the API consumers' perspective, they simply use version 1 or version 2. They don't care about the second level of versioning (NONBREAKING); they only need the BREAKING digit.

> **NOTE** Remember that a breaking change is a non-backward-compatible change. It could be an obvious modification of the interface contract or a more insidious modification of the invisible contract.

If removing or renaming a goal leads to a major version bump, it might not be that obvious to do the same thing thing for the invisible modification we discussed in section 9.1.6. It will have to be discussed for each case, and we must evaluate its true impact on consumers in order to determine if releasing a new version is necessary in such cases.

If only a single level of versioning matters for consumers, we can use anything as version names. We could use ISO 8601 dates, such as 2017-10-19 for version 1 and 2018-22-12 for version 2. If we wanted, we could even use famous anime soundtrack composers' names, such as Yoko Kanno and Kenji Kawai for versions 1 and 2, respectively.

API and implementation versioning are different, and consumers (mostly) only care about the version changes announcing breaking changes. But how do consumers actually tell which version of an API they want to use?

9.2.2 *Choosing an API versioning representation from the consumer's perspective*

The Banking Company has rolled out its brand-new Banking API v2.0, which is not completely backward-compatible. Hopefully, the transfer-related goals are backward-compatible, so consumers using those in the previous version of the API will only have to tweak their requests a little to switch to this new version. Figure 9.11 shows the different possibilities the Banking Company might choose to actually expose the different versions of the API.

The Banking API could use the resource's path to handle the API's version. Consumers wanting to list transfers might send a GET /v1/transfers or GET /v2/transfers request on the same api.bankingcompany.com domain to use version 1 or 2, respectively, of the API. A similar approach would be to use different domains or subdomains for each version of the API: here, api.bankingcompany.com for version 1 and apiv2.bankingcompany.com for version 2.

The version of the API used can also be indicated via a query parameter (GET /transfers?version=2) or a custom header (Version: 2). Or the Banking API could propose to indicate the version of the API desired using content negotiation, as you

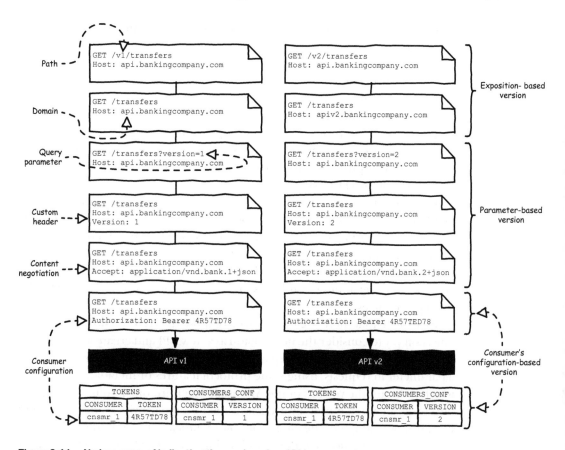

Figure 9.11 Various ways of indicating the version of an API in a request

learned in section 6.2.1. For this, consumers indicate a custom media type in the standard `Content-type` header, such as `application/vnd.bank.2` to indicate that they want to use version 2 of the API.

And last but not least, the version of the API used can be indirectly indicated in the request. Because the API is secure, consumers have to send some credentials with each request; with this approach, the request contains an `Authorization` header with a token (here, `4R57TD78`). According to the data stored by the provider in the `TOKENS` table, this token has been generated for the `cnsmr_1` consumer (obviously in the real world, nobody would ever store such sensitive data without encryption). The version of the API used by this consumer is indicated in the `VERSION` column of the `CONSUMERS_CONF` table.

That's six different ways of indicating the version for an HTTP-based API. Which one should you choose? Obviously, this choice must be made from the consumer's perspective.

The simplest options are path and domain versioning. Changing a domain name or path in a URL is quite straightforward, especially if the API is tested with a browser or a `curl` command line. Consumers can see what version is being used by looking at the URL they use. These are probably the most used options; and, based on what you learned in section 6.1.4, it's worth taking those into consideration. Your consumers, who are probably already familiar with these mechanisms, will find them easy to use.

Query parameter versioning is also a quite simple option; but, from an API designer's perspective, I don't recommend it because it is not really clean. For example, if we add a currency filter as in `GET /transfers?currency=eur&version=2`, the query mixes a purely technical parameter with a functional one.

`Content-type` versioning is interesting from an HTTP expert's perspective, but many people are reluctant to use HTTP headers despite the fact that it is not complicated at all. This problem is exacerbated with the custom HTTP header option because it's not part of the HTTP standard.

The consumer configuration option is totally consumer-friendly in that there's no need for consumers to modify their code. One small drawback is that it requires updating the configuration to switch from one version to another, which can be cumbersome when testing different versions of the API.

What would your preferred choice(s) be? Personally, I prefer path and consumer configuration versioning, but let's step back and look beyond REST, HTTP, and personal preferences.

We can see that there are three ways to expose different versions of an API. The first one is simply to consider the new version as a new API and create a new exposition endpoint. The second one is to keep a single endpoint for the various versions but to pass a parameter in requests, using some protocol features or metadata in the request data, which indicates the version of the API used. The third one also uses a single endpoint, but stores the version used by each consumer on the provider side. Whatever the technical solution adopted, the choice of how to indicate the version of the API used must take into consideration standards and usability in order to ensure that consumers will be able to understand it and use it easily.

So far, we've talked about API versioning. But is versioning an entire API the only option?

9.2.3   *Choosing API versioning granularity*

Versioning an API as a whole is the most common practice, but not the only one. Depending on the use case and type of API, other options can be more effective.

For REST APIs, besides at the API level, versioning can be done at the resource level, the goal/operation level, and the data/message level. Figure 9.12 compares API versioning and resource versioning when breaking changes are introduced. Note that the breaking changes in this example could be avoided based on what you have learned in section 9.1.

To keep the example simple, the Banking API is reduced to three goals: transfer money, list transfers, and delete transfer. The left side shows what happens when versioning the API as a whole, and the right side, what happens when versioning each resource identified by its path. On both sides, the version number is located on the first path level. Take a look at the top of this figure. On the left, the API version is v1. On the right, the version of the two transfer resources (`/v1/transfers` and `/v1/transfers/{id}`) is v1.

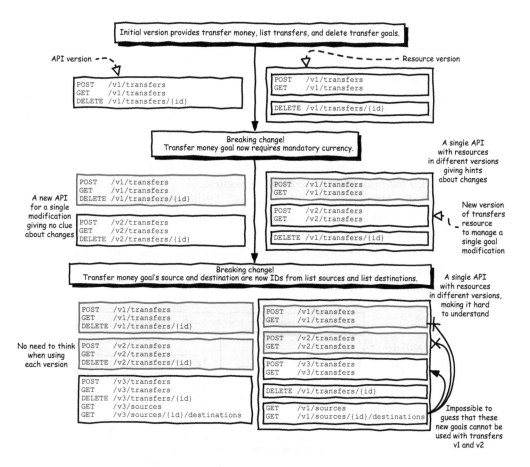

Figure 9.12 API versioning versus resource versioning

The transfer money goal expects a `source` and a `destination` account number, and an amount of money. A first breaking change is introduced by adding a new mandatory currency property to the input of this goal. On the API versioning side, this single breaking change forces us to create a new v2 of the API. If consumers compare the goals of the two versions, they will have absolutely no clue about what has changed without reading the API's release notes.

On the resource versioning side, no new API is created, but a new `/v2/transfers` resource is added in order to manage the modification of the `POST /v2/transfers` operation. That gives consumers a hint, but it is impossible to know which operation on the transfer resource has been modified without reading the release notes.

NOTE Even if there must always be release notes, these are not always available when needed, and some people don't read them at all! Being able to detect changes could be beneficial for consumers or people involved in the project.

Two new goals are also introduced, and the transfer money goal is modified in order to facilitate money transfers and manage transfers to external accounts. The list sources goal allows a consumer to list all possible sources for a money transfer, and list destinations gives possible destinations for a selected source. Introducing these two new goals is not a breaking change. But unfortunately, the sources and destinations are each identified by a number, which is different from the string account numbers expected by the transfer money goal. Its input data is modified, thereby introducing a breaking change.

On the resource versioning side, a new v3 transfer resource is added with the `/v3/transfers` path, along with `GET /v1/sources` and `GET /v1/sources/{id}/destination` operations. The API now comprises three different versions of the transfer resource, and the new source and destination resources can only be used with version 3. That's not easy for consumers to guess.

On the API versioning side, a new v3 API is again created, but there's no need to think about which versions can be used together. Each independent API version contains a set of compatible resources.

Let's go now to a deeper level of versioning—at the goal or operation level. Figure 9.13 compares API versioning and goal/operation versioning when the same breaking changes are introduced.

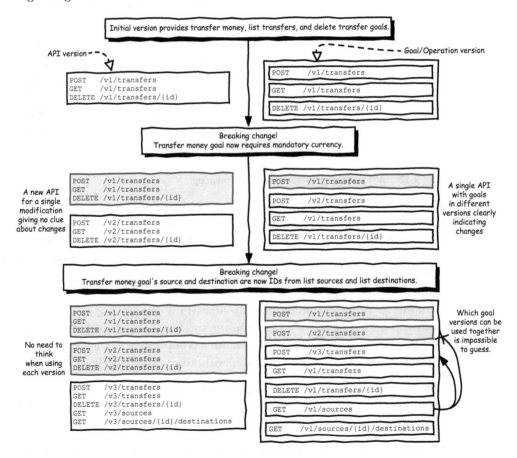

Figure 9.13   **API versioning versus goal (or operation) versioning**

The API versioning side is exactly the same; but on the other side, each operation is now versioned independently, still using the vX in the path. On each breaking change to the transfer money goal, a new request is added to the API (POST /v2/transfers then POST /v3/transfers). That's useful because it clearly indicates which goal has been modified. But as with the resource versioning use case, the API ends up with three different versions of the transfer money goal, and consumers have absolutely no clue that GET /v1/sources and GET /v1/sources/{id}/destinations can only be used with POST /v3/transfers. That is definitely not consumer-friendly.

Now let's look at the last level of versioning: the data/message level. Figure 9.14 shows what could happen to the transfer money goal using this versioning strategy. Note that this strategy only works on the data that is located in request and response bodies; headers and query parameters are out of its scope.

Figure 9.14 **Data (or message) versioning with content negotiation**

Because the Banking API uses the HTTP protocol, we can take advantage of the content negotiation feature to version the requests and responses for each goal. In the API's initial version, POST /transfers requests and responses use the application/ vnd.transfer.request.v1+json custom media type. When the transfer money goal's input is modified, its media type's version bumps to v2 (application/vnd.transfer .request.v2+json), then v3 (application/vnd.transfer.request.v3+json). The response version is modified only on the second breaking change to v2.

In both cases, the versions of requests and responses are not correlated anymore, and with the second update, it becomes unclear which versions of requests and responses work together. Note that we could perfectly correlate request and response message versions by simply bumping request's and response's versions together no matter which one is modified. In that case, this strategy is close to the goal/operation versioning strategy. Table 9.3 sums up the pros and cons of each level of granularity.

Table 9.3   Choosing a versioning granularity for REST APIs

Granularity	Pros	Cons	Recommended?
API	No need to think about which versions of operations or resources work together	API version change on single breaking change, no clue about the changes	By default for REST APIs (common practice)
Resource	Gives hints about changes	Impossible to guess which versions work together	Not recommended for REST APIs; use only when resources are completely independent
Goal/operation	Indicates which goals have changed	Impossible to guess which versions work together	Not recommended for REST APIs; use only when operations are completely independent
Data/message	Indicates which data/messages have changed	Impossible to guess which versions work together; limited to request/response bodies when using HTTP	Not recommended for REST APIs; can be used in conjunction with API-level granularity

Each level of granularity has its pros and cons, but at least in REST API world, the most commonly used strategy is API-level versioning. Choosing any other granularity must not be done lightly because most consumers are not used to these versioning strategies. But that does not mean that they must never be used, especially if the API you are designing is not a REST one.

You might sometimes need to mix different versioning granularities. For example, if you work in the banking industry, you might have to work with the ISO 20022 standard that defines XML (and soon, at the time of writing of this book, JSON) messages. Messages come in versioned request/response pairs. If you were to design an API using these messages, you would have to deal with the versioning of both your API and the ISO 20022 messages.

API versioning should hold few secrets for you now. But as an API designer, you must be aware of its impact beyond API design.

9.2.4 *Understanding the impact of API versioning beyond design*

What is discussed here is mostly the concern of API product managers, tech leads, and architects; but as API designers, it's good to be aware of these matters too (plus, sometimes APIs designers have more than one role). Even if the changes introduced in the

API are not breaking ones, each of them must be carefully recorded so that you are able to communicate the list of changes to consumers.

You should understand by now that changing the version of an API—or more precisely, introducing a breaking change—has consequences on the consumer side, and that consumers might not be happy with that. Creating new versions of an API means that multiple versions of the API will run at the same time, and consumers might not be willing to make the effort to switch to a newer version if the older one they are using is still running. Therefore, the breaking changes that are introduced in the API have to be carefully chosen.

For example, introducing a breaking change that does not bring any value to the consumers, such as switching from an OAuth 1 to 2 security framework, is definitely not a good idea. To make the switch less inconvenient, it would be better to introduce new features that consumers want along with such boring breaking changes.

Regarding implementation, having to expose multiple versions of the API might require extra work and, therefore, choosing how many versions will be supported and for how long is important. This depends on your context. Some API companies providing their services only as an API might choose to indefinitely support all versions. On the other hand, for a private API, some companies might only support two versions. There is no silver bullet; it's up to you to choose an adapted solution.

On the technical level, there are broadly two options to manage versioning in the implementation. The first option is for each version to be handled by a specific implementation. This means development of each older version of the implementation will go on (at least to fix bugs and security issues, for example) for as long as those versions remain in use. The infrastructure supporting each older version must also be maintained. Depending on the context of your company, this may or may not be a problem. This context will definitely have an impact on how long you let consumers use older versions of an API. The second option is for all versions to be handled by a single implementation. Again, depending on the context, having one implementation manage all possible versions of your APIs may or may not be a problem.

As you can see, versioning can be challenging. Are there ways to lessen the risk of breaking changes that necessitate a change of API version?

9.3 Designing APIs with extensibility in mind

We know how to avoid introducing breaking changes when possible and how to version APIs when such changes are unavoidable. That's good, but we must not forget one of the fundamental principles of software design: extensibility.

> *"Extensibility is a software engineering and systems design principle where the implementation takes future growth into consideration. The term extensibility can also be seen as a systemic measure of the ability to extend a system and the level of effort required to implement the extension. Extensions can be through the addition of new functionality or through modification of existing functionality. The central theme is to provide for change—typically enhancements—while minimizing impact to existing system functions."*
>
> *Wikipedia*

By carefully designing data, interactions, and flows, and choosing the appropriate level of granularity for versioning, we can design extensible APIs that facilitate evolutions and, more importantly, lessen the risk of breaking changes.

9.3.1 Designing extensible data

Figure 9.15 shows how to design data envelopes in order to make an API extensible.

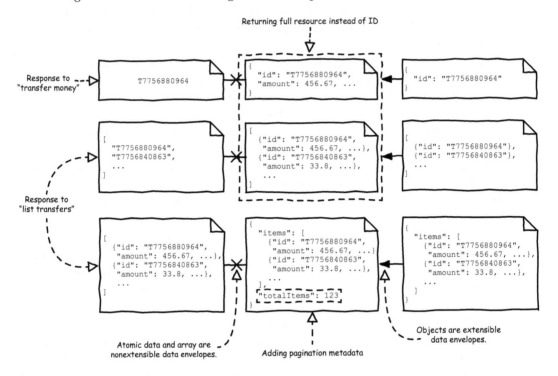

Figure 9.15   Choosing extensible data envelopes

What do you think will happen if the transfer money goal just returns the money transfer's ID, such as `"T775688964"`, as a raw string? At first, consumers might be puzzled because they get a response whose `Content-type` is `text/plain` instead of the usual `application/json` or `application/xml` used in all the other goals. That's awkward, but they might get used to it ... until the Banking Company decides to return the entire resource that was created in order to avoid many subsequent calls to the list transfers goal. Instead of a `text/plain` response containing a raw string, they now get an `application/json` response containing an object. That's a breaking change. If the response had been an object containing an `id` property from the start, adding the other transfer properties wouldn't be a problem at all. The same goes for the list transfers goal returning a list of transfer IDs as strings.

Speaking of lists, returning one of those is not a good idea either. What would happen if metadata had to be added in order to provide information about pagination, such as the total number of items? It's a breaking change, again. The way to avoid that is by encapsulating the list in an `items` property inside an object.

So, as you can see, all high-level data (the resources in a REST API) must be enveloped inside an object to ensure extensibility and lessen the risk of breaking changes. But what about the data inside this envelope? As figure 9.16 shows, you should beware of Booleans and provide self-descriptive data.

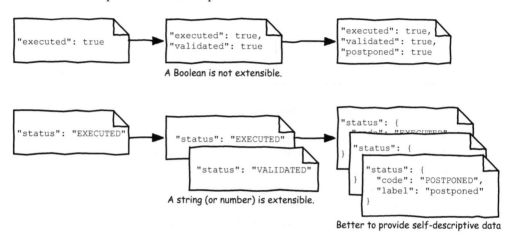

Figure 9.16 Choosing types wisely and using self-descriptive data

When a money transfer is created using the transfer money goal, it is not executed immediately. In order to provide information about this transaction, there's an executed Boolean property that is `true` when the money transfer is executed and `false` otherwise. What happens if a new state is introduced?

Let's say that some money transfers need to be validated before execution for some reason. How do we handle this? We can add a `validated` Boolean property to signify this. But then what happens if a third `postponed` state is introduced? Should we add another Boolean property? Adding these new properties in a response does not introduce a breaking change, but consumers won't be aware of these new states if they don't update their code.

To avoid adding multiple Boolean status properties, we can instead add a single `status` property. This allows us to add new statuses as needed without adding new properties. This status could be a number or a string. Note that a Boolean is less extensible than a number, which is less extensible than a string. But as you saw in section 9.1, adding values to an enum could provoke a breaking change. Making the status a self-descriptive object with a code and an easily interpretable label might lessen this risk.

So choose your property types carefully in order to ensure extensibility, and always think about providing self-descriptive data in order to lessen the risk of breaking changes. All this works only if a single property is sufficient to replace multiple ones. Figure 9.17 shows what to do when it is not.

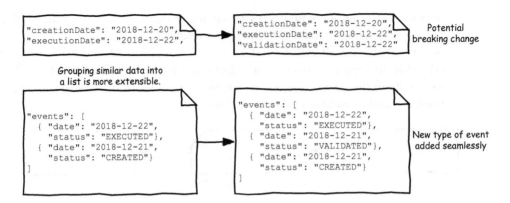

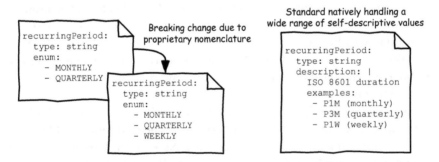

Figure 9.17   Grouping similar data in a list

A money transfer has `creationDate` and `executionDate` properties, corresponding to the dates when it was created and then executed. To provide information about the new validation state you have just seen, a `validationDate` property could be added. But then the same problems we have just seen would arise. These different dates could be replaced by an `events` list property, its elements each consisting of a `date` and a `status` (`EXECUTED` for the execution date, for example). Adding new dates to the list is quite simple; and, of course, the `status` could be provided in a self-descriptive format.

If the properties are similar, always consider whether you can put them into a list, possibly using self-descriptive data, which will facilitate the addition of elements and lessen the risk of breaking changes. Speaking of self-descriptive formats that lessen the risk of introducing breaking changes, figure 9.18 shows how we can use standards to design extensible APIs.

Figure 9.18   Using standards and a wider range of self-descriptive values

A proprietary nomenclature could be used to describe a recurring money transfer period. The values could be ready-to-use ones like `MONTHLY` or `QUARTERLY`, but adding a new value such as `WEEKLY` would inevitably introduce a breaking change. This approach is also quite rigid. What if a customer wanted to trigger a money transfer every 10 days? You'd have to add a new value. Using the ISO 8601 duration format might solve the problem. It can describe any duration using a simple format; for example, `P1M` corresponds to `MONTHLY` and `P10D` corresponds to 10 days.

In a similar manner, you've already seen the benefits of using ISO 4217 currency codes to facilitate not only understanding but also extensibility. If the Banking API needs to manage new currencies, consumers will be able to understand these easily because they understand ISO 4217. So using standards and a wider range of self-descriptive values instead of a finished list facilitates extensibility and lessens the risk of breaking changes.

9.3.2 Designing extensible interactions

Postel's law states

> *"Be conservative in what you do, be liberal in what you accept from others."*[1]
>
> *Postel's law (Robustness principle)*

Applied to API design, the robustness principle could be understood as "Be consistent in what you return and try to avoid errors." You saw how to be consistent and ensure extensibility regarding the data returned by an API in section 9.3.1, so let's focus on errors.

Concerning error data and being consistent in what we return, we can apply what we have learned in order to be as generic as possible. You saw in section 5.2.3 that to provide informative feedback, we can type errors as shown in the following listing.

Listing 9.2 An informative error message

```
{
  "errors": [
    { "source": "amount",
      "type": "MISSING_MANDATORY_ATTRIBUTE",
      "message": "Missing mandatory amount" }
  ]
}
```

Because this type is generic, we can reuse it for another property that becomes mandatory. If the type were `MISSING_AMOUNT`, we would not be able to reuse it and would instead be forced to introduce a new type of error that consumers would not be able to interpret without updating their code. In general, the more generic the `type` values are, the more extensive the error feedback is.

As for trying to avoid errors, what would happen if a consumer provided an unknown `test=2` parameter when requesting to list transfers? The API could be strict and return an error saying, "Sorry, we do not understand the `test` parameter." Providing informative error feedback is consumer-friendly, but the API could also simply not take this unknown parameter into account, process the request, and return a result. That is still a consumer-friendly design, but also an extensible one. Indeed, if this `test` parameter had actually existed in a previous version, non-updated consumers might still send it, and it would bother them that their queries now trigger some unexpected error. Note that works only if ignoring `test` actually has no negative side effect on the consumer side.

---

[1] This is often reworded as "Be conservative in what you send, be liberal in what you accept."

Let's consider some other types of errors. What should the Banking API do if a consumer sends a `pageSize=150` parameter with a list transfers request, but the maximum size of a page is 100? For the same reasons, the API should not return an error but a page of 100 elements. Then, if one day (perhaps for performance reasons) the maximum size is reduced to 50, no consumers will be bothered. The pagination metadata should provide all needed information in order to let consumers seamlessly use the modified goal; but if necessary, some warning metadata could be added along with the response using the same format as errors to signify the modifications made to the requests.

And what should the Banking API do if a consumer sends an `amount` of `15000`, which is above the maximum transfer amount of $10,000 (regardless of source account balance and owner privileges)? Should we trigger a $10,000 money transfer instead of a $15,000 one? Obviously not! As API designers (and implementers), we should try to avoid returning errors, but not at all costs.

As you can see, this is the implementation's business. But as an API designer, you'll have to define a policy regarding errors and unknown or invalid parameters (query parameters, headers, or properties in bodies). Will you not take the issue into account and use a default value to lessen the risk of breaking changes? Or will you be strict and return errors to be more secure and favor consumer accuracy (if they break, they will update)? Your approach will depend on the context of the API and the context of each goal.

9.3.3 *Designing extensible flows*

How you design each goal in a flow and the flows themselves will impact the extensibility of your API. The Banking API was initially created for the Banking Company's mobile application. With this application, end users making a money transfer have to select a source account, then a destination, and then provide an amount.

From the API's perspective, this means using the list sources goal to list possible sources of a money transfer. After that, list destinations can be used to get the accounts and registered beneficiaries that can be used as the destination for a money transfer using a specific source's ID. Finally, the transfer money goal can be used to make the transfer with a provided amount and source and destination IDs.

Now suppose some people within the Banking Company decided to build a money transfer tool for the back office. They were quite happy when they discovered that there already was a money transfer API. In their implementation, they already had the source and destination account numbers, so they simply called the transfer money goal using these values. Unfortunately, all their calls ended with an "Unknown source account" error.

After some investigation, they realized that the transfer money goal expected source and destination IDs, which were not regular account numbers. They had to call list sources to find the ID corresponding to their source account number and then follow the same flow as in the mobile application. What a pity. If the flow had not been so focused on the mobile application use case, and if the various goals involved in the money transfer flow had used regular account numbers, it would have been far simpler.

As you can see, extensibility in design is not only about ensuring that modifications can be done with a low risk of breaking changes. Extensibility is also about ensuring that the API can be used in a wide range of use cases, not only the one it was originally created for.

Always try to see beyond the specific use case you are working with and ensure that the flows you design, especially UI flows, are not correlated to a specific process. Also, try to design each step so it can be used in a standalone way. Choosing widely adopted inputs and outputs, especially IDs, helps to achieve that.

9.3.4 *Designing extensible APIs*

Last but not least, how can we ensure extensibility at the API level? What will happen if the Banking API grows to provide several dozen goals covering various topics such as account information, banking services subscriptions, money transfers, and personal finance management, among others? Obviously, breaking changes will occur, even if all the design principles we have seen so far are applied. Why? Simply, because it is big!

The bigger an API gets, the higher the number of evolutions, and therefore, the higher the risk of breaking changes. That's quite simple to understand, and the solution is obvious: instead of building big APIs, we should build smaller ones.

It's not always that simple to define relevant groups of goals that can be combined easily, however. This is not specific to API design; it's a common challenge in software design. Hopefully, if you remember section 7.2.3, you already have the basics that can help you to organize goals and split an API into smaller parts. You will also have to analyze each goal you add to an existing API in order to evaluate whether the goal you are adding should instead be part of a different API using the same principles.

Summary

- Each API evolution must be carefully designed in order to avoid breaking changes, which can cause problems not only on the consumer's but also the provider's side.
- API designers might have to live with previous poor design choices in order to avoid introducing benevolent but breaking changes.
- Depending on the context, breaking changes might be acceptable (for example, private APIs with consumers under the organization's control).
- API versioning is a design + implementation + product management matter.
- Designing APIs with extensibility in mind eases the design of evolutions, lessens the risk of breaking changes, and favors API reusability.

Designing a
network-efficient API

This chapter covers

- Web API network communication concerns
- Using compression, caching, and conditional requests
- Optimizing API design to make fewer calls and exchange less data

So far, we've focused on designing APIs that provide usable, secure, and evolvable representations of goals that make sense for consumers and hide internal concerns. But in reality, we've learned to design ideal laboratory APIs, ignoring most of the context in which they are used—especially the network context.

Network communication efficiency is an important topic that any API designer must be aware of. Indeed, communication efficiency is important in our day-to-day lives. When you have a conversation with someone, either by speaking or by instant message or email, sometimes you want the full story to get all the possible background information, and sometimes you want the person you communicate with to get straight to the point and tell you only the bit you need to know. If you get the full story, but you wanted just a specific bit of it, you will have to waste time listening to or reading all of it to get what you want. This can be frustrating, and it can even have serious consequences, like missing out on an opportunity.

Choosing the wrong way of communicating information can have negative impacts in our daily lives. The same is true for APIs that provide inefficient network communications, as shown in figure 10.1.

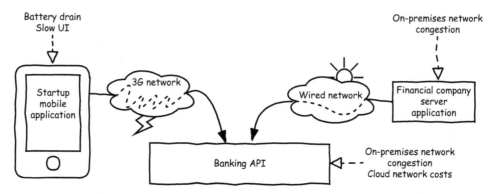

Figure 10.1   Network concerns influence API design

On mobile phones, network-inefficient APIs can have a significant impact on the developer experience, making it hard or even impossible to consume these without slowing the user interface and draining the device's battery, which also negatively impacts the user experience. Even with modern devices and networks, this is less of a concern than it once was for server consumers. Such inefficient APIs can have a significant impact on network bandwidth usage. This can be problematic for on-premise infrastructures with limited capacity. There can be impacts on the provider side too. Providers can face network congestion on on-premise infrastructures or excessively large bills on cloud infrastructures.

Network communication efficiency can be a major concern, and as an API designer, you contribute to it. API designers must have some basic knowledge about network communication concerns. This includes an understanding of how to avoid or solve network problems by taking advantage of the API's underlying protocol or by creating APIs that are network-efficient by design.

10.1   Overview of network communication concerns

This book is about remote APIs and web APIs, in particular. In section 1.1, you saw that such APIs allow consumers to interact with a provider over a network. We may forget it, but if network capabilities keep growing and growing, network communication efficiency can still be an important matter on both sides of the wire in certain contexts.

As an API designer, you must be aware of network communication concerns because they can have an impact on your designs. To investigate this topic, we will analyze from a network perspective how the Awesome Banking App, a mobile application running on a mobile phone connected to a not-so-good 3G network, uses a slightly modified version of the Banking API.

10.1.1   Setting the scene

Let's set the scene to begin. Figure 10.2 shows the goals provided by the Banking API, and figures 10.3 and 10.4 show how the three different screens of the Awesome Banking App use all of these.

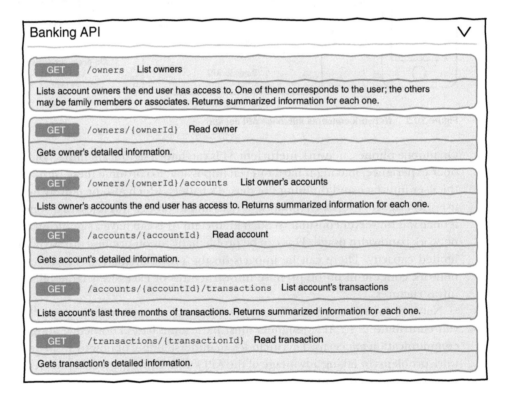

Figure 10.2   The Banking API

The dashboard screen (figure 10.3) shows all owners whose accounts the user has access to and highlights the one corresponding to the user. For each owner, it shows their title and name, the combined balances of their checking and savings accounts, and the sum of all their account transactions for both types of accounts for the last three months (for simplicity's sake, we'll assume all transactions are withdrawals).

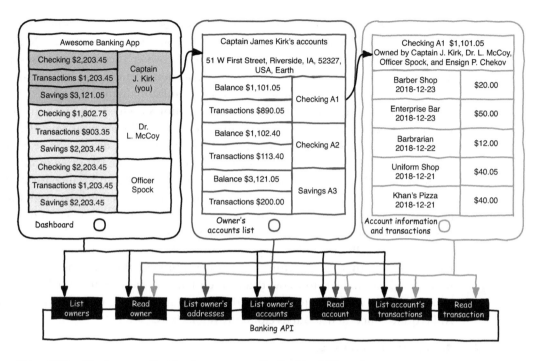

Figure 10.3   The Awesome Banking App consumes the Banking API's goals.

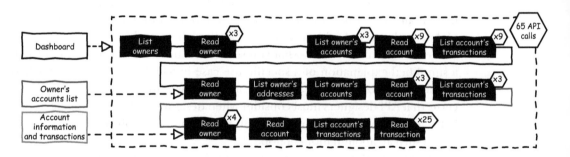

Figure 10.4   The Awesome Banking App makes too many calls.

To do that, it first lists owners to get their IDs and names and the user flag, which indicates which owner corresponds to the user. For each owner listed, it uses the read owner goal to get their title. Then it lists accounts to get the IDs and balances of each owner's accounts. Next, it uses the read account goal to get the account type for each account. And finally, it lists transactions for each account to get their amounts and sum them all.

When the user taps an owner line, the application switches to the owner's accounts list screen. This screen shows the selected owner's title, full name, home address, and owned accounts. For each account, it shows its type (checking or savings), ID (A1, for example), balance, and transaction sum for the last three months.

The application begins by using the read owner goal to get the account owner's title and full name. It then lists addresses to get the owner's home address. Next, it lists accounts to get the IDs and balances of each of the owner's accounts and uses the read account goal to get the account type for each account. And finally, it lists transactions for each account to get the transaction amounts and sum them.

When the user taps an account line, the application switches to the account's detailed information and transactions screen. This screen shows the account type, ID, balance, and owner(s), which the application gets by using the read owner and read account goals. It then lists all the recent transactions, precisely, for the last three months, using the list transactions goal and retrieving the transaction ID and balance for each. And finally, for the last 25 transactions only, it uses the read transaction goal to get the labels and dates. It displays the five most recent transactions (more transaction detail information will be fetched if users scroll through the list).

That's many API calls—65 to be precise. Your API designer's sense is probably already telling you that there is something wrong here. Indeed, the Awesome Banking App's users complain that it is too slow, drains their battery, and uses too much of their data allowance. And it's no better on the other side! The Banking Company providing the API is quite concerned about its cloud provider's bills.

10.1.2 Analyzing the problems

Why do the Awesome Banking App's users complain? Why is this application slow and inefficient? And why is the Banking Company concerned about its cloud provider's bills? It all comes down to the number and frequency of network calls and the volume of data exchanged. In this section, we'll analyze these problems.

Please bear in mind that what you see here is not an exact reflection of reality; it's a simplified explanation of a specific use case in which all possible issues have been grossly emphasized in order to provide an overview of the network communication concerns that API designers must consider when designing APIs. The mobile application's behavior and the API design are actually pretty dumb, and obviously no one would ever create such an abomination—I hope!

Let's start by decomposing an API network call made over the mobile network. Figure 10.5 shows what happens when the Awesome Banking App lists an account's last three months of transactions.

The first step is to connect to the server hosting the Banking API. That consists of various actions involving the phone's radio antenna, low-level network communication

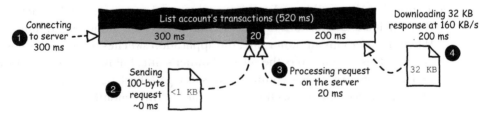

Figure 10.5   Decomposing an API call made over a mobile network

initiation, and encryption. We will assume that it always takes around 300 ms, but know that depending on the type of mobile network, the radio signal quality and what happened before this call can take up to several seconds. This time is often called the *latency*.

Once the connection is established, the API request can be sent. Because it is a simple `GET /accounts/{accountId}/transactions` request, its size is only around 100 bytes, so it takes far less than 1 ms to upload or send it to the API server. When the server receives the request, it has to process it, load the transactions from the database, and generate a JSON document. We'll assume that this takes 20 ms, but the actual time depends on what is requested and the server's capabilities.

Finally, the fourth step consists of downloading the server's response. We'll assume the generated JSON document's size is around 32 KB, so it takes 200 ms to download it at 160 KB/s (which is advertised as 1.3 Mb/s). Like the latency, the *download speed* depends heavily on the type of network and the radio signal quality. The overall request takes 520 ms. It's a bit long, but given the hostile network conditions, we have to live with that. This single request alone is not that bad, but let's see what happens when the Awesome Banking App actually uses the API to populate the dashboard screen for the simplest use case: a user corresponding to a single owner who has a single account.

Figure 10.6 shows which API calls are made and how. To simplify the explanation, we will take it for granted that the network bandwidth is 160 KB/s, the latency is always 300 ms, sending the request always takes 0 ms, and it always takes 20 ms for the server to process a request.

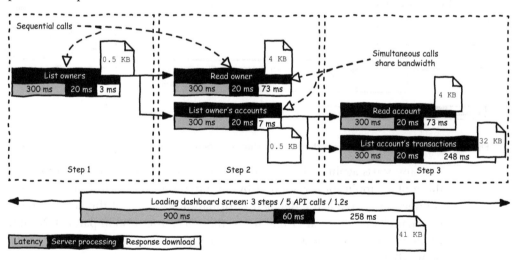

Figure 10.6   A basic use case with a user who has access to a single account owner who owns a single account

To load the data shown on the dashboard screen, the Awesome Banking App lists the owners whose accounts the user is authorized to view; here, it returns a single owner corresponding to the user. Then it reads this owner's detailed information and lists the owner's accounts in parallel. Once the application has gotten the list, which consists of a single account in this case, it reads that account's detailed information and lists its transactions, also in parallel.

The whole API call chain consists of five API calls, distributed in three steps thanks to the parallel calls. Unfortunately, it takes 1.2 s, which is above 500 ms, the top end of the acceptable *latency range* (the time above which a human brain tolerates latency). And this is for a simple use case! Now let's see how it goes with a more complex one. Figure 10.7 shows what happens for another user who has access to four owners and their eight accounts.

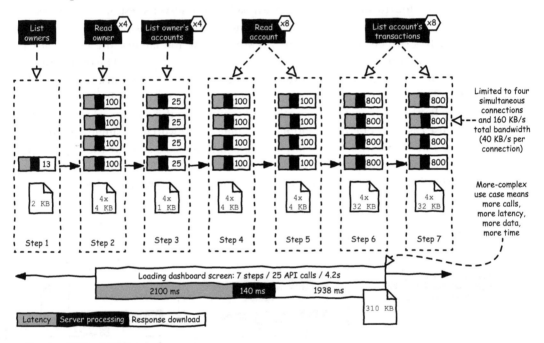

Figure 10.7   A complex use case with a user who has access to four owners and their eight accounts

The app starts again by listing owners, but this time there are four of them. Because the mobile application is limited by the operating system to four concurrent HTTP connections, it reads the detailed information for each of the account owners using four parallel requests; after that it lists their accounts, also in parallel. Note that if the whole network bandwidth is 160 KB/s, each parallel request is made at a quarter of it, or 40 KB/s.

Next, the application reads the detailed information for the owners' eight accounts and their transactions in four steps of four parallel requests. So, in this case, there are 25 API calls done in seven sequential steps, taking 4.2 s and retrieving 310 KB of data. That's 20 more calls and ~7.5 times more data than in the previous use case, and the whole chain takes 3.5 times longer. This is a very long delay, and even if the application shows a spinner, users will definitely get bored before the screen loads.

Each screen the application displays can have the same kind of problems. I'll let you imagine what happens on the account screen when the application has to make individual calls to get detailed information for each transaction. And it gets worse. The users might navigate through the application to see all of their data, and this can raise some other problems, as shown in figure 10.8.

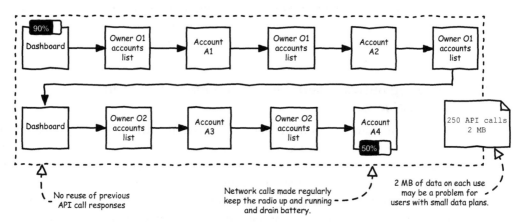

Figure 10.8   An average navigation through the Awesome Banking App

The Awesome Banking App team has dug into its analytics data, and it seems that an average user has access to two owners and that each owner has, on average, two accounts. The team has also determined that these average users typically navigate through all their data when using the app. Unfortunately, the app does not reuse previous API call responses because it does not know if the data can be reused. Therefore, new API calls are made on each screen even if the data has already been retrieved. This results in many API calls being made (around 250 per session, on average) and a considerable amount of data being exchanged (around 2 MB). Depending on how often users check their accounts, the Awesome Banking App could use around 60 to 90 MB of data per month.

Nowadays data use isn't really a problem for most users in most countries, but that's not true for all users everywhere. And for users who are traveling abroad, each KB can matter, because data is worth gold in that case. But beyond the data plan, the most annoying thing is that all the API calls made on each screen drain the device's battery because they keep the radio up and running for a longer period of time. Clearly, the number of calls, their length, and the data volume exchanged can be of concern on the consumer's side, but the same can be true on the provider's side.

Let's say the Banking API is hosted on the Barbrarian cloud service (which started life as an online book seller, but that's another story). The API is implemented using the brand new serverless service called Functions. Each goal is coded independently as a function, and there is no more need to worry about servers, applications, and scaling. The systems handle everything; when calls arrive, each corresponding function is run. The pricing of the service is based on the number of calls received, the processing time, and the outgoing data volume. This means that the more API calls are made, and the bigger they are, the more the Banking Company will have to pay. So, optimizing all that can be important and even vital.

These are only two examples. APIs can have different contexts than those we have just seen, but the network efficiency dimensions will usually resolve around these factors: speed, data volume, and number of calls. As API designers, we have to be aware of that and try to find a balance between the need for efficiency and an *ideal* design. Next, we will investigate how we can seek this balance and optimize network communication at the protocol level.

10.2   Ensuring network communication efficiency at the protocol level

Network communication optimization begins at the protocol level. Indeed, by taking advantage of the underlying protocol, it's possible to create a network-efficient API without having to tinker too much with your ideal design. For HTTP-based APIs, activating compression and persistent connections can reduce data volume and latency. Enabling *caching* (letting consumers know if they can save a response to reuse it and for how long) and *conditional requests* (allowing consumers to check if the data they have is still fresh enough to avoid retrieving it again) can reduce not only the data volume but also the number of calls.

10.2.1   Activating compression and persistent connections

For HTTP-based APIs, there are two fairly common optimizations that can be done without impacting design: activating compression and enabling persistent connections. Once compression is activated on the Banking API server, the 310 KB of data retrieved for the four account owners and their eight accounts in our second use case can be reduced to less than 2 KB. For the Awesome Banking App running on a mobile phone connected to a not-so-good 3G network, this means less data and shorter calls. Smaller responses will be downloaded faster, and the app will not use up the end user's data allowance. Most if not all consumers using a standard HTTP library can take advantage of this feature without having to modify anything in their code.

This server modification also benefits the consumer side. If the Banking API is hosted on an on-premises infrastructure, less data means less risk of network congestion because the overall bandwidth used is lower and network connections will be open for less time. For cloud infrastructures, this simply means smaller bills.

Once persistent connections are enabled on the Banking API server, the use case that required 25 calls distributed in seven steps taking a total of 4.2 s can be reduced to 2.4 s by removing 6 × 300 ms of latency. When persistent HTTP connections are enabled, only the first API call will have to suffer the connection latency; the subsequent calls are made using the same connection. The connection stays open for a given number of calls or a given time, determined by the server's configuration.

Switching to HTTP/2 can also be an option; out of the box, it offers efficient persistent connections, parallel requests, and binary transport, and the icing on the cake is that it is backward-compatible with HTTP/1.1! From an API design perspective, using

HTTP/2 has roughly the same effect as activating compression and persistent connections. It is transparent and requires no modifications. In both cases, the idea is to reduce the latency and the exchanged data volume and, therefore, the length of the API calls.

> **NOTE**   If API designers are not the tech leads, architects, or developers who usually handle these kinds of optimizations, they must be at least aware of the possible protocol optimizations (such as persistent connection or compression, for example) in order to propose solutions to possible network communication performance problems.

It's important for API designers to verify with the API team whether such optimizations have been considered prior to modifying an existing design because of network communication performance problems. Ideally, such optimizations must be done from the start, and optimizing communication for efficiency can have important effects on the design. Indeed, depending on the context, it could be wise to use different types of APIs and even different ways of communicating.

10.2.2 Enabling caching and conditional requests

A second way to optimize communications is simply to not communicate at all or, at least, to communicate less. In section 10.1.1, you saw that the Awesome Banking App was making many unnecessary calls because it did not reuse the responses of previous calls. In particular, to build the dashboard screen, the Awesome Banking App loaded a lot of data that could be reused when showing an owner's accounts list. Figure 10.9 shows the API calls made without and with response caching.

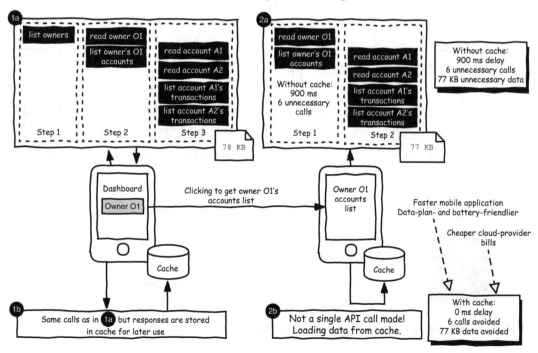

Figure 10.9   Reducing the number of calls with caching

The scenario at the top of the figure shows a totally unoptimized Awesome Banking App that does not reuse API call responses. In the scenario at the bottom of the figure, the application caches the responses of all the requests made on the dashboard screen. By doing so, it avoids six API calls when showing an owner's accounts list screen because it can get the needed data from the cache. This is good for the Awesome Banking App and its users: the application reacts faster when going from the dashboard to the accounts list screen, and it uses less of the network, the battery, and the data plan. It's also good for the Banking Company that provides the API; by avoiding the six unnecessary API calls in this scenario, the traffic to the Banking API is cut by 46% for calls and 50% for data volume.

As you can see, caching can be a great help in making network communications more efficient. This is what any mobile developer would do without even thinking about it. Consumers can choose to cache any of an API's responses, but the API can help them do it correctly and efficiently. The API designer is responsible for determining what data should be cached and for how long. Figure 10.10 shows how this can be done using the HTTP protocol.

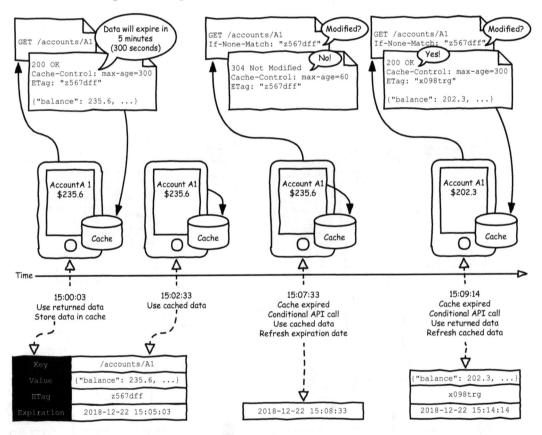

Figure 10.10   Using the HTTP protocol's caching features

When the Awesome Banking App gets the first account's information with a GET / accounts/A1 HTTP request, the API returns a 200 OK response along with the data and the Cache-Control and ETag HTTP headers. The Cache-Control header's value is max-age=300, which means that this response can be cached for 300 s (5 min). So if the application needs to show this account's data again in the next five minutes, it will use the cached response instead of making a call to the API.

Once the five minutes have passed, the cache has expired; therefore, the application will have to make another GET /accounts/A1 HTTP request if it needs the first account's information again. Rather than sending the exact same request as the first time, however, it can send a conditional request that basically says, "Give me account A1's data only if it has been modified." This is done by using the z567dff ETag value returned by the first call. An If-None-Match: "z567dff" header is sent along with the second request.

When the Banking API server receives the request, it uses the z567dff value to check if the account's data has been modified. This value describes the state of the resource that was sent with the first request. It could be a hash of the data, a date or a version number, or any other value that allows the server to know which version of the resource was provided earlier. Consumers do not need to know what this value actually is.

If the data has not been modified, the server returns a 304 Not Modified response without any data and, therefore, avoids loading data unnecessarily. The application updates the cache expiration date, which can be different from the first call, thanks to the Cache-Control header returned with the 304 response. The ETag header is not modified because the data has not changed.

The same request made later might get a 200 OK response, which says, "Yes, the data has been updated, here it is." This response contains the updated data along with the Cache-Control and ETag headers. In our example, the Cache-Control value is max-age=300, as before, but the ETag value is now x098trg. Its value has changed because the data of the resource has changed.

If the application only wants to know if the first account's data has changed but does not actually want to load the new data, it can send a HEAD /accounts/A1 request instead of GET /accounts/A1. The HEAD HTTP method is identical to GET except for the fact that the server does not return the resource content, only the headers.

REST constraints: Caching

The REST architectural style states that a response to a request must indicate if it can be stored (so a client can reuse it instead of making the same call again), and for how long. This is definitely a must have for any API to ensure that consumers will not have to make unnecessary calls and also to ensure that providers do not send too many resources for nothing, but return data that consumers already have. We've only seen a few of the possibilities of HTTP caching here; if you'd like to learn more, there is a dedicated RFC on that subject: RFC 7234 (https://tools.ietf.org/html/rfc7234).

By returning and accepting some metadata, but also by providing ways of getting only that metadata without the data, an API can enable the caching of its responses and propose conditional requests that greatly optimize network communications by reducing the number of calls and the volume of data returned. Caching also guarantees a certain freshness and accuracy of the data.

If your chosen protocol/API type provides these features natively, don't hesitate to use them. Be warned, however, that just because a response from the API can be cached, this does not mean that consumers will actually cache it. Furthermore, caching features might not always be available (for example, at the time of this book's writing, the gRPC framework does not provide these features). In such cases, if you decide caching is really important, you have two options. The first one is to reconsider your choice of protocol and API type; check if it was really the better one according to the context. The second is to recreate equivalent features in your API at the risk of providing a solution that is so custom or unusual (or inefficient) that consumers don't use it at all.

When designing an HTTP-based REST API, caching seems relatively simple; we only need to add the appropriate HTTP method, status code, and headers to the API description. But there's a little more to it than that. Where does the 5-minute cache duration come from? Why not 15 minutes or 2 days? Why is caching even allowed? The tricky thing about caching is that the caching possibilities must be evaluated for each goal and, more precisely, for each property returned by a goal.

10.2.3 *Choosing cache policies*

The data returned when a consumer requests an account's information might be its creation date, its name, and its balance. The creation date never changes. The name could change, but this rarely happens. In contrast, the balance is updated whenever a transaction occurs for that bank account. Because balance is the property that will change more often than any other, it is its *time to live* that determines the cache duration of the bank account data returned by this goal. So, how do we determine the correct cache duration value? Well, it depends.

How long data can be cached can depend on how often it is updated. In the beginning, the Banking Company only updated an account's transactions list and, therefore, the account balance a few times per day. So, a long caching duration of one hour was practicable. But the Banking Company has now improved its system: the transactions with other banks are still processed in batches a few times per day, but now all internal transactions are processed in real time. Therefore, in order to provide accurate data, the appropriate cache duration should be determined not only by how the banking system works but also by how people actually use their bank accounts.

The Banking Company has determined that statistically, a five-minute cache offers a good balance between accuracy and efficiency when getting account information.

In the near future, when all interbank communications will be done in real time and people will be used to always getting their banking information that way, caching data might not be possible at all. In that case, the `Cache-Control` header's value will be `"0"`, but at least it will still be possible to make conditional requests using the `ETag` value in order to avoid loading unchanged data.

How data can be cached can also depend on other matters. For example, presenting an inaccurate balance, even through a third-party application, can cause some problems from a legal or security perspective. Therefore, the Banking API's documentation might state that consumers must use fresh data. As with real-time balance information, in such a scenario, the API would provide a `Cache-Control` header with a value of `"0"` but can still make use of conditional requests.

Legal or security considerations might also prevent consumers from storing data, or there might be a middle ground where caching is allowed but not storage. In this scenario, the `Cache-Control` value could be `"60", no-store`, meaning data can be cached in a volatile storage for 60 s but cannot be stored in a non-volatile storage (`no-store`).

In a nutshell, as you've already seen in section 8.4.1, you might have to get some advice from the security people and the legal department when designing your API. So, although enabling conditional requests is quite simple, in order to be efficient and accurate some work is required to determine whether caching is actually possible and, if so, what is the best cache duration to choose.

These kinds of optimizations can be built in from the beginning, but they can also be implemented when the API is already being consumed without much impact on the interface contract or much work for the API designers. But API designers have far more responsibilities than just checking whether compression and persistent connections are activated and if consumers are actually using the cache. Indeed, the API design itself can be the cause of inefficient network communication between consumers and providers.

10.3 Ensuring network communication efficiency at the design level

Just because communication between consumers and providers can be optimized at the protocol level doesn't mean we can be careless at the design level. Fundamentally, the design of an API dictates the number of calls consumers need to make to achieve their goals and the amount of data exchanged between consumers and providers. By applying what you learned in previous chapters, you can design APIs that provide accurate goals, optimized data granularity and organization, and enough flexibility to ensure communication efficiency. As a reminder, we will work on the Banking API, whose current state is shown in figure 10.11.

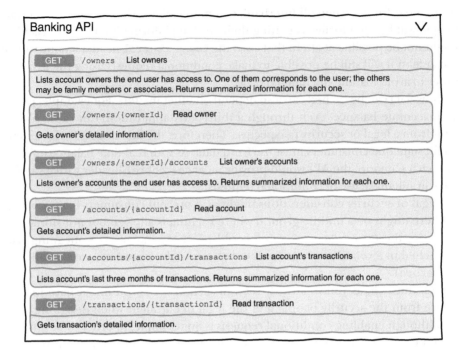

Figure 10.11   The Banking API goals

This design is quite easy to understand and seems, at least on the surface, relevant and well organized. But from a network communication efficiency perspective, it's far from perfect. Let's take a look at some strategies we can use to optimize the number of calls and the volume of data exchanged when the Banking API is used by the Awesome Banking App or any other consumer.

10.3.1 *Enabling filtering*

Providing filtering options is a good way to reduce the exchanged data volume because it allows consumers to get just what they really need. The list transactions goal always returns the last three months' worth of transactions, sorted from the latest (most recent) to the earliest (least recent). In the Awesome Banking App context, such data depth is needed when showing the cumulative sum of the transaction amounts on the dashboard and accounts list screens, even if users will probably never scroll through all these transactions. Thanks to caching possibilities, we can reuse this huge transactions list on the account screen. But unfortunately, when the cache expires, the application has to reload all three months' worth of transactions again, even if only one transaction has been added. It looks like this goal was tailor-made for the specific needs of the Awesome Banking App's dashboard and accounts list screens, but the result is not really efficient.

You learned in section 6.2.3 that always providing all the data might not be a good idea because consumers might not need all the data in all situations. Proposing filtering options makes an API more usable and more efficient by allowing consumers to request only the data they actually need—and this is what we desperately need here. Every byte saved improves communication efficiency in a hostile network context.

Based on what you have learned, you could add `page` and `size` query parameters to provide offset-based pagination features, but note that the goal can still return all three months' worth of transactions without these parameters to stay backward-compatible if the API is already being consumed. It seems that the account screen could make good use of this feature. A `GET /accounts/A1/transactions?page=1&size=25` request would return only the latest 25 transactions for the A1 account. If users scroll down, the application can request the next page with `GET /accounts/A1/transactions?page=2&size=25`. But what happens if new transactions occur between these two requests? Some transactions from the first page will shift to the second one, so the second request will return already retrieved transactions. It will be up to the consumer to check if it has already gotten each transaction and to ignore the duplicate ones.

This might not happen that much, but it can lead to providing inaccurate information, which is not tolerable for the Banking Company. This way of paginating transactions does not work well in this use case and context, and it doesn't solve the problem of reloading all three months' worth of transactions on the other screens. So what kinds of filters could we provide to solve this problem?

Consumers, whoever they are, basically need to be able to retrieve any transactions before or after a selected one to get exactly the data they want. Figure 10.12 shows how this could be done using cursor-based pagination.

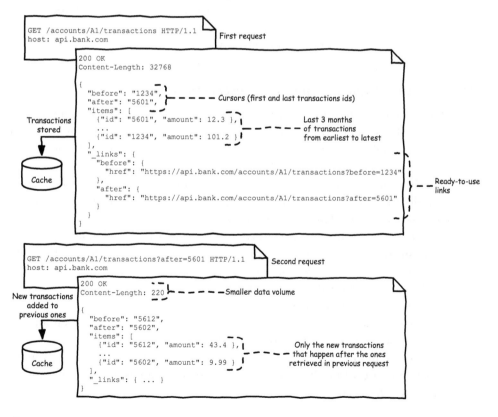

Figure 10.12 Cursor-based pagination to retrieve transactions

The Awesome Banking App still sends an initial request to get the last three months' worth of transactions using GET /accounts/{accountsId}/transactions, but now the response contains pagination metadata. The before and after properties are cursor values that can be used to retrieve the transactions before or after the retrieved set. Their values are the IDs of the first (latest) and last (earliest) transactions of the set, respectively. To only retrieve transactions that occurred after the current transaction set was retrieved, the application has to send a second request like this:

```
GET /accounts/{accountId}/transactions?after={latestTransactionId}
```

The after value is the last known transaction ID, or the previously provided cursor. Better yet, consumers can use the ready-to-use before link. Because the response to this request contains only the new transactions, its size is far smaller. Such a design greatly diminishes the volume of data downloaded by the Awesome Banking App and also improves response time, both because there's less data to download and because the requests take less time to process on the server side.

This solution also works on the account's transactions list screen in the unlikely event of users scrolling beyond the three months' worth of cached transactions. In that case, this request using the before link

```
GET /accounts/{accountId}/transactions?before={earliestTransactionId}&size=25
```

retrieves the 25 transactions that took place *before* the one identified by earliest-TransactionId. Providing filtering options is a good strategy to lessen the volume of data exchanged and improve usability. But in order to provide accurate and efficient filters, it's important to consider the nature of the data and the contexts of use.

10.3.2 *Choosing relevant data for list representations*

Which data you choose to return in lists can have a big impact on communication efficiency. The Banking API is not as efficient as it could be because it does not provide all the relevant data in lists. As shown in figure 10.13, the Awesome Mobile Banking App shows account owners' titles and names on its dashboard screen.

If the owners' names can only be retrieved using the list owners goal, the summarized data does not provide the titles. To get this information, the application has to read each owner's detailed information. This is an indicator of an incorrect balance between the summarized representation of resources, usually returned in lists, and the detailed one, usually returned when accessing a specific resource. By simply adding the title to the summarized version, we can avoid the calls to read owner.

The same goes for the list accounts goal, which does not return the account types and, therefore, requires extra calls to the read account goal to get this fundamental information. Adding the type property into the summarized representation returned by list accounts prevents any additional API calls.

We could modify the list transactions goal the same way, but we'll go even further. As shown in figure 10.14, the account screen needs to call list transactions and then read transaction for each one.

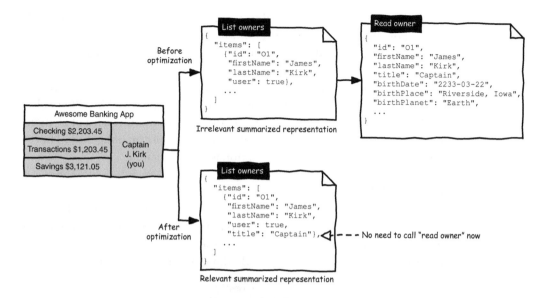

Figure 10.13 Choosing relevant summarized representations in lists

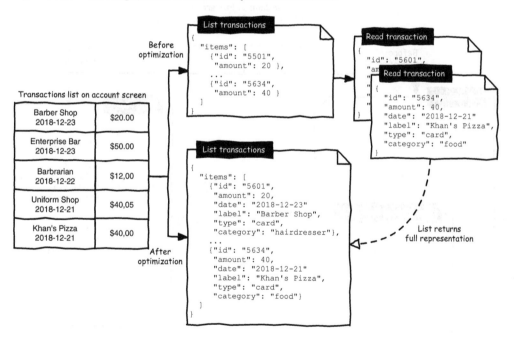

Figure 10.14 Using full representations in lists

The summarized transaction representation returned in the list only contains an ID and a label; the amount and transaction type are missing. This requires the consumer to request detailed information about each transaction. Given the nature of transactions, which are usually numerous and reviewed in batches, the list transactions goal should return the complete representation of each transaction instead of just a summary.

Why not do the same modification for other lists, like the owner's list? The owner resource contains much more data, and most of it is not relevant when working with a list. But returning all the data in the owner's list would increase the data volume unnecessarily.

Choosing a relevant representation including the most representative and useful properties of a resource is the best way not only to create a usable API but also to avoid many API calls after getting the list's data. Although requesting a list of elements usually returns a summarized version of each element, this is not an obligation. There are cases when returning a complete representation is more efficient.

10.3.3 *Aggregating data*

Fine-grained resources provide a flexible and precise way to get different subsets of data from a concept, but they can lead to many API calls when consumers need to get all the data. Without taking into account the previous optimizations we have made, figure 10.15 shows how the Awesome Banking App loads an owner's data.

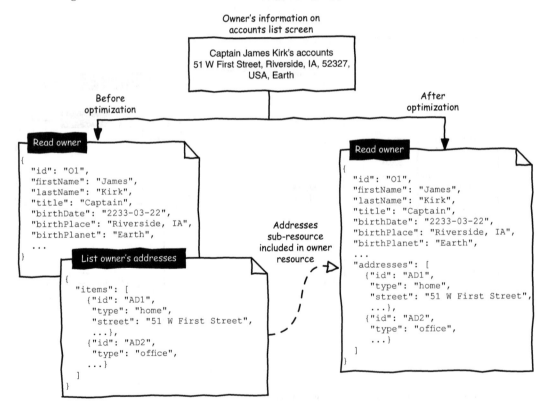

Figure 10.15   Aggregating subresources and the parent resource

The owner's data is split between the owner resource, available via the read owner goal, and the addresses resource, available via the list addresses goal. Consumers can get one subset or the other, but this means two API calls are needed to get two closely related and quite small sets of data. This is cumbersome; and in a hostile network context, we can't afford this additional call. We've already seen a similar use case in section 7.2. A better design would be to include the list of addresses with the rest of the owner's data so a single call to the read owner goal would return all the required data.

Taking this a step further, why not aggregate accounts and their transactions? This is not a good idea, however, for several reasons: there are likely to be many transactions for each account, consumers might want to filter transactions by type or date, and most importantly, the transactions list is regularly updated. Aggregating the list of addresses into the owner's data was OK because the data volume is relatively low and the addresses do not change too frequently. Even if consumers need to select a given type of address, they just need to filter a list of 10 elements at most. And if the data changes, there won't be too much data to retrieve. For account transactions, however, it's better to keep dedicated access.

So, we can't aggregate transactions into the account's data, but what about trying a bigger aggregation on the other side of the tree? Why not get all the data except the transactions list with a single call? Figure 10.16 shows the impact of such an aggregation for the use case involving a user having access to four owners and their eight accounts.

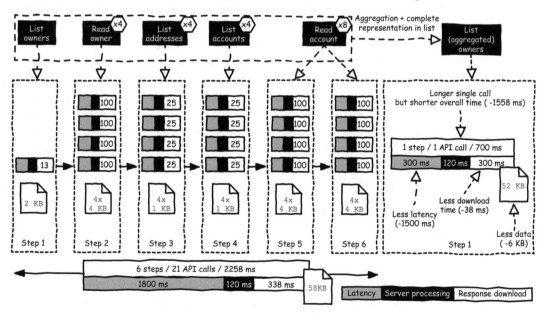

Figure 10.16   Extended aggregation has an impact on communication.

Retrieving all account data except the transactions in one call would mean returning full account representations into the accounts list, aggregating all this data into the owner resource along with the list of addresses, and returning a complete representation of each owner in the owners list. What do we gain by replacing these 17 API calls (distributed in six steps, taking 2.2 s, and representing 58 KB of data) with a single call?

The latency time is reduced from 1,500 ms to 300 ms because there is a single step instead of six. Surprisingly, there is also less data downloaded: 52 KB instead of 58 KB. This is because the duplicated data returned in summarized lists is not downloaded anymore; the data is returned only once with the read owner or read account goal. The server processing time is still 120 ms; but in reality, it would probably be reduced too. The overall time is reduced from 2.2 s to 700 ms. Now, instead of several short calls, we have one longer one. That's quite an impressive result; the response time is cut by almost 70%!

We could keep this new list of the aggregated owners goal and the list transactions goal and remove all the other goals in the Banking API. But keep in mind that the diminution mostly concerns the latency time; if persistent connections are enabled on the API server, the aggregation might not be quite as effective.

In certain contexts, aggregation can also hinder caching possibilities. The time-to-live of the aggregated data is the smallest value of all the individual properties (in this case, the account's balance, which can change quite often). Therefore, when the balance of a single account changes, consumers will have to reload a lot of data. Although this might not seem like a big deal, in hostile network conditions having one very long call instead of several shorter ones can be problematic. The longer a request lasts on a 3G network, the higher the risk of losing the connection, and if the connection is lost when 95% of the download has been completed, the consumer will have to download all the data again.

Finally, in addition to performance, aggregation can have an impact on usability. It might not be easy for consumers to understand how an API works when providing only list owners and list transactions goals. So aggregating data can be a valid solution to possible communication performance problems, but it must be done carefully with a good view and understanding of all the implications. When designing resources and goals, choose their granularity wisely to ensure the API is not only usable but also efficient.

10.3.4 *Proposing different representations*

By wisely using aggregation or using more complete representations in lists, we can design a more efficient API. But that is quite a rigid solution; all consumers might not need all data in all cases. How can we make our API more adaptable and provide consumers with a way to choose the representation that best fits their needs?

You already know the answer to this question: we can use content negotiation, the capability of providing different representations of a resource, as you discovered in section 6.2.1. As shown in figure 10.17, we could provide three different levels of representations of our resources: summarized, complete, and extended.

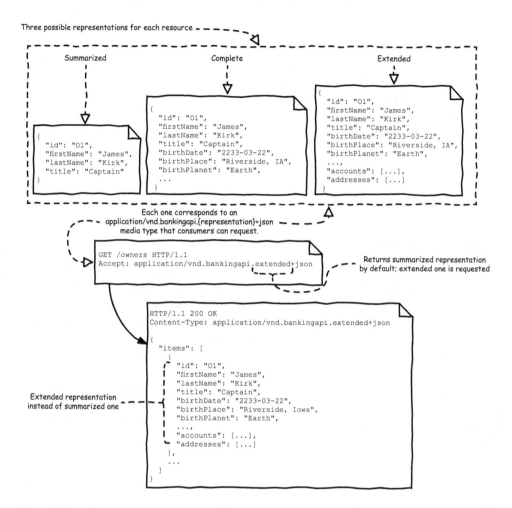

Figure 10.17   Using content negotiation to get an appropriate representation

We are used to getting a complete representation when reading a specific resource, as with the read owner goal (`GET /owners/{ownersId}`). The summarized representation provides a subset of the complete representation's data. It's the one we are used to getting in lists using the list owners goal (`GET /owners`, for example). Finally, the extended representation is an aggregation of the resource's and its subresources' data. Here, it provides the complete data for the owner resource along with its subresources' data—the complete representations of the accounts and addresses resources.

Now, when the Awesome Banking App requests to read owners on its dashboard screen, it can indicate that it wants the extended representation of each owner instead of the default summarized one by sending an `Accept` header whose value is `application/vnd.bankingapi.extended+json`. This way, it can avoid separate calls to read owners, list accounts, and read account.

The positive and negative impacts on speed, caching, and risk of lost connections are the same as those you saw in section 10.3.3; but now other consumers have the option of choosing to get only the summarized representation of each owner if that's all they need. Also, to get an updated account balance, consumers can send a `GET /accounts/{accountId}` request along with an `Accept: application/vnd.bankingapi.summarized+json` header to get only the data required instead of the regular complete representation.

There is no standard way of handling this mechanism. The `application/vnd.bankingapi.{representation}+json` media types shown here are totally custom ones. Their names use the standard `vnd` prefix, which stands for *vendor*. The `+json` suffix is also standard and states that this custom media type basically is JSON data. Providing different representations of a resource can help to provide a more efficient and more flexible API, but we can do better.

10.3.5 *Enabling expansion*

Using content negotiation, we can design a much more flexible API providing, for example, three different representations of an owner. But that's still a bit rigid. What if consumers only need to get summarized representations of owners along with their accounts but without their addresses? This isn't possible unless we add a fourth, not-so-summarized, representation of an owner. Let's try something else: a technique called *resource expansion*, illustrated in figure 10.18.

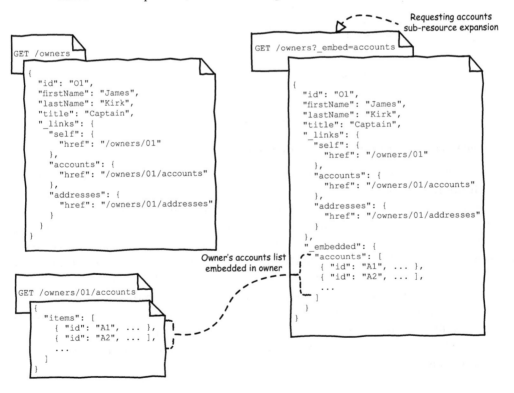

Figure 10.18   Expanding the owner's accounts subresource in the owners list

On the left, we can see a list owners request (`GET /owners`), which returns a summarized representation of owners, and a list accounts request (`GET /owners/01/accounts`), which returns a summarized representation of accounts. Note that in this representation, we provide HAL links in the `_link` property (see section 6.3.2).

On the right, the list owners request includes an `_embed=accounts` query parameter, which means "Please embed all owners' accounts lists in the response." The response actually includes this information in the `_embedded.accounts` property.[1] If consumers send a request with an `_embed=accounts, addresses` query parameter, the returned owner representations include lists for both accounts and addresses under the `_embedded` property. This `_embed` parameter allows us to trigger subresource expansion or embedding. Again, drawbacks can include longer requests, bigger responses, and caching inefficiency.

There is no standard way of proposing such a mechanism; what is presented here is totally custom. The query parameter could be named `embed`, `expand`, or any other name you choose. Depending on how the data is organized and which hypermedia format is used (HAL, Siren, custom, and so forth), the way the subresources are included can vary.

Resource expansion is another way of reducing the number of calls consumers might have to make to retrieve a data tree. However, further economies are possible through querying.

10.3.6 Enabling querying

If every single byte and millisecond really matters, we can make our API even more adaptable by letting consumers query the data they want, property by property, in order to reduce the data volume and, possibly, the number of API calls. For example, a `GET /owners?_fields=id` request could return a list of owners; but for each owner, the consumer would get only the owner's ID. There is no standard way of proposing such a mechanism with a REST API, but it's usually done with a query parameter named `fields` or `properties` (or something similar), whose value is a list of property names (like `title`), or with JSON paths (like `$.accounts[*].id`, for example, to get all account IDs).

Alternatively, if more complex queries are needed, to reduce the data volume, you can consider another option: an existing query language. REST is not the only way of doing APIs. We've already briefly talked about gRPC, but here's another style of API that might be of interest: GraphQL. Created by Facebook in 2012 and open-sourced in 2015, GraphQL is

> *"A query language for APIs and a runtime for fulfilling those queries with your existing data."*
>
> *https://graphql.org*

This section is not intended to teach you how to build GraphQL APIs; it is only meant to provide an example of an existing API query language that you could use to let consumers query the data they want instead of creating your own. The following listing shows a basic GraphQL call that queries the owners list. It's equivalent to a `GET /owners?_fields=id` request.

---

[1] This representation conforms to the HAL specification (https://tools.ietf.org/html/draft-kelly-json-hal-06#section-4.1.2).

Listing 10.1   A GraphQL API call and its response

```
POST /graphql

{
 "query": "{ owners { id } }"
}

HTTP/1.1 200 OK
{
  "owners": [
    {"id": "01"},
    {"id": "02"},
    ...
  ]
}
```

A GraphQL API call consists of a POST request on a generic graphql path. Its body is a JSON document that, when reading data, contains a query string property. This property's value is the actual GraphQL query that will be executed to retrieve data.

Don't be fooled by the curly braces; this query is not written in JSON! The { owners { id } } query states that we only want each owner's ID. The following listing shows a longer GraphQL query, which goes in the query property, retrieving some additional data about owners and their accounts.

Listing 10.2   Retrieving some owner and account data

```
{
  owners {
    id
    title
    firstName
    lastName
    accounts {
      id
      balance
    }
  }
}
```

This request returns a list of owners containing the selected data. To do this using the REST Banking API (not providing aggregated data), we would need to chain multiple API calls. We would first list owners with GET /owners and then list each owner's accounts with a GET /owners/{ownerId}/accounts request.

Now imagine that the Banking API proposes a goal allowing us to retrieve a list of nearby ATMs. With a REST API, we would use a request like

```
GET /atms?latitude=48&longitude=2&distance=2
```

to get the ATMs within two miles of the specified location. But as shown in the next listing, we could run two queries using a single GraphQL API call to retrieve the owners and their accounts as well as the list of nearby ATMs.

Listing 10.3   Executing multiple queries

```
{
  owners {
    id
    title
    firstName
    lastName
    accounts {
      id
      balance
    }
  }
  atms (latitude: 48, longitude: 2, distance: 2) {
    address
    longitude
    latitude
  }
}
```

Consumers can easily select exactly the data they want and make multiple queries in a single call. But because GraphQL only uses the POST HTTP method, requests cannot be cached using HTTP's standard caching mechanism, whereas a GET /atms?latitude=48&longitude=2&distance=2 request can.

At the time of this book's writing, GraphQL does not propose any caching mechanism; it is up to the consumers to guess how long they can cache data. And as with data aggregation, caching the response as a whole might not make sense because it can contain heterogeneous data with very different time-to-live values. There are other implications that must be evaluated before choosing such a solution; we will talk a little bit more about these in section 11.3.1.

Enabling data querying might be appropriate in some scenarios, but not all. It can reduce the volume of data transferred and the number of API calls, but at the possible expense of caching possibilities.

10.3.7 *Providing more relevant data and goals*

As you've just seen, the Awesome Banking App could retrieve all the data needed for any of its screens in a single call using an API query language. But before we consider changing the Banking API's type from REST to GraphQL, we should reconsider its design. Indeed, inefficient communication can be a symptom of a design that does not fulfill consumers' actual needs.

We've already seen in sections 10.3.2 and 10.3.3 that our choices about resource granularity and what data we include in summarized representations have an impact not only on communication efficiency but also, more importantly, on usability. But providing a design that is both usable and network-efficient requires more than just selecting which data to return in lists and how to carve up resources—providing *relevant* data and goals is the key to creating such a design.

When consumers need to get information about an account, they usually need its type, name, balance, and transaction history. The Banking API provides all of that, thanks to the read account and list transactions goals. But the balance of an account is modified every time a new transaction occurs.

Using the current design, updating this information can be done by requesting the latest transactions using cursor-based pagination (see section 10.3.1) or with a conditional request (see section 10.2.2). If there are new transactions, consumers then have to read the account again to get the updated balance, even though all the other account data has probably not changed at all. Banking API consumers will probably never use the transactions list without the account's balance.

These are definitely closely related data: the balance is based on the transaction amounts. As shown in the following listing, adding the updated account balance to each transaction could simplify this.

Listing 10.4   Adding an updated balance to transactions

```
{
  "items": [
    {"id": "5601", "date": "2018-12-23", "amount": 20,    "balance": 202.3,
      ...},
    {"id": "5550", "date": "2018-12-23", "amount": 20,    "balance": 222.3,
      ...},
    {"id": "5548", "date": "2018-12-22", "amount": 23.7, "balance": 246,
      ...},
    ...
  ]
}
```

When retrieving new transactions, consumers will now automatically get the updated account balance each time without having to read the account again. As a bonus, this modification provides interesting historical information: consumers can see how the balance has changed over time. Note that it is not because the account's balance has been added to transactions that it should be removed from the read account account goal; the balance is useful in both places.

Providing relevant data also means not providing all the available data. Indeed, focusing on the consumer's perspective can help to limit data volumes (remember section 2.4.1). In our case, the Banking API's owner and account resources could probably omit a few uninteresting properties that only matter for the API provider's implementation.

> **NOTE**   Adding the right data to the right resources and focusing on the consumer's perspective to provide only data that's actually relevant can improve both usability and network efficiency.

At the root of the Banking API resources tree organization is the accessible owners list; all consumers have to pass by this root to do anything. This seems appropriate for the Awesome Banking App, whose screens show the data with the same organization as the API. But that means all consumers have to list owners with a GET /accounts/ {ownerId}/accounts call to know which accounts are accessible. That could be annoying for those who don't really care about the account owners. But when advisors want to get an overview of all accounts of all their customers, it could be useful to add a GET /accounts to the API, which would return all the accounts that can be accessed by current users (whomever they are).

Also, among the owners returned by the list owners goal, one corresponds to the end user. With the current design, consumers only wanting to get data about the end user have to list owners and search for the one having the endUser flag set to true in the returned list. By using a magic resource ID such as me, consumers could directly read the end user's information using the read owner goal with a GET /owners/me request without having to list owners first to determine the user's ID.

As you can see, adding more goals providing different access to the same resources or more direct access can also improve usability and efficiency in different contexts. For example, the way the Awesome Banking App builds its main dashboard screen could lead to the addition of data to existing goals or even the creation of more specific goals. The aggregation of transaction amounts and account balances by owner could be done by the API's implementation and added to the owner's data. The aggregation of transaction amounts could also be added to the data returned by read account and list transactions, alongside the account's balance.

If it makes sense for other consumers, we could also consider adding a read dashboard goal accessible via a GET /dashboards/me request that would return the data needed by the Awesome Banking App's dashboard screen. If many consumers are likely to benefit from such a modification, it should be added to the API.

Also be aware that consumers will probably use your APIs in unexpected ways. Whether because of blatant holes in the initial design or because some consumers simply have ideas you would never have dreamed of, it's wise to analyze such unexpected uses and modify the design as needed in order to provide the most efficient experience. Indeed, it's crucial for API designers to evaluate the efficiency of their API designs.

As you saw in section 10.1.2, depending on the use case, the Banking API's efficiency varies greatly: loading the dashboard data could take 5 API calls completing in 1.2 s or 25 calls completing in 4.2 s. When evaluating communication efficiency, you must not think only about basic use cases. An API's goals flows can look perfect with a very basic hypothetical use case but become nightmares when confronted with reality or edge cases. API designers must always test their designs with actual use cases in order to truly evaluate their efficiency.

10.3.8 *Creating different API layers*

Trying to optimize APIs for network communication efficiency is a good thing, but API designers must know when to say no. Optimizing an API design in order to provide efficient communication must not be done at the expense of usability and reusability. Trying to please all consumers by making specific modifications here and there or adding multiple highly specific goals will probably lead to a complex API that will not be reusable. Fortunately, by using the various techniques described in this chapter, you should be able to design an efficient API, and this should give you the confidence to push back when necessary.

If consumers really have specific needs, they should build their own APIs on top of the provider's. In the mobile app and website world, such a component is called a *BFF* (not "best friends forever" but "backend for frontend"). The Awesome Banking App's developer team could, for example, build a GraphQL-based BFF relying upon the Banking API. Doing so is quite simple; there are GraphQL libraries that can help developers do this without having to code much.

Providers can also provide such APIs themselves, creating a new API layer in their systems. Such specialized APIs are sometimes called *experience APIs* (regardless of their type—REST, GraphQL, or whatever), and their design is optimized for a specific context of use from a functional or technical (network, usually) perspective.

Below the experience APIs, you might find *original/not specialized APIs*. These are APIs whose design is consumer-oriented but that are not really confined to a specific context of use. And below this layer, you might find *system APIs* providing access to core systems. If you remember the microwave oven example in section 2.1, such an API would give access to the magnetron.

In the next chapter, we will fully explore the context surrounding the API from both the consumer's and provider's sides in order to design APIs that are more fully usable and implementable.

Summary

- API designers have a role to play in network communication efficiency.
- The very first step of network optimization is at the protocol level, not the design level.
- API granularity and adaptability have impacts on network efficiency.
- Network efficiency problems can be a sign of missing or inadequate goals in the API.
- API design optimizations must not be done at the expense of usability and reusability; providing different API layers can help to avoid such booby traps.

Designing an API in context

This chapter covers

- Adapting communications to goals and data
- Considering needs and limitations of consumers and provider
- Choosing an API style based on context

In the previous chapter, we started to discover that the APIs we were designing were created ignoring most of the context in which they exist. We explored the network context and how it can impact the design of APIs. But there are other contextual elements to consider in order to design APIs that will actually fulfill all your consumers' needs and also be implementable. As we've seen, designing APIs requires us to focus on the consumers first, but it also requires us to keep an eye on the provider's side.

Do you know how the QWERTY keyboard layout was invented at the end of the 19th century? The most common story is that it was created to solve a mechanical problem. On a typewriter, letters are mounted on metal arms that can clash and jam if two neighboring keys are pressed at the same time or in rapid succession. To avoid this mechanical problem and allow users to type faster, commonly used letter pairs were placed far away from each other. This story, if true, means that the

QWERTY design was influenced by internal concerns. But according to Koichi Yasuoka and Motoko Yasuoka from Kyoto University[1]

> *"The early keyboard of Type-Writer was derived from Hughes-Phelps Printing Telegraph, and it was developed for Morse receivers. The keyboard arrangement very often changed during the development, and accidentally grew into QWERTY among the different requirements. QWERTY was adopted by Teletype in the 1910's, and Teletype was widely used as a computer terminal later."*
>
> *Koichi Yasuoka and Motoko Yasuoka*

According to this research, the design was in fact influenced by the context in which typewriters were used. Regardless of its origin, the funny thing is that this relic of the past is still widely used today. I have inspected my smartphone and did not find any metal arms behind its touchscreen; but in most countries, Latin or Roman alphabetic digital keypads still use the QWERTY layout or their local version, like AZERTY in France, for example. Even if does not make sense anymore, people are used to it, and the few who dared to try to change their habits were not really successful. So how objects are built and how they work, how they are used and what their users are used to, can influence their design, and the same goes for APIs, as shown in figure 11.1.

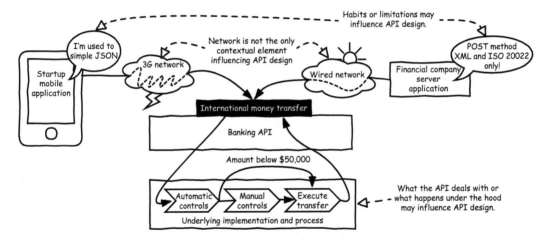

Figure 11.1   Provider and consumer contexts influence API design.

While most developers might be used to consuming JSON-based APIs, taking full advantage of the HTTP protocol, there are dark corners of the software industry where XML still rules, and POST is the only possible HTTP method. The banking industry is used to ISO 20022 standard messages, which could be considered

---

[1]   Koichi Yasuoka and Motoko Yasuoka, "On the Prehistory of QWERTY," Kyoto University, March 2011 (https://doi.org/10.14989/139379).

complex and not user-friendly, but trying to provide APIs supporting other simpler formats to banking companies can cause more problems than the ones these formats are supposed to solve.

Context impacting design is not reserved to consumer contexts, either. The provider's context can also influence design, even if API designers do everything they can to hide the provider's perspective (see section 2.4). Representing a goal involving human controls (such as some cases of international money transfers) with a synchronous request/response mechanism might not be the best option. That is why when we design APIs, we must choose the best way to communicate, taking into account both consumers' and providers' potential limitations and even considering other styles of APIs beyond REST. If we do not do that, the APIs we design might not be fully usable or implementable.

11.1 Adapting communication to the goals and nature of the data

So far, we have been talking about synchronous web APIs that allow consumers to send requests to providers and get responses immediately. But depending on the nature of an API's goals and data, a unitary and synchronous request/response-based mechanism might not be the most efficient representation. You might have to deal with long processing times, send events to consumers, or process multiple elements in one shot. As an API designer, you must have tools other than synchronous request/response in your toolbox to deal with such cases.

11.1.1 Managing long processes

A synchronous request/response mechanism is not always the best option to represent a goal. Sometimes you might have to provide asynchronous goals. For example, the Banking API provides a transfer money goal that allows both national and international money transfers. But according to banking regulations, depending on which country and bank the target account is located in and the transfer amount, some documents might have to be provided in order to explain the nature of the transaction. Therefore, the consumer (the Awesome Banking App, for example) must provide the source and destination for each transfer (see section 5.3). To determine the valid sources and destinations, it uses the aggregated list sources and destinations goal.

The data returned by this goal not only describes all possible source and destination combinations and their minimum and maximum amounts, but also indicates in which cases documentation justifying the transaction must be provided. If documentation is required, the consumer can use the upload transfer document goal to send that and get a reference. Figure 11.2 shows what happens afterwards: validation by a human.

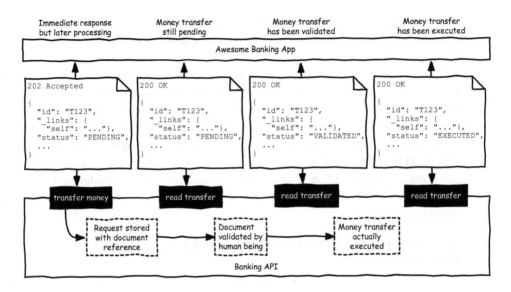

Figure 11.2   A money transfer requiring human validation

Once the document is uploaded, the consumer can use the transfer money goal, indicating the source account, the destination account, the amount, and the document reference. Unfortunately, the money transfer cannot be triggered immediately because the provided document has to be validated by a human being. So in this case, the money transfer response status is `202 Accepted` (instead of `201 Created`, which would be the response if no validation was required). This means the money transfer request has been accepted but will be processed later.

The returned data indicates the current status of the money transfer (`PENDING`), the transfer's ID (`T123`), and the `"self"` URL in `_links`. The consumer can later use the read transfer goal using the provided ID or `self` URL to check the transfer's current status. This status can be either `PENDING` (if no action has yet been performed), `VALIDATED` (if the document has been validated by a human being, but the transfer has not yet been performed), or `EXECUTED` (if the money transfer has been completed). Note that when accessing the transfer's status using a `GET /transfers/T123` HTTP request, cache directives (see section 10.2.2) can provide some hints about when is it wise to retry this call to get updated information.

As you can see, depending on the nature of the goal, what actually happens from a functional perspective using a synchronous request/response mechanism might not be possible. Here, it would mean consumers waiting for several minutes (or even hours, if not days) to get a response, which obviously is unthinkable. In such cases, the API has to provide a goal to receive the request, which can take quite a long time to process, and then a way to get the status of this request's processing later. Providing information about when to make another request by taking advantage of protocol features or by simply returning data benefits both consumer and provider by avoiding unnecessary calls.

11.1.2 *Notifying consumers of events*

Consumer-to-provider communication is not always the most efficient way of communicating. Indeed, sometimes it can be useful to let the provider take the initiative.

In the previous section, we saw that consumers might have to make repeated API calls to ask, "Is this money transfer done?" Such behavior is called *polling*, and it can be quite annoying for both consumers and providers: many unnecessary calls can be made. It would be great if the Banking API could instead tell its consumers when a money transfer is actually done.

Reversing the consumer/provider communication can be done using a *webhook*, which is often described as a "reverse API." Figure 11.3 shows how such a mechanism could be used with the Awesome Banking App to notify the consumer of an executed money transfer.

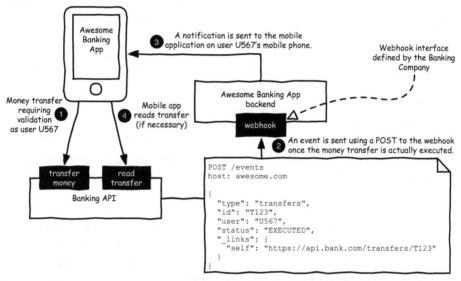

Figure 11.3   Using a webhook to notify the consumer of the execution of a money transfer

As before, the Awesome Banking App calls the Banking API to request a money transfer that requires (human) validation (1). The Banking API again responds with a 202 Accepted status to indicate that the request has been accepted and will be processed later. Now the mobile application does not have to poll (regularly make calls to) the Banking API to get the transfer's status. Instead, once the money transfer has actually been executed, the Banking API (or more probably another module managed inside the Banking Company's systems) sends a POST request to the Awesome Banking App's webhook URL, https://awesome-banking.com/events (2). The request's body contains some data about the event that occurred, like the ID of the user who initiated the money transfer, the transfer ID, the event's status, and the transfer's "self" link, for example.

When the Awesome Banking App backend implementing the webhook receives this event, it can look for the mobile phone identifier corresponding to the user and send a notification using the iOS or Android notification system to the mobile application to signify that money transfer T123 has been executed (3). Finally, the mobile application can use the read transfer goal to get further information that was not included in the event or notification (4).

Such a mechanism is not restricted to an asynchronous communication initiated by the consumer. It can also be used to notify consumers of events that are generated without any consumer interaction. For example, events could be sent when new transactions occur on a bank account. The Awesome Banking App could take advantage of this for its dashboard, owner, and account screens (see section 10.2). It could also rely on cached data as long as no such event is sent.

More specific and custom events could be sent too. For example, the Banking API could provide an alerting system that sends events based on transactions or balance data. Using such a feature, the Awesome Banking App could allow its users to configure alerts like, "Let me know when my account balance is below $200" or "Let me know when a card payment above $120 is made." The Banking API would send these alert events through the webhook only for users who have configured those.

This looks great, but how does the Banking Company, the provider of the Banking API, know the Awesome Banking App's webhook URL and its interface? In section 8.1, you saw how consumers have to register to be able to consume an API and how they are identified when they send a request. When registering the Awesome Banking App on the Banking API developer portal, its developer team indicated its webhook URL, which can be used to notify the consumer of events.

This webhook is an API that is implemented by the Awesome Banking App team, but its interface contract and behavior are defined by the Banking API team in order to ensure that all consumers expose the same webhook API. It would obviously be a nightmare for the Banking Company to let each consumer design its own webhook interface contract as it would have to code specifically the webhook calls for each of its consumer.

Like any APIs, you have to design webhook APIs to hide the provider's perspective and make them usable and evolvable. Depending on your needs, a single webhook might receive all possible events, or there might be multiple webhooks: one for each event type. Each event might provide a little data or a lot. It will be up to you to decide what's appropriate.

Having a single webhook that receives lightweight, generic events is usually a good strategy. Such a webhook API is quite simple to implement and to consume, and adding new events is easy. You should always decide on what design to use according to your context.

There is another important characteristic that must not be overlooked when dealing with webhook APIs—security. A webhook can be exposed on the internet, and some malicious people might try to send *false* events in order to hack the provider's systems. That's one of the reasons why using lightweight, generic events is a good option; consumers have to call the provider to get detailed information.

It's crucial that the access to the webhook API be secured in order to ensure that only the API provider can actually use it. Securing a webhook can be done using various techniques, such as provider IP address whitelisting (bear in mind that such whitelists might be hard to maintain), sending a secret token when posting to the webhook, encrypting and signing the request, using mutual TLS, and so on.

As you saw in chapter 8, API designers don't have much to say about the technical side of API security, but they heavily contribute from a functional perspective. You have to ensure that events do not contain sensitive data and that the data provided allows consumers to react securely. For example, if an event concerns a specific user, an API's consumers must be able to identify that user through the event's data. Otherwise, a user can get undue access to other users' data. This again promotes the use of lightweight events to limit the damage that can be done if this should occur.

> ## WebSub
>
> There is no webhook standard. Although you can design your API as you wish, the W3C has issued a WebSub recommendation (https://www.w3.org/TR/websub/) that you can take advantage of when building webhook-based systems:
>
> *"WebSub provides a common mechanism for communication between publishers of any kind of Web content and their subscribers, based on HTTP web hooks. Subscription requests are relayed through hubs, which validate and verify the request. Hubs then distribute new and updated content to subscribers when it becomes available. WebSub was previously known as PubSubHubbub."*
>
> W3C WebSub recommendation
>
> Basically, the WebSub recommendation describes how an API provider (the publisher) can expose its event capabilities and let consumers (the subscribers) register for and receive events, all in a secure way. Being inspired by this recommendation, the Banking API could provide a standard API to let consumers register for events like the alerts mechanism discussed earlier in this section.

Webhooks basically are APIs implemented by API consumers but defined and used by API providers to send notifications of events. These events can be triggered by consumer or provider actions. This is not the only way of implementing notifications, but with this model, providers can notify consumers about events when they happen and don't have to wait for the consumers to make API calls themselves.

11.1.3 Streaming event flows

When an API provides data that always changes to consumers using a basic request/response goal, you can be sure that they will poll it continuously, making repeated API calls in order to get new or updated data. Suppose the Banking API provided data about stocks for trading account portfolios. There are different options for doing so, as shown in figure 11.4.

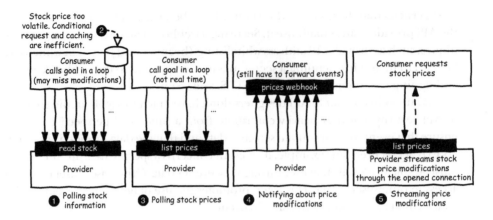

Figure 11.4   How the Banking API could provide stock information

The Banking API could offer a read stock goal that provides detailed information about a specific stock and its price (1). Consumers wanting to always have the latest stock price might call this goal in a *loop* (once they get the new data, they trigger another call, endlessly).

In section 10.2.2, you discovered caching and conditional requests (2). Could these be of any help? Unfortunately, those would be useless, at least when the stock exchanges are open, because the stock prices can change every second (if not more frequently). The cache's time-to-live would be so short that caching would be ineffective and conditional requests would always return updated data. This data is so volatile that even using polling, consumers might not be aware of all price variations as the price could vary between calls.

In section 10.3.7, you saw that sometimes we have to check if a goal really fulfills consumers' needs. Maybe this goal is not the right one. What about adapting the API's design and providing a list stock prices goal returning the *n* latest price variations and offering cursor-based pagination (3)? Consumers could indicate the last price ID they received and, in that way, be sure to not miss any price variations. That could be an interesting option if consumers are willing to get not-quite-real-time data, but consumers would still poll this goal endlessly.

A change in stock price looks like an event that consumers could be notified of. So what about a webhook (4)? Because the provider knows when a stock price changes, it can post that event to consumers' webhooks as soon as it occurs. But that means always sending price variations of all stocks to all consumers.

Using a WebSub system or a custom WebSub–like one, as we discussed briefly in the previous section, consumers could subscribe to a few stock price variation feeds instead of receiving notifications about all of them. They would still get this data all the time, though.

But what about consumers that want to show real-time data for only a small period of time, while their end users are looking at their portfolios or at a specific stock, for example? They would have to find a way to forward these event flows. How could an API server (like the Banking API's) send a stream of events requested by a consumer (5)? Figure 11.5 contrasts a basic request/response API call and a Server-Sent Events (SSE) stream that can be used in such cases.

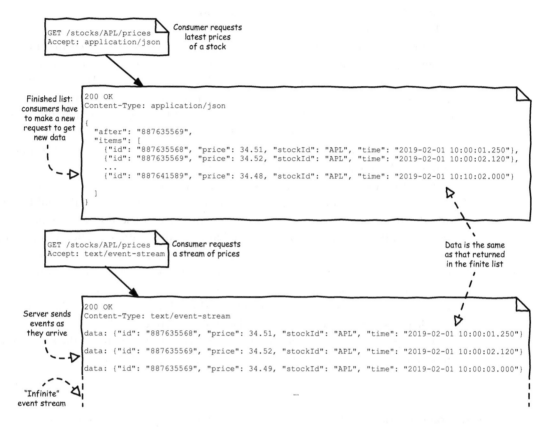

Figure 11.5   Streaming events to consumers with HTTP SSE

At the top of the figure, the consumer requests the latest prices of the APL stock as an application/json document using a GET /stocks/APL/prices request with the appropriate Accept header. By default, the server returns the list of prices for the last five minutes. The document has an items attribute containing the list of prices. To get more recent data, the consumer will have to make another request using cursor-based pagination.

The bottom of the figure shows how all this could be handled with an SSE stream. The request is almost the same, but the consumer now indicates that it wants the data as a text/event-stream document. The server responds with a 200 OK success status and a document whose content type is text/event-stream as requested. Each price event is represented by a line starting with data:, and it contains the same data as provided previously in the finished list.

The huge difference in this approach is that now the price events are provided as a stream; the returned document is not a static and finished one anymore. The server adds a `data:` line for each new price event occurring for the APL stock. It will go on doing this until there are no more events or until the consumer closes the connection. Using SSE, a server can send event data to consumers.

Regarding the design of the event data, you'll recall that in the webhook use case, I recommended that you put the least possible amount of data in events and that consumers get additional data with another regular call to the API. But in such a streaming use case, regardless of the technology used (SSE or something else), it is usually better to provide as much data as possible because consumers will want all the data without having to make another independent call to the API. As always, though, this is not mandatory; it can depend on the context. Everything else you have learned in this book applies too: events and their data must make sense for consumers and must be easy to understand and use, to evolve, and to secure.

Note that using content negotiation and providing both `application/json` and `text/event-stream` media types is not required; the Banking API could only provide the streaming version. It is also not mandatory to use the same path to provide these two different representations. The Banking API could use different paths such as `/stocks/{stockId}/prices` and `/stocks/{stockId}/price-events`. The API could also provide a way of getting price events for multiple stocks with a request like `GET /stock-prices?stockIds=APL,APA,CTA`. In the response to this request, each event sent via a `data:` line will concern one of the APL, APA, or CTA stocks; the consumer will be able to tell which one by checking the `stockId` property value.

Although the SSE specification provides more features than just the `data:` lines, it's quite simple. The following listing shows the various possibilities.

Listing 11.1   The complete SSE specification[2]

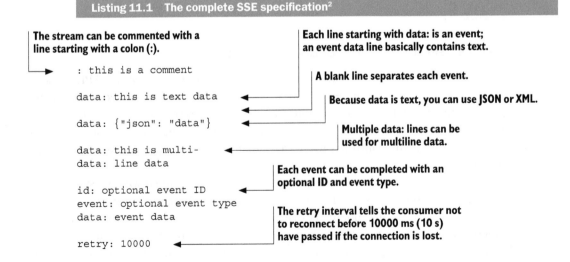

---

2   "W3C Working Draft," April 2009, Eds. Ian Hickson, Google, Inc. (https://www.w3.org/TR/2009/WD-eventsource-20090421/#event-stream-interpretation).

There are a few other things to know about SSE:

- It relies on the HTTP protocol but is not part of it; it was created as a standard for HTML5 by the W3C.
- It is quite simple to use for browser-based consumers because it was designed for them, but there are libraries available for almost any language.
- The event data can only be text (simple text, JSON, XML, and so on). If you need to send binary data, like images, you have to encode that in text.
- An SSE stream can take advantage of HTTP compression. It is a unidirectional stream, which means that once the connection is established, the consumer cannot send data to the server using this connection.

Because it relies on the HTTP protocol, no specific infrastructure is required to host an API using this technology, but be warned: using SSE means that HTTP connections remain open for quite a long time. Therefore, the infrastructure hosting the API has to be tuned to support long parallel connections. Even so, it might be useful to use a single SSE stream to send different types of events. To do so, you can take advantage of the `event` property.

Now, suppose the Banking Company wants to provide some chat features to allow end users to discuss their accounts with humans or bots. In this case, it might be preferable to provide for bidirectional communication, allowing both the consumer and provider to send events. Unfortunately, SEE only allows unidirectional communication from server to consumer; but thankfully, there are other solutions. Such a need is usually met using the WebSocket protocol as defined by RFC 6455 (https://tools.ietf.org/html/rfc6455), which is widely adopted for chats and games. We will not go into detail on the infrastructure, but know that this approach requires more work on the infrastructure side than the HTTP-based SSE stream.

A WebSocket relies on a raw TCP connection, which might not be allowed to pass through corporate proxies without modifying their configuration. Regarding the messages that could be exchanged with this protocol, it is up to you, the API designer, to do your job without relying on any standard. But remember that you can copy what others have done.

Most WebSocket APIs rely on typed messages as with SSE, except that in this case, both the consumer and the provider can send messages. If you need to link an event request sent through the WebSocket to its event response, you just need to add some unique identifier to the messages.

NOTE A WebSocket can also be used for unidirectional communication as in the SSE use case.

There are different ways of streaming events. The important thing for an API designer is to know that a request/response mechanism is not the only option. When dealing with high-volatility data and real-time data, streaming events not only from provider to consumer but also from consumer to provider is an option that should be considered.

11.1.4 *Processing multiple elements*

The various API examples you have seen so far have provided two ways of reading data. Some goals can provide access to single elements and others to multiple ones. For instance, the Banking API allows consumers to read a single account with the read account goal or multiple ones with the list accounts goal. But when it comes to creation-, modification-, or deletion-related goals, we have only seen goals that work on a single element. Depending on the elements being manipulated and the context, it might be useful to be able to process multiple elements with a single API call instead of having to make many API calls, each processing a single element at a time.

To explore this topic, let's add some more personal financial management features to the Banking API. We can let consumers modify transactions to define personalized categories, add comments about them, and also check them; checking a transaction is similar to marking an email as read. To do so, we'll add an update transaction goal represented by a `PATCH /transactions/{transactionId}` request. The following listing shows the JSON schema of the expected body.

Listing 11.2   The JSON schema of the update transaction goal's body

```
openapi: "3.0.0"
...
components:
  schemas:
    ...
    UpdateTransactionRequest:
      description: |
        At least one of the comment, customCategory, or checked
        properties must be provided
      properties:          ◄──────────────────────────────   The body is composed of three
        comment:                                             properties: comment,
          type: string                                       customCategory, and checked.
          example: My new Ibanez electric guitar
        customCategory:
          type: string
          example: Music Gear
        checked:
          type: boolean
          description: |
            Checking a transaction is similar to marking an email as read.
            True if the transaction has been checked, false otherwise.
```

The `comment`, `customCategory`, and `checked` properties are all optional; consumers can update one, two, or all of them. The transaction's ID is also not needed in the body because it is provided in the `/transactions/{transactionId}` resource's path. No other properties of a transaction, like its amount or date, can be updated in this case.

Providing a 'Mark all as checked' or a 'Mark all selected as read' feature in the Awesome Banking App requires us to update each transaction. Depending on the transaction count, having to make an API call to update each transaction might be a problem. As we saw when reading data (section 10.3), we could try to aggregate all these unitary calls into a single one. That is, we could allow consumers to update multiple transactions in a single API call by proposing an update transactions (with an *s*) goal. As shown in figure 11.6, such a goal could be represented by a PATCH /transactions request. Listing 11.3 shows the JSON schema of its body.

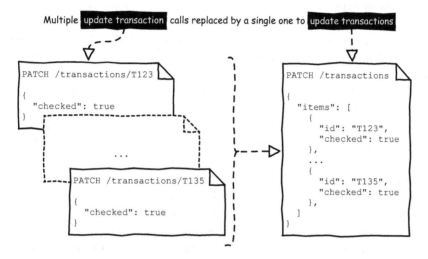

Figure 11.6   Checking multiple transactions in one call

Listing 11.3   The JSON schema of the update transactions goal's body

```
openapi: "3.0.0"
...
components:
  schemas:
    ...
    UpdateTransactionsRequest:
      properties:
        required:
          - items
        items:
          type: array
          minItems: 1                    No more than 100 updates at a time
          maxItems: 100
          items:
            allOf:                       Same data as unitary call plus the
              - required:                transaction ID; allOf aggregates
                - id                     provide JSON schemas
                properties:
                  id:
                    type: string
                    description: Transaction ID
              - $ref: "#/components/schemas/UpdateTransactionRequest"
```

The updated data for all transactions is provided as an object containing an items property, which is a list of 1 to 100 transactions. This is the same kind of representation used in the response body of a list *something* goal, such as list transactions. The properties provided for each transaction are the same as the ones provided for the unitary goal (`comment`, `customCategory`, and `checked`), plus the `id` because the transaction ID cannot be in the resource path. To check multiple transactions in one call, consumers need to provide `id` and `checked` properties for each checked transaction.

That's for the request, but what about the response? When updating a single transaction, the update transaction goal can signify that the update has been done with a `200 OK` HTTP status, that there was something wrong with the request with a `400 Bad Request` status, or that the transaction ID is unknown with a `404 Not Found`. When processing multiple transactions simultaneously, if all the transactions are successfully updated, a `200 OK` status could be returned.

The same goes in the case of an error: a `400 Bad Request` response could be returned even if the problem is an invalid transaction ID. A `404` status code can only be returned if the resource's path is unknown, which would not be the case here. This is slightly different from the unitary update. And what if some transactions can be updated and some cannot? Should the Banking API implementation stop at the first error and return a `400` response without processing any valid transaction updates?

If you remember our discussion in section 5.2.4, you know that the answer to this question is no because this would make the API less usable. Consumers would have to do many calls to fix each error one by one (and an API not processing the valid updates could be quite infuriating). The update transactions goal must return all errors, process all valid transaction updates, and also indicate which updates were successfully done. That means returning multiple statuses; fortunately, there is an HTTP code for that:

> *"The 207 (Multi-Status) status code provides status for multiple independent operations...."*
>
> *WebDAV*

The `207` status is defined in RFC 4918, which allows clients to perform remote web content authoring operations.[3] It provides new methods, headers, media types, and statuses to facilitate resource management and especially to manipulate multiple resources in one call—thanks to this `207` status. The following listing shows an example of what a WebDAV server should return, according to RFC 4918, in a `207` response when deleting multiple resources.

Listing 11.4   A `207 Multi-Status` response as described in RFC 4918

```
<?xml version="1.0" encoding="utf-8" ?>
<d:multistatus xmlns:d="DAV:">
  <d:response>
    <d:href>http://www.example.com/container/resource3</d:href>
    <d:status>HTTP/1.1 423 Locked</d:status>
    <d:error><d:lock-token-submitted/></d:error>
```

---

[3] "HTTP Extensions for Web Distributed Authoring and Versioning (WebDAV)," L. Dusseault, Ed., June 2007 (https://tools.ietf.org/html/rfc4918).

```
    </d:response>
    <d:response>
      <d:href>http://www.example.com/container/resource4</d:href>
      <d:status>HTTP/1.1 200 OK</d:status>
    </d:response>
</d:multistatus>
```

This is an XML document containing a list, with each element composed of an `href` (the URL of the processed resource), a `status` (the unitary HTTP status), and an optional `error` message. Note the compression and encoding handled at the upper level (the response sent by the API server); each response must use the same encoding and compression.

The RFC 4918 describes various `207` responses for specific HTTP methods (such as `PROPPATCH` and `PROPFIND`), but these are XML-based—too specific to the WebDAV context—and cannot be reused in other contexts. That is why I chose to just keep the `207` status and define my own (JSON) format for request and response bodies for the update transactions goal, as shown in figure 11.7.

A `207 Multi-Status` response to an update transactions request is an object with an `items` property, which is a list containing as many elements as are in the `items` list provided in the request. The response list is ordered exactly like the request one: the response to the third request is in the third position in the response list. For each element, consumers get exactly the same information they would have gotten making a unitary call. Here, that means a `status` and a `body` containing the HTTP status and the response body for each transaction update attempt.

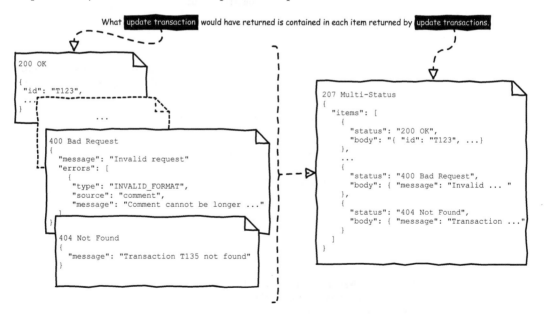

Figure 11.7   Contrasting multiple responses to the update transaction goal with a single response to the update transactions goal

The first status in the list is a success status (200 OK), and its body contains the updated resource. The last two requests were not processed because of a comment that was too long and an unknown transaction ID. For each of these, the body contains the error data structure (seen in section 5.2.4) that would have been returned for a unitary call. If the consumer sends an invalid list in its request (with more than 100 elements, for example), the status will be 400 Bad Request. Also, if headers are usually returned for unitary calls, we could add a headers map for each element. Listing 11.5 shows the complete JSON Schema, and listing 11.6 shows an example.

Listing 11.5   **The multi-status response's JSON Schema**

```
openapi: "3.0.0"
...
components:
  schemas:
    MultipleStatusResponse:
      required:
        - items
      properties:                    Contains one element for each
        items:          ◀───────     transaction of the request
          type: array
          minItems: 1
          maxItems: 100
          items:
            required:
              - status
            properties:              The HTTP status
              status:   ◀────────
                type: string
                description: HTTP status
                example: 404 Not Found
              headers:                        A <string, string> map for the headers
                additionalProperties:  ◀──    (it could also be a name, value list).
                  type: string
                description: HTTP headers map
                example:
                  My-Custom-Header: CUSTOM_VALUE
                  Another-Custom-Header: ANOTHER_CUSTOM_VALUE
              body:
                description: |
                  Transaction if status is 200 OK, Error otherwise
                oneOf:
                  - $ref: "#/components/schemas/Error"
                  - $ref: "#/components/schemas/Transaction"
                example:
                  message: Transaction T135 not found
```

The body—a Transaction if status is 200
OK or an Error otherwise (one of the
provided JSON Schemas)

```
{
  "items": [
    {
      "status": "404 Not Found",
      "headers": {
        "My-Custom-Header": "CUSTOM_VALUE",
        "Another-Custom-Header": "ANOTHER_CUSTOM_VALUE"
      },
      "body": {
        "message": "Transaction T135 not found"
      }
    }
  ]
}
```

Remember that what is shown in figure 11.7 and listings 11.5 and 11.6 is my own interpretation of what the content of a 207 Multi-Status response might look like. We can use the same design to replace or delete multiple resources with a PUT /resources or a DELETE /resources?ids=1,2,5,6,9 request. To create multiple resources at a time, there are a few things to consider.

We could use a POST /resources request, but what if we also want consumers to be able to create a single resource at a time? As long as a create resources goal can create one or more resources, a consumer could pass a single resource in the list. We could also accept a list of resources and a single resource in the request body (you should try to describe such an operation, its request body, and the various responses using the OpenAPI Specification as described in chapter 4). But what if we want to make a clear separation for security concerns, for example, between the create resource and create resources goals using different paths?

It is not uncommon to see POST /resources/batch requests to create multiple resources in one call; such paths break the /collection/{resourceId} pattern, but at least consumers will understand at first sight what they can do. Depending on how security is handled, providing two different paths might be unavoidable. In an ideal world, however, I would prefer to provide a single POST /resources path, accepting a list of resources or a single resource, with consumers having the batch resource creation scope only being allowed to send requests containing a list of resources.

Be warned that the partial processing strategy (processing valid items even if the provided list contains invalid ones) discussed in this section might not be the one to choose in all cases. There are some cases where processing only a portion of the provided items can cause problems. So before introducing such behavior, always check the consequences of such partial processing. If partial processing does not make sense, the API can return a more classical 200 OK on success and 400 Bad Request, for example, if the request is invalid.

As you can see, APIs are under no obligation to provide only ways to process single resources; there are contexts in which processing multiple resources in a single call can be useful. Whatever the solution you design, remember that consumers must get the same data, including protocol data like headers or status codes for HTTP and errors that they would have gotten for unitary requests. They must be able to make the connection between each element of their request and each element of the API's response. And do not forget to handle global controls and errors; for example, limiting the number of elements that can be provided in the request.

11.2 *Observing the full context*

You saw in section 10.1 that designing APIs requires us to think about how the APIs will actually be used by consumers, mostly for the consumers' sake but also for the provider's. And now we have discovered that it also requires us to care about the true nature of goals or data in order to provide efficient, usable, and also implementable APIs (see section 11.1). All this means is that designing APIs requires more than just focusing on consumer needs and avoiding the provider's perspective. Designing APIs requires us to fully observe the context in which these will be consumed and provided in order to ensure that these fulfill all consumers' needs in the best possible way—and actually be implementable by providers.

11.2.1 *Being aware of consumers' existing practices and limitations*

Fulfilling all consumers' needs means designing APIs that provide all the needed goals in an easy-to-understand and easy-to-use way; it also means being careful about some aspects that could be called *nonfunctional requirements*. These nonfunctional requirements basically concern how the API goals and data will actually be represented. Consumers can be used to certain practices or have some limitations that must be taken into account when designing APIs.

You saw in section 5.1 and in sections 6.1.3 and 6.1.4 that APIs designed using simple representations and standards, and following common practices, are easier to understand, easier to use, and more interoperable. But this can go far beyond just using crystal-clear names and standard date formats or applying commonly used path patterns. Existing practices can have a deeper impact on API design.

For example, suppose the Banking Company wants to provide a bank details verification API that confirms if an account number actually exists at any bank and belongs to a given person. Such a service could be useful to companies using direct debit for payments. To be paid, companies withdraw funds from their customer's bank account. When doing so, companies would be glad to be sure that the provided information actually matches an existing bank account belonging to their customer before selling them any goods or products.

Such an API seems quite simple to design. It proposes a single verify bank details goal. This goal expects an account number in IBAN format and the account owner's first name and last name. It returns a simple OK feedback in the case of success and provides detailed information in the case of an error; for example, if the account number exists but the owner name does not exactly match because of a typo. Based on what you have learned, how would you represent such a goal? Figure 11.8 shows three ways of doing so.

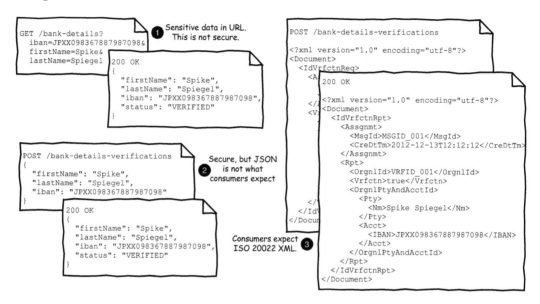

Figure 11.8 Adapting design to what consumers are used to

Based on what you have learned in section 8.4, you know that it is not a good idea to represent this bank details verification goal with a GET /bank-details request with firstName, lastName and iban query parameters (1). Indeed, IBANs (account numbers) and first and last names as sensitive data cannot be passed as query parameters— they could be logged anywhere! So you would probably represent this goal with a POST /bank-details-verification request (2), its body being a JSON object containing iban, firstName, and lastName mandatory properties. If the request is a valid one, it can return a 200 OK response with its body containing the status of the verification, indicating if the provided bank details are valid or not. If the request is invalid (for example, if an IBAN with an invalid format has been provided or a lastName property has not been provided), a 400 Bad Request response containing a JSON object with an informative message and details about the problem(s) encountered can be returned, as you saw in section 5.2.4.

Such an API seems easy to understand and easy to use by anyone. But before designing this API, we did not check the actual consumers' context; and in this case, this is a critical mistake. The targeted consumers are the Banking Company's corporate consumers, who will consume the API using financial COTS (commercial off-the-shelf) software. The people working with such financial software (and the software itself) are not used to custom JSON data; rather, they are used to standard ISO 20022 financial XML messages (3). Let's take a closer look at this third design option: both request and response are based on ISO 20022 financial XML messages as shown in listings 11.7 and 11.8.

Listing 11.7   An ISO 20022 IdentificationVerificationRequestV02 XML message

```xml
<?xml version="1.0" encoding="utf-8"?>
<Document>
  <IdVrfctnReq>
    <Assgnmt>
      <MsgId>MSGID_001</MsgId>
      <CreDtTm>2012-12-13T12:12:12</CreDtTm>
    </Assgnmt>
    <Vrfctn>
      <Id>VRFID_001</Id>
      <PtyAndAcctId>
        <Pty>
          <Nm>Spike Spiegel</Nm>        ◄── Account holder's first
        </Pty>                               name and last name
        <Acct>
          <IBAN>JPXX098367887987098</IBAN>  ◄── Account's IBAN
        </Acct>
      </PtyAndAcctId>
    </Vrfctn>
  </IdVrfctnReq>
</Document>
```

Listing 11.8   An ISO 20022 IdentificationVerificationReportV02 XML message

```xml
<?xml version="1.0" encoding="utf-8"?>
<Document>
  <IdVrfctnRpt>
    <Assgnmt>
      <MsgId>MSGID_001</MsgId>
      <CreDtTm>2012-12-13T12:12:12</CreDtTm>
    </Assgnmt>
    <Rpt>
      <OrgnlId>VRFID_001</OrgnlId>           ◄── Verification status
      <Vrfctn>true</Vrfctn>
      <OrgnlPtyAndAcctId>                     ◄── Verified information
        <Pty>                                      (name and IBAN)
          <Nm>Spike Spiegel</Nm>
        </Pty>
        <Acct>
          <IBAN>JPXX098367887987098</IBAN>
        </Acct>
      </OrgnlPtyAndAcctId>
    </Rpt>
  </IdVrfctnRpt>
</Document>
```

The `IdentificationVerificationRequestV02` message shown in listing 11.7 is a standard bank details verification request. It contains an IBAN in the `Document.IdVrfctnReq.Vrfctn.PtyAndAcctId.Acct.IBAN` property and the owner's first name and last name in `Document.Vrfctn.PtyAndAcctId.Pty.Nm`. There is also a request ID and date and a verification ID.

The `IdentificationVerificationReportV02` message shown in listing 11.8 is the standard response to such a request. It contains the original request data and a Boolean flag that is `true` if the verification succeeds and `false` otherwise (`Document.IdVrfctn-Rpt.Rpt.Vrfctn`).

As the ISO 20022 standard only describes messages, not how they are transmitted, we can at least keep the spirit of the second version of the API. The verify bank details goal could still be represented by a `POST /bank-details-verifications` request, but now its body is an `IdentificationVerificationRequestV02` ISO 20022 XML message. The response could still be `200 OK` if the `IdentificationVerificationRequestV02` input message is a valid one, but now the response body is an `IdentificationVerification-ReportV02` message. If the request is invalid, a `400 Bad Request` response is returned along with a custom XML message mapping to the JSON error message that we are used to (the ISO 20022 standard does not describe how such errors are to be handled).

The resulting API design is not that bad, but according to what you have learned, especially in section 5.1, such ISO 20022 XML messages could be considered complex (and we could also consider that XML is not really trendy anymore). But in this context, the targeted consumers natively speak using ISO 20022 XML messages; and therefore, the API must use them. Consuming the XML API within the financial COTS software used by the targeted consumers would be quite easy. If the API used custom JSON messages, consuming the API might require more work on the consumer side and, in some cases, might not be possible. But when in Rome, do as the Romans do.

Choosing a suitable representation is not about choosing what we as API designers are used to or what we might consider good design or fashionable; it is about choosing what is appropriate in the desired context. Always check if the targeted domain or consumers have specific practices that you should follow in your API design. Such practices could be the use of standards or the way they represent data, name things, manage errors, or anything else.

That takes care of the existing practices that might influence the design of APIs, but what about the limitations? Let's say that the Banking Company also wants to target noncorporate/nonfinancial consumers, who are definitely not used to ISO 20022 XML and are more used to simple JSON. A smart API design could take advantage of content negotiation (see section 6.2.1) to handle that. Consumers would just have to set the `Content` and `Accept` headers to `application/xml` when they want to use the ISO 20022 standard and `application/json` to use the simple JSON format. That's great; the API is adaptable enough to fulfill the needs of two different types of consumers.

But unfortunately, after interviewing some of the developers of the financial COTS systems used by the targeted customers, it seems that most of them cannot handle content negotiation easily. It would be wiser, then, to consider the API's default format to be XML, or perhaps to allow consumers to specify which format they want to use when registering on the developer portal. Not being able to pass a simple header seems quite ridiculous, but that can happen.

Don't take it for granted that all consumers can do what you are used to. Consumers might have technical limitations, like the COTS software being unable to add headers to an HTTP request, but there are many other possibilities. Some consumers might not be able to use any HTTP method other than GET or POST. You saw in section 10.1 how mobile applications can be limited by network capabilities. And in section 11.1, we talked about webhooks. Not all consumers can implement those easily.

In order to avoid discovering too late existing practices or limitations that go against what you are used to, you will have to show empathy toward your targeted consumers. Don't hesitate to talk to them, question them, discuss your designs with them—you won't regret it.

Of course, as discussed in section 10.3.8, all this must not be done at the expense of usability and reusability. Do not try to please a few consumers with highly specific needs in a single API. Instead, consider creating different API layers or letting consumers create their own backend for frontend APIs.

11.2.2 *Carefully considering the provider's limitations*

In section 2.4, you learned to design APIs while avoiding exposing purely internal concerns to consumers. But avoiding exposing the provider's perspective does not mean wearing blinders and totally ignoring it. Indeed, when designing an API, we have to take into consideration what is happening behind the API in order to propose a design that will actually be not only usable, but also implementable. Figure 11.9 shows some examples.

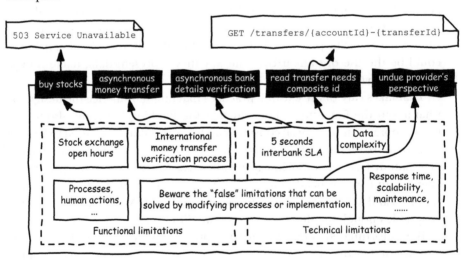

Figure 11.9   Provider's limitation examples

If the Banking Company wants to provide trading-related goals like buy stocks or sell stocks, its API designers must be aware that stock exchanges are not always open in order to create an adequate design. A consumer trying to buy stocks on a closed stock exchange should get an error telling them that the operation is not possible at the moment. Such an error could be represented by a `503 Service Unavailable` HTTP status code. As you learned in section 5.2.3, the error should be accompanied by some data that will help the consumer, such as the stock exchange's opening time. And as discussed in section 5.3.2, it could also be useful to add goals listing the available stock exchanges or providing details on a stock exchange's market calendar and trading hours to prevent such errors.

> **NOTE** If you don't take care of functional limitations, the resulting API will be incomplete and less consumer-friendly.

Stock trading is outside the scope of our Banking API, but we saw an example of a functional limitation that impacted the API's design in section 11.1.1. An international money transfer above a given amount must be validated by a human being; and, therefore, it cannot be represented by a basic request/response goal: an asynchronous representation must be used instead. It might be worth investigating if a solution can be found to omit the human-verification step in the international money transfer process. This would allow us to provide a real-time and more consumer-friendly synchronous goal instead of an asynchronous one.

But provider limitations are not only functional—they can also be technical. The bank details-verification service you saw in section 11.2.1 relies not only on the Banking Company itself, but also on other banks. To verify that a bank account exists at another bank, the Banking Company has to communicate with that bank. This service relies on an asynchronous, standardized, interbank messaging service. This interbank bank details verification system's service-level agreement states that a verification must take less than five seconds.

Building a synchronous request/response API goal on top of such a system could be problematic. It would mean that the consumer might have to wait for up to five seconds for a response, which could seem like an eternity (especially for mobile consumers). Therefore, instead of a synchronous request/response goal, the API should let consumers send a verification request and then get the result later or even be notified by a webhook that a result is available.

Some limitations can be quite trivial, like "Oops, we don't have an existing unique ID to identify transfers." Don't panic; in that case, you might want to use composite IDs composed of the various IDs or values needed to identify something. In this example, an `accountId` and a `transferId` could be used in a `GET /transfers/{account Id}-{transferId}` request. Note that if this composite ID is your business only, your visible interface contract might be opaque and only show a `GET /transfers/{id}`, the value of `id` being a composite ID returned by the list transfers goals.

Like functional limitations, technical limitations on the provider's end must be questioned—but they must be questioned *carefully*. Don't be fooled by the true technical limitation example you've just seen. Unlike functional limitations, which usually tend to be true problems that are not easily solved, technical ones are more often than not *false* limitations that can be solved with little effort through changes to the implementation. Such little effort avoids major impacts on the API design and, most importantly, the consumers.

I can't count how many times I've heard things like, "We can't aggregate this data; unitary calls already take too much time!" when all that was needed was to activate compression (see section 10.2.1), add missing indexes in the database, or optimize some database requests. Such a simple change can often result in awesome performance, allowing designers to implement the supposedly impossible feature.

As another example, not so long ago, in big, old companies discovering that the web was not only about websites that just used POST and GET HTTP methods, you might have heard that using the DELETE HTTP method is impossible; it's blocked by firewalls. All that was needed to solve this problem was to talk to the people in charge of network security and explain the new needs so they could modify the firewalls configurations to allow the use of an HTTP method other than POST and GET. (Note that this specific HTTP method problem shouldn't exist anywhere anymore; at least, I hope so!)

As an API designer, this means you should be aware of the whole chain between consumers and the point where the API is exposed and its actual implementation, and what is happening inside while designing, so that you can spot technical limitations as soon as possible and solve these problems either within the implementation or by adapting the design.

Technical limitations will usually revolve around response time, the scalability or availability of underlying systems, and network restrictions. For example, it is quite annoying to discover in production that an API request takes more than two seconds to complete, and this problem could have been solved by adding more CPU, optimizing the implementation, or, as a last resort, adapting the API's design. Consumers could be unpleasantly surprised to discover that your API is unavailable for 15 minutes every day at midnight thanks to a daily reboot or backup procedure. It could also be unnerving to realize that each of your carefully crafted 5XX errors is replaced by a generic 500 Server Error whose body is an HTML page, thanks to a zealous old-fashioned firewall or a misconfigured API gateway.

The important thing to remember is that designing an API requires you to have a *deep* understanding of what really happens before and after requests are made so that you can spot possible functional or technical limitations. Any potential limitation must be questioned because it might be possible to totally or partially resolve the issue through the implementation (in a broad sense) without impacting the API's design. Only through careful consideration of the problem will you be able to adapt the API design appropriately, should that become necessary.

Functional or technical limitations on the provider's end can take many forms and have as many solutions based on adapted communication or adequate goals, input/output properties, or error handling. But whatever the solution, you must always conceal the provider's perspective as much as possible in order to provide easy-to-understand and easy-to-use APIs.

11.3   *Choosing an API style according to the context*

When you've mastered or are used to using a tool like a hammer, it's very tempting to treat all problems like nails. This is a cognitive bias called the law of the instrument, the law of the hammer, or Maslow's law (https://en.wikipedia.org/wiki/Law_of_the_ instrument). Such a bias can also have another effect: screwdriver users might think that a screwdriver is a better tool than a hammer, while hammer users might think the opposite. This could be called the *fannish folk law.*

But a hammer will not solve all problems, and a screwdriver is not better than a hammer; each tool is as useful as the other, but in different contexts. This book is about web API design, not carpentry or woodworking, but the same concerns apply in the tech industry too. Choosing which tool(s) you will use to design a remote API must not be done based on what you are used to, what is fashionable, or your personal preference; it must be done according to the context. And being able to choose the right tool requires you to know more than one.

Web APIs can easily be reduced to unitary and synchronous request/response + REST + HTTP 1.1 + JSON web APIs, which is nowadays one of the most commonly used ways to enable software-to-software communication in order to expose goals fulfilling targeted users' needs. Therefore, API designers could be tempted to use this set of tools in all situations, in all contexts. In this book, this toolset is only used to expose fundamental API design principles that you can use when designing other types of remote APIs.

We've already discovered some other tools that can be added to our toolboxes to be used in the appropriate contexts. In section 6.2.1, for example, you saw that JSON was not the only possible data format for APIs; you can use XML, CSV, PDF, or many other formats. You also saw in section 11.2.1 that sometimes it might even be counterproductive to use JSON in a context where consumers are used to an existing standardized XML format. In section 10.3.6, you learned that REST APIs are not the only option when creating web APIs. Using a query language might bring more flexibility when requesting data (but less caching possibilities). In section 11.1, you discovered that a synchronous request/response consumer-to-provider mechanism is not the only way of enabling communication between two systems. We can create asynchronous goals, notify consumers of events, stream data, and even process multiple elements in one call. And in section 10.2.1, you learned that HTTP 2 can be used instead of the good old HTTP 1.1 protocol.

We already know that context plays an important role in the choice of tools, and we already know about several different tools. But as API designers and software and systems designers, in general, we need to broaden our perspective in order to be sure to avoid the law of the instrument. In order to do so, we will explore some alternatives to REST APIs and web APIs in this section.

11.3.1 Contrasting resource-, data-, and function-based APIs

At the time of this book's writing, there are three main ways of creating web APIs: REST, gRPC, and GraphQL. Will they still be there in five or 10 years? Will they still be the same? Only time will tell.

Is one of them better than the others? No! It depends on needs and context. The approaches shown in figure 11.10 represent three different visions of APIs: REST is resource-oriented, gRPC is function-oriented, and GraphQL is data-oriented, and each of these has its pros and cons.

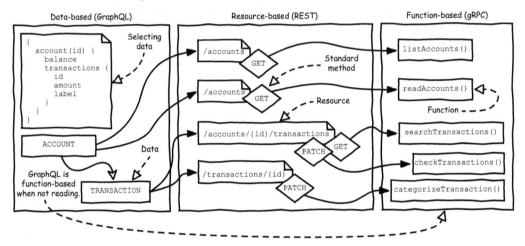

Figure 11.10   Contrasting resource-, data- and function-based APIs

You should know by now what a REST API is. As you have seen throughout this book, and especially in section 3.5.1, a REST API—or RESTful API—is an API that conforms (or at least tries to conform) to the REST architectural style introduced by Roy Fielding.[4] Such an API is resource-based and takes advantage of the underlying protocol (the HTTP protocol, in this case). Its goals are represented by the use of standard HTTP methods on resources with the results being represented by standard HTTP status codes.

In the Banking API, reading an account's details could be represented by a GET / owners/123 request, returning a 200 OK HTTP status along with all the customer's data if this 123 owner exists or a 404 Not Found HTTP status if not. Updating the same owner's VIP status could be done with a PATCH /owners/123 request, whose body would contain the new value.

Relying on an existing protocol favors consistency and makes APIs predictable, as you saw in section 6.1. Indeed, upon seeing any resource, a consumer might try to use the OPTIONS HTTP method to determine what can be done with it, or even try the GET

---

[4] See his PhD dissertation "Architectural Styles and the Design of Network-Based Software Architectures" at https://www.ics.uci.edu/~fielding/pubs/dissertation/fielding_dissertation.pdf.

method to read it or PUT or PATCH to update it. Even the most obscure 4XX HTTP status code will be understood as an error on the consumer's end by any consumer. Such an API can also take advantage of all the existing features of HTTP, such as caching and conditional requests; designers do not have to reinvent the wheel. Server-to-consumer streaming capabilities can be added too, using SSE (see section 11.1.3). But this does not make the design of the API simple.

You have seen throughout this book that even if the HTTP protocol provides some kind of framework, it does not magically prevent us from creating terrible REST APIs. It is still up to designers to choose resource paths (/owner or /owners?) and to decide how to represent data, provide informative feedback on errors or successes beyond HTTP statuses, and more.

The gRPC framework was created by Google. The *g* stands for Google and *RPC* stands for Remote Procedure Call. An RPC API simply exposes functions.

In a function-based API, reading the 123 owner could be done by calling the read-Owner(123) function, and updating that owner's VIP status could be done by calling updateOwner(123, { "vip": true }). The gRPC framework uses the HTTP 1.1 or 2 protocol as a transport layer, without using its semantics. It does not provide any standard caching mechanism. Note that it can take advantage of the HTTP 2 protocol to propose bidirectional and streaming communication. It can also use the Protocol Buffer data format, which is less verbose than XML or JSON (you can also use this format in a REST API).

Whereas in a resource-based API case, the underlying protocol provides some kind of framework, especially to describe what kind of action is being taken and what the result is, in a function-based API, it is usually up to the designers to choose their own semantics for almost everything. So, how would you represent a goal such as list owners? Should it be a listOwners(), readOwners(), or retrieveOwners() function? The same goes when it comes to modifying data. Should the API provide a saveOwner() or updateOwner() function?

For errors, the gRPC framework provides a standard error model including a few standard codes that map to HTTP status codes (https://cloud.google.com/apis/design/errors). For example, when calling readOwner(123), a NOT_FOUND code (mapping to a 404 Not Found HTTP status) can be returned along with an Owner 123 does not exist message. The error model can be completed with additional data in order to provide more informative feedback. As with a REST API, it is up to the designers to choose how to do that (see section 5.2.3) and also how to represent data.

We covered GraphQL briefly in section 10.3.6; it's a query language for APIs created by Facebook. A GraphQL API basically provides access to a data schema allowing consumers to retrieve exactly the data they want. It is protocol-agnostic, meaning that any protocol that lets us send requests and get responses could be used; but because the HTTP protocol is the most widely adopted, it usually is the chosen one.

Like gRPC, GraphQL does not provide any standard caching mechanism. A POST /graphql request with the { "query": "{ owner(id:123) { vip } }" } query in its body would only return owner 123's VIP status. And when it comes to creating or updating data, GraphQL behaves like any RPC API. It uses functions that are called *mutations*. Updating owner 123's VIP status would require us to call the updateOwner mutation, which takes the owner's ID and an owner object containing the new VIP status.

GraphQL also comes with a standard error model that can be extended. Listings 11.9 and 11.10 show a query and a response with a standard error, respectively.

Listing 11.9   A GraphQL query

```
{
  owner(id: 123) {
    vip
    accounts {
      id
      balance
      name
    }
  }
}
```

Listing 11.10   A GraphQL response with an error

```
{
  "errors": [
    {
      "message": "No balance available for account with ID 1002.",
      "locations": [ { "line": 6, "column": 7 } ],
      "path": [ "owner", "accounts", 1, "balance" ]
    }
  ],
  "data": {
    "owner": {
      "vip": true,
      "accounts": [
        {
          "id": "1000",
          "balance": 123.4
          "name": "James account"
        },
        {
          "id": "1002",
          "balance": null,
          "name": "Enterprise account"
        }
      ]
    }
  }
}
```

Points to error in query → (pointing to "locations": [{ "line": 6, "column": 7 }],)

Indicates the result property affected by the error ← (pointing to "path": ["owner", "accounts", 1, "balance"])

The actual property affected by the error ← (pointing to "balance": null,)

The query shown in listing 11.9 requests owner 123's VIP status and account IDs, balances, and names. Unfortunately, as shown in listing 11.10, the balance could not be retrieved for the second account. The standard error model contains, for each error, a human-readable `message`, the possible sources of the error in the GraphQL query in `locations` (balance is on the sixth line and starts at the seventh character of the query), and the optional `path` of the affected property in the returned `data` (the `null` balance is in `data.owner.accounts[1].balance`).

Such an error seems to be the provider's fault and not the consumer's, but this is not indicated. It's up to the designers to choose how to add information to this standard error model in order to provide fully informative feedback. And obviously, like in REST and gRPC APIs, it's up to the designers to choose how to design the data model.

From a design perspective, we can see that these three different ways of creating APIs have three different ways of envisioning representations of an API's goals: resources (REST), functions (gRPC and also creations and modifications in GraphQL), and data (reads in GraphQL). Fundamentally, representing any read goal is possible in any of these API styles. When it comes to create, modify, delete, or do goals, they can be represented by a resource/method couple or a function. Each approach comes with more or less standardized elements favoring consistency and, hence, facilitating usability and design.

> **NOTE** An API strictly following the underlying protocol's rules is the most consistent one out of the box.

But whatever the provided framework, designers still have a lot of work to do in order to design decent APIs. Regardless of the API style they choose, designers still have to identify users, goals, inputs, outputs, and errors, and choose the best possible consumer-oriented representations while avoiding the provider's perspective.

From a technical perspective, we have three different API tools or technologies that can be used over the HTTP protocol. The use of the HTTP protocol is important because it is widely accepted, and you usually do not need many, if any, modifications to your infrastructure to host or use an HTTP-based API. There are some differences between the three tools, however.

REST APIs rely on the HTTP protocol and can benefit from features such as content negotiation, caching, and conditional requests. GraphQL and gRPC do not provide such mechanisms but have some other interesting features. Thanks to the use of HTTP 2 and the ProtoBuf data format, gRPC-based APIs can provide high performance. They also provide streaming and bidirectional communication between consumer and provider. (Note that REST APIs can provide one-way streaming from provider to consumer with SSE.) And as seen in section 10.3.6, GraphQL's querying capabilities let consumers get all the data they want, and only the data they want, in a single request, but at the expense of caching capabilities.

Concerning the provider's context and especially the implementation, you obviously don't have much control over the queries that could be made by consumers in a data-based API. In non-infinitely-scalable systems, too many complex requests could result in a load higher than the underlying systems can support and terribly long response times if the implementation is not ready to prevent that. With a resource- or function-based

API, it is quite easy to avoid such problems. Because each goal's behavior is usually predictable, the solicited systems are known, and rate limiting can be used to protect the underlying systems. You can specify that each consumer cannot make more than x requests per second on the API, and even specialize this rate limiting by consumer and/ or goal.

For data-based APIs, you could limit the number of queries or their size, but that would be pointless because it would not prevent unexpectedly complex queries from being made. You could limit the number of nodes in a request (containing one or more queries) or accept only preregistered requests, but that would be done at the expense of flexibility, making the data-based API choice almost useless. In all cases (REST, gRPC, GraphQL), a good practice would be to limit the number of items returned by default in lists.

So, which approach should you use? Such a choice cannot be made prior to analyzing your context and needs. Once you know who your consumers are and understand their contexts, the goals they need, and how they will be used, and you understand the provider's context, you can choose what kind of API will be the most appropriate. Although each context will be different, nowadays the rule of thumb is to choose REST by default. If there are very specific needs that cannot be fulfilled by a well-designed REST API, you might want to try GraphQL or gRPC.

Choosing REST by default could be seen as an example of the law of the instrument or fannish folk law, but the REST approach is capable of fulfilling most needs. It is the most widely adopted way of creating APIs, and most developers are used to it (remember section 11.2.1). Choose GraphQL for private APIs in mobile environments only if a well-designed REST API hosted in a well-configured environment is not possible (see section 10.2), and if

- You actually need advanced querying capabilities.
- You do not plan to make your API public or share it with partners.
- You do not care about caching.
- You are sure to be able to protect the underlying systems through the implementation or through infinite scalability.

Finally, choose gRPC APIs for internal-application-to-internal-application communication only if milliseconds really matter, if you do not care about caching or you are willing to handle it without relying on HTTP, and if you do not plan to make the API public or share it with partners. Also bear in mind that this choice might not be exclusive. You have already seen in section 10.3.8 that different layers of an API can fulfill different needs. Building a mobile BFF exposing a GraphQL API or a more specialized REST API is totally legit. An application can also expose a gRPC interface for internal consumers and a REST interface for external ones.

11.3.2 *Thinking beyond request/response- and HTTP-based APIs*

As API designers, we must be aware that request/response HTTP-based APIs are not the only way of enabling communication between applications. We talked about events and streaming in section 11.1, but mostly from an HTTP perspective. When you build an event-based system, a provider can notify consumers about events using a webhook or WebSub system, both HTTP-based. But this could also be done using a messaging system such as RabbitMQ. If it's for internal purposes, it might be more effective to directly connect providers and consumers to such tools.

When dealing with the Internet of Things (IoT), energy consumption efficiency is a key concern, and two-way communication over unreliable networks or with sleeping devices is almost a standard. The Message Queuing Telemetry Protocol (MQTP) is a message-based protocol designed to deal with such constraints. When streaming events, you can use SSE over HTTP for provider-to-consumer communication. But this could also be done using the WebSocket protocol, which is not HTTP-based (as seen in section 11.1.3). And if you need to process a massive flow of events, Kafka Streams could be an option.

An entire book would be needed to talk about the design and architecture of event-based systems, and that is not this book's purpose. But you can at least take advantage of what you have learned in this book to design the event notifications and streams. The point to remember here is that HTTP-based communication is not the only option; and, in certain contexts, it should actually be avoided at all costs. In the next chapter, you will discover the different types of API documentations and how designers can participate in their creations.

Summary

- Unitary request/response, consumer-to-provider communication is not the only option; you can also design asynchronous goals, notify consumers of events, stream data, and process multiple elements in one call.
- Designing APIs requires us to be aware of the consumers' contexts, including their network environments, habits, and limitations.
- Designing APIs requires us to carefully consider the provider's limitations, to spot these earlier, and to solve problems without impacting the design (if possible) and adapting the design (if not).
- Designing APIs requires us to ignore fashion and personal preferences. Just because you like or know a certain tool/design/practice doesn't mean that it will be the ideal solution for all API design matters.

Documenting an API

This chapter covers

- Reference documentation
- User guides
- Implementer specifications
- Change logs

In previous chapters, you discovered that designing APIs requires more than just designing usable APIs doing the job. Indeed, we have to take care of the whole context surrounding the API when designing it. But this context goes beyond that of the API itself—its interface contract, its implementation, and how and by whom it is used. API designers have to participate in various aspects of API projects, and a very important one is documentation.

The best designs of even the simplest things need documentation. As shown in figure 12.1, everyday objects can come with various types of documentation to help users understand how to use them, as well as to help the people in charge of building those objects to actually build them.

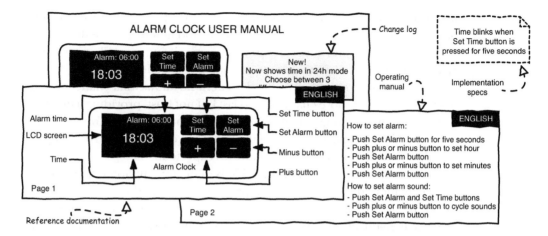

Figure 12.1 Different types of documentation

Page 1 of the Alarm Clock User Manual shows an annotated figure of the alarm clock. Thanks to that, users know what the components of the user interface are and their roles, even if the device's user-friendly design makes this fairly obvious. But this first page of documentation alone is not enough to operate the alarm clock. That's why page 2 shows its various functions, such as how to set the alarm by using the Set Alarm and plus and minus buttons.

The user manual's cover is also a kind of documentation: it advertises, "Now shows time in 24h mode" to indicate a new feature that was not present in the previous version. (This might not be of interest to new users, but it will be to people who owned the earlier version.) Without this documentation, most users, especially if they've owned one before, would be able to use the alarm clock because of its design. But some users, the absolute beginners, might struggle at first to guess how to operate it.

We've mentioned three different types of documentation that are user-oriented, but there is another kind of documentation. Although this user manual provides all the information needed to use the alarm clock, it's not sufficient to actually build one. For example, the user manual does not state that the time on the LCD screen blinks when the Set Time button is pressed for five seconds, but it actually does that. The people in charge of building the alarm clock got the documentation from its designers in the form of *implementation specifications* describing such behavior. Without such documentation, there is little chance that a design will be implemented as expected by the designers. Without relevant documentation, all the effort that's put into a design can be worthless.

As API designers, you will have to create or at least participate in the creation of such documentation for the APIs you are designing. The best-known API documentation is the reference documentation that describes the interface contract of the API. It lists the available goals and describes their inputs and outputs. This is what you have to describe when designing an API, which can be sufficient for very basic APIs if all use cases fulfilled by the API can be accomplished using a single goal. But if that's not the case, only supplying reference documentation is like only providing the list of ingredients for a recipe without some indication of what to *do* with those ingredients—an edible result might be quite hard to achieve from that. That is why an API must also come with an operating manual describing various use cases and how to achieve them.

Additionally, as with any software, when modifying an API, even if no breaking changes are introduced, it is wise to provide a change log indicating the features that have been changed or added. As the designer who knows what changes you have made, it is up to you to list those changes. And last but not least, providing a description of the API might not be enough to allow someone to implement it. You might also have to provide additional specifications to the people in charge of the API's implementation in order to ensure that the result behaves as expected.

Your involvement in each of these kinds of documentation depends on the type of documentation, the size of your company or team, and the type of API (private, partner, or public). In a big company and/or team, technical writers might be available to produce high-quality documentation; you only have to provide support and raw inputs. Relying on technical writers is especially important for consumer-facing documentation of public APIs; writing usable and user-friendly documentation requires experts in order to ensure a top-quality developer experience. For private APIs, the expectations might be lower, and the documentation might be less eye-catching, but the developer experience should still be a major concern. Documentation for internal developers must at least be readable and exhaustive. Exhaustively documenting APIs has a nice side effect—it is testing the design. If you are unable to document how to use the API or how to implement it, it can be a sign of improper design.

In this chapter, we will discover what reference documentation, operating manuals, implementation specifications, and change logs might contain, and how we as API designers can contribute to them by taking advantage of our work during the design of the API. What you learn to do here might be sufficient for wholly documenting private APIs; for consumer-facing partner or public APIs, your work will be a good input for more experienced technical writers.

12.1   Creating reference documentation

API reference documentation like that shown in figure 12.2 is like the annotated alarm clock schema in figure 12.1: it lists and describes each available component of the interface.

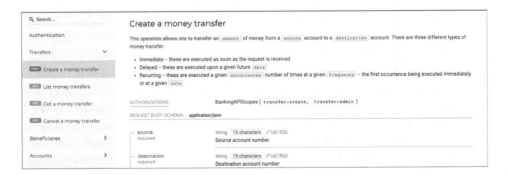

Figure 12.2   Reference documentation generated from an OpenAPI Specification file using the ReDoc open source tool

For an API the components are, at minimum, the available goals and their inputs and outputs for both success and error cases. (In the case of the alarm clock, these components were its buttons and LCD screen.) Documentation of the API should also contain a simple description of it and provide information about security. All this information could be written in any format, from a simple text file to a wiki page. Some people even dare to use spreadsheets (please don't!). Any custom format could do the job, but you saw in section 6.1.3 that using standards is better when designing an API, and this is also the case when creating API documentation.

You learned about some of these standards in chapter 4. Indeed, API description formats such as the OpenAPI Specification are the perfect companion when you want to create API reference documentation. These formats are made to describe what is needed in such documentation; and, as seen in section 4.1.2, they can be easily stored, versioned, and most importantly, used to generate a human-friendly representation. The tool used to generate the reference documentation based on the OpenAPI Specification file shown in figure 12.2 is called ReDoc.

Running ReDoc CLI

All of this chapter's API documentation screenshots have been created with the `redoc-cli` command-line utility (https://github.com/Rebilly/ReDoc/tree/master/cli) using the following command line:

```
redoc-cli serve <path to OpenAPI file> --options.showExtensions
```

This utility also lets you generate standalone HTML documentation using the following command line:

```
redoc-cli bundle <path to OpenAPI file> --options.showExtensions
```

These are only a few of the possibilities for ReDoc. Its documentation (https://github.com/Rebilly/ReDoc) provides all needed information to use it and integrate it into any existing web applications.

ReDoc is one tool among many. Many API tools, especially API developer portals, natively understand the OpenAPI Specification (and others) and so can generate such renderings without you having to code anything. But format alone isn't enough. If the description of your API does not contain all the needed information, the generated documentation will be incomplete, even if these tools are able to guess a few things by themselves.

What follows is illustrated with the OpenAPI Specification and ReDoc, but you can use other API description formats and rendering tools. The important things to remember here are what information is needed in the reference documentation and what you should expect from API description formats and renderers. We will start by documenting the data model, then the goals (paths and HTTP methods, input, outputs). After that, we will deal with security; and finally, we will see how to add some useful information about the API itself.

12.1.1 Documenting data models

Figures 12.3 and 12.4 show a detailed data model and an example of the request body parameter, respectively, needed to create a money transfer.

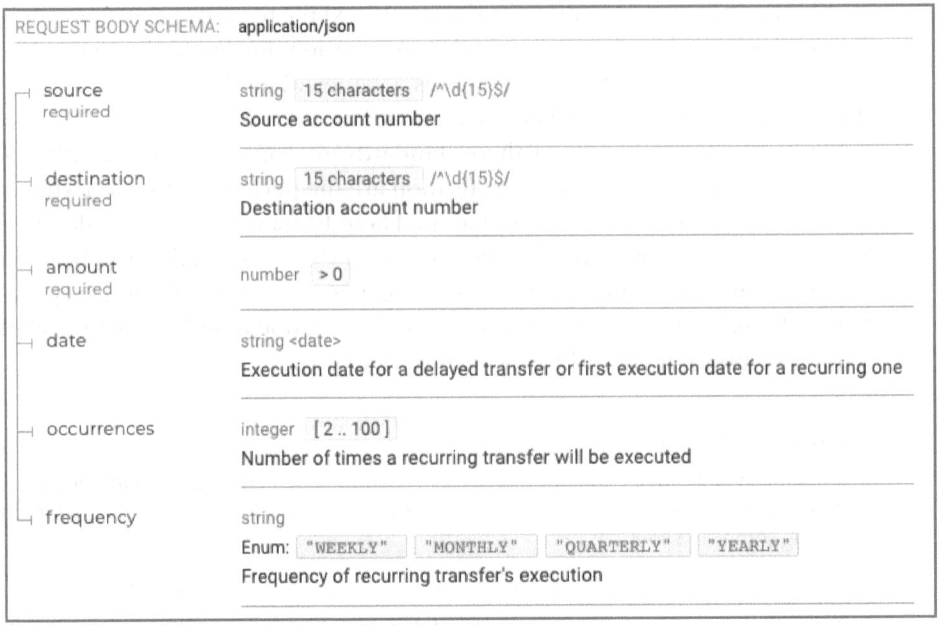

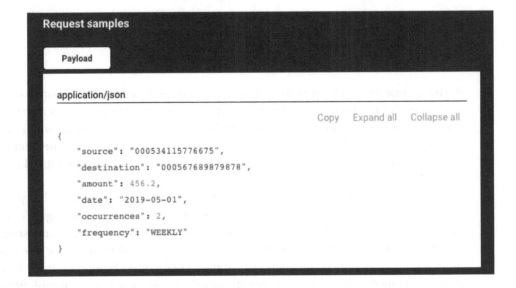

Figure 12.3   Data model reference documentation

Figure 12.4   Data model reference example

The reference documentation in figure 12.3 shows us that this data model is composed of source, destination, amount, date, occurrences, and frequency properties. They are all of type string except for amount, which is a number, and occurrences, which is an integer; additionally, source, destination, and amount are mandatory (required) properties. This is the most fundamental information needed in reference documentation, as it is when describing an API in the design phase (see section 3.3.1).

But this reference documentation does more than just provide the minimum: it also provides useful functional and technical descriptions and examples. The documentation gives detailed information about each property's format and value. The source and destination properties must be 15 characters long and contain only digits, according to the /^\d{15}$/ regular expression. The amount is an exclusively positive number, and the value of occurrences must be between 2 and 100. The possible values of the frequency property are "WEEKLY", "MONTHLY", "QUARTERLY", and "YEARLY". The example shown in figure 12.4 helps us to visualize what each property looks like.

Furthermore, the date, occurrences, and frequency descriptions give useful information about how these properties can be used for creating delayed or recurring transfers. Note that amount has no description because its name and the context make it clear that it specifies the amount of money to transfer from source to destination.

All this information comes from a JSON Schema defined in the underlying OpenAPI Specification file (two excerpts are shown in listings 12.1 and 12.2). You already learned in section 4.3.2 how to define a property's name, type, and description; how to state if a property is mandatory; and how to provide an example.

Listing 12.1 A very complete description of a property with an example

```
components:
  schemas:
    TransferRequest:
      description: A money transfer request
      required:
        - source
        - destination
        - amount
      properties:
        source:
          type: string
          description: Source account number
          minLength: 15
          maxLength: 15
          pattern: ^\d{15}$
          example: "000534115776675"
```

Minimum length for source property → minLength: 15

Maximum length for source property → maxLength: 15

Format for source property (a regular expression) → pattern: ^\d{15}$

An example value → example: "000534115776675"

The source property's length is 15 because its minLength and maxLength values are both 15. Its exact format (a string composed of 15 digits) is defined by pattern, which contains the ^\d{15}$ regular expression (000534115776675, for example).

ReDoc is actually able to guess the property's length based on the regular expression, but not all tools take advantage of this information. The source's value shown in figure 12.4 comes from the example provided in listing 12.1, but documentation tools can also guess example values based on descriptions, as show in the following listing.

Listing 12.2   Documentation tools rely on descriptions to generate examples

```
[...]
date:
  type: string
  format: date          ◄──┐  The date property is a string using a date
  description: |            │  format (YYYY-MM-DD); today's date is
    Execution date for a delayed transfer   used in the documentation.
    or first execution date for a recurring one
[...]
frequency:
  type: string
  description: Frequency of recurring transfer's execution
  enum:    ◄──────────────┐  Possible values for frequency; a random
    - WEEKLY              │  value is shown in the documentation.
    - MONTHLY
    - QUARTERLY
    - YEARLY
```

The date property uses the date format, which means the value will be a YYYY-MM-DD ISO 8601 full date: 2019-03-23, for example. The frequency property's possible values ("WEEKLY", "MONTHLY", "QUARTERLY", and "YEARLY") are defined in the enum list. There are no examples set for the date and frequency properties, but the reference documentation still provides some: these have been generated based on the JSON Schema.

For the date property, being a date, ReDoc simply uses today's date (2019-05-01 in figure 12.4), and for frequency, it uses a random value from the enum (WEEKLY in figure 12.4). I'll let you find out for yourself how the other properties have been described.

More about the OpenAPI Specification

As mentioned in section 4.1.1, you can easily explore the whole OpenAPI format by using my OpenAPI Map and by reading its specification.[a] Note that there are specific additional JSON Schema properties that can be used to make fine descriptions of any atomic types and also arrays (for example, how many items can be used in an array).

---

[a]   For the OpenAPI Map, see https://openapi-map.apihandyman.io/. For the OpenAPI Specification, see https://github.com/OAI/OpenAPI-Specification/tree/master/versions.

As you can see, basic but valuable reference documentation for an API's data model can be created by just reusing the work done during the API's design. Simply listing properties, their types, and if they are mandatory, without even providing examples or extensive descriptions, could be sufficient for simple data models. Consumers might not thank you for providing such basic reference documentation, but be sure that they will curse you if you do not provide any at all.

If you add examples and, more importantly, detailed and relevant descriptions, including both machine-readable (like formats or possible values) and human-readable ones, the resulting reference documentation will be of help to anyone using it on either the consumer's or the provider's side. There is no need for "Captain Obvious" descriptions like "amount: the transfer's amount" or, even worse, "amount: the amount."

> **NOTE** A relevant human-readable description explains the nature of the property, including its roles and relationships with others and when it is used.

If stating a property's name, type and context is sufficient for a user to understand its meaning; there is no need to add a description. If the API description format and rendering tool you use support formatted human-readable descriptions (using Markdown, for example), do not hesitate to use this feature to make long descriptions easier to read.

12.1.2 Documenting goals

A goal's reference documentation describes the goal's purpose, what is needed to use it, what kind of feedback consumers get in the event of success or failure, and if it is part of a group of goals. For example, figure 12.5 gives an overview of the transfer money goal.

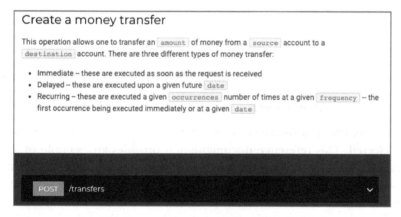

Figure 12.5 An overview of the transfer money goal

As you can see, the goal is represented by a POST /transfers request. According to the description, this goal allows users to create immediate, delayed, or recurring money transfers. Each type of transfer is explained from a functional point of view, and there is also information about the use of the various properties that can be shared by all types or those specific to one. All types of transfers need an amount, source account, and destination account. We can also see that a delayed transfer is executed on a given future date, and that a recurring transfer requires a date as well as a number of occurrences and a frequency.

All the information provided in this description could be inferred by analyzing the request body data model previously shown in figure 12.3, but it's better to provide a more human-readable description instead of simply saying, "Create a money transfer" or "Create an immediate, delayed, or recurring money transfer." Such a description makes documentation very user-friendly, but this can be even better. Look at the request samples shown in figure 12.6.

Figure 12.6   Multiple goal input examples

There are Immediate transfer, Delayed transfer, and Recurring transfer tabs, the latter being selected. This reference documentation provides an example of a request for each type of money transfer. This is a must-have! Users don't have to think to get almost-ready-to-use examples for various use cases; they just have to tweak the provided values. That's for the inputs, but an API reference documentation must also provide detailed information about possible responses, as shown in figure 12.7.

For each response, there is a human-readable description and the response body description (using the same format as the request body). The reference documentation shows that in the case of success, a 201 or 202 HTTP status can be returned. A 201 Created HTTP status is returned when a transfer is accepted, and no date property has been provided (for immediate or recurring transfers with the first occurrence executed immediately). A 202 Accepted HTTP status is returned when a transfer is accepted, and

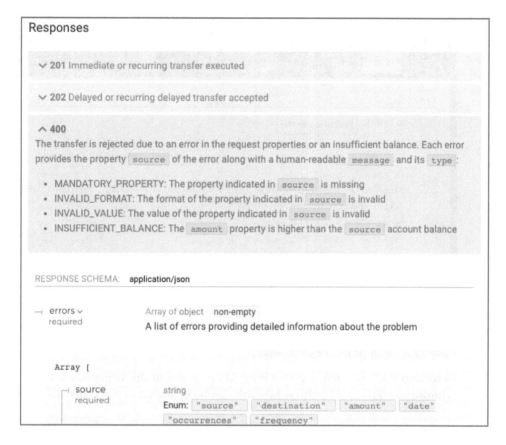

Figure 12.7 **Goal outputs**

a date property has been provided (for delayed or recurring transfers with a delayed first occurrence). Note that the response body schemas are not visible; this is to keep the screen capture small.

In the case of an error in the transfer request, a 400 Bad Request HTTP status is returned. Its response body is partially shown (again to keep the screen capture small). The interesting thing here, though, is the description, which provides details about all the possible errors and how they are represented.

As for the input, multiple examples can be provided for each response, as shown in figure 12.8. Here, 202 is selected. Delayed and recurring transfer samples are available, and the latter is selected.

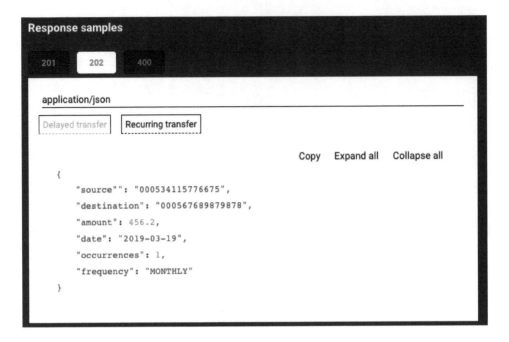

Figure 12.8   Multiple goal output examples

In section 7.1.3, you learned that if an API provides multiple goals, their organization is important. Figure 12.9 shows how this can be managed in reference documentation.

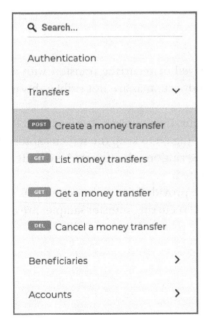

Figure 12.9   Goal organization

Figure 12.9 shows the reference documentation's menu (left column in figure 12.2). Goals are organized in various categories, with the Transfers category comprising all transfer-related goals ("Create a money transfer" or "Cancel a money transfer," for example). As with the data model reference documentation, everything that is shown comes from an underlying OpenAPI Specification file. The following listing puts into practice what you learned in section 4.2.3 to describe a goal.

Listing 12.3 The transfer money goal's basic reference documentation

```
[...]
paths:                      The resource path         The HTTP method used on the resource.
  /transfers:    ◄
    post:    ◄                                        A short description of the
      summary: Creates a money transfer    ◄          (resource, method) couple
      requestBody:    ◄
        content:                        The goal's input
          "application/json":    |
            schema:
              $ref: "#/components/schemas/TransferRequest"    The goal's
      responses:    ◄                                          possible outputs
        201:
          description: Immediate or recurring transfer executed
          content:
            "application/json":
              schema:
                $ref: "#/components/schemas/TransferResponse"
        [...]
        400:                                          A brief description
          description: Transfer rejected    ◄         of the feedback
          content:
            "application/json":
              schema:                                 A reference to the
                $ref: "#/components/schemas/Error"    ◄  feedback data model
[...]
```

The goal is described with a brief summary, and all the possible responses and their data models are listed without much detail. The various reference documentation screenshots you have seen provided more information. That's because the OpenAPI Specification file used obviously contains more information. The next listing shows the underlying detailed description of the transfer money goal.

Listing 12.4 The transfer money goal overview's OpenAPI Specification file

```
paths:
  /transfers:
    post:                               A multiline description
      summary: Transfers money          in Markdown
      description: |    ◄
        This operation allows one to transfer an `amount` of money from a
        `source` account to a `destination` account.
        There are three different types of money transfer:
          - Immediate, they are executed as soon as the request is received
```

```
      - Delayed, they are executed upon a given future `date`
      - Recurring, they are executed a given `occurrences` number of
      times at a given `frequency`, the first occurrence being executed
      immediately or at a given `date`
```

Here, after the summary (short description), a complete multiline description taking advantage of the Markdown format is provided. The next listing shows how to provide multiple examples of the transfer money goal's request body.

Listing 12.5   Multiple examples of the transfer money goal's request body

```
[...]
paths:
  /transfers:
    post:
[...]
      requestBody:
        content:
          "application/json":
            schema:
              $ref: "#/components/schemas/TransferRequest"
            examples:              ◄────┐
              immediate:                │  Multiple examples for the request body
                [...]
              delayed:                     An example comes with a summary,
                [...]                       description, and value
              recurring:       ◄───────┘
                summary: Recurring transfer
                description: |
                  The money transfer is executed at a
                  given date recurringly
                value:
                  source": "000534115776675"
                  destination: "000567689879878"
                  amount: 456.2
                  date: "2019-03-19"
                  occurrences: 1
                  frequency: "MONTHLY"
              [...]
[...]
```

The Request Samples pane in figure 12.6 showed three tabs: Immediate transfer, Delayed transfer, and Recurring transfer. Their content came from the examples property after the schema property. Each example has a summary (tab name), description, and value (tab value). Unfortunately the description of each example is not shown in ReDoc.

> **NOTE**   Be aware that all tools might not support all API description format features.

Providing multiple examples can be done for other types of input parameters too (query or header parameters, for example), as well as response bodies. Speaking of responses, remember that you learned in section 5.2.2 that we should list all possible errors. These obviously must be documented beyond just listing the possible 4XX or 5XX status codes in the reference documentation. The next listing shows how to take advantage of a complete multiline-formatted description to do so.

Listing 12.6   A detailed error description

```
[...]
paths:
  /transfers:
    post:
      [...]
      responses
        [...]
        400:
          description: |
            The transfer is rejected due to an error in the request
            properties or an insufficient balance. Each error provides the
            property `source` of the error along with a human-readable
            `message` and its `type`:

            - MANDATORY_PROPERTY: The property indicated in `source`
            is missing
            - INVALID_FORMAT: The format of the property indicated in
            `source` is invalid
            - INVALID_VALUE: The value of the property indicated in
            `source` is invalid
            - INSUFFICIENT_BALANCE: The `amount` property is higher than
            the `source` account balance
          [...]
[...]
```

For the goal groups, there's nothing new. You learned in section 7.1.3 how to define them, as shown in the next listing.

Listing 12.7   Describing tags

```
[...]
tags:                                                    Optional tags definition
  - name: Transfers                                      and description
    description: Everything you need to transfer money

paths:
  /transfers:
    post:
      summary: Create a money transfer       Tags to which the goal belongs
      tags:
        - Transfers
[...]
```

So good reference documentation for an API goal, like the data model, requires a relevant human-readable description and relevant examples (the more, the better). A good description of the possible errors is especially important. Besides providing multiple examples, this is basically what you have to describe when you design the API, so this kind of reference documentation is easy to create once the API has been designed.

12.1.3 Documenting security

Reference documentation must also contain information about security, as shown in figures 12.10 and 12.11.

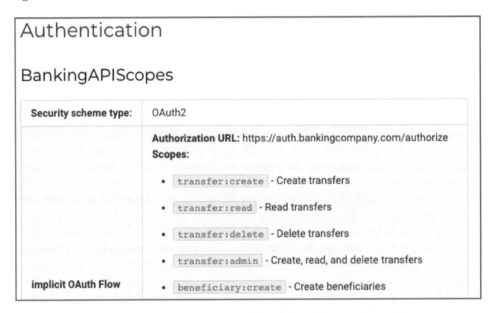

Figure 12.10   How the Banking API is secured and what the available scopes are

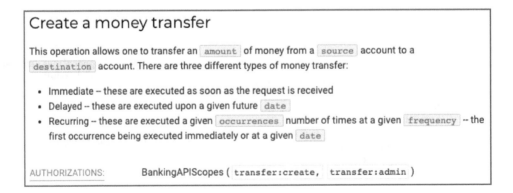

Figure 12.11   Which scopes are needed to create a money transfer

The Authentication section in figure 12.10 shows that the Banking API is secured using the OAuth 2.0 implicit flow, and the (visible) available scopes are `transfer:create`, `transfer:read`, `transfer:delete`, `transfer:admin`, and `beneficiary:create`. On the Create a money transfer screen in figure 12.11, the Authorizations section states that consumers must have the `transfer:create` or `transfer:admin` scope to be authorized to use the transfer money goal. There's nothing new here; you saw how to describe API security using the OpenAPI Specification in section 8.2.4. The following listing shows an excerpt of the underlying OpenAPI Specification file.

> **Listing 12.8   Defining API security and attaching scopes to a goal**

```
[...]
components:                        Security and scope definitions
  securitySchemes:      ◄────────┘
    BankingAPIScopes:
      type: oauth2
      flows:
        implicit:
          authorizationUrl: "https://auth.bankingcompany.com/authorize"
          scopes:
            "transfer:create": Create transfers
            "transfer:read": List transfers
            [...]
[...]
paths:
  /transfers:
    post:
      summary: Create a money transfer
      security:      ◄─────────────────┐
        - BankingAPIScopes:
          - "transfer:create"          Scopes needed to use the goal
          - "transfer:admin"
[...]
```

ReDoc automatically adds an Authentication menu showing everything defined in the `components.securitySchemes` section of the OpenAPI Specification file. If `security` is defined on a goal, ReDoc also shows an AUTHORIZATIONS: entry.

Again, because you have to define how the API is secured when designing it, not much effort is needed to provide basic reference documentation describing how the API is secured, the available scopes, and which scopes are needed to use each goal.

12.1.4 *Providing an overview of the API*

Last but not least is the API-level reference documentation. Figure 12.12 shows how ReDoc uses the `info` section of an OpenAPI Specification file (shown in listing 12.9) for this.

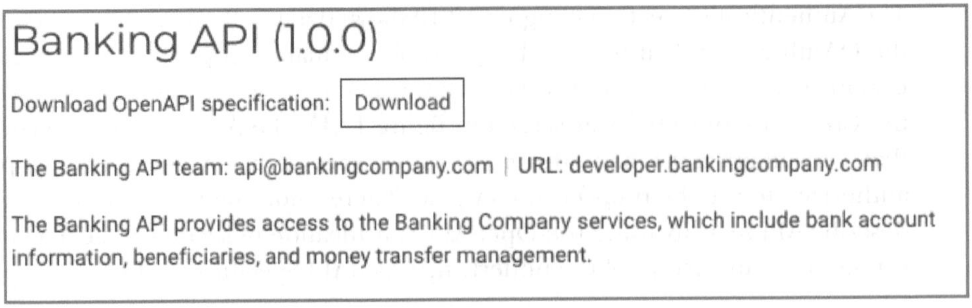

Banking API (1.0.0)

Download OpenAPI specification: | Download |

The Banking API team: api@bankingcompany.com | URL: developer.bankingcompany.com

The Banking API provides access to the Banking Company services, which include bank account information, beneficiaries, and money transfer management.

Figure 12.12   An API's short description and contact information in the reference documentation

Listing 12.9   The `info` section of the underlying OpenAPI Specification file

```
info:
  title: Banking API
  version: "1.0.0"
  description: |
    The Banking API provides access to the
    [Banking Company](http://www.bankingcompany.com) services, which
    include bank account information, beneficiaries, and money transfer
    management.
  contact:
    name: The Banking API team
    email: api@bankingcompany.com
    url: developer.bankingcompany.com
```

You learned how to define an API's name (`title`) and `version` when describing an API using the OpenAPI Specification in section 4.2.1. Here we've added a `description` and some `contact` information. The `description` provides an overview of the Banking API and takes advantage of the Markdown format to provide a link to the Banking Company's website. The `contact` information consists of the `name` of the team managing the API, their `email` address, and the API's developer website's `url`.

Providing a brief description of the API is mandatory in an API's reference documentation; it helps consumers understand what can be done using the API if its name alone is not enough. The contact information is optional, but you should always provide users a way of getting more information or help.

12.1.5 *Generating documentation from the implementation: pros and cons*

Documentation can be generated from the implementation code alone or code plus annotations; that was the original intent of the Swagger framework (see section 4.1.1).

Such a strategy has the advantage of keeping implementation and documentation synchronized, but know that it has a few drawbacks:

- I do not recommend only relying on a pure generation based on code, as the resulting documentation will be far from complete.
- Existing annotation frameworks, at least the one I have been working with, do not allow the same flexibility as you get when working directly with an API description format (for example, providing examples adapted to various contexts when using generic data structures shared across the API is impossible).
- Including documentation in the code implies that you will actually modify the code to fix the documentation. That could be a problem depending on who works on what (documentation versus code) and your organization and your confidence level when modifying the code (yes, not all organizations in the world are able to push all applications automatically into production on every single commit without fearing anything).
- In the early stages, code has to actually be written to generate documentation. If you remember the beginning of this book, you know how this can expose the provider's perspective.

Obviously, keeping the documentation outside the code can also have some drawbacks; the major one, being able to keep documentation and code synchronized. Know that there is no good or bad strategy regarding this matter; you have to choose one that works for you and your organization.

So, whatever the means, as an API designer, you can create good API reference documentation without much effort, especially if you take a little time to provide detailed machine- and human-readable descriptions and (multiple) examples. Like design, writing good documentation requires practice, and reference documentation is a good place to start. Remember that seasoned technical writers might be needed if this documentation is for a partner or public API.

12.2 Creating a user guide

Complete reference documentation listings and describing every component of an API is a must-have, but as mentioned earlier, when following a recipe, if you only have the ingredients list, you can struggle to achieve something edible. An API user guide, like the example in figure 12.13, is meant to explain how to actually use the API. It describes how to use the API as a whole, as well as its principles and how to get access to it (registration and getting access tokens). When you're providing public APIs, this documentation can be fairly dynamic.

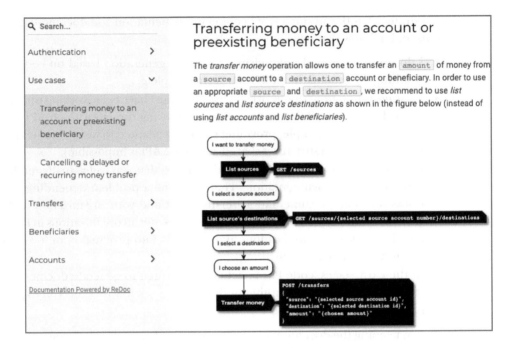

Figure 12.13   An API user guide

12.2.1 *Documenting use cases*

In figure 12.13, there is a Use cases menu in the left pane. It contains two items: Transferring Money to an Account or Preexisting Beneficiary and Canceling a Delayed or Recurring Transfer. The first option is selected. Each item is obviously intended to describe a use case that exposes how various goals of the API can be combined in order to achieve something.

In the right pane, showing the transfer money use case, there is some text explaining what a money transfer is, the concept of source and destination accounts, and which goals should be used to select appropriate values for these properties. There is also a diagram below the text showing how to proceed:

1 Call the list sources goal.
2 Select a source account in the resulting list.
3 Call the list source's destinations goal for the selected source.
4 Select a destination account in the returned list.
5 Decide on an amount.
6 Call the transfer money goal with the selected source and destination and the amount.

Does that not seem familiar? This looks like the information you learned to gather in section 2.3 and put in an API goals canvas like the one shown in figure 12.14.

Whos	Whats	Hows	Inputs (source)	Outputs (usage)	Goals
Customer	Transfer money	Select source account	Customer ID (security data)	Source accounts usable for a money transfer (list source's destinations, transfer money)	List sources
		Select a destination account or beneficiary	Source account (list sources)	Valid destination accounts or pre-registered beneficiaries for selected source (transfer money)	List source's destinations
		Request money transfer	Source account (list sources), destination account or pre-registered beneficiary (list source's destinations), and amount (customer/consumer input)	Money transfer ID	Transfer money

Figure 12.14   An excerpt of the API goals canvas made while designing the Banking API.

An API goals canvas describes use cases that can be achieved using various goals. This means that, again, the work done during the design of the API can be reused to document the API. The API goals canvas can be reused more or less as is for private APIs and as a raw input for partner or public APIs.

Describing use cases in an API user guide can be done in many different ways, using many different tools. For basic user guides, all you need is to be able to write formatted text and, possibly, add some diagrams or images. You can use a simple content management system (CMS), a developer portal (which usually include CMS features), or even build your own custom website. For illustration purposes here, I'll continue to use ReDoc and the OpenAPI Specification file shown in the following listing.

Listing 12.10   How ReDoc takes advantage of the OpenAPI Specification file

```
[...]
info:
  title: Banking API          The description of the API
  version: "1.0.0"
  description: |        ◄──

    The Banking API provides access to the
    [Banking Company](http://www.bankingcompany.com) services, which
    include bank account information, beneficiaries, and money transfer
    management.

    # Use cases      ◄──────  A Markdown level 1 header

    ## Transferring money to an account          A Markdown level 2 header
           or preexisting beneficiary   ◄─────

    The _transfer money_ operation allows one to transfer an `amount` of
    money from a `source` account to a `destination` account or
    beneficiary.
    In order to use an appropriate `source` and `destination`, we recommend
    to use _list sources_ and _list source's destinations_ as shown in the
    figure below (instead of using _list accounts_ and
    _list beneficiaries_).
```

This description includes an image.

```
![Diagram](http://developer.bankingcompany.com/diagrams/transfer.svg)

## Canceling a delayed or recurring       A simple text-based description
                money transfer

 - List money transfers: To list existing money transfers and select the
   one to delete
 - Cancel a money transfer: To cancel the selected money transfer
[...]
```

I've added some text and included an image in the `info.description` section of the OpenAPI Specification file, taking advantage of the Markdown format. If the description contains level 1 and 2 headers, ReDoc automatically adds them to the left pane as menu items and submenus. If it contains an image (`![Text](URL)`), it is shown as long as the URL can be accessed by the browser in which the ReDoc documentation runs. Diagrams can definitely be of great help for consumers (as the saying goes, a picture is worth a thousand words), but you can also simply use text, as shown in the second use case (Canceling a delayed or recurring money transfer).

Code your diagrams

If you want to create diagrams but struggle with drawing tools, note that the diagram shown in figure 12.13 was generated using a tool called PlantUML (or sometimes PUML) available at http://plantuml.com. This tool lets you create diagrams using code. You can find the transfer money diagram code in this book's source code (https://www.manning.com/books/the-design-of-web-apis). I'll let you explore the tool's website to discover how to use this awesome format.

Including the user guide in an API description file can be complex to manage in the long run for big APIs with many use cases. The people in charge of maintaining the API description might not be the ones maintaining the user guide, and the two forms of documentation might not have the same lifecycle. If you use a completely different tool or system for the API user guide, don't forget to use `info.contact.url` or add a link in the description pointing to where it is located.

12.2.2 *Documenting security*

Another topic that is important in an API user guide is what consumers have to do to actually make an API call. It would be a pity if consumers knew which API calls to make to trigger a money transfer, but couldn't actually make those calls because they didn't know how to get a security token. An API user guide *must* include advice about how to register as a developer, register a consumer app, and get tokens using the available OAuth flows or whatever other security system/framework is in use (see section 8.1).

Unfortunately, there is nothing much to reuse here from the design phase (the scopes list is not of great help); but fortunately, such documentation should be almost the same for all of your APIs, and there are literally thousands of existing resources that can be used as inspiration to explain how to get an access token using an OAuth flow once the consumer application is registered.

12.2.3 Providing an overview of common behaviors and principles

An API user guide can also contain information about all of the API's common behaviors and principles; security is but one of these. Such documentation can explain how errors are handled (see section 5.2.3), the available data formats and languages supported, or how pagination is handled (see section 6.2). In sum, you should include everything that is common to your API goals and worth mentioning to consumers in order to facilitate the use of the API.

12.2.4 Thinking beyond static documentation

This topic is totally out of the scope of this book, but know that static documentation is not the only option. The most-praised (public) APIs usually provide awesome developer portals, including high-quality reference documentation and user guides—and all of this is constructed in a totally dynamic way.

For example, while browsing the reference documentation of such an API, you might see a Try It! button that lets you actually call the API using a prefilled request, with the developer portal handling all the security business under the hood. Similarly, some user guides allow you to test use cases, step-by-step, inside the developer portal.[1]

12.3 Providing adequate information to implementers

We've explored how to document an API for consumers, but before any of them start to actually consume the API, it has to be implemented. And what do the people in charge of the implementation need? They obviously need a detailed description of the interface contract and, possibly, how it is supposed to be used; but that's not enough. They also need a description of what happens under the hood.

> **NOTE** The events depicted in the story that follows are fictitious. Any similarity to any person living or dead or any existing or previous organization is merely coincidental.

When the Banking API was implemented, the resulting API was not exactly the expected one. For example, the account balances were implemented as objects containing a value as a number and a currency as a string. Unfortunately, for a $123.45 balance, the value was 12345 (the balance in cents, as it is stored in the banking system) and the currency was "C123" (the internal $ currency code). Also, the returned balances were not the real-time ones, but the daily ones, updated once a day at midnight.

There were also problems with error handling. For example, when a money transfer request was missing both a destination account and an amount, the error feedback only indicated the first problem. And if the account's balance was insufficient, the error type was the internal error code "0002". More frightening, if a consumer using a security

---

[1] Look at Twilio (https://www.twilio.com) and Stripe (https://stripe.com) to discover first-class documentation.

token linked to a given customer requested an existing account with a `GET /accounts/`
`{accountNumber}` request, and it did not belong to the consumer, the consumer got
a `200 OK` response with the account instead of a `404 Not Found`. It was fortunate that
someone had the idea of conducting tests that uncovered these issues (we will talk more
about that in section 13.3.5).

After some investigation, the project team realized that the developers in charge
of the implementation did not get enough information about the API contract, how
it should map to the underlying system, and what the expected security controls were.
More importantly, they lacked knowledge of API security in general. All of the problems were solved by enhancing the API description (the OpenAPI Specification file) as
shown in figure 12.15 and listing 12.11, and by providing training and guidance.

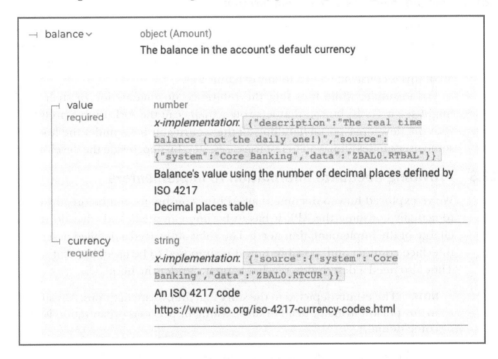

Figure 12.15   API description with enhanced description and implementation information

Listing 12.11   Adding custom properties into an OpenAPI Specification file

```
[...]
properties:
  value:
    description: |
      Balance's value using the number of decimal places as defined
      by ISO 4217
    externalDocs:          ◄──────┤ A link to some documentation
      description: Decimal places table
      url: https://www.currency-iso.org/en/home/tables/table-a1.html
```

```
    type: number
    x-implementation:
      description: The real time balance (not the daily one!)
      source:
        system: Core Banking
        location: ZBAL0.RTBAL
currency:
    description: An ISO 4217 code
    externalDocs:
      url: https://www.iso.org/iso-4217-currency-codes.html
    type: string
    example: USD
    x-implementation:
      source:
        system: Core Banking
        location: ZBAL0.RTCUR
[...]
```

Custom data ignored by standard parsers

A link without a description

The data format problems were due to an incomplete description of the amount's data model in the API description file. If the description for the amount's `value` property had stated that the number of decimal places was the one defined by the ISO 4217 standard, that would have given a hint about its format. The same goes for the `currency` description, which should have stated that this value was an ISO 4217 three-letter code. For both properties, links to external documentation (`externalDocs`) about ISO 4217 have been added. Note that the first link to the decimal places table has a description that ReDoc uses to render the link.

For the balance information, because the Banking API is used by non-expert consumers, there was no need to state in its description that it is the real-time balance. This means that it must be stated in another place only visible on the provider's side. The team (including the designer and developers) chose to define it in the OpenAPI Specification file using a custom (or vendor) extension `x-implementation`, containing a detailed description about the source of the data (the system and location).

Standard OpenAPI Specification parsers ignore all properties starting with x-, so the `x-implementation` property's name and format are totally custom and were defined by the team. Tools such as ReDoc might render the data contained in such a property, but as you can see in figure 12.15, it is rendered as a JSON object. To get a more human-friendly rendering, you have to customize the tool. The OpenAPI Specification file also has been enhanced to contain information about security controls, as shown in the next listing.

Listing 12.12 Security controls information on the get account goal

```
[...]
paths:
  /accounts/{id}:
    get:
      summary: Get an account
      x-implementation:
        security:
```

```
        description: |
          Only accounts belonging to user referenced in security data;
          return a 404 if this is not the case
        source:
          system: security
          location: jwt.sub
        fail: 404
[...]
```

The x-implementation property contains a description of the security controls that have to be performed, the security data to use, and which HTTP status to return in case of failure. Besides this detailed implementation documentation, developers have been trained to understand API security concerns, and they also have been provided with guidelines (we talk more about this in section 12.2). The error problems were fixed by adding more detailed information in the consumer-oriented documentation (as seen in section 12.1.1) and by also explaining error-handling principles (as seen in section 12.1.2).

> **NOTE** The consumer-facing documentation must not show the x-implementation information; it must be stripped from the OpenAPI Specification file before it's published to the developer portal.

So, the first step in providing relevant documentation to the API implementers is providing detailed consumer-facing documentation (a reference documentation and user guide). This documentation does not have to be flashy and eye-catching, but it must be exhaustive. But this is not enough.

The implementers also need *provider-facing* documentation about what actually happens under the hood. They need information about the data mapping (which system each piece of data comes from), error mapping (how to transform internal errors into consumer-facing errors), security data and controls, and expected behaviors based on internal business/technical rules.

As you've seen, this information can be documented within the API description file, but this is only one option. Choosing how to provide this information is up to you, as the API designer, and the people you are working with. Besides the actual API documentation, the implementers' documentation also consists of general guidance and training (see section 12.2).

12.4 *Documenting evolutions and retirement*

You learned in section 9.1 how to handle API design and evolutions in order to limit the introduction of breaking changes. But changes, breaking or not, will inevitably happen, and they have to be documented.

Such documentation is useful for consumers to keep them aware of new features and let them know if they need to modify their code in the event that elements are deprecated (or worse, retired). It can be also useful for all the other people involved in the project, providing them with an overview of upcoming changes in the next version.

And who is the best person to document or at least list all these changes? You! As the person who designed the changes, you know best what you have done. Figure 12.16 shows a very basic *change log* describing the latest modifications made to the Banking API.

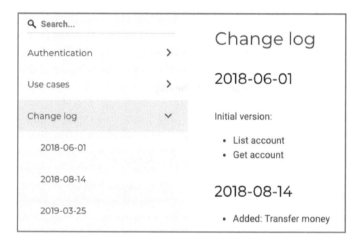

Figure 12.16   A simple change log listing modifications made in each version

A change log should state which elements (data model properties, parameters, responses, security scopes) have been added, modified, deprecated, or retired. Here, we simply take advantage of the info.description section of an OpenAPI Specification file to add a Change Log level 1 header containing level 2 sections for each version, as we did for the use cases. API description formats do not, at least at the time of this book's writing, propose ways of describing such a change log, but they can at least provide ways of indicating deprecated elements, as shown in figure 12.17.

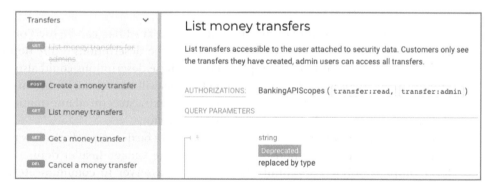

Figure 12.17   Indicating deprecated elements using the OpenAPI Specification file

The List money transfers for admins goal in the lefthand menu is struck through, and the t query parameter of the List money transfers goal, shown in the right pane, is indicated as deprecated; they both have a deprecated flag set to true in the OpenAPI Specification file, as shown in listings 12.13 and 12.14.

Listing 12.13   Deprecating the List money transfers for admins goal

```
/admin-transfers:
  get:
    summary: List money transfers for admins
    tags:
      - Transfers
    description: Redirects to GET /transfers
    deprecated: true      ◄──────┐
  responses:                     │ Goal deprecation flag
    "200":
        description: Transfers list
        content:
          "application/json":
            schema:
              $ref: "#/components/schemas/TransferList"
```

Listing 12.14   Deprecating the t query parameter

```
/transfers:
  get:
    summary: List money transfers
    parameters:
      - name: t
        in: query
        description: replaced by type
        deprecated: true      ◄──────┐
        schema:                      │ Parameter deprecation flag
          type: string
      - name: type
        in: query
        description: transfer type
        schema:
          type: string
```

According to the OpenAPI Specification, the `deprecated` flag can be used on parameters, goals, and properties in data models. Here, the descriptions of the deprecated elements indicate what to use as replacements. These descriptions could also provide an indication about when the deprecated elements will be retired (if they are to be). You can also use some `x-` custom properties to add extra structured information about the deprecations instead of using text in the descriptions.

Documenting deprecated elements can sometimes be done in a dynamic way by providing metadata in API responses. For example, the `Sunset` header defined by RFC 8594 (https://tools.ietf.org/html/rfc8594) allows a server to communicate the fact that a resource is expected to become unresponsive at a specific point in time. If the Banking Company introduces a version 2 of the Banking API on August 4, 2019, and lets all consumers take six months to update their code, any call made on any resource of version 1 (like a `GET /v1/accounts` request) can return the response shown in the following listing, stating that the resource will not be available after February 4, 2020.

Listing 12.15   A response with a `Sunset` header

```
200 OK
Sunset: Tue, 4 Feb 2020 23:59:59 GMT

{ "items": [ ... ] }
```

In the next and final chapter, we will expand even more the context around API design in order to be able to work as API designers on a long-term basis on many APIs, even ones we do not actually design.

Summary

- API designers must participate in the creation of different types of API documentation.
- A detailed reference documentation is a good thing, but it is not enough. We must also create a user's guide.
- User guides must provide all needed information to use the API as a whole, including how to obtain credentials and tokens.
- Leveraging an API description language such as the OpenAPI Specification can be of great help when creating documentation.
- It is important to keep track of modifications in order to inform users of changes.
- Creating documentation helps to test the API design.

Growing APIs

This chapter covers

- API lifecycle
- API design guidelines
- API reviews
- Communication and community

Throughout this book, we have expanded our vision of API design and APIs in general beyond simple application programming interfaces floating in the air. This is especially true of the four previous chapters. In chapters 10 and 11, you saw how to pay attention to not only the consumer's but also the provider's context to design realistic APIs that will be implementable and will fulfill consumers' needs in the most efficient way. And by thinking beyond an API's current version, you learned in chapter 9 to create API designs that reduce the risk of introducing breaking changes when modifying them.

Designing APIs requires us to think beyond the APIs themselves because they are just one part of the whole. We started to uncover this whole in chapter 12. Indeed, you discovered that API designers can do more than just create APIs by participating in the making of different types of documentation. In this last chapter, we will explore three other API-design-related topics that any API designer must be aware of, and sometimes master, in order to grow their APIs in the long run.

We will talk first about the API lifecycle: how APIs are born, live, and are eventually retired. Then we will explore API guidelines, which are mandatory when designing multiple APIs or multiple versions of a single API, whether working alone or with other designers. After that, we will take a look at the different ways of reviewing APIs in order to ensure that a design conforms to the organization's API surface, fulfills expectations, is implementable, and pleases consumers. We will finish by talking about communication and sharing your APIs, their evolutions, and your API practices.

13.1 *The API lifecycle*

Growing APIs requires that we know the API lifecycle and understand that it runs in parallel with others, as shown in figure 13.1. As you can see, API design is only a part of the API lifecycle: how APIs are born, live, and eventually retire.

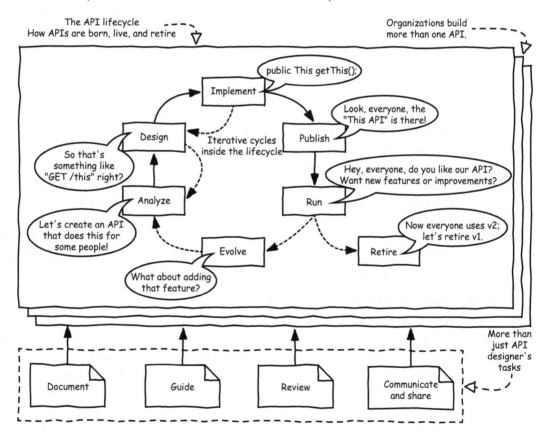

Figure 13.1 The API lifecycle

The API lifecycle starts with the *analyze phase*, where a company/organization/team/individual thinks providing an API might be of interest for business or technical reasons. During this phase, topics are explored, such as the API's goals, what needs it is supposed to fulfill, what consumers it targets, who needs it, and what benefits it offers. Then comes the *design phase*, in which the ideas resulting from the Analyze phase are deeply investigated and transcribed into a programming interface contract. After that, during the *implement phase*, an application exposing this contract is built.

The analyze, design, implement journey is actually an iterative process; you might have to go back and forth according to new discoveries, new questions, or simply because you change your mind on a given design solution. After all this, the API is made available to the targeted consumers in the *publish phase*. The API will run this way until it evolves to provide new features. But it can also be retired because a new version introducing breaking changes is needed, with the previous version being replaced by the new one. Unfortunately, APIs can also be retired because they were unsuccessful or are simply not needed anymore.

An entire book, if not several, would be necessary to explore the full API lifecycle in depth. In the rest of this chapter, we will focus on topics relevant to API design and designers, but these topics are not confined to the design phase. More often than not, API designers must intervene in various stages of the API lifecycle and do more than just design APIs.

To guarantee success, designers must work closely with stakeholders, product owners, technical writers, and developers or testers. They also have to work closely with consumers, either directly or through the API's developer relations team. And when working on an API, API designers participate in the creation of different types of documentation (as you saw in the previous chapter), take part in various reviews on both the provider's and the consumer's side, and can also have a hand in communications about the API.

But organizations rarely build a single, never-changing API; instead, they typically produce multiple, always-evolving APIs. The API designers have to work together to build a consistent API surface for the organization (see section 6.1). API designers must share what they do, helping each other by providing guidance when designing and reviewing APIs. Even lone API designers have to guide themselves by keeping an eye on their past work in order to be consistent in their design.

13.2 *Building API design guidelines*

Put two API designers in a meeting room and ask them how to handle pagination in a REST API. You'll probably witness a lively discussion with each one proposing different methods and assessing the pros and cons of the other's suggested solutions. And in the end, you might be presented with several options, all valid, and some different from the one(s) used in your existing organization or team's APIs, which were created by either the same designers or other ones.

You saw in section 6.1 that consistency is a key concern when designing APIs. APIs have to be consistent with themselves, with the rest of the organization/team's APIs, and also with the rest of the world in order to be easy to use. Being consistent over time when working alone on a single API is easier said than done, but when many API designers are working on an organization's API surface, which is composed of many APIs, it's hard to keep this surface totally smooth. We are humans; we all have our own preferences and backgrounds, and sometimes we change our minds without even noticing.

When new designers arrive, they have to discover how your APIs need to be designed in order to be consistent. But without proper guidance, they might not succeed. Similarly, if people who have never designed APIs before want to do so, it would be wise to provide them with adequate guidance to avoid API design catastrophes.

Defining *guidelines*, a set of rules that will be used by all designers, is a must to ensure consistency within and across the organization/team's APIs. It's also a good way to avoid wasting time with endless debates where everyone is right, but a single solution has to be chosen, and to focus on what really matters: providing the easiest to understand and easiest to use representations of APIs that fulfill consumers' needs. What's more, guidelines are a wonderful tool to help beginning API designers. Let's see what the contents of such guidelines might look like and how to actually create them.

13.2.1 *What to put in API design guidelines*

API design guidelines can be composed of three different layers: *reference guidelines* that focus on describing the foundations of the API designs, *use case guidelines* that explain how to apply these foundations through various uses cases, and *design process guidelines* that provide guidance about how to design APIs. Such guidelines can also provide information that goes beyond the interface contract, such as details about software architecture and implementation principles. Let's take a closer look at each possible layer of the design guidelines, what it contains, and why you should think about including it in your API's guidelines.

REFERENCE GUIDELINES

Being consistent in API design requires the definition of principles and rules that should be applied when designing APIs. Reference guidelines are the minimum API design guidelines that you must create: these list and describe all of the principles and rules. Figure 13.2 shows an excerpt of the Banking Company's reference guidelines.

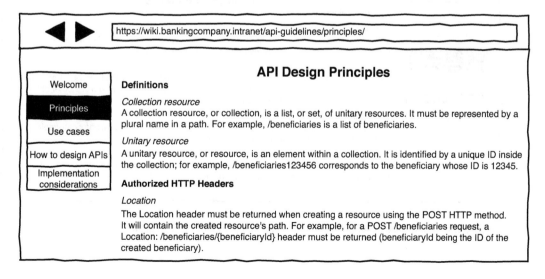

Figure 13.2   The Banking Company's API design principles

The most basic reference guidelines might, for example, describe which HTTP methods, status codes, or headers can be used and when; the format of the resources' paths; what data formats are returned in the case of errors; and how to handle pagination. Such guidelines should also provide clear and shared definitions of the vocabulary used when designing APIs; for example, what is an API, what is a resource or a collection, what is a path, and what is a version? If you have heard of domain-driven design, this could be compared to the ubiquitous language that has to be used by all people involved in the design of APIs.

The reference guidelines can be compared to the API reference documentation: it lists and describes all the elements that you need when designing APIs. Like reference documentation, these can be quite indigestible alone, and it might not be that easy to design APIs that actually respect them. That is why you should also consider adding use case guidelines.

USE CASE GUIDELINES

You should know by now that usability and the user's point of view matter when you design anything. You have witnessed that when learning to design APIs, as well as their documentation. Obviously, API design guidelines are no exception: you must create those with usability and simplicity in mind. If you don't do this, it's better not to write them at all because at best, some people might read them but not fully follow them; and at worst, nobody will want to read them at all! The use case guidelines provide ready-to-use "recipes" or solutions as shown in figure 13.3.

The Create an Element page describes a use case using ordinary vocabulary, providing variants of a typical create, and then explains how to do that in a REST API using a shared vocabulary. It describes which parameters are expected, their format, and what

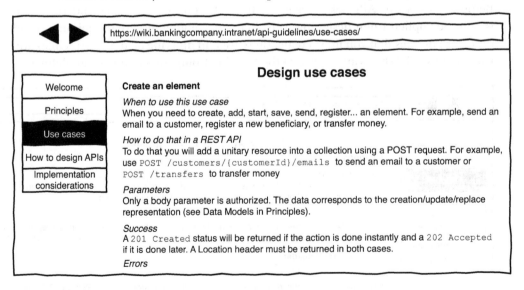

Figure 13.3   A use case description in the Banking Company's API design guidelines

kind of feedback should be provided, mentioning only the needed rules or principles coming from the reference guidelines.

Such documentation is really important for beginners, but it is also useful to seasoned API designers too. Some API designers might only do this work from time to time, and they might not be comfortable with technical API designers' vocabulary. Some of them might stick to the CRUD actions and find it hard to design a goal that is not something like create *xyz*; they're usually tempted to use POST /do-this. They might also not know which HTTP status to choose if the reference guidelines only provide an inventory of authorized HTTP status codes without many details about when exactly to use them. If they haven't read all the principles, they might have missed that a Location header was supposed to be returned when creating a resource (even seasoned API designers can forget this!).

Both beginners and seasoned designers will be more efficient and happier if they can find all the information they need in a single page without having to scan through all the principles and rules. But how did the designers know that they had to add a create *something* goal to the API?

DESIGN PROCESS GUIDELINES

Designing APIs requires methods, tools, and processes. It can be useful to add design process guidelines to your API guidelines, as shown in figure 13.4.

The idea is not to copy and paste text from this book or some other software design book into your guidelines. Such guidelines can simply provide a design canvas or links to existing documents or checklists, or to training sessions provided by seasoned API designers. You learned in chapters 10 and 11 that designing an API is not simply a

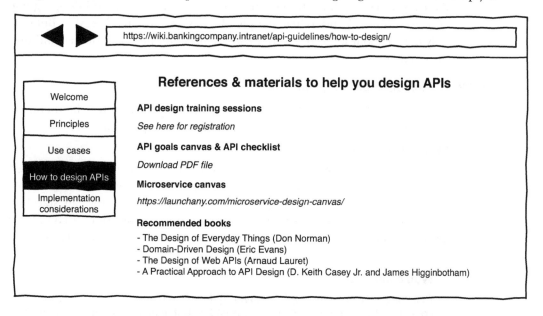

Figure 13.4 The Banking Company's How to Design APIs page in the design guidelines

matter of designing an interface contract floating in mid-air. There are many considerations around the creation of APIs that could be included in your guidelines.

MORE THAN INTERFACE DESIGN GUIDELINES

Extended API design guidelines could contain information about security, network concerns, or implementation, as shown in figure 13.5. These might include details on the standard data attached to security tokens, which OAuth flow to use in a given context, or how to configure frameworks in order to actually get the expected results when implementing the API.

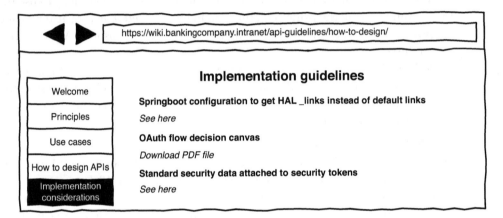

Figure 13.5 The Banking Company's Implementation considerations page in the design guidelines

Basically, you can put anything you think is relevant in your API design guidelines to ensure consistency and to help people who design and build the APIs. But so far, we've only talked about what to put in the guidelines, not how to actually build them. We'll turn to that next.

13.2.2 *Continuously building guidelines*

Building API design guidelines requires us not only to actually write them, but also to evolve them and make people aware of them and accept them.

START SMALL AND ACCURATE

When writing API design guidelines, don't try to construct the best possible guidelines covering every possibility and every edge case in one shot. You will waste your time and end up producing rambling, low-quality documentation. Instead, start by covering basic, necessary topics in a simple and straightforward way. Aim for completeness and accuracy. This is not the time to start inventing fancy ways of using HTTP!

Web concepts

Designing APIs and building API design guidelines requires a solid understanding of web concepts like HTTP headers and status codes. But finding which RFC contains the most up-to-date source of truth about a specific header or other concept so you can use it accurately is not always simple. Fortunately, Erik Wilde has created the Web Concepts website (http://webconcepts.info/) to help with this task.

"The Web's 'Uniform Interface' is based on a large and growing set of specifications. These specifications establish the shared concepts that providers and consumers of Web services can rely on. Web Concepts is providing an overview of these concepts and of the specifications defining them.

One example for how this works is HTTP/1.1 Caching, which defines 5 HTTP Header Fields, 7 HTTP Warn Codes, and 12 HTTP Cache Directives. Web Concepts provides a structured, quick, and interlinked overview of these and many more concepts that together establish the 'Web surface.'"

Erik Wilde

As mentioned in section 6.1.4, you can also be inspired by others, especially your favorite APIs. If there are APIs that you really love to use, why not copy their style? Similarly, you can take advantage of existing API guidelines that other companies share publicly, instead of inventing your own.

The API Stylebook

The API Stylebook (http://apistylebook.com) is a website in which I collect and analyze API design guidelines. It aims to help API designers solve API design matters and build their own API design guidelines by providing quick and easy access to topics covered in the guidelines on the site. Instead of reinventing the wheel or searching the web for hours, API designers can browse the API Stylebook to quickly find solutions and take inspiration from these existing guidelines.

If your API design guidelines start small, that means they will evolve. Indeed, they must be allowed to evolve to include new contents related to situations that were not covered in the beginning.

EVOLVE, ADAPT, AND FIX

Rather than progressively adding everything that comes into your head in your API design guidelines, the idea is to only add field-proven content that has been used to solve an actual design question. Guidelines might also have to be fixed if some rules, use cases, or other content is revealed to be a burden to apply or inconvenient in the long run. And you might realize that you need different types of guidelines depending on the context. You could, for example, choose to use gRPC APIs internally and REST ones over the internet.

Evolving API design guidelines obviously means dealing with breaking changes, versioning, and change logs. The guidelines basically describe APIs, so remember what you learned in section 9.1 when modifying existing rules. You need to be aware of possible breaking changes and version your guidelines accordingly. Don't forget to list the changes made in each version to avoid having designers keep trying to do things the way they were described in the previous version.

BUILD COLLECTIVELY, NO DOGMA

Just because you write guidelines does not mean that all the API designers in your team/organization/company will magically be aware of them or accept them. What will happen if you write guidelines and just put them on a shelf or in a wiki? Absolutely nothing. You will have to communicate; you will have to promote those. You have to tell the designers that guidelines exist, and that they are there to help people avoid wasting time reinventing the wheel and to help them solve design problems. You will have to explain why consistency matters. You might have to explain why a specific rule has been chosen (by the way, it's a good idea to write down in your rules why they exist!).

But simply saying all this might not be sufficient to make people accept your guidelines. After all, we all have our own backgrounds and points of view. You might be tempted to bluntly enforce the use of your guidelines and cross over to the dark side of governance. Please don't.

Building API design guidelines is not something that should be done alone by a single designer, or worse, by someone who has never put an API into production. The guidelines should be built collectively by actual designers for actual designers, without dogma, always willing to adjust/add/fix/evolve and even derogate when necessary. API design guidelines must not be enforced at all costs by the API police, and they should not reflect the ideas and preferences of a single individual. A whole book would be needed to thoroughly explain how exactly to proceed, but I think you get the idea.

13.3 *Reviewing APIs*

What could go possibly wrong when creating APIs? Everything. Even if you've read this book. Well, it might be less risky if you've read it, but things can still go wrong if the APIs are not reviewed. Let's illustrate this with another story.

One day, at the Banking Company, someone decided they needed to be able to send emails to customers. So they designed an API to do so. The idea was to later add other functions, like sending SMSs or notifications. That sounded like a good plan at first.

The API design was submitted to the company's API designers' guild for some advice. But before even analyzing the proposed design, someone in the guild asked why this send email goal was used and in what context. The answer was that when customers modified their personal data via the mobile application or website, such as changing their mailing or email address, they needed to receive an email confirming that the modification had been made and informing them that if they had not requested the change, they should immediately contact the Banking Company. The goal was supposed to be called by the website or mobile app after the update customer goal was called. This was considered a problem because it could mean that it was up to consumers to know that an email must be sent when updating the customer's information. Analyzing the design revealed other significant problems.

The send email goal was represented as a `POST /send-email` request awaiting an email address and a message. Such a request does not respect the company's API guidelines: consumers would need to know the customer's email address and what message should be sent to use it. But all that was nothing compared to the security hole that this API would have caused. The API would have exposed on the internet a way to send emails with any content to anyone on behalf of the Banking Company!

APIs have to be reviewed (validated, analyzed, scrutinized, checked, tested, and so on) at various stages of the API lifecycle to ensure that they work as intended. First and foremost, the needs have to be clearly identified and well understood, and it must be verified that creating an API is actually the best solution.

Once the API is designed, its interface contract must be *linted* in order to check that it's free of errors and, in the case of modifications, free of breaking changes. Then it must be validated from the provider's perspective: does it fulfill the identified needs, and is it secure, implementable, and evolvable? It must also be validated from the consumer's perspective: is it understandable and usable in the consumers' contexts? And last but not least, once the API is implemented, the implementation has to be tested in order to ensure that it actually exposes the expected interface contract.

API designers typically participate actively or at least have a say in all these reviews. Designers should obviously participate in reviews of the APIs they are working on, but they can also give a hand with reviews of other APIs. Getting feedback from others is always rewarding and helps ensure quality. Also, getting feedback from experienced API designers helps beginners to improve. Conversely, helping with the design of other people's APIs is rewarding because it's a good way to broaden one's perspective and discover new design use cases and ideas.

As an API designer, it is your job to question, challenge, investigate, validate, and analyze everything regarding the design of your APIs. But you must also keep an eye on the overall context—everything around the design—to ensure that the directions taken are the right ones. (Remember chapter 11 where you learned how to design an API in context?)

The idea is to absolutely not act as a hostile expert who knows everything and impose your will on everyone else, but rather to participate in growing the APIs beyond their design in the best possible manner, as everyone in the team/organization should be seeking to do.

13.3.1 *Challenging and analyzing needs*

In the send email use case, asking why and in what context this goal was to be used revealed that the imagined need was not the actual need and that the proposed solution was not secured at all. The real need was not to send an email but to notify customers of activity in their profiles. And in the end, the implemented solution was not a REST web API but a publish/subscribe system (see section 11.3.2).

Indeed, it was eventually decided to create a new Customer Notification server application relying on events sent by the Customer application. With this solution, the

Customer application, which exposes the API with the update customer goal, sends a customer updated event when a customer's data is modified. The Customer Notification application subscribes to these events. It holds all knowledge about how to notify customers, like their preferred channel (email, mobile app notification, or SMS), and the related data, such as their email address and phone number. It only reacts to selected events: in this first version, an update of the customer's data.

Such a decoupled architecture separates concerns, is flexible, and can easily evolve, while at the same time being secure and fulfilling the actual need. The implemented solution is completely different from what was imagined at first. It's a good thing the Banking Company's API guild conducted a review before starting to code! The send email API was designed for nothing, and this waste of time could have been avoided if the review had been carried out earlier.

You learned in chapter 2 that an API must fulfill consumers' needs to avoid creating terrible Kitchen Radar APIs, or worse, insecure send email goals as we have just seen. These perceived consumer needs have to be carefully evaluated and challenged in order to spot the real needs and find adequate, implementable, and secure solutions.

So before thinking about which URLs or HTTP methods to use, before even thinking about filling in an API goals canvas, you have to challenge and analyze the identified needs. And this should be done as early as possible. Once needs have been vaguely identified, they must be discussed and evaluated prior to anything else. Figure 13.6 shows an example of a checklist that can be used to challenge and analyze the needs you identify; it is based on this book's contents, but feel free to adapt it to your own situation.

Analyzing needs is not reserved to APIs. Clearly identifying the needs or problems to solve must be done when building anything. There is no single best approach for challenging and analyzing needs; you can use your favorite method.

Asking questions, such as why something needs to be done, what the context is, and how it will be used, usually helps to identify the real need or needs hidden by the first demand. The 5 Whys method is also a good way of doing this: you simply ask "why?" and get a response, then ask "why?" again about the response to go deeper into the analysis. Doing this five times in a row is usually sufficient to find the real root need. All these elements impact the design of the solution and the API.

After that, you must also investigate the consumer's and provider's contexts (see chapters 10 and 11) and think about security (see section 8.1.4). All of this is an iterative process that should be undertaken with various participants (those who are involved in defining the needs, implementation, security, and so on).

Clearly identifying the needs and investigating the context will ensure that the most appropriate solution is designed, whether it involves adding new goals to an existing API, creating a new API, or building something that is not an API or where an API is only part of the solution. If an API *is* the solution, having clearly identified needs will ensure that the goals the API helps to achieve are actually the right ones.

Challenging and Analyzing Needs Checklist (from *The Design of Web APIs*)	

Analyzing needs	
Question/Tool	Description
What do you want to do? What is the context?	These are the very first questions to ask to get an overview of the needs and start to understand their context.
How will "it" be used?	Do not forget to explicitly ask how the "solution" is supposed to be used; this gives more details about the context.
Who are the targeted consumers?	Knowing who the consumers and end users are will give direction to the design (for example, using a specific industry standard) and may raise questions about security (see the security section below).
Who are the targeted end users?	Knowing who the possible end users are (if any) may give direction about the design (for example, supporting internationalization and localization) and security (see the security section below).
5 Whys method	The 5 Whys is a simple tool that can be used to identify the root cause of a "problem," need(s) in our case, and therefore identify the real need(s). Ask "Why?" and get a response, then ask "Why?" again about the response to go deeper in the analysis. Doing this five times in a row is usually sufficient to find the real root need.
API goals canvas	Use the API goals canvas once you have a good overview of the "real" needs.

Investigating the consumer's(s') context(s)	
Question	Description
Who are the target consumers?	Knowing who the consumers are will give direction to the design (for example, using a specific industry standard) and may raise questions about security (see the security section below).
Who are the targeted end users?	Knowing who the possible end users are (if any) may give direction about the design (for example, supporting internationalization and localization) and security (see the security section below).
Do consumers have limitations?	Some consumers may only be able to use XML or may not be allowed to use the PATCH HTTP method, for example.
Is there an industry standard? Is it used by the targeted consumers?	Instead of reinventing a custom wheel nobody will want to use, favor standards if they exist and are actually used by the targeted consumers. Note that an API can support different formats (standard and custom), so you can also propose different APIs to different types of customers.
What is their network environment?	Depending on the network environment, some extra care may be necessary when designing the API. Experience APIs (or backend-for-frontend components) may also be needed.

Investigating the provider's context	
Question	Description
Which existing systems/APIs/teams/partners are needed under the hood?	Identifying the dependencies early allows you to avoid discovering too late that they are unable to do what they were supposed to do, as well as their limitations. Dependencies could be in-house systems, human teams, or partners' systems. Also, new needs may be fulfilled by existing APIs as they are, or you may need to evolve existing APIs.
Are there technical limitations?	Dependencies may have limited capabilities or specificities that will impact the design (not run 24/7, only asynchronous, long processing time, long response time, not scalable ...).
Are there functional limitations?	Dependencies may have existing business rules that are incompatible with the needs.
Are humans involved?	If there's a human process under the hood, it may need to be automated or the design may need to be adapted.
What type(s) of communication are needed?	Depending on the needs and context, you have to identify the type(s) of communication that will be needed (synchronous, asynchronous, streams, events).
What type(s) of API are needed?	Depending on the needs and context, you have to identify the type(s) of API that you will need.
Is an API the solution?	Depending on the needs and context, an API may not be the solution, or it can be only a part of the solution.

Investigating security concerns	
Question	Description
Does the API deal with sensitive material?	Depending on the sensitivity of the data and actions, and who the consumers and end users are, the design (and also the implementation) may have to be adapted.

Figure 13.6   Challenging needs checklist

13.3.2 *Linting the design*

Was the proposed POST /send-email request awaiting an optional email as a string and msg as a number a valid one? It uses a resource path that doesn't look like what you learned to use in section 3.2.3, but maybe the Banking Company's API design guidelines say that APIs have to be function-based (see section 11.3). Still, for clarity, shouldn't msg be called message and shouldn't it be a string? And is it normal to have all the expected properties be optional? Linting the proposed design will give answers to all these questions:

> *"Lint, or a linter, is a tool that analyzes source code to flag programming errors, bugs, stylistic errors, and suspicious constructs. The term originates from a Unix utility that examined C language source code."*
>
> *Wikipedia*

Just like code, an API design can contain errors (for example, using the wrong type for a property) and might have to be written (designed) following conventions like using the errorMessage property name instead of err_msg. Linting the API will help detect these kinds of errors and others.

API linting consists of checking for bugs in the design, as well as verifying that it conforms to the design guidelines and is consistent with any preexisting elements (we explore what those are in a moment). While linting an API design, you should also check its security and documentation. That is, you basically lint anything that you would put in an API description file; indeed, you have to check every aspect of the interface contract. Figure 13.7 shows an example of a linting checklist.

Basically, you have to analyze each model and its properties and each goal and its parameters and responses. You also have to analyze the goal flows and security definitions. Most of these checks are quite simple and binary, but there are three types of verification that you should take particular care with: checking the documentation, checking flows, and (most importantly) checking consistency with preexisting elements.

Checking the documentation of the interface contract is important because having an exhaustively documented interface contract will facilitate design reviews from both the provider's and the consumer's perspective. We talk about this in the following sections (13.3.3 and 13.3.4).

Checking flows is basically what you learned to do in section 2.3 and section 3.3.4. It's quite simple, but critical, to ensure that the API actually works. It would be embarrassing, if not disastrous, if consumers could not use the API because they were unable to provide some parameters.

Checking consistency with preexisting elements is perhaps the most difficult check, but it's a very important one. Verifying that a name, data model, or goal's behavior is consistent with preexisting elements requires concentration and detailed knowledge of what actually exists inside and beyond the API that is being linted. Otherwise, you can end up with, for example, three different address formats, two different standard ways of representing countries, too many ways of showing that an amount is invalid, and a totally custom way of representing phone numbers.

Goals

Check	Description
Categorized	This is not an obligation, but categorizing goals facilitates understanding of an API.
Valid path	Path's format conforms to guidelines and is consistent with preexisting elements. It also conforms to the success response type. If path parameters are defined, they must be present.
Valid HTTP method	HTTP method conforms to guidelines and preexisting elements and is appropriate for what the goal is supposed to do.
Handles success and errors	Goal returns all needed responses to handle both success and error conditions.
Secured	Each goal is covered by a security mechanism.

Goal's parameters

Check	Description
Valid name	Parameter's name conforms to guidelines and is consistent with preexisting elements.
Valid required status	Parameter's optional/required status conforms to guidelines and is consistent with preexisting elements and its location (path parameter must be required). If all of the body parameter's properties are optional on a creation/replacement, it is probably an error (but it can happen).
Valid type and format	Parameter's type and format conform to guidelines and preexisting elements and are valid according to its location (for example: no objects in query parameters, no URL forbidden characters in path ones).
Valid description	Parameter's human- (the description property) and machine-readable (minimum, and so on) descriptions are valid and accurate, conform to guidelines, and are consistent with preexisting elements.
Valid location	Parameter's location conforms to guidelines, is consistent with preexisting elements, and conforms to the HTTP status method (no body parameter on a delete request, for example).
Can be provided	Consumers must be able to provide each goal's parameters (because they know them or they got them from another goal).

Goal's responses

Check	Description
Valid HTTP status	Response's HTTP status conforms to guidelines and preexisting elements and is appropriate for the type of response (success, consumer failure, provider failure).
Valid body	Response's body type and format conform to guidelines and preexisting elements and are appropriate for the HTTP status (for example: standard error model for 4XX or 5XX).
Valid headers	Response's header names, types, and formats conform to guidelines and preexisting elements.
Is used	Data provided in each goal's response is actually used.
Success valid description	Response's and its body's and headers' human- (the description property) and machine-readable (model definition) descriptions are valid and accurate, conform to guidelines, and are consistent with preexisting elements.
Error valid description	Response's and its body's and headers' human- (the description property) and machine-readable (model definition) descriptions are valid and accurate, conform to guidelines, and are consistent with preexisting elements. Detailed information about possible errors should be provided in the human- and, if possible, machine-readable descriptions.

API Linting Checklist (from *The Design of Web APIs*)

Evolution (applies to all topics)

Check	Description
Breaking change introduced	If a modification implies a breaking change, check if it is really necessary. If so, apply your versioning policy.

API's security definitions

Check	Description
Is used	Each security definition must be used. If not, check if it was forgotten on a goal. If not, remove it.
Is valid	Relevant machine-readable information must be provided according to the security type, and it must conform to the guidelines.
Valid description	Relevant description of each scope must be provided.

API's goal flows

Check	Description
Is valid	Flow of goals (use case) and its behavior conforms to guidelines and preexisting elements.
Valid description	Flow of goals (use case) is accurately described in the API or goal descriptions.

Models

Check	Description
Is used	Each model definition must be used. If a definition is not used, it may have been forgotten on a goal. If not, remove it.
Valid name	Model's name conforms to guidelines and is consistent with preexisting elements.
Valid data structure	Model's data structure/organization and depth conform to guidelines and are consistent with preexisting elements.
Valid description	Model's human-readable description (the description property) is present (and accurate) if necessary.

Model's properties

Check	Description
Valid name	Property's name conforms to guidelines and is consistent with preexisting elements.
Valid required status	Property's optional/required status conforms to guidelines and is consistent with preexisting elements. If all properties are optional, this is probably an error (but it can happen).
Valid type and format	Property's data type (atomic or model) and format (ISO 8601 date, for example) are valid according to its name, value, or description. They should also conform to guidelines and be consistent with preexisting elements.
Valid description	Property's human- (the description property) and machine-readable (minimum, and so on) descriptions are valid and accurate, conform to guidelines, and are consistent with preexisting elements.

Figure 13.7   An example API linting checklist

Preexisting elements mostly come from the API itself, other APIs from the organization, and standards; they can be names, types, data models, and even behaviors. To verify that an API is consistent with preexisting elements in the API itself or other APIs from the same organization, you can rely partly on your API designer's sense. Also, if you've had the good fortune to participate in reviews of other APIs, you might have a few memories of what you have seen. But it's hard to keep up with everything that can be happening across the organization's API surface, so you should also rely on available API documentation. It can be helpful to enable a search mechanism across all of your APIs' documentation to facilitate such an analysis.

Regarding identifying standards that could be used instead of custom formats, this is up to you, your API designer's sense, and your favorite search engine. There are obvious standards you will have heard of, like ISO 8601 for dates and ISO 4217 for currencies, but you can't possibly be aware of *all* the existing standards. For example, did you know there's a standard for representing phone numbers? It's the E.164 format, defined by the International Telecommunication Union (ITU).

You should always check if a standard exists to represent a given data item. If you find one, add it to your guidelines immediately. It might be a burden at the beginning; but in the long run, it will make your life easier as you will quickly catalog all the standards you need for your APIs. And in case of evolution of an existing API, do not forget to check if you are introducing some breaking changes. If they cannot be avoided, you will have to apply your versioning policy.

Linting can be partially automated by running some tools on a machine-readable API description format, but a human will still need to be involved. It's fairly simple to check path formats or if an HTTP status code is authorized, but it's quite complex to check that a human-readable description is relevant. While it's not possible to fully automate the process, taking advantage of automation for linting is highly recommended so reviewers can focus on the checks that actually need human beings.

Finally, be aware that linting an API design only validates the form, not the substance. It only ensures that the designed interface contract respects certain design rules. It absolutely does not validate that the API fulfills all of the provider's requirements and that consumers will actually want and be able to use it. Once linted, an API must therefore be reviewed in depth from both the provider's and consumer's perspectives.

13.3.3 *Reviewing the design from the provider's perspective*

Just because you have identified the real needs and contextual elements required to design an API, and its design has been fully linted, doesn't mean everything is OK from the provider's perspective. Indeed, you have to check with the whole team that the resulting API design actually fulfills all of the provider's requirements. You'll want to confirm that the design satisfies all the identified needs and that it is secure, implementable, and extensible. Figure 13.8 shows another example of a checklist inspired by this book's content that you can use for this purpose. Again, feel free to adapt it to your needs.

Goals	
Check	Description
Valid purpose	Conform to needs.
Secure path	Do not expose undue sensitive data, and expose sensitive data with secure representations.
Exhaustive successes	Conform to needs (all expected success responses are defined).
Exhaustive errors	Conform to needs (handle all possible surface control errors, functional errors, security errors, and technical errors).
Secured	Covered by expected scope(s) and security mechanism(s), and do not provide undue access.
Can be implemented	Can actually be implemented (directly or via a dependency).
Valid performance estimates	Match needs (corollary to "can be implemented").
Extensible	Reasonably take future evolutions into consideration.

Goal's parameters	
Check	Description
Valid required status	Conform to needs.
Valid type and format	Conform to needs.
Secure data	Do not require undue sensitive data, and require sensitive data with secure representations or locations.
Valid location	Conform to needs and security concerns (see secure data). URL cannot contain sensitive data.
Extensible	Reasonably take future evolutions into consideration.

Goal's responses	
Check	Description
Valid success data	Conform to needs.
Secure success data	Do not expose undue sensitive data, and expose sensitive data with secure representations.
Existing success data	Can actually be provided by the implementation (directly or via a dependency).
Valid error data	Conform to needs and are exhaustive.
Secure error data	Do not expose undue sensitive data, and expose sensitive data with secure representations.
Existing error data	Can actually be provided by the implementation (directly or via a dependency).
Extensible	Reasonably take future evolutions into consideration.

Provider Review Checklist (from *The Design of Web APIs*)

API's security definitions	
Check	Description
Relevant scopes	Defined scopes match the security partitioning needs.

API's goal flows	
Check	Description
Valid purpose	Conform to needs.
Valid performance estimates	Match needs (cumulated performance).
Extensible	Reasonably take future evolutions into consideration.

Models	
Check	Description
Valid data structure	Conform to needs (actually represent the expected concept).
Extensible	Reasonably take future evolutions into consideration.

Model's properties	
Check	Description
Valid required status	Conform to needs.
Valid type and format	Conform to needs.
Valid value	Conform to needs.
Secure value	Do not expose undue sensitive data, and expose sensitive data with secure representations.
Existing value	Can actually be provided by the implementation (directly or via a dependency) or requested if used as a parameter.
Extensible	Reasonably take future evolutions into consideration.

Figure 13.8 Checking the design from the provider's perspective

If you have used the API goals canvas, created exhaustive documentation, and applied what you have learned in this book to design the interface contract, such a review should not be a problem at all. The API goals canvas will help to link initial needs and

API goals. The documentation is important here to facilitate the review for all the people involved who don't have your extensive knowledge of the API.

The various goal flows must match the identified needs, and each goal must behave as expected, returning the correct data and triggering the correct errors. Each element should be reasonably extensible (remember section 9.3). Also, don't forget to check that each goal, behavior, or returned response can actually be handled by the implementation and that the performance of each goal and flow matches expectations. But this review only concerns the provider's perspective; we must not forgot to also check that everything is OK from the consumer's perspective.

13.3.4 *Reviewing the design from the consumer's perspective*

Last but not least in the design analysis is the review from the consumer's perspective. Is the API easy to use, easy to understand, and efficient? Does it take care not to unduly expose the provider's perspective? If not, all the effort you've put into creating the API will be worth nothing because nobody will want to use the resulting product (see section 1.2.3). Hopefully, all that you have learned in this book should make this review a piece of cake. Figure 13.9 shows an example checklist for reviewing an API's design from the consumer's perspective, based on this book's content. As usual, feel free to adapt it to your needs.

During this review, you have to take the place of a consumer who does not know anything about the API. Check that each goal and its parameters and responses (especially the errors) make sense for consumers and are not a vile exposition of what's happening under the hood (the despised provider's perspective). Verify that each required parameter is really required in order to request minimal data. Pay particular attention to the names and descriptions: check that they are not provider's jargon. Check also that the goal flows are simple and efficient, without too many steps and with goals that prevent errors. And don't forget to check that the performance estimates (for single goals and goal flows) are valid for both basic and complex use cases (see section 10.1).

> **TIP** Don't hesitate to submit your design to people outside the team and, if possible, potential consumers for review; their feedback will be valuable and increase the quality of the design.

Finally, once all the verifications have been done—API linting (see section 13.3.2), provider review, and consumer review—the API can at last be implemented. But your job does not necessarily stop here. You might have to help verify that the implementation actually implements the designed interface contract as expected.

13.3.5 *Verifying the implementation*

I will not explain how to actually test the implementation of an API because that's outside the scope of this book. There are many tools out there for doing so, and some of them even allow you to generate tests based on API description files. But these tests are usually insufficient to verify that the implementation does everything that is expected, so tests will have to be written.

Consumer Review Checklist
(from *The Design of Web APIs*)

Goals

Check	Description
Valid path	Path structure and names or parameters used can easily be understood.
Valid purpose	Meaningful for consumers.
Valid performance estimates	Match consumers' needs.

Goal's parameters

Check	Description
Valid required status	Minimal required properties.
Valid name	Name can easily be understood ("source" instead of "ts," for example).
Valid type and format	Type and format can easily be understood and used (for example: ISO 8601 dates instead of Unix timestamps, "CHECKING" instead of "2").
Valid value	Values are ready to use (account numbers instead of technical IDs, for example).
Can be provided	Consumers must be able to provide each goal's parameters (because they know them or they got them from another goal).

Goal's responses

Check	Description
Valid success data	All needed data is returned along with informative data (like what has been done and what to do next).
Valid error data	Exhaustive and informative error feedback that actually helps to solve all problems is provided.

API's security definitions

Check	Description
Relevant scopes	Meaningful for consumers.

API's goal flows

Check	Description
Prevent errors	Goals prevent errors (like a goal providing possible destinations for a source account when transferring money, for example).
Shortest	The number of steps is the shortest possible.
Valid performance estimates	Match consumers' needs.
Valid purpose	Each step (goal) is meaningful for consumers.

Models

Check	Description
Valid data structure	Adequate organization, depth and granularity favoring understanding and use. Minimal properties for parameters.
Valid name	Name can easily be understood ("Account" instead of "aDTO", for example).

Model's properties

Check	Description
Valid required status	Minimal required properties (for parameters).
Valid name	Name can easily be understood ("source" instead of "ts," for example).
Valid type and format	Type and format can easily be understood and used (for example: ISO 8601 dates instead of Unix timestamps, "checking" instead of "2").
Valid value	Values are ready to use (for example: adding age along with birth date, code with localized labels, account numbers instead of technical IDs).

Figure 13.9 Checking the design from the consumer's perspective

The implementers might rely on various levels of testing (usually unit tests and API tests) to entirely validate an API. What I want to do here is show you a few things that should particularly be taken care of and warn you about a few traps.

NEVER BYPASS SECURITY TESTING

Security testing for APIs is mandatory. You must ensure that access controls and sensitive data are actually handled in the proper way.

For access control, the first level of testing consists of ensuring that only registered consumers can access the API and that they cannot do anything outside of the granted scopes. The second level of testing concerns consumer/end user permission controls. For example, if a consumer requests a list of accounts on behalf of an end user, only that user's accounts must be returned. And if the same consumer requests account 12345, the API must only return it if the end user is actually authorized to get it.

Regarding sensitive data, you have to ensure that undue sensitive data is not returned. If sensitive data has to be requested or returned, you must ensure that it is properly secured (using a nonsensitive representation or encryption, for example) as discussed in section 8.4.

BE CAREFUL WHEN USING GENERATED DOCUMENTATION TO VALIDATE THE IMPLEMENTATION

Some implementation frameworks allow you to generate an API description file from the code at runtime or while building the application. This generated file could be compared to the original API description file to validate that the interface contract exposed by the implementation conforms to the expected one. But such validation can only be done on elements that do not come from annotations specifically made to generate the API description file.

If, for example, I add in my code an API description-specific annotation to indicate that the possible values for a `type` attribute are `checking` and `savings`, there is no guarantee that my code will actually only return these values. This information is only declarative.

Some tools can leverage standard annotations that are prescriptive, however. For example, if I develop a web application exposing an API with the Java Spring Boot framework, I can use a standard annotation to declare that a method maps to the `POST / transfers` request. Such values can be used in a comparison between an original API description file and a generated one.

CHECK THE INTERFACE CONTRACT AT RUNTIME

Even if you find a magic trick, framework, or tool that allows you to generate the actually implemented interface contract, you must test the implementation at runtime to validate all expected behaviors. Just because the generated and valid interface contract states that a `400 Bad Request` response is returned in the case of a missing mandatory attribute doesn't mean it's actually the case.

CHECK PROPERTIES' CHARACTERISTICS IN RESPONSES

When the interface contract says that a property is required or mandatory in a returned data model, it must always be returned. The same is true if the API description provides information about minimum and maximum values, number of items in arrays, and so on. Do not forget these tests.

CHECK THE WHOLE NETWORK CHAIN

When testing your API, you must make test calls encompassing the whole network chain in front of the implementation. This network chain can include firewalls, proxies, and VIP or API gateways, for example. Firewalls are good purveyors of bugs; misconfigured ones can, for example, block `DELETE` HTTP requests or replace HTTP `5XX` status codes with `500` responses or return an HTML page (no kidding) instead of data in case of error.

Also, misconfigured API gateways can implement some controls on behalf of the implementation based on the API description file used to expose the API, but not necessarily in the best way. For example, these can return one error at a time or use the wrong error format (using the gateway standard error format which happens to be different from the API's one, or worse, an HTML page—again, no kidding).

13.4 Communicating and sharing

The end is near; this is the last section of the last chapter of the book. I want to take this opportunity to talk briefly about communicating and sharing as an API designer. As you might have noticed while reading this last chapter, API designers do not work alone. An API designer has to work, at the least, with the people who want to create the APIs or think that an API could be the solution, the consumers, the people in charge of developing the implementation, the people in charge of security, those in charge of documentation, and other API designers.

As an API designer, you have to be able to share what you do, your design material. To make it easy to do so, you should at least use a standard API description format. You might also want to take advantage of a source control system like Git to store your files, use wikis for less-structured descriptions, build a custom API catalog, or use an off-the-shelf developer portal.

To ensure consistency, your company's guidelines (that you contribute to) should be easily accessible and known to all the API designers. All the existing APIs and data models should at least be easily findable (hence the source control system, wiki, or API catalog) and, if possible, searchable.

To design with confidence, never hesitate to have your designs reviewed by peers. It could also be useful and informative to create or participate in an API designer community (or API guild). And most importantly, make sure your designs are reviewed by actual consumers.

Summary

- Documentation is vital to designing, building, and validating APIs.
- Consistency is impossible without API design guidelines and documentation.
- Designing APIs must not be done alone: work with others on reviews and/or build a designers community.
- API designers participate in the whole API lifecycle.
- In order to design effective and useful APIs, API designers must challenge and deeply analyze the needs their APIs are intended to fulfill.

index

RELATED MANNING TITLES

Irresistible APIs
Designing web APIs that developers will love
by Kirsten L. Hunter

> ISBN: 9781617292552
> 232 pages, $44.99
> September 2016

GraphQL in Motion
by Tyler Reckart

> Course duration: 2h 44m
> 28 exercises, $59.99

HTTP/2 in Action
by Barry Pollard

> ISBN: 9781617295164
> 416 pages, $49.99
> March 2019

OAuth 2 in Action
by Justin Richer and Antonio Sanso

> ISBN: 9781617293276
> 360 pages, $49.99
> March 2017

For ordering information go to www.manning.com